C.I.P.A. GUIDE TO THE PATENTS ACTS

FIFTH EDITION

FOURTH CUMULATIVE SUPPLEMENT

AUSTRALIA
Law Book Co.
Sydney

CANADA and USA
Carswell
Toronto

HONG KONG
Sweet & Maxwell Asia

NEW ZEALAND
Brookers
Wellington

SINGAPORE and MALAYSIA
Sweet & Maxwell Asia
Singapore and Kuala Lumpur

C.I.P.A. GUIDE TO THE PATENTS ACTS

FIFTH EDITION

FOURTH CUMULATIVE SUPPLEMENT

Up to date to January 1, 2005

PREPARED BY
STEPHEN F. JONES

with the assistance of
ALAN W. WHITE
(Editor 1982–2001)

FOR
THE CHARTERED INSTITUTE
OF PATENT AGENTS

Founded 1882
Royal Charter 1891

LONDON
SWEET & MAXWELL
2005

First Edition 1980
Second Edition 1984
Third Edition 1990
Fourth Edition 1995
Fifth Edition 2000

Published by Sweet & Maxwell Ltd of
100 Avenue Road, Swiss Cottage, London NW3 3PF
http://www.sweetandmaxwell.co.uk
Typeset by Interactive Sciences Ltd, Gloucester
Printed and bound in Great Britain by
Antony Rowe Ltd, Chippenham, Wiltshire

No natural forests were destroyed to make this product;
only farmed timber was used and replanted.

A CIP catalogue record for this book is available from the British Library

ISBN Main Work 0 421 650109
Supplement 0 421 876905

Notice to Readers

Attention is drawn to the statement of purpose for this book on page xii of the Main Work, namely that the book (and therefore also this Supplement) is truly intended as a "guide" and is not a substitute for the exercise of professional judgment. In particular, it is too optimistic to think that the book (and this Supplement) contains no errors. All such errors are regretted. Those readers who find any, or who feel that they can contribute to improvement of the work from their own experience, are invited to write to the Editor (c/o The Chartered Institute of Patent Agents, Staple Inn Buildings, High Holborn, London WC1V 7PZ), so that appropriate correction or addition can be made in the next cumulative supplement. In this way, the value of the book to other patent practitioners can be enhanced.

C.I.P.A. Guide to the Patents Acts

FIFTH EDITION

Fourth Cumulative Supplement

INTRODUCTION

This Supplement mainly comments on cases reported and other material which became available after the text for the Fifth Edition was finalised, and attempts to state the law up to January 1, 2005. Some matter has also been included by way of addition to that contained in the Main Work or the Third Supplement.

The main reason for the additional length of this Supplement compared to the previous one is of course the additions required to be made to the text of the Third Supplement to set out the amendments to the 1977 Act made (sometimes prospectively) by the Patents Act 2004, as well as the further amendments made by the Regulatory Reform (Patents) Order 2004 and the Patents (Amendment) Rules 2004, all coming into force on January 1, 2005. I am indebted to Alan White, the Editor of the Main Work, for his hard work in compiling the text of the amendments and the commentary on them, and for his other assistance very generously given and gratefully received, including as ever the advance copies of his regular notes on cases for the CIPA Journal.

Each entry in this Supplement has a marginal reference in bold type to the section (§) of the Main Work to which it relates, identified by headings and sub-headings corresponding to those in the Main Work. The Supplement also contains prefatory Supplementary Tables to the Tables in the Main Work, as necessary, together with a Supplementary Index at the end of the Supplement, each to be read in conjunction with the corresponding Table or Index in the Main Work, each against the section (§) number quoted therein.

Marginal sidelines indicate the entries in this Supplement which are additional to, or different from, the entries in the Third Supplement.

This should be the last Cumulative Supplement before the publication of a new Edition. The present Supplement has been compiled by Stephen Jones and Alan White under the aegis of the Publications and Textbooks Committee of the Chartered Institute of Patent Agents. Thanks are again due to the patents judges, in particular Judge Michael Fysh QC of the Patents County Court, for providing copies of judgments, to the staff of the Patent Office for their input, to Richard

v

Lloyd for his headnotes and of course to the people at Sweet & Maxwell, especially Jacqui Mowbrey. The Editor once again thanks the partners and staff of Baker & McKenzie for their support, and to all the others who have helped him cope with the task of producing this present Supplement during an eventful year.

ERRATA

The following errors of a minor, usually typographic, nature have been noted in the Main Work. It is suggested that these be entered in manuscript into this Main Work. Where more significant errors have been discovered, these are noted in the following commentary sections of this Supplement.

Section	Page	Paragraph	Line(s)	Old wording	Correct wording or amendment
Table of Cases	lii	Minnesota	22	BL O/237/00	BL O/237/00 (The citation in the Main Work is correct, despite the indication to the contrary in the First Supplement, now deleted.)
Table of Statutory Instruments	cxiv	Entry for S.I. 1978 No.621	8	132.09	132.07
Table of EPO Decisions	lxxix	T 2/83	8	/Simethicon	/Simethicone
Table of EPO Decisions	xci	Plant Genetic Systems	30	T 326/93	T 356/93
Table of EPO Decisions	xciii	T361/87	29	Wrongly indexed with 1997 decisions	
§ 2.10	46	4	1	Beechsm	Beecham
§ 2.10	46	5	4	§ 3.46	§ 3.41
§ 2.20	57	2	5	§ 3.46	§ 3.41
§ 2.32	69	5	7	§ 2.36	§ 2.37
§ 3.21	99	4 (indent)	6	3. . . . starting form the	3. . . . starting from the
§ 5.03	131	1	1	initially signed in 1878	originally signed in 1883

Section	Page	Paragraph	Line(s)	Old wording	Correct wording or amendment
§ 5.17	150	2	2	§ 5.17	§ 5.18
§ 5.17	150	2	4	§ 5.18	§ 5.19
§ 7.06	159	5	7	BL O/237/00	The reference to BL O/237/00 for the *Minnesota Mining* case is correct, despite the indication to the contrary in the First Supplement, now deleted.
§ 8.13	171	1	4	§ 8.06	§ 8.04
§ 11.02	177	*Note*	1	rule 11(2)	rule 13(2)
§ 12.05	183	3	2	EPCa. 61(b)	EPCa. 61(1)(b)
§ 13.04	186	1	4	§ 32.04	§ 32.03
§ 13.09	189	4	6	PF 11/77	PF 7/77
§ 13.12	192	4	1	(notified	notified
§ 15.08	238	1	last	§ 14.33	§ 14.12
§ 17.08	259	3	1	20(15)	20(14)
§ 17.08	259	3	2	20(13)	20(12)
§ 17.11	262	2	4	three months before the beginning of the "rule 34 period"	three months before the end of the "rule 34 period"
§ 17.12	263	2	3	§ 17.19	§ 17.20
§ 17.18	266	5	5	can proceed	can, but usually will not, proceed
§ 17.18	266	5	6	section 16.	section 16, see § 16.04.
§ 17.18	266	5	9–10	although a limited . . . is possible,	[*delete these words*]

Section	Page	Paragraph	Line(s)	Old wording	Correct wording or amendment
§ 17.20	267	3	7	subsection (1)	subsection (6)
§ 19.12	288	2	1	§§ 18.02 and 32.05	§§ 19.02 and 32.04
§ 23.01	303	2	1	subsection (4)(6)	subsection (3)(b)
§ 29.08	351	1	3	PF 19/77	PF 15/77
§ 32.02	365	Heading	2	RE-REGISTRATION RULES)	RE-REGISTRATION) RULES
§ 37.04	394	*Note*	2	rule 33(4)	rule 33(5)
§ 37.08	399	5	last	BL O/237/00	BL O/237/00 (The citation in the Main Work is correct, despite the indication to the contrary in the First Supplement, now deleted.)
§ 48A.06	488	2	9	§ 48A.05).	§ 48A.05.
§ 48B.01	492	1	1	**48.—(1)**	**48B.—(1)**
§ 48B.02	494	2	1	, in may cases,	, in many cases,
§ 50.02	500	2	1	Whether of not	Whether or not
§ 51.06	505	3	4	§ 49A.02)	§ 48A.02)
§ 60.04	547	4	4	§ C15	§ D15
§ 60.04	547	4	8	§ C17	§ D11
§ 60.11	552	2	last	§§ C02–C05 . . . § C15	§§ D03–D05 . . . § D15
§ 60.18	558	2	8	it may here by noted	it may here be noted
§ 60.19	559	3	last	§ C15	§ D13
§ 60.25	563	Heading		*Joint tortfeasance*	*—Joint tortfeasance*
§ 61.22	581	3	3	§§ 125.10 and 125.15	§§ 125.13 and 125.21

Section	Page	Paragraph	Line(s)	Old wording	Correct wording or amendment
§ 61.25	584	1	2	, other that damages	, other than damages
§ 61.61	627	2	1	§ 25.12–25.15	§§ E25.12–E25.15
§ 72.32	687	Table of Rules	Entry for rule 107	72.34	72.33
§ 73.04	708	1	4	in subsection (3)	in subsection 76(3)
§ 76.16	742	3	6	modification of the feature	modification of the features
§ 78.01	763	Title		**filing and application**	**filing an application**
§ 89.02	797	Title		117–122	117–120
§ 89.25	811	4	1	if if an appeal	Delete repeated word "if"
§ 89.28	814	3	16	has been filed	had been filed
§ 96.02	866	Heading		**SUPREME COURT ACT 1982**	**SUPREME COURT ACT 1981**
§ 117.12	938	2	4	rule 38	rule 36
§ 123.32	983	2	6	rule 41(1)— opposing restoration	rule 41(1)— application for restoration
§ 130.03	1069	Designate	Definition	78.06	78.03
§ 132.06	1081	2	5	77.10	77.09
§ 132.06	1081	2	8	380	391
§ 139.01	1097	Heading	Heading	Section	Rule
§ 139.01	1102	1	4	123.02	123.15
§ E33.3	1340	(aa)	2	witness evidence	hearsay evidence
§ E43PD.1	1347	1	4	4	1.4

TABLE OF CASES

(Supplemental to the Table of Cases in the Main Work)

Cases are listed according to the section (§) numbers of the Main Work to which they refer, as supplemented by the contents of this Supplement likewise referring to the same paragraph numbers. Abbreviations are used as in the Main Work, see page cxl *thereof.*

An asterisk against a case indicates that it is also cited in the Main Work and † indicates a case or citation omitted from mention in the Table of Cases in the Main Work.

AB Hässle's Patents [2002] FSR 564 and [2003] FSR 413; [2003] IP&T
    266 (CA) 61.60, 97.19
ABB PATENT/Transformer (OJEPO 2004, 16) (EPO Decision T 1173/00) ... 14.29
Abbott Laboratories' SPC Application BL O/302/02 .... 123.36, B12
Abdulhayogu's Application [2000] RPC 18 .... 107.05
Admiral Management Services v. Para Protect Europe, *noted The Times*,
    March 26, 2002) 61.35
AEI Rediffusion v. Phonographic Performance [1999] 1 WLR 1507 .... 61.35
Adair v Young (1879) L.R. 12 Ch. D. 13, CA 60.02
ADVANCED SEMICONDUCTOR PRODUCTS/Limiting Feature OJEPO
    1994, 541; [1995] EPOR 97 (EPO Decision G 1/93) 76.13
Affymetrix Inc v Multilyte Ltd (BL C/9/04) [2004] EWHC 291; [2005] FSR
    1; Ch D (Patents Ct) 61.46
ALBANY/Pure Terfenidine (EPO Decision T 728/98) [2002] EPOR 1 ..... 125.15
ALKO/CBH II [2003] EPOR 414 (EPO Decision T 816/90) 125A.24
American Home Products v. Novartis [2000] RPC 547 and [2001] RPC 159
    (CA) 2.03, 2.34, 14.29, 61.45, 125.07, 125.18, 125.19
— v. — (No. 2) BL C/53/00, *noted* IPD 24010; [2001] FSR 784 (CA) 61.49
AMERICAN HOME PRODUCTS/Canine coronavirus (EPO Decision
    T 977/93) [2001] EPOR 274 .... 2.12
American Photo Booth's Patent BL O/457/02 .... 4.03
Amersham v. Amicon C/49/00, *noted* IPD 24011 ..... 3.10, 61.60, 125.16, 125.19
— v. — (CA) BL C/32/01, *noted* IPD 24078 .... 125.19
AMOCO/Olefin Catalyst (EPO Decision T 124/93) [1996] EPOR 624 ..... 14.27
Anaesthetic Supplies v. Rescare [Australia] (1994) 28 IPR 383 .... 4.04
Ancare's Patent [New Zealand] [2001] RPC 335 .... 75.06
— — [2003] RPC 139 (Privy Council) 3.09
Anderson's Application BL O/297/02 .... 15.13
Apotex v. SmithKline Beecham [2004] EWHC 964; [2004] EWHC 2051;
    [2004] FSR 523 .... 61.35, 61.60

xi

Approved Prescription Services v. Merck BL C/3/03, *noted* IPD 26025 .... 61.13,
71.04
APV ANHYDRO/Granulation by spray drying (EPO Decision T 79/96)
[2001] EPOR 309 .... 3.23, 3.25, 125.14
* Arbiter Group v. Gill Jennings & Every [2001] RPC 67 .... 274.09
Arjo and Impro v. Liko BL C/52/01, *noted* [2001] *CIPA* 575, 628 and IPD
25006 .... 71.05, 125.19
Arrow Generics v. Generics UK BL C/52/02 .... 61.60
Asahi Medical v. Macapharma BL C/46/00 and C/15/02, *noted* IPD
25037 .... 3.10
Ash & Lacy v. Fixing Point PCC July 24, 2002 .... 72.33
Ash & Lacy's Patent No. 2240558 [2002] RPC 939; [2002] IP&T 709 ..... 71.08,
72.33, 72.39, 107.05
— — — No. 2240559 BL O/60/02 and O/144/02 .... 72.37, 72.53
Associated Newspaper v. Impac [2002] FSR 293 .... 61.35
AT&T/Computer system (EPO Decision T 204/93) [2001] EPOR 300 ...... 1.15

Baker Hughes' Patents BL O/1/01 .... 72.42
— — — BL O/332/02 and C/49/02, *noted* IPD 26003 ... 27.05, 27.06, 27.07, 27.08,
76.08, 97.06, 117.06
I BALFOUR/Feedstuff [2004] EPOR 73 (EPO Decision T 73/92) 14.27
* Balmoral Group v. CRP [2000] FSR 860 .... 5.10
BASF v. BIE (ECJ Case C–258/99) [2002] RPC 274 .... B09
* BASF/Zeolites (EPO Decision T 219/83) OJEPO 1986, 211 .... 14.23
* BBC/Television signal (EPO Decision T 163/85) OJEPO 1990, 379; [1990]
EPOR 599 .... 1.16
BELOIT/Digester (EPO Decision T 37/96) [2002] EPOR 308 .... 2.23
"Biegevorrichtung" (German Supreme Court) [2002] GRUR 231 .... 64.06
Bilgrey Samson's Application BL O/577/01 .... 1.14, 14.28
Biogen v. Medeva [1997] RPC 1 (HL) 3.04, 5.10, 14.17, 97.19
* Bonzel v. Intervention (No. 2) [1991] RPC 231 .... 61.50
* — v. — (No.3) [1991] RPC 553 .... 72.26, 76.07
Bourns v. Raychem [2000] FSR 841 .... 61.54
Bradford Hospital's Application BL O/37/01 and O/85/01 .... 12.05, 39.08
* Bristol-Myers Squibb v. Baker Norton [1999] RPC 253 .... 4.04
* — v. — (CA) [2001] RPC 1; [2004] FSR 330, CA 2.11, 2.13, 2.34, 3.10, 4.04,
64.03, 91.03, 125.24, 125.26, 130.09, 130.11
British Horseracing Board v. William Hill [2001] RPC 612 .... D12
— v. — (CA), *noted* IPD 24059 .... D12
* BRITISH TECHNOLOGY/Contraceptive method (EPO decision T 74/93)
[1995] EPOR 279 .... 4.03
British Telecommunications' Applications BL O/402/01 .... 12.04
* Buchanan v. Alba Diagnostics [Scotland] [2000] RPC 367 and [2001] RPC
851 (Inner House) and [2004] RPC 681 HL 31.05, 60.02, 125.15
I Building Product Design Ltd v. Sandtoft Roof Tiles Ltd (No.1) [2004] FSR
823; [2004] FSR 834, PCC 60.21, 61.42

Cadcam Technology v. Proel, BL CC/61/00 .... 61.60, 125.15, 291.06
Calix Technology's Patent BL O/62/03 .... 27.07
* Cartonneries de Thulin v. CTP White Knight [2001] RPC 107 ... 3.15, 72.26, 76.14,
125.07, 125.15
Cairnstores v. AB Hässle BL C/15/01; [2002] FSR 564 .... 72.15
Celltech (Adair's) US Patent *see* Celltech Chiroscience v. Medimmune
Celltech Chiroscience v. Medimmune BL C/36/01, *noted* IPD 24074 and
[2003] FSR 433; [2004] EWHC 1124, BL C/55/04 Ch D (CA) 125.26
Central Research Laboratories' Application BL O/419/00 .... 15.13, 21.06

I   Chiron and Novo-Nordisk's SPC Application BL O/343/04 .... B10

CIL International v. Vitrashop [2002] FSR 67 .... 61.36

City Technology v. Alphasense BL C/42/00; [2001] IP&T 326, *noted* IPD
23102 and BL C/13/02; [2002] IP&T 767, *noted* IPD 25038 ...... 125.16, 125.20

CIUFFO GATTO/Trade mark (EPO Decision T 480/98) [2000] EPOR
494 .... 14.28, 76.10

Classlife's Patent BL O/278/00 .... 28.05

Clear Focus Imaging v. Contra Vision BL C/54/01, *noted* IPD 25009 .... 75.13,
97.09, 97.12, 97.16

I *   Coflexip v. Stolt Comex [2001] RPC 182; [2004] FSR 118; [2004] FSR
708 .... 61.22, 72.28, 97.16, 125.13, 125.15, 125.21

— v. — BL C/34/02 and [2003] EWCA Civ 296, (March 13, 2003) 61.25

Collag v. Merck [2003] FSR 263 .... 8.09

Collins' Patent BL O/322/01 .... 28.12

I   Comet Technology's Patent (BL O/337/03) 28.06

CYGNUS/Surgical Device (EPO Decision T 964/99) OJEPO 2002, 4;
[2002] FSR 272 .... 4.08

D.I. BV v. H.S. [Germany] [2000] ENPR 194 .... 60.08

I   Datadot v. Alpha Microtech [2004] 59 IPR 402 .... 65.03

Degüssa-Huls' Application BL O/180/04 .... 20.05

Dell USA's Application No. 0005904.8 BL O/177/02 .... 1.14

— — — No. 0127329.1 (Divisional) BL O/377/02 .... 1.14

— — — No. 9919949.9 BL O/432/01 .... 1.14

I   Dendron GmbH v. University of California [2004] EWHC 1163; [2004]
FSR 842; [2004] FSR 861; Ch D (Patents Ct) 67.03, 67.04

Denman's Patent BL O/369/01 .... 71.05

Designer's Guild v. Russell Williams [2001] FSR 113 at 122; [2001] IP&T
277 (HL) 3.04, 97.19

DISCOVISION/Rotation apparatus for information storage (EPO Decision
T 362/86) [2002] EPOR 90 .... 3.16

DSM NV's Patent [2001] RPC 675 ... 3.11, 3.19, 14.17, 76.10, 125.05, 125A.14,
125A.19, 125A.25

Duncan and Harcombe's Applications BL O/426/01 .... 20.07

DU PONT/Fibre-filled elastomer (EPO Decision T 345/96) [2001] EPOR
123 .... 3.25

Dyson v. Hoover [2001] RPC 473, and [2002] RPC 465 .... 2.11, 3.06, 3.13, 3.14,
125.10, 125.13, 125.15

— v. — (No. 2) [2001] RPC 544 .... 60.12, 61.22, 61.24

— v. — (No. 3) [2002] RPC 841 .... 61.55

— v. — (Costs) [2003] FSR 394 .... 61.38

Dyson's Patent [2003] RPC 473 .... 29.06

ELI LILLY/Naizatidine (EPO Decision T 55/99) [2000] EPOR 430 .... 125.13

—/Serotonin receptor (EPO Decision T 241/95), OJEPO 2001, 103; [2001]
EPOR 292 .... 14.28

I   ENICHEM/Amorphus TPM [2003] EPOR 73 (EPO Decision T 20/94) 14.27

Entertainment UK's Patent BL [2002] RPC 291 .... 40.09, 40.16

ETA/Request with review to revision (EPO Decision G1/97) OJEPO 2000,
322; [2001] EPOR 1 .... 77.10

*   Eveready Battery's Patent [2000] RPC 852 .... 32.21, 123.23

EXPANDABLE GRAFTS/Surgical Device (EPO Decision T 775/97)
[2002] EPOR 24 .... 4.07

Festo Corp v. Shoketsu Kinzoku (US) [2003] FSR 154 .... 125.26

xiii

Fieldturf's Divisional Application BL O/192/02 .... 76.11
FUJISAWA/Alpha-human ANP (EPO Decision T 202/95) [2002] EPOR
   34 .... 3.11
Fujitsu's Application BL O/317/00 .... 1.12, 1.14
—— —— No. 9720151.1 BL O/459/02 .... 1.15
FUJITSU/Removal of organic resist (EPO Decision T 311/91) [2000]
   EPOR 488 .... 76.16
* Furr v. Truline [1985] FSR 553 .... 125.26

* Gale's Application [1991] RPC 304 .... 1.15
GASCO/Solid lipid microspheres (EPO Decision T 79/99) [2000] EPOR
   419 .... 123.13
GALDERMA/Benzimidazole derivatives (EPO Decision T 1129/97)
   OJEPO 2001, 273, [2001] EPOR 478 .... 14.28
GENENTECH/Vaccines (EPO Decision T 187/93) [2002] EPOR 221 ...... 14.17
General Electric v. Enercom, Laddie J., February 17, 2003 [2003] EWHC
   1248 (Ch) 61.46
| GENETIC SYSTEMS/Synthetic antigen [2004] EPOR 127 (EPO Decision
   T 451/99) 76.10
GEORGETOWN UNIVERSITY/Pericardial access (EPO Decision
   T 35/99) OJEPO 2000, 447 .... 4.05
* Gerber Garment v. Lectra Systems [1995] RPC 383 and [1997] RPC 443 .... 61.22
* Gibbons' Patent [1957] RPC 158 .... 72.30
| Glaxo Group's Patent [2004] RPC 843 .... 3.11, 61.60
* Greater Glasgow Health Board's Application [1996] RPC 207 .... 39.08

Haberman v. Comptroller, *unreported*, March 5, 2003 .... 118.14
Hardman's Patent BL O/423/02 .... 28.06
* Harris's Patent [1985] RPC 19 .... 39.10
—— —— BL O/100/01 .... 28.06, 28.08
Hartington Conway Ltd's Patent Applications *See* Xtralite (Rooflights) Ltd
   v. Hartington Conway Ltd
| * HETTLING-DENKENT [2004] EPOR 38 (EPO Decision T 686/90) 1.11
Hewlett Packard v. Waters BL C/42/01; [2002] IP&T 5, *noted* IPD 24071
   and BL C/18/02; [2003] IP&T 143, *noted* IPD 25044 ... 2.11, 3.02, 3.04, 125.08
Hidalgo's Patent BL O/243/02 .... 28.09
HITACHI/Automatic auction system, unreported (EPO Decision T
   258/03) 1.14
* HOECHST/Thiochloroformates (EPO Decision T 198/84), OJEPO 1985,
   209 .... 2.20, 3.23, 3.38
Hoechst Marion Roussel v. Kirin-Amgen, *see* Kirin-Amgen's Patent
Hoerrman's Patent BL O/7/02 .... 28.10
HOYA/Intraocular lens (EPO Decision T 494/96) [2002] EPOR 131 .... 2.23
Hsiung's Patent [1992] RPC 497 .... 27.06
Hutchins' Application [2002] RPC 264 .... 1.15

IBM/Automatic sales control [Germany] [2000] ENPR 309 .... 1.14
Icon Health v. Precise Exercise Equipment BL C/29/01, *noted* IPD 24054 ... 70.02
ICOS Corp. (EPO Opposition Division Decision) [2002] OJEPO 293 ...... 1.10
IMPERIAL TOBACCO/Smoking article (EPO Decision T 524/98) [2000]
   EPOR 412 .... 14.25
* Impro's Patent [1998] FSR 299 .... 71.05, 125.19
Inhale Therapeutics v. Quadrant Healthcare [2002] RPC 419 ..... 2.09, 2.18, 3.08,
   3.18, 60.14
Inline Logistics v. UCI Logistics BL C/14/02; [2002] IP&T 444 .... 61.35

Instance v. CCL [2002] FSR 430; [2002] IP&T 721 .... 27.07
* Instance v. Denny Bros. [2000] FSR 869 .... 3.02, 3.13†, 61.54
— v. — (CA) [2002] RPC 321 .... 3.02, 3.04, 97.19
INSTITUT PASTEUR/Lympdenopathy-associate virus (EPO Decision
    T 824/94) [2000] EPOR 436 .... 76.20
International Business Machines' Applications BL O/390/01, O/399/01 .... 1.12,
    1.15
Intel v. Via Technologies [2003] FSR 175 and 574 .... 61.34
— v. — BL C/36/02, noted IPD 26007 .... 61.55
Intel's Patent [2002] RPC 957 .... 72.42, 72.44
Interfilta (UK)'s Patent [2003] RPC 411 .... 72.33
ITP SA v. Coflexip Stena Offshore Ltd 2004 SLT 1285; The Times, Novem-
    ber 29, 2004, IH (1 Div) 77.10

Jessen v. Coopervision BL C/31/00 .... 289.04

Kaiser's Patent BL O/279/00 .... 27.06, 27.07
Kalsep v. X-Flow BL C/13/01 .... 274.09
Kavanagh Balloons v. Cameron Balloons [2004] RPC 87 .... 2.23
Kenburn Waste Management v. Bergmann [2002] FSR 696 and 711 (CA) ... 70.02
* Kimberly-Clark v. Procter & Gamble (No. 2) [2001] FSR 339 ... 3.08, 14.20, 27.08,
    125.13
Kimberley-Clark v. Procter & Gamble (Pat 040109, 30.7.04; BL O/91/04,
    IPD 27099) 289.03
KIMBERLY-CLARK/Training pant (EPO Decision T 411/98) [2002] EPOR
    331 .... 3.33
* Kingdom of the Netherlands v. European Parliament (Case C–377/98 ECJ)
    [2002] FSR 574; OJEPO 2002, 231; [2002] IP&T 121 .. 1.19, 1.20, 125A.09
Kirin-Amgen v. Roche Diagnostics (No.1) [2002] RPC 1; [2003] RPC 31;
    (2001) 24(8) IPD 24050; [2004] UKHL 46; (2004) 148 SJLB 1249, HL ... 1.10,
              14.17, 14.19, 14.23, 14.27, 63.03, 125.10, 125.13, 125.15, 125.16
Kirin-Amgen v. Transkaryotic Therapies [2003] RPC 31 and [2005] RPC
    169 (CA) 14.17, 14.23, 61.22
— v. — (No. 2) [2002] RPC 203 .... 61.22, 61.24, 96.12, 125.15, 125.16, 125.26
— v. — (No. 3) [2002] RPC 851; [2002] IP&T 331 .... 61.22
Kirin-Amgen's Patent [2002] RPC 851 .... 63.03, 75.06
Kodak v. Jumbo Markt (Swiss Federal Court) [2001] ENPR 321 .... D16
KOMAG/Divisional claim conflicting with parent (EPO Decision T 587/98)
    OJEPO 2000, 497 .... 15.14
Koninkijke Philips Electronics NV v. Princo Digital Disc GmbH BL
    C/24/03 [2003] EWHC 1598, Ch D (Patents Ct) 2.24, 3.15
* Kooltrade v. XTS [2000] FSR 158 .... 70.03
— v. — [2002] FSR 764 .... 70.06

* LATCHWAYS/Unlawful applicant (EPO Decision G 3/92) OJEPO 1994,
    633; [1995] EPOR 141 .... 12.05
LELAND STANFORD/Modified Animal (EPO Opposition Division Deci-
    sion) [2002] EPOR 16 .... 1.20
Levi Strauss v. Tesco (ECJ) see Zino Davidoff v. A&G Imports
LG Electronics v. NCR Financial Solutions [2002] FSR 428 .... 68.04
Lilly Icos v. Pfizer see Pfizer's Patent
Lilly Icos v. Pfizer [2002] FSR 809 .... 61.55
Lionweld Kennedy's Application BL O/258/00 .... 18.15
LUBRIZOL/Flourohydrocarbons [2004] EPOR 85 (EPO Decision
    T 525/99) 76.10

Luk Lamellan's Patent BL O/379/02 .... 27.10, 72.30
Lundbeck v. Lagap BL C/5/03, *noted* IPD 26027 .... 70.04

Magill v. European Commission [1995] ECR I, 743 .... 61.34
Magill's Application BL O/256/00 and O/362/00 .... 12.03, 36.03, 37.06
Marshalltown Trowel v. Ceka Works [2001] FSR 633 .... 61.60
Matelect's Patent, BL O/458/00 .... 28.09
Machinery Developments Ltd v. St Merryn Meat Ltd (2004) 27(10) IPD
    27086, PCC 125.26
MacMullen's Application (BL O/307/03) 123.34
McGarry and Lawson's Application (BL O/262/03) 107.05
* McGriskin's Patent BL O/36/99, O/135/00 and O/410/00 .... 37.11
McGhan Medical v. Nagor BL C/6/01 .... 2.12
— v. — [2002] FSR 162 .... 61.35
Meijer's Plant Variety Right, *noted* [2002] EIPR N–38 ....48A.04
Melkris Ltd v. Denman *see* Denman's Patent
| * Memco-Med's Patent [1992] RPC 403 .... 40.09
Menashe v. William Hill [2002] RPC 950 and [2003] RPC 575; [2003]
    IP&T 32; [2003] 1 All ER 279 (CA) 60.08
| Merck v. Generics [Alendronate product] [2003] FSR 498; [2004] FSR 330;
    [2004] RPC 607 .... 2.34, 4.04, 61.35, 61.41, 61.59, 97.19, 125.08, 125.16
Meunier's International Application BL O/13/01 .... 123.34
Micromatic v. Dispense Systems BL C/20/01 .... 61.60
Minnesota Mining v. ATI Atlas [2001] FSR 514; [2001] IP&T 535 .... 3.18
Minnesota Mining's Application BL O/259/00 .... 1.12, 1.15
— — International Application [2003] RPC 541 .... 36.04, 37.06
* — — Patent BL O/247/00 and O/452/00 .... 7.06, 37.08
MITSUI/Photocurable resin composition (EPO Decision T 922/94) [2002]
    EPOR 208 .... 3.34
MODINE/Heat exchanger [2004] EPOR 303 (EPO Decision T 422/00) ... 76.13
Monitoring Technologies Ltd v. Bell Group Plc [2003] EWHC 3136; (2004)
    27(2) IPD 27015, Ch D (Patents Ct) 61.36
MONSANTO/Insect-resistant tomato plants (EPO Decision T 425/96)
    [2002] EPOR 45 .... 3.11
* Monsanto v. Merck [2000] RPC 709 ..... 2.10, 2.17, 2.34, 3.10, 3.11, 5.10, 14.29,
        60.03, 61.43, 72.26, 76.08, 76.11, 76.13, 125.16, 125.20, 125A.25
— v. — (CA) *see* Pharmacia v. Merck (BL C/62/01)
— v. — [Ireland] *see* Searle and Monsanto's Patent [2002] FSR 381
— v. Schmeiser [Canada] 12 CPR (4th) 204 .... 60.02

* N.N./Percarbonate (EPO Decision W 11/99) OJEPO 2000, 186; [2000]
    EPOR 515 .... 14.31
| * Niche Generics v. Lundbeck BL C/17/03 .... 61.57
| * Norling v. Eez-Away [1997] RPC 160 .... 75.04
Novartis' Supplementary Protection Certificates BL O/44/03 and Pumfrey,
    J., May 5, 2003 .... B14
* Nutrinova v. Scanchem [2001] FSR 797 .... 60.06
— v. — (No. 2) [2001] FSR 831 .... 27.08, 61.22, 61.35, 65.03

Omnicell's Patents BL O/329/02 .... 28.06
* Oxford Gene Technology v. Affymetrix and Beckman [2000] FSR 741 and
    [2001] FSR 136 .... 60.19
— v. — (No. 2) [2001] RPC 310 .... 27.06, 61.50
Oystertec's Patent BL O/298/02 and [2003] RPC 559 .... 72.15
— — BL O/525/02 .... 72.53, 107.02

Panduit v. Band-It BL C/11/01 and [2003] FSR 127 (CA) 3.13
* PASSONI/Stand structure [1992] EPOR 79 .... 2.30
PBS PARTNERSHIP/Controlling pension benefits system EPO Decision
    T 931/95 OJEPO 2001, 441 [2002] EPOR 522 .... 1.11, 1.14, 1.15
Peet's (unpublished) Application BL O/360/00 .... 1.05
Pfizer's Patent [2001] FSR 201 .... 3.11, 3.12, 3.18
— — BL C/36/00, noted IPD 23089 .... 61.60
— — BL C/2/02; [2002] IP&T 244, noted IPD 25022 .... 3.11, 3.12, 3.18
* Pharmaceutical Management v. Commissioner of Patents [New Zealand]
    [1999] RPC 752 and [2000] RPC 857 .... 4.04
Pharmacia v. Merck [2002] RPC 775; [2002] IP&T 828 ... 2.10, 2.17, 3.11, 3.36,
             5.10, 14.17, 14.29, 60.03, 61.35, 72.26, 76.08, 76.11, 76.13, 97.19,
                           125.15, 125.16, 125.20, 125A.25
* PHILIPS/Data structure product (EPO Decision T 1194/97) OJEPO 2000,
    525; [2001] EPOR 193 .... 1.16
Pico's Patent BL O/303/00 .... 37.09
Pilat's International Application [2003] RPC 253 .... 123.34
Pintos Global Services' Application BL O/171/01 .... 1.14
Poulton v. Adjustable Cover & Boiler Block Co [1908] 2 Ch 430; (1908) 25
    RPC 529 and 661: CA 72.28
PPG/Disclaimers (EPO Decision T 507/99) OJEPO 2003, 225; [2003]
    EPOR 291 .... 76.10
Practice Direction (Form of Judgments, Paragraph Marking and Neutral
    Citation) [2001] 1 WLR 194; [2001] 1 All ER 193 .... 123.48
Practice Direction (Neutral Citations) [2002] 1 WLR 346 .... 123.48
Practice Notice (Patent Office) "Interpreting section 1(2)" ([2002] RPC
    774) 1.14

Quantum Glass v. Spowart [Scotland], noted [2001] CIPA 99 .... 37.08

R v. Comptroller-General ex parte Ash & Lacy Building Products see Ash
    & Lacy's Patent No. 2240558
Reeves Wireline's Application BL O/454/01 .... 117.05
Requirement for claiming priority of the "same invention" (EPO Decision
    G 2/98) OJEPO 2001, 413; [2002] EPOR 167 .... 5.10, 5.13
Richard Pearson's Patent BL C/78/01 .... 28.06
Richardson's Application BL O/368/00 .... 4.03
RIJKSUNIVERSITEIT LEIDEN/Monocotyledonous plants (EPO Decision
    T 612/92) [2002] EPOR 79 .... 14.17
Robinson Wiley's Patent BL O/228/02 .... 72.39
Rockwater v. Coflexip BL C/46/02, noted IPD 25085 .... 61.53
— v. — BL C/15/03 .... 125.13, 125.21
* Rocky Mountain Traders v. Hewlett Packard [2000] FSR 411 and [2002]
    FSR 1 (CA) 2.09, 3.13, 125.16
* Rohm & Haas v. Collag [2001] FSR 426 and [2002] FSR 445 ..... 71.07, 125.18,
                                  125.26
Russel Finex v. Telsonic [2004] EWHC 474 (Pat), BL C/26/04; IPD
    27050 .... 125.23, 125.26

S.B. v. S.J.M. [Germany] [2000] ENPR 177 .... 2.05
Sabaf SpA v. MFI Furniture Centres Ltd; sub nom. Sabaf SpA v. Mene-
    ghetti SpA [2003] RPC 264 and [2005] RPC 209 HL 3.14, 3.15, 3.16, 60.04,
                                  60.18, 60.25
Sapey v. Trianco Redfyre, unreported July 31, 2001 .... 3.10
* Sara Lee v. Johnson Wax [2001] FSR 261 .... 27.05, 125.12

Sara Lee v. Johnson Wax (CA) BL C/60/01, *noted* IPD 25008 ... 125.11, 125.13, 125.16, 125.19

| Schering Corp v. Cipla Ltd [2004] EWHC 2587; BL C/134/04; IPD 28009; *The Times*, December 2, 2004, Ch D 61.43, 61.61

Searle and Monsanto's Patent [Ireland] [2002] FSR 381 .... 61.46

SEARLE/Cyclooxygenase 2 inhibitors (EPO Decision T 812/00) [2002] EPOR 443 .... 76.13

* SEKISUI/Shrinkable sheet (EPO Decision T 472/92) OJEPO 1998, 161; [1997] EPOR 432 .... 2.23

SEQUUS/Liposome composition (EPO Decision T 04/98) [2002] EPOR 371 .... 4.04

Shanley's Application BL O/422/02 .... 1.11

Smart Card Solution Application BL 0/80/02 .... 18.15

* Smith Kline & French v. Evans Medical, [1989] FSR 561 .... 27.06, 72.44

| SmithKline Beecham v. Apotex [2003] FSR 524 and 544 and [2004] FSR 523 .... 61.13, 61.60, 63.02

— v. — BL C/7/03, *noted* IPD 26031 .... 61.54

— v. Generics UK BL C/50/01 *noted* [2001] *CIPA* 628 and IPD 25005 ... 61.13

SmithKline Beecham's [Paroxetine Anhydrate] Patent BL C/28/02, *noted* IPD 25083 and BL C/27/03 (CA) 2.09, 125.12

— — [PMS] Patent BL C/24/02 and [2003] RPC 114 (CA) 2.24

— — — [2003] RPC 607 and [2003] EWCA Civ 861 (June 25, 2003) ... 2.09, 2.12, 2.24, 61.59

* SOLATRON/Fluid transducer (EPO Decision T 1149/97) OJEPO 2000, 259 [2001] EPOR 33 .... 76.22

Solenzaro's Patents BL O/156/01 .... 37.11

Speeches of Welcome for His Honour Judge Michael Fysh Q.C. [2002] FSR 79 ....287.04

Sporting Exchange's Application BL O/280/02 .... 1.14

Spring Form v. World's Apart BL C/22/01 .... 3.04

— v. Toy Brokers BL [2002] FSR 276 .... 61.29, 69.04

* Stafford Engineering's Licence of Right (Copyright) Application [2000] RPC 797 .... 107.04

Stafford Rubber Company's Application BL O/255/02 .... 8.11

Stannah Stairlifts v. Freelift (Patents County Court, July 4, 2002) 3.11

| Stead v. Anderson (1847) 4 CB 806; 136 ER 724 .... 60.02

Stena v. Irish Ferries [2002] RPC 990 and [2003] RPC 668 .... 60.16

— v. — (No. 2) [2003] RPC 681 .... 61.35

STERLING/S(+)ibuprofen (EPO Decision T 315/98) [2000] EPOR 401 ...... 2.34

| Storage Computer Corp v. Hitachi Data Systems Ltd [2003] EWCA Civ 1155; BL C/41/03; IPD 26063, CA (Civ Div) 3.06, 61.43

— — v. — BL C/35/01 *noted* IPD 24066 .... 61.46

* Stoves v. Baumatic BL C/27/00, *noted* IPD 23086 .... 3.10, 72.26, 125.20

| Sumitomo Rubber's Patent BL 0/35/03 .... 28.06

SUMITOMO/Superconductive film (EPO Decision T 348/94) [2001] EPOR 161 .... 2.05

| Swansea Imports v. Carver Technology BL O/170/04 .... 48A.07

* Swintex v. Melba Products [2000] FSR 39 .... 75.11

Takeda Chemical Industries' SPC Application [2003] EWHC 649 (Pat) [2004] RPC 37 .... B09

| Takeda Chemical Industries Ltd's SPC Application (No.2) [2004] RPC 20, PO B10

TECNICA/Ski boot lining (EPO Decision T 554/98) [2000] EPOR 475 ...... 3.22, 3.33

| Technip's Patent [2004] RPC 919 .... 61.53, 72.28, 125.13, 125.15, 125.21

Thibierge & Comar v. Rexam [2002] RPC 37937 .... 13, 97.09
Thibierge & Connor's Application BL O/345/01 .... 37.13
Tickner v. Honda BL C/68/01, *noted* IPD 25020 ... 3.06, 14.17, 61.60, 76.13, 76.22,
125.15
Tribunal Practice Notice 1/2003 (revised) O.J. August 20, 2003 .... 97.12

ULTRAFEM/Feminine hygiene device (EPO Decision T 1165/97) [2002]
EPOR 384 .... 4.03, 4.05
UNILEVER/Disclaimer (EPO Decision T 323/97) [2002] EPOR 427 .... 76.10
UNILEVER/Emulsions (EPO Decision T 384/94) [2000] EPOR 469 .... 3.33
Unilin Beheer BV v. Berry Floor [2005] FSR 56; [2004] FSR 238; [2004]
EWCA Civ 1021; (2004) 27(8) IPD 3; (2004) 148 SJLB 975, CA (Civ
Div) 5.04, 5.10, 61.55, 61.59
* United Wire v. Screen Repair Services [2001] RPC 439 (CA and HL) 60.20
University College London's Application BL O/381/02 .... 8.11, 12.04
UNIVERSITY OF CALIFORNIA/Ice nucleating (EPO Decision T 391/91)
[2002] EPOR 70 .... 14.21
I UNIVERSITY OF EDINBURGH/Stem Cells (Patent No. 069535) 1.19
University of Southampton's Applications [2002] RPC 906 .... 72.44
— — — BL O/444/02 and O/456/02 .... 118.19
— — — [2004] EWHC 2107; [2005] RPC 220 .... 13.04
* UNIVERSITY PATENTS/Herpes simplex virus (EPO Decision T 377/95)
OJEPO 12999, 11; [1999] EPOR 211 .... 2.30
— —/Six-month period (EPO Decision G/3/98) OJEPO 2001, 62, [2001]
EPOR 249 .... 2.30

Vericore's Patent BL O/125/02 and C/4/03, *noted* IPD 26026 ..... 2.06, 2.12, 3.11

Warheit v. Olympia Tools Pumfrey J., February 2, 2001 .... 60.25
— v. — (CA) [2003] FSR 95 .... 61.35
Wesley Jessen Corp. v. Coopervision BL C/31/01 .... 289.04
— v. — [2003] RPC 355 .... 125.19, 125.26
West Glamorgan's Application BL O/235/01 .... 39.10, 39.11
West Pharmaceuticals International Application BL O/58/02 .... 37.09
WEYERSHAEUSER/Cellulose (EPO Decision T 727/95) [2001] EPOR
265 .... 14.21
* Wheatley v. Drillsafe BL C/66/99 and [2001] RPC 133 .... 3.02, 3.06, 125.18,
125.19
Woolard's Application BL O/513/01 and [2002] RPC 767; [2002] IP&T
897 .... 2.26

Xtralite (Rooflights) Ltd v. Hartington Conway Ltd; *sub nom.* Hartington
Conway Ltd's Patent Applications [2004] RPC 161; [2003] EWHC
1872; [2004] RPC 161; Ch D (Patents Ct) 61.04

Young and Chatwin's Application BL O/70/01; O/174/01 .... 8.11

Zbinden's Application [2002] RPC 310 .... 2.26
ZENECA/Enantiomer (EPO Decision T 1046/97) [2002] EPOR 325 .... 2.20
Zino Davidoff v. A&G Imports (ECJ) [2002] RPC 403 .... D16

TABLE OF EPO CASES

(Supplemental to the Table of EPO Cases in the Main Work)

Cases are listed according to the section (§) numbers of the Main Work to which they refer, as supplemented by the contents of this Supplement likewise referring to the same paragraph numbers. Abbreviations are used as in the Main Work, see page cxl thereof.

An asterisk against a case indicates that it is also cited in the Main Work and † indicates that a case has been omitted from mention in the Table of Cases in the Main Work.

Note that where an EPO decision is recorded as "unreported", the full text of that decision (in its original language only) can be found on the "Espace-Legal" CD-ROM produced by the EPO and also on the EPO web site "www.european-patent-office.org".

Opposition Division Decision (ICOS Corp.) [2002] OJEPO 293 .... 1.10
Opposition Division Decision (LELAND STANFORD/Modified Animal) [2002] EPOR 16 .... 1.20

G 1/93 ADVANCED SEMICONDUCTOR PRODUCTS/Limiting Feature OJEPO 1994541; [1995] EPOR 97 .... 76.13
G 1/97 (ETA/Request with review to revision) OJEPO 2000, 322; [2001] EPOR 1 .... 77.10
* G 2/98 (Requirement for claiming priority of the "same invention") OJEPO 2001, 413; [2002] EPOR 167 .... 2.24, 5.10, 5.13, 76.10
* G 3/98 (UNIVERSITY PATENTS/Six-month period), OJEPO 2001, 62, [2001] EPOR 249 .... 2.30

† T 128/82 (HOFFMANN-LA ROCHE/Pyrrolidine-derivatives) OJEPO 1984, 164 .... 2.33
* T 219/83 (BASF/Zeolites) OJEPO 1986, 211 .... 14.23
* T 198/84 (HOECHST/Trichloroformates) OJEPO 1985, 209 .... 2.20
* T 163/85 (BBC/Television signal) OJEPO 1990, 379; [1990] EPOR 599 .... 1.16
T 362/86 (DISCOVISION/Rotation apparatus for information storage) [2002] EPOR 90 .... 3.16
* T 686/90 HETTLING-DENKENT [2004] EPOR 38 .... 1.11
T 816/90 ALKO/CBH II [2003] EPOR 414 .... 125A.24
T 311/91 (FUJITSU/Removal of organic resist) [2000] EPOR 488 .... 76.16
T 391/91 (UNIVERSITY OF CALIFORNIA/Ice nucleating) [2002] EPOR 70 .... 14.21
T 73/92 BALFOUR/Feedstuff [2004] EPOR 73 .... 14.27

T 612/92 (RIJKSUNIVERSITEIT LEIDEN/Monocotyledonous plants) [2002] EPOR 79 .... 14.17

* T 472/92 (SEKISUI/Shrinkable sheet) OJEPO 1998, 161; [1997] EPOR 432 .... 2.23

* T 74/93 (BRITISH TECHNOLOGY/Contraceptive method) [1995] EPOR 279 .... 4.03

* T 124/93 (AMOCO/Olefin Catalyst) [1996] EPOR 624 .... 14.27

T 187/93 (GENENTECH/Vaccines) [2002] EPOR 221 .... 14.17

T 204/93 (AT&T/Computer system) [2001] EPOR 300 .... 1.15

T 977/93 (AMERICAN HOME PRODUCTS/Canine coronavirus) [2001] EPOR 274 .... 2.12

I T 20/94 ENICHEM/Amorphus TPM [2003] EPOR 73 .... 14.27

T 348/94 (SUMITOMO/Superconductive film) [2001] EPOR 161 .... 2.05

T 384/94 (UNILEVER/Emulsions) [2000] EPOR 469 .... 3.33

T 824/94 (INSTITUT PASTEUR/Lympdenopathy-associate virus) [2000] EPOR 436 .... 76.19

T 922/94 (MITSUI/Photocurable resin composition) [2002] EPOR 208 ... 3.34

I * T 145/95 BTG/Newcastle disease virus [2003] EPOR 390 .... 125A.19

T 202/95 (FUJISAWA/Alpha-human ANP) [2002] EPOR 34 .... 3.11

T 241/95 (ELI LILLY/Serotonin receptor), OJEPO 2001, 103; [2001] EPOR 292 .... 14.28

* T 377/95 (UNIVERSITY PATENTS/Herpes simplex virus), OJEPO 1999, 11; [1999] EPOR 211 .... 2.30

T 727/95 (WEYERSHAEUSER/Cellulose) [2001] EPOR 265 .... 14.21

T 931/95 (PBS PARTNERSHIP/Controlling pension benefits system) OJEPO 2001, 441 .... 1.11, 1.14, 1.15

T 37/96 (BELOIT/Digester) [2002] EPOR 308 .... 2.23

T 79/96 (APV ANHYDRO/Granulation by spray drying) [2001] EPOR 309 .... 3.23, 3.25, 125.14

T 345/96 (DU PONT/Fibre-filled elastomer) [2001] EPOR 123 .... 3.25

T 363/96, noted IPD 23094 .... 2.23

T 425/96 (MONSANTO/Insect-resistant tomato plants) [2002] EPOR 45 ... 3.11

T 494/96 (HOYA/Intraocular lens) [2002] EPOR 131 .... 2.23

T 323/97 (UNILEVER/Disclaimer), [2002] EPOR 427 .... 76.10

T 775/97 (EXPANDABLE GRAFTS/Surgical Device) [2002] EPOR 24 .... 4.07

T 1046/97 (ZENECA/Enantiomer) [2002] EPOR 325 .... 2.20

T 1129/97 (GALDERMA/Benzimidazole derivatives) OJEPO 2001, 273, [2001] EPOR 478 .... 14.28

* T 1149/97 (SOLATRON/Fluid transducer) OJEPO 2000, 259; [2001] EPOR 33 .... 76.22

T 1165/97 (ULTRAFEM/Feminine hygiene device) [2002] EPOR 384 .... 4.03, 4.05

T 1194/97 (PHILIPS/Data structure product) OJEPO 2000, 525; [2001] EPOR 193 .... 1.16

T 04/98 (SEQUUS/Liposome composition) [2002] EPOR 371 .... 4.04

I T 254/98 (MINGATI/Vertical lathe) [2003] EPOR 316 .... 2.23

T 315/98 (STERLING/S(+)ibuprofen) [2000] EPOR 401 .... 2.34

T 411/98 (KIMBERLY-CLARK/Training pant) [2002] EPOR 331 .... 3.33

T 480/98 (CIUFFO GATTO/Trade mark) [2000] EPOR 494 .... 14.28, 76.10

T 524/98 (IMPERIAL TOBACCO/Smoking article) [2000] EPOR 412 ... 14.25

T 554/98 (TECNICA/Ski boot lining) [2000] EPOR 475 .... 3.22, 3.33

T 587/98 (KOMAG/Divisional claim conflicting with parent) OJEPO 2000, 497 .... 15.14

T 728/98 (ALBANY/Pure Terfenidine) [2002] EPOR 1 .... 125.15

T 35/99 (GEORGETOWN UNIVERSITY/Pericardial access) OJEPO 2000, 447 .... 4.05

T 55/99 (ELI LILLY/Naizatidine) [2000] EPOR 430 .... 125.13
T 79/99 (GASCO/Solid lipid microspheres) [2000] EPOR 419 .... 123.13
T 451/99 (GENETIC SYSTEMS/Synthetic antigen) OJEPO 2003, 334 .... 76.10
T 507/99 (PPG/Disclaimers) OJEPO 2003, 225; [2003] EPOR 291 .... 76.10
I T 525/99 LUBRIZOL/Flourohydrocarbons [2004] EPOR 85 .... 76.10
T 964/99 (CYGNUS/Surgical Device) OJEPO 2002, 4; [2002] EPOR
   272 .... 4.08
I T 422/00 MODINE/Heat exchanger [2004] EPOR 303 .... 76.13
T 812/00 (SEARLE/Cyclooxygenase 2 inhibitors) [2002] EPOR 443 .... 76.13
I T 1173/00 ABB PATENT/Transformer (OJEPO 2004, 16) 14.29

* W 11/99 (N.N./Percarbonate), OJEPO 2000, 186; [2000] EPOR 515 ...... 14.31
I T 258/03 HITACHI/Automatic auction system, unreported, ... 1.14

TABLE OF STATUTES

(Supplemental to the Table of Statutes in the Main Work)

References are to section (§) numbers and bold type indicates a reprinted section. An asterisk indicates that the citation is additional to the corresponding citation in the Main Work and † indicates a citation omitted from the Main Work.

❙ *	1939	Import, Export and Customs Powers (Defence) Act (2 & 3 Geo.6, c. 69) 22.14
*	1975	Evidence (Proceedings in Other Jurisdictions) Act (c. 34) E34.21
	1977	National Health Service Act (c. 49)

Sched. 8A 56.01

* Patents Act (c. 37) 0.03A, F63.1, F63.3, F63PD.2
[References below to "R" refer to a section of this Act as subsequently replaced; and the use of asterisks has been discontinued for entries to the 1977 Act]

s. 2(3)	5.19
s. 2(4)	8.11
s. 2(6)	**2.01**, 2.34, 4A.02
s. 4	1.01, **4.01**
s. 4A 1.01, 2.01, 2.33, 2.34, 4.01, **4A.01**, 4A.02	
s. 5	**5.01**
s. 5(2) **5.01–5.02C**, 15.09, 17.02, 20A.03	
s. 5(2A) 5.01, 5.02A, 5.07, 5.07A, 17.09, 20A.01, 78.01,78.04, 89B.05	
s. 5(2B) **5.01**, 5.03, 17.09	
s. 5(2C) **5.01**, 5.03, 17.09, 20A.03	
s. 5(5) 15.01, 15.06, 76.03	
s. 8(3) **8.01**, 8.11, 12.05	
s. 8(7) F63.11	
s. 11(3A) **11.01**, 11.04	
s. 12(2) F63.11	
s. 12(6) 8.11, 12.01, 12.05	
s. 13(2) 15A.01, 15A.03, 81.02, 81.03	
s. 14(1) 15.01	
s. 14(1A) **14.01**, 14.08, 15.01, 130.01	
s. 14(10) **14.01**	
s. 15R **15.01**, 15.06, 15.08	
s. 15(1)R 76.01	
s. 15(2)–(4)R 15.08	

s. 15(5)–(6)[R] 15.02
s. 15.(7)[R] 15.02
s. 15(8)[R] 15.06
s. 15(9)[R] ... 5.07, 15.02, 15.05, 15.13, 15.15, 18.02, 18.03, 72.01, 72.25,
                                                                76.01, 123.08
s. 15(10)[R] 14.01, 14.08, 15.01A, 15.04, 15.06, 15.08, 15.10,15.11,
                    15A.01, 15A.03, 76.01, 76.03, 81.02, 81.03, 89A.02
s. 15A 14.08, 15.01, 15.24, **15A.01**–15A–03, 17.01–17.03, 17.06,
                                                    81.08, 89B.01, 89B.16
s. 15A(2) 15.09
s. 15A(6) 76.01, 76.03
s. 16 .... 16.01, 16.03, 16.07, 89B.08
s. 16(1) 5.02, 5.02A
s. 17 .... 15A.01, 15A.03, **17.01**, 17.06
s. 17(1) **17.01**, 17.02
s. 18 .... 15.01
s. 20 .... 117B.01
s. 20A 5.07A, **20A.01**–20A.03, 20B.01, 112.31
s. 20B 20A.03, **20B.01**, 20B.02, 60.01, 78.05, 117A.02
s. 22 .... 16.01, **22.01**
s. 23 .... **23.01**
s. 23(1A) **23.01**, 23.02
s. 23(3A) **23.01**, 23.02
s. 24(4) **24.01**, 24.08
s. 25(3) **25.01**, 25.07, 25.08, 46.01
s. 25(4) **25.01**, 25.08, 62.04
s. 27(6) **27.01**, 27.05, 75.06
s. 28 .... F63.15
s. 28(3) 25.08, **28.01**, 28.06
s. 28A 20A.02, 20B.02, 80.01, 80.07, 117A.02
s. 30(6)–(6A) **30.01**, 30.06
s. 32 .... **32.01**, 74A.02, F63.1
s. 36(3) **36.01**, 36.05, 72.15
s. 37(8) F63.11
s. 38 .... 11.04
s. 38(3) **38.01**, 38.05
s. 38(5) **38.01**, 38.05
s. 40 .... **40.01**, 106(2)
s. 40(1) **40.01**, 40.09, F63.12, F63PD.13
s. 40(2) 40.01, 40.09, F63.12, F63PD.13
s. 40(5) F63.11
s. 41(1) **41.01**, 61.39
s. 43(4) 43.01
s. 43(5) **43.01**
s. 43(5A) **43.01**
s. 46(3) 25.08, **46.01**, 46.18
s. 46(3B) **46.01**, 46.18
s. 50A **50A.01**, 50A.02
s. 51 .... 50A.02, **51.01**
s. 53(1) **53.01**
s. 53(2) 50A.02, **53.01**
s. 58(6) 27.05, **58.01**, 58.05
s. 58(9A) **58.01**, 58.05, 63.04
s. 60(4) **60.01**, 60.11
s. 60(6) 60.01, 60.17
s. 61 .... **61.01**, 106.02

s. 61(1) 74B.01–74B.03
s. 61(5) F63.11
s. 61(7) 41.03, **61.01**, 61.39
s. 62(2) **62.01**
s. 62(3) 27.05, 58.05, **62.01**, 63.03
s. 63(2) 27.05, 58.05, **62.01**
s. 63(4) 58.05, **63.01**, 63.03, 63.04
s. 64 ....20B.01
s. 69 ....20B.02
s. 70 .... 70.01, F63PD.2
s. 70(2) **70.01**, 70.05
s. 70(2A) **70.01**, 70.05
s. 70(4) **70.01**
s. 70(5) **70.01**
s. 70(6) **70.01**, 70.08
s. 71 .... 106.02
s. 71(1) 74B.01–74B.03
s. 72 .... 15.01, **72.01**
s. 72(1) **72.01**, 74B.01–74B.03
s. 72(4) **72.01**
s. 72(4A) **72.01**, 72.27
s. 72(7) F63.11
s. 74(1) 74B.02
s. 74(2) 74B.02
s. 74(8) **74.01**, 74.03, 74A.02, 74B.02
s. 74A 74.01, 74.03, **74A.01**–74A.03, 74B.01–74B.03
s. 74B 74.03, 74A.02, **74B.01**–74B.03
s. 75 .... **75.01**, F63.10
s. 75(5) 27.05, **75.01**, 75.06
s. 76 .... 15.01, 15A.01, 15A.03, **76.01**, 76.03
s. 76(1A) 15.08, **76.01**, 76.03
s. 76(4) **76.01**, 76.03
s. 77(5) **77.01**, 77.12
s. 78 .... 15.01
s. 78(3) 5.03, **78.01**, 78.04
s. 78(5A) **78.01**, 78.05
s. 78(6)–(6C) **78.01**, 78.05, 80.07
s. 80 .... **80.01**
s. 80(4) **80.01**, 80.07
s. 80(5)–(7) **80.01**, 80.07
s. 81 .... 5.02B, 5.18, 15.01, **81.01**
s. 81(1) 81.06
s. 81(2) 81.09
s. 86 .... 86.01
s. 87 .... 87.01
s. 89(3) 89A.02
s. 89(4) 89.01, 89.11, 89A.02
s. 89A 15.01
s. 89A(3) 15.01, 89A.23, 89B.01
s. 89B **89B.01**
s. 91 .... **91.01**
s. 93 .... 41.03, 61.39
s. 95 .... **95.01**
s. 97(4) 74B.02
s. 101 ....74A.02
s. 103 .... **103.01**, 103.02

	s. 105	101.01, **105.01**, 105.02
	s. 106	61.35, **106.01**, 106.02
	s. 106(1A)	**106.01**, 106.02
	s. 107	41.03, 61.39, **107.01**, 107.05
	s. 117(1)	14.01, 14.07, 14.34
	s. 117(3)	**117.01**, 117.03, 117A.01
	s. 117(4)	**117.01**, 117.03, 117A.01
	s. 117A	14.34, 20B.02, 60.01, 78.05, 117.03, **117A.01**, 117A.02, 123.31
	s. 117B	18.15, 20A.03, **117B.01**, 117B.03, 123.31
	s. 120	**120.01**, 120.04, 123.15
	s. 121	**121.01**, 121.02, 123.15
	s. 123(2)	13.04, **123.01**, 123.41
	s. 123(2A)	**123.01**, 123.05, 123.15, 123.19
	s. 123(4)	123.25
	s. 123(5)	123.30
	s. 123(6)	F63.10
	s. 124A	14.02, 14.03, 14.05, 14.09, 17.04, 27.15, 77.03, 123.05, 123.05A, **124A.01**–124A.03
	s. 130(1)	15.01, 78.03, **130.01**
	s. 130(4A)	89.11, 89.29, **130.01**, 130.07
	s. 130(5A)	27.03, 75.03, **130.01**, 130.07
	s. 131	**131.01**
1969	Official Secrets Act (c. 6)	22.13
* 1981	Supreme Court Act (c. 54)	
	s. 6	F63.1
	s. 37	61.22
	s. 70	F63PD.10
* 1985	Administration of Justice Act (c. 61)	103.01
* 1988	Copyright, Designs and Patents Act (c. 48)	F63.1
1994	Welsh Language Act (c. 38)	14.12
1997	Plant Varieties Act (c. 66)	48A.04
1998	Human Rights Act (c. 42)	15.13
1999	Access to Justice Act (c. 22)	97.06
	Youth Justice and Criminal Evidence Act (c. 23)	
	Sched. 6	32.01
2000	Electronic Communications Act (c. 7)	130.01
* 2000	Finance Act (c. 17)	
	s. 17	126.01
	s. 129	126.01
	Sched. 40, Pt III	126.01
	Postal Services Act (c. 26)	119.04
I 2001	Regulatory Reform Act (c. 6)	22.01A
	Health and Social Care Act (c. 15)	
	s. 28	56.01
	Sched. 5, para. 4	56.01
2002	Export of Goods Control Act (c. 28)	22.14
	Enterprise Act (c. 40)	44.04, 50A.01, 50A.02, 51.01, 53.01, 135.01
2003	Health and Social Care (Community Health and Standards) Act (c. 43)	56.01
	Criminal Justice Act (c. 44)	32.01, 292.04

2004 Patents Act (c. 16) 0.03A, 1.01, 2.01, 4.01, 4A.01, 8.01, 11.01, 12.01,
            16.01, 22.01, 23.01, 24.01, 25.01, 28.01, 28.07, 32.01, 36.01, 38.01,
            40.01, 41.01, 43.01, 46.01, 53.01, 60.01, 61.01, 62.01, 63.01,
            70.01, 72.01, 74.01, 74A.01, 74A.02, 74B.01, 74B.02, 75.01,
            77.01, 78.01, 80.01, 81.01, 86.01, 87.01, 89.01, 89B.01, 91.01,
            95.01, 103.01, 105.01, 106.01, 107.01, 117A.01, 121.01, 123.01,
                            123.16, 130.01, 131.01, 132.03,
        s. 17 .... 0.03A, 132.03

TABLE OF STATUTORY INSTRUMENTS

(Supplemental to the Table of Statutory Instruments in the Main Work)

References are to section (§) numbers and bold type indicates a reprinted rule. An asterisk indicates that the citation is additional to the corresponding citation in the Main Work and † indicates a citation omitted from the Main Work.

*   1978   Patents Act 1977 (Isle of Man) Order (S.I. 1978 No. 621) 132.02

*   1990   Patents Act 1977 (Isle of Man) (Variation) Order (S.I. 1990 No. 2295) 132.02

*   1991   Patent Office Trading Fund Order (S.I. 1991 No. 1796) ... 121.02, 123.16

            Solicitors' Incorporated Practices Order (S.I. 1991 No. 2684) 103.01

*   1992   Patents (Supplementary Protection Certificate for Medicinal Products) Regulations (S.I. 1992 No. 3091) F63.1

*   1995   Patents Rules (S.I. 1995 No. 2093)

            References below to "R" refer to a rule of these rules as subsequently entirely replaced; and the use of asterisks has been discontinued for entries to the 1995 Rules]

            r. 2 .... 15.08, 20B.02, 89A.19, **123.03**, 123.18

            r. 3^R **123.04**

            r. 4^R **123.05**

            r. 6^R ... 5.02, 5.03, 5.07, 15.05, 15.11, 15A.02, 17.09, 123.11, 123.42

            r. 6(2)^R 5.07, 15.11, 123.09A

            r. 6(4)^R 5.07

            r. 6(6) 5.07, 123.42

            r. 6A 5.02, **5.02A**, 5.03, 5.07, 5.07A, 15.05, 15.11

            r. 6B 5.02, **5.02B**, 5.02C, 5.03, 5.07, 5.18, 15.05, 15.11, 15A.02, 17.09, 123.09C, 123.11

            r. 6C 5.02, **5.02C**, 5.03, 5.07, 5.19, 15A.02, 17.09, 123.11

            r. 7(3) 123.09B

            r. 8(3) 123.09B

            r. 8(5) 123.09B

            r. 8(6) 123.09B

            r. 9^R **8.04**

            r. 9(2) 123.09B

            r. 12(2) 123.09B

            r. 13^R **11.02**

            r. 13(2) 123.09B

            r. 14(3) 123.09B

            r. 15^R **13.03**, 123.09C, 123.09D

r. 16 .... **14.02**, 14.08, 15.08, 123.09C, 123.09D, 123.11
r. 16(1A)–(1C) **14.02**, 14.08
r. 16(2) 14.02, 14.09
r. 16(5) **14.02**, 14.08
r. 16(6) **14.02**, 14.08
r. 22A 15.01, **15.01A**, 15.08
r. 23R **15.02**, 15.09, 15.11, 123.09C
r. 24 .... 15.03, 123.09D
r. 25R 14.08, **15.04**, 15.11, 15.15, 89A.23, 123.09–123.09C, 123.09D
r. 26R 15.05, 15.11, 123.09A, 123.09C, 123.09D
r. 28R **15A.02**, 15A.03, 17.02
r. 28AR 15A.02, **17.02**, 17.06, 17.09
r. 29R 15A.03, **17.03**, 17.06, 17.09
r. 30 ....15A.03
r. 31 .... 15A.03, 17.06
r. 32 .... 17.05
r. 33 .... 123.09C, 123.09D
r. 34 .... 18.03, 123.09C, 123.09D
r. 36A **20A.02**, 20A.03, 72.09, 123.09A, 123.11
r. 40 .... 27.02, 27.16, 123.09A, 123.09B
r. 41(1) 123.09A
r. 41(4) 123.09A
r. 43(2) 123.09A
r. 43(4) 123.09B
r. 45 .... **32.04**, 32.18
r. 46 .... **32.05**, 32.18
r. 47 .... **32.06**, 32.20
r. 54 .... 123.09B
r. 56 .... 123.09B
r. 57R **38.02**, 38.04
r. 57(1) 123.09B
r. 58R 38.03, 38.04
r. 58(2) 123.09B
r. 59 .... 123.09A, 123.09B
r. 62 .... 123.09B
r. 64(1) 123.09A
r. 65(2) 123.09A
r. 70 .... 123.09B
r. 71 .... 123.09B
r. 72 .... 123.09B
r. 73 .... 123.09B
r. 74 .... 123.09B
r. 75 .... 123.09B
r. 77 .... 123.09B
r. 78(2) 123.09A
r. 81 .... 15.04, **81.02**, 123.09A, 123.09C, 123.09D, 123.11
r. 82 .... 15.04, **81.03**, 123.09A, 123.09C, 123.09D, 123.11
r. 83 .... 123.09D
r. 85 .... **89A.02**, 89A.21, 123.11
r. 85(7) 15.04, **89A.02**, 89A.16, 123.09C, 123.09D, 123.11
r. 85(7A) 15.04, **89A.02**, 89A.16, 123.09C, 123.09D, 123.11
r. 91(3A) **117.02**
r. 91(4) 123.09A
r. 98 .... 120.01, 120.04
r. 99 .... 120.01, 120.04
r. 102 .... **123.08**

r. 107 .... 20A.03, 72.09, 72.23
r. 110ᴿ 89A.35, **123.09**, 123.31–123.34, 123.36
r. 110(4)ᴿ 14.08
r. 110(7)ᴿ 123.33
r. 110(8)ᴿ 14.08, 15.11, 123.31, 123.33
r. 110(9)ᴿ 123.36
r. 110(11)ᴿ 72.34, 123.09C, 123.31
r. 110A **117B.02**, 117B.03, 123.09A
r. 112(3)–(5) **123.11**
r. 112A 5.02C, 5.18, 15.08, 15.09, **123.10A**
r. 113 .... **123.11**, 123.42, 123.43
r. 113(6) **123.11**
r. 113A 27.16, **123.11A**, 123.43
r. 115 .... 120.04, **123.13**, 123.18
Sched. 2, para. 2 .... 123.09C
Sched. 4, para. 5 .... 77.05, 123.09A, 123.43
Sched. 4A 89A.35
Sched. 4A, Part 1 ...... 5.07, 5.07A, 15.11, 20A.03, 123.05, **123.09A**,
              123.31, 123.32, 125A.30
Sched. 4A, Part 2 .... 123.09B, 123.31, 125A.30
Sched. 4A, Part 3 .... 5.07, 5.18, 15.11, 89A.35, 123.09, **123.09C**,
              123.31, 123.33
Sched. 4A, Part 4 ... 15.11, 28.05, 89A.35, 123.09, **123.09D**, 123.31,
              123.33

*   1996   Patents (Supplementary Protection Certificate for Plant Protection
          Products) Regulations (S.I. 1996 No. 3120) F63.1
*   1997   Patents (Supplementary Protection Certificates) Rules (S.I. 1997 No.
          64) F63.1
     1999   Visiting Forces and International Headquarters (Application of Law)
          Order (S.I. 1999 No. 1736) 55.01, 56.01, 57.01, 57A.01, 58.01
          Scotland Act 1998 (Consequential Modifications) (No. 2) Order
          (S.I. 1999 No. 1820) 131A.01
     2001   Patents (Amendment) Rules (S.I. 2001 No. 1412) ... 15.05, 89A.02, 123.09,
              125A.02–125A.07, 125A.27–125A.30
          Patents (Convention Countries) Amendment Order (S.I. 2001 No.
          2126) 90.03
     2002   Patents and Plant Variety Rights (Compulsory Licensing) Regula-
          tions (S.I. 2002 No. 247) 1.21, 48.04
          Patents (Amendment) Rules (S.I. 2002 No. 529) 15.04, 18.02, 89A.02
     2003   Patents Act 1977 (Electronic Communications) Order (S.I. 2003 No.
          512) 124A.01, 124A.02
          Patents (Electronic Communications) (Amendment) Rules (S.I.
          2003 No. 513) 14.02, 14.03, 14.05, 17.04, 27.02, 75.02, 77.03,
              123.05, 123.19, 124.02, 140.11
          Patents Act 1977 (Isle of Man) Order (S.I. 2003 No. 1249) 0.03, 1.01,
              5.01, 22.01, 23.01, 41.01, 44.01, 45.01, 48.01, 48A.01, 48B.01,
              50.01, 51.01, 52.01, 53.01, 54.01, 58.01, 60.01, 76A.01, 93.01,
              96.01, 97.01, 107.01, 109.01, 124A.01, 125A.01, 130.01, 132.02,
              137.01, 138.01
          Export of Goods, Transfer of Technology and Provision of Technical
          Assistance (Control) Order (S.I. 2003 No. 2764) 22.02, 22.14
     2004   Patents Act 2004 (Commencement No. 1 and Consequential and
          Transitional Provisions) Order (S.I. 2004 No. 2177) ... 120.01–120.04,
              123.01, 123.03, 123.05, 123.15, 123.18, 139.02

Regulatory Reform (Patents) Order (S.I. 2004 No. 2357) "the
RRO" 5.01, 14.01, 15.01, 15.15, 15A.01, 17.01, 18.01, 20A.01,
28.01, 28.06, 30.01, 60.01, 72.01, 76.01, 78.01, 81.01, 89B.01,
117.01, 117A.01, 117B.01, 130.01, 132.03
Patents (Amendment) Rules (S.I. 2004 No. 2358) 5.02–5.02C, 13.03,
14.02, 15.01–15.05, 15A.02, 17.02, 17.03, 20A.02, 27.02,
32.04–32.06, 81.01, 81.03, 89A.02, 117.02, **123.09–123.09D**,
123.11A, 123.14, 139.02, 140.01, 140.09A
Patents Act 2004 (Commencement No. 2 and Consequential, etc.
and Transitional Provisions) Order (S.I. 2004 No. 3205 (C.140) 8.01,
8.04, 11.01, 11.02, 12.01, 16.01, 22.01, 23.01, 38.01–38.03, 40.01,
41.01, 43.01, 53.01, 60.01, 61.01–62.02, 63.01, 70.01, 75.01,
86.01, 87.01, 89.01, 89B.01, 91.01, 95.01, 103.01, 105.01, 106.01,
121.01, 123.16, 130.01, 131.01, 139.02
Patents (Convention Countries) Order (S.I. 2004 No. 3335) 90.03

TABLE OF COURT RULES

(Supplemental to the Table of Court Rules in the Main Work)

References are to section (§) numbers. An asterisk indicates that the citation is additional to the corresponding citation in the Main Work and † indicates a citation omitted from the Main Work.

*	CPR 6	F63.16
	CPR 6.19	F63.16
*	CPR 7	F63.5
	CPR 15.4	F63.6
	CPR 15.8	F63.6
	CPR 16PD	E16PD11, E16PD12, E16PD14
	CPR 18PD	E18PD.5
*	CPR 20	F63.5, F63.9
	CPR 20PD	E20PD.3
	CPR 22.1	E22.1
	CPR 22PD	E22PD.1, E22PD.5
|	CPR 25.13	107.05, E25.13
	CPR 26	F63.7
	CPR 29.3	F63.7
*	CPR 29.4	F63.7
	CPR 29.5	F63.7, F63PD.4
†	CPR 29.6	**E29.6**
	CPR 29.7	**E29.7**, F63PD.4
†	CPR 29.8	**E29.8**
	CPR 30.5	F63.4
*	CPR 31	F63.8
	CPR 31PD.5	E31PD.5
	CPR 31PD.7	E31PD.7
*	CPR 31PD.8	**E31PD.8**
	CPR 34.21	92.03, 92.04, **E34.21**, E50.0
	CPR 35.1–35.4	E35PD.0–E35PD.5
	CPR 35.5	E35PD.0–E35PD.5, 63PD.10
	CPR 35.6	E35PD.0–E35PD.5, 63PD.10
	CPR 35.12	E35.12

*	CPR 35.14	E35.14
	CPR 35.15	E35.15
| *	CPR 44	61.35, E44.2–E44.14, 106.02
	CPR 44.13	E44.13
	CPR 44.14	E44.14
	CPR 44 PD.11	E44PD.11
	CPR 48.8	E48.8
	CPR 49EPD	E49EPD.0, F00
| *	CPR 49 PD16	97.12
	CPR 49 PD16.3	97.12
	CPR 52	20.05, 72.52, 97.12, 97.16
	CPR 52.2	97.12
	CPR 52.3–52.4	97.12
	CPR 52.5	20.05, 72.52, 97.12, 97.16
|	CPR 52.6	97.12
	CPR 52.11	97.09
|	CPR 52.13.1	97.06
|	CPR 52 PD.5	20.05, 72.52, 97.12
	CPR 52, PD5.1	97.12
	CPR 52 PD.7–52PD.16	20.05, 72.52
	CPR 52 PD.17	20.05, 72.52, 97.12
	CPR 52 PD.18–52PD.21	20.05, 72.52
	CPR 63	34.21, 41.10, 58.08, 61.41, 70.09, 71.09, 72.13, 72.31, 80.12, 96.06, 97.18, 99A.05, 131.03, 291.04, E00.3, E49EPD.0, E63.0
	CPR 63.1	32.15, 40.14, 61.05, 96.07, B–09, **F63.1**
	CPR 63.2	40.14, 61.05, 96.07, B09, **F63.2**
	CPR 63.3	40.14, 55.11, 56.02, 58.02, 61.05, 96.07, B09, **F63.3**

CPR 63.4 .... 40.14, 61.05, **F63.4**
CPR 63.5 ...37.15, 40.14, 61.05, 61.42,
       F63.5, F63PD.3
CPR 63.6 .... **F63.6**
CPR 63.7 .. 61.41, 61.42, 61.62, **F63.7**,
       63PD.4
CPR 63.8 ...61.49, 61.50, 61.54, 72.44,
    280.05, 291.04, **F63.8**, 63PD.5
CPR 63.9 ....61.42, **F63.9**, 63PD.11
CPR 63.10 ....75.08, 75.11, 75.12,
      F63.10, F63PD.12
CPR 63.11 ....37.15, 40.14, 61.39,
      F63.11
CPR 63.12 ....40.06, 40.14, 40.17,
    41.09, 41.10, 106.02, **F63.12**,
      F63PD 13
CPR 63.16 ....32.15, 61.42, 70.09,
    71.09, 96.11, 97.19, **F63.16**
CPR 63.17 ....20.05, 40.17, 41.10,
    72.52, 97.02, 97.12–97.14,
      97.16, **F63.17**
CPR 63PD 58.08, 61.41, 70.09,
    71.09, 72.13, 72.31, 80.12,
    96.06, 97.18, 99A.05, 131.03,
    291.04, E00.3, E49EPD.0,
      F63PD.1–F63PD.16
CPR 63 PD.2 .... 61.05, 70.09, **F63PD.2**
CPR 63 PD.3 .... 61.05, **F63PD.3**
CPR 63 PD.4 ....61.41, 61.42, 61.62,
      F63PD.4
CPR 63 PD.5 ....3.14, 3.44, 61.49,
    61.50, 61.54, 61.55, 61.60,
    61.62, 72.44, 280.05, **F63PD.5**
CPR 63 PD.6 .... 61.62, **F63PD.6**
CPR 63 PD.7 .... 61.62, **F63PD.7**
CPR 63 PD.8 .... 61.62, **F63PD.8**
CPR 63 PD.9 ....60.14, 61.59, 61.62,
      F63PD.9
CPR 63 PD.10 .... 61.60, **F63PD.10**
CPR 63 PD.11 ....2.21, 61.42, 61.57,
    72.13, 72.18, 72.37, 77.18,
    80.12, **F63PD.11**

CPR 63 PD.12 .... 75.08, 75.11,
      F63PD.12
CPR 63 PD.13 .....40.06, 40.14, 40.17,
    41.09, 41.10, 106.02,
      F63PD.13
CPR 63 PD.14 .... 94.05, **F63PD.14**
CPR 63 PD.15 .... 34.06, **F63PD.15**
CPR 63 PD.16 .... 34.06, 37.15,
      F63PD.16
Patents Court Guide (new) 61.41,
    70.09, 71.09, 72.13, 72.31,
    96.06, 131.03, 291.06,
      G00–G22A.19
para. 1 .... **G01**
para. 2 ....61.62, **G02**
para. 3 ...34.06, 61.41, 61.62, 97.14,
      G03
para. 4 .... **G04**
para. 5 ....61.41, **G05**
para. 6 ....61.41, **G06**
para. 7 ....97.12, 97.13, **G07**
para. 8 ....61.18, **G08**
para. 9 ....61.42, **G09**
para. 10 ... 61.41, 61.60, 61.62, **G10**
para. 11 ....61.62, 77.18, **G11**
para. 12 ....61.41, 61.42, **G12**
para. 13 ....61.42, 61.58, **G13**
para. 14 ....61.62, **G14**
para. 15 ....61.41, **G15**
para. 16 ....34.06, 61.41, **G16**
para. 17 ....61.41, **G17**
para. 18 ....96.06, **G18**
para. 19 ....96.06, **G19**
para. 20 ....61.62, **G20**
para. 21 ....61.09, **G21**
para. 22 .... **G22**
Annex ...61.36, 61.41, 61.59, 61.60,
    61.62, **G22A.1–G22A.19**

TABLE OF INTERNATIONAL CONVENTIONS, TREATIES AND RELATED RULES AND REGULATIONS

(Supplemental to the Table of International Conventions, Treaties and Related Rules and Regulations in the Main Work)

COMMUNITY TREATY
Art. 81 .... D20
Art. 81(1) D20, D28
Art. 81(3) D20
EUROPEAN COMMUNITY DIRECTIVES
2004   Dir. 2004/27/EC (O.J. L136/34)
Art. 10(6) 60.14
Dir. 2004/28/EC (O.J. L136/358)
Art. 13(6) 60.14
EUROPEAN COMMUNITY REGULATIONS
1965   Reg. 19/65/EEC d27
1996*   Reg. 240/96 TTR D20
2001   Reg. 44/2001 [2001] OJEC L12 12/1   Jurisdiction and Enforcement of
   Judgements 107.05
2004   Reg. 772/2004   Technology Transfer Block Exemption D20, D21
Art. 1 .... **D21**, D29
Art. 2 .... **D23**, D30
Art. 3 .... **D23**, D30
Art. 4 .... **D24**, D31
Art. 5 .... **D25**, D30
Art. 6 .... **D26**, D32
Art. 7 .... **D26**, D32
Art. 8 .... **D27**, D30
Arts 9–11 .... **D28**
Art. 10 .... D33
EUROPEAN PATENT CONVENTION
a. 53 .... 4A.01, 4A.02
a. 54 .... 4A.01, 4A.02
a. 79 .... 78.03, 78.05, 89.11, 89.29
a. 105A 27.03, 27.05, 63.04, 72.27, 75.03, 130.07
a. 112A 77.12, 78.05
a. 123 .... 27.05
EUROPEAN PATENT CONVENTION RULES [EPC r.]
r. 38 .... 5.02B, 5.02C

TABLE OF FORMS

(References are to section numbers wherein a particular form is mentioned)

Note The forms for use in Patent Office proceedings are now regulated by directions issued by the Comptroller, see §140.00 below. Here it is explained that these forms are now readily accessible on the Patent office web site and, accordingly, this Supplement contains no reprinting of these forms and pages 1105–1151 of the Main Work are now redundant.

AF1 .... 14.08
PF 1/77 ....14.08, 14.09, 15.08, 89A.23,
                                   140.00, 142.02
PF 3/77 ... 5.02, 5.02A, 5.03, 5.07, 5.07A,
                                   140.00, 142.02
PF 7/77 .... 89A.16, 89A.28
PF 9A/77 ....17.02, 17.05, 17.07, 81.09,
                                          142.02

TABLE OF EPO GUIDELINES

(Supplemental to the Table of EPO Guidelines in the Main Work)

References are to section (§) numbers. An asterisk indicates that the citation is additional to the corresponding citation in the Main Work and † indicates a citation omitted from the Main Work.

| † | C–II, 4.14 | 14.14 |
| | C–IV, 56 (B1) | 3.16 |

In this Table in the Main Work (page cxxxix), the references to Guidelines B–VII, 5 and C–III, 6.3 should be deleted.

TABLE OF ABBREVIATIONS

(Supplemental to the Table of Abbreviations in the Main Work)

BSLR   BioScience Law Review
IP&T   Intellectual Property and Technology Cases
RRO   The Regulatory Reform (Patents) Order 2004 (S.I. 2004 No. 2357)
USC   United States Code of Law

Patents Act 1977 (c. 37)

The long title to the Act, its Sections and Schedules   **0.02**

On page 8 of the Main Work, add after "124. Rules ..." the new entry "124A. Use of electronic communications", and add after "131. Northern Ireland." the new entry, "131A. Scotland."

Amendments to the Patents Act 1977   **0.03**

The following further amendments have been made to this Act:

Year	Enactment	Sections affected
1991	Solicitors' Incorporated Practices Order (S.I. 1991 No. 2684)	103
1999	Youth Justice and Criminal Evidence Act (c. 23) [Sched. 6]	32
	Visiting Forces and International Headquarters (Application of Law) Order (S.I. 1999 No. 1736) [Art. 6 and Sched. 4(2)]	55–58
	Scotland Act 1998 (Consequential Modifications) (No. 2) Order (S.I. 1999 No. 1820) [Art. 4 and Sched. 2, Part I, para. 58]	131A
2000	Finance Act (c. 17) [s. 156 and Sched. 40, Part III]	126
2001	Health and Social Care Act (c. 15) [s. 67 and Sched. 5, para. 4]	56
2002	Enterprise Act (c. 40) [Sched. 25(8)]	50A, 51, 53
2003	Health and Social Care (Community Health and Standards) Act (c. 43) [Sched. 11(6)]	56
	Criminal Justice Act (c. 44) [Sched. 37(6)]	32

Year	Enactment	Sections affected
	Patents Act 1977 (Electronic Communications) Order (S.I. 2003 No. 512)	124A
	Patents Act 1977 (Isle of Man) Order (S.I. 2003 No. 1249)	1, 5, 22, 23, 41, 44, 45, 48, 48A, 48B, 50, 51, 52, 54, 58, 60, 76A, 94, 96, 97, 107, 124A, 125A, 130, Scheds. A1 and A2
2004	Patents Act 2004 (c. 16)	1, 2, 4, 4A, 8, 11, 12, 16, 20B, 22–25, 27, 32, 36, 38, 40, 41, 43, 46, 50A, 53, 58, 60–63, 70, 72, 74–74B, 75, 77, 78, 80, 81, 86, 87, 89, 89B, 91, 95, 103, 105–107, 117A, 117B, 120. 121. 123, 130, 131, 132
	Regulatory Reform (Patents) Order (S.I. 2004 No. 2357)	5, 14, 15, 15A, 17, 18, 20A. 20B, 28, 30, 60, 72, 76, 78, 81, 89B, 117, 117A, 117B, 130

0.03A *Effect of Patents Act 2004 (c. 16)*

The Patents Act 2004 (c. 16. s. 17) contains the following provisions which have effect to provide for subsequent further amendment of the provisions of that Act (or the 1977 or other Act in relation thereto) by secondary legislation, subject (except in the case of amendment under subsection (4)(a)) to affirmative resolution by each House of Parliament:

17.—(4) order under this section may make—
(a) any supplementary, incidental or consequential provision, or
(b) any transitory, transitional or saving provision,
that the Secretary of State considers necessary or expedient for the purposes of, in consequence of or for giving full effect to any provision of this Act.

(5) A statutory instrument containing provision made by virtue of subsection (4) is subject to annulment in pursuance of a resolution of either House of Parliament, unless the only such provision it contains is transitory, transitional or saving provision.

(6) The provision that may be made under subsection (4) includes provision amending or repealing any enactment or instrument.

(7) A statutory instrument containing an order under this section that adds to, replaces or omits any part of the text of an Act is not to be made unless a draft of the instrument has been laid before and approved by a resolution of, each House of Parliament; and subsection (5) does not apply to such an instrument.

PART I [SECTIONS 1–76A]—NEW DOMESTIC LAW

SECTION 1—Patentable inventions   1.01

The Patents Act 2004 (c. 16, Sched. 2(2)) prospectively amended subsection (1)(d) by adding the words "or section 4A" before the word "below". This amendment will be brought into effect when the EPC revisions agreed in 2000 come into force. It is a consequence of the relocation from section 4 into new section 4A of the unpatentability of methods of medical or surgical treatment or of diagnosis, for which see § 4A.02 *infra*.

Note
   4. The amendments to subsections (4) and (5) have been applied to the Isle of Man (S.I. 2003 No. 1249).

COMMENTARY ON SECTION 1

General considerations concerning the treatment of subject-matter excluded   **1.05**
from patentability under subsection (2)

Subsection (2) is declaratory in form and, while it lists certain types of subject-matter to be excluded from patentability under the Act, the categorisation of these types is not exhaustive in view of the phrase "among other things" in the preamble to the subsection. In *Peet's (unpublished) Application* (BL O/360/00), this phrase was used to exclude patentability for matters which, if not exactly matters categorised in paragraphs (c) or (d) were sufficiently akin thereto, the application being directed to real or fantasy games organised and performed in accordance with specified procedures; and, although these operations involved computerised actions, they could also be carried out manually.

—Discoveries, scientific theories and mathematical methods (subs. (2)(a))   **1.10**

In *Kirin-Amgen Inc. v. Roche Diagnostics GmbH* ([2002] RPC 1), the court held that although the essential feature of the patent was a discovery (of a certain DNA sequence) it was a discovery that made a technical contribution. Claim 1 was to an application of the discovery which was capable of industrial application.

EPO (Opposition Division) Decision (ICOS Corp.) [2002] OJEPO 293 holds that DNA sequences with indications of function that are not substantial, specific and credible shall not be patentable inventions according to Art. 52(1) because they lack technical character. Thus a claim to a DNA sequence encoding a protein without a credible function was held not patentable. Reference was made to the Biotechnology Directive Recital 23.

1.11   —*Aesthetic creations (subs. (2)(b))*

Claims to partitions for buildings intended "to provide a different appearance" in the finished building were refused in *Shanley's Application* (BL O/422/02) although subclaims introducing technical features were allowed to proceed, subject to amendment. An argument that the main claim should be allowed on the basis of *EPO Decision T* 931/95, *PBS PARTNERSHIP/Controlling pension benefits system* was rejected.

EPO Decision T 686/90, *HETTLING-DENKEN/Translucent building materials*, referred to in the Main Work, has been reported at [2004] EPOR 38.

1.12   —*Mental acts (subs. (2)(c) in part)*

In *Minnesota Mining's Application* (BL O/259/00), the collection of data was seen as a rule, scheme or method for performing a mental act, it being possible to collect the same data using pen and paper, see also § 1.15; and, in *Fujitsu's Application* (BL O/317/00), an application concerned with systems for handling conflicting demands for resources, such as reservations for meeting rooms, particularly involving "queuing" criteria, was denied patentability as directed to mental acts being "the mere automation of a manual method of prioritisation of human actions". In this *Fujitsu* case, the application was also seen as an unpatentable method of doing business, see § 1.14 *infra*.

International Business Machines' Applications (BL O/390/01 and O/399/01) are further examples of applications being refused as directed to methods of performing mental acts. In O/390/01 (which was concerned with a method allowing a computer to identify the human language of a computerised document by breaking down words into all their constituent letter pairs, and comparing those with corresponding letter pairs of preselected words from the chosen languages under consideration), the agent for the applicant argued that there was a technical effect, being the electronic recognition of the language of the document, but had to concede that this argument was weakened by the fact that the documents being handled remained unchanged by the process. The Comptroller considered the operations performed by the computer to be "a purely intellectual exercise" and held that "no matter how broad an interpretation is put on the terms technical contribution, technical effect, or technical consideration, I cannot find such a contribution, effect or consideration in the invention of the present application." A similar result was reached in O/399/01 in which the invention related to a method of translation. It was held irrelevant that the claims were directed to a translation "system", as (following *Merrill Lynch*) "substance must prevail over form and it is therefore necessary to construe each claim carefully to determine whether it relates to an excluded matter in the guise of some other article".

The Notice in the O.J. of April 24, 2002 referred to in § 1.14 *infra* as regards business methods, also applies in relation to inventions deemed to relate to mental acts as such.

1.14   —*Methods of doing business (subs. (2)(c) in part)*

The Patent Office has published a practice notice relating to the handling of applications for business method patents (O.J. 6027, 24.11.04, [2004] *CIPA* 634, which indicates that the examiner will refer the matter to a hearing officer at an early stage if he is of the opinion that there is no prospect of a patent being granted despite the applicant's response to the first official action. The applicant will be given the opportunity for an oral hearing but the examiner will not enter into correspondence about other matters that might be outstanding. These will be deferred pending the hearing officer's decision on patentability. Also, hearing officers may issue abbreviated decisions without necessarily giving detailed reasons for rejecting each of the arguments advanced if those are, in essence, the same as those that have been rejected in previous decions. The notice gives a list of ten previous decisions by way of example.

An application concerned with systems for handling conflicting demands for resources, such as reservations for meeting rooms, particularly involving "queueing" criteria, was denied patentability as essentially directed to a method of doing business (*Fujitsu's Application* BL O/317/00), see also § 1.12. However, the German Federal Patent Court has accepted that a method of automatic sales control involving adjusting selling prices from sales prediction data is not merely an automatic method of putting a business method into effect and has technical character and so is not inherently unpatentable (*IBM/Automatic sales control [Germany]* [2000] ENPR 309).

Pintos Global Services' Application (BL O/171/01) was directed to an "apparatus" for controlling a pension benefit system and was rejected, following *Merrill Lynch*, because the fact that the claim was formally directed to "apparatus" was not conclusive: it essentially involved a method of doing business as such. This was despite *EPO Decision T 931/95, PBS PARTNERSHIP/Controlling pension benefits system* (OJEPO 2001, 441 [2002] EPOR 522) which also involved a pension benefits system, and in which the EPO would apparently have allowed the claims but for (in their view) the lack of an inventive step of a technical character. In the event of any apparent conflict between the EPO and United Kingdom decisions the Comptroller held that he was bound by the decisions of the United Kingdom courts.

In *Applied Psychology's Application* (BL O/208/04) and *Venner's Application* (BL O/193/04), it was argued that the Comptroller's approach to recent cases was not in conformity with decisions of the EPO Boards of Appeal, particularly in not following *T* 931/95 (*supra*). However, the Hearing Officer saw the UK and EPO approaches as being "consistent" as a matter of law, although, in *Venner*, it was accepted that *T* 931/95 "is not consistent with established UK principles". The required "technical contribution" could arise from either the nature of the problem to be solved or the means of solving that problem and the efforts made in doing so.

In *Dean's Application* (BL O/274/04), the hearing officer set out the principles underlying statutory patentability under section 1(2) as:

> "First, in deciding whether an invention is excluded, it is the substance of the invention that is of importance rather than the form of claims adopted. Second, the effect of the final part of section 1(2) is that an invention is only excluded from being patentable if it amounts to one of the excluded areas "as such". Following decisions of the UK courts and the EPO Boards of Appeal, an invention is not considered to [be] one of those things "as such" if the invention makes a technical contribution. Third, whether an invention makes a technical contribution is an issue to be decided on the facts of the individual case. Finally, it is desirable that there should be consistency between the Patent Office's interpretation of the Patents Act and the EPO's interpretation of the EPC."

In *Ultrasonic's Application* (BL O/273/04), it was argued that UK decisions should produce the same effect as those given by the EPO Boards of Appeal and attention was drawn to *EPO Decision T* 258/03, *HITACHI/Automatic auction system* (unreported), where it had been held that it is sufficient for patentability under Article 52 for an invention to have a "technical character", whereas the English decisions had required patentability under section 1(2) to be dependent upon the existence of a "technical contribution". The Hearing Officer considered patentability using first the UK approach, and then that of the EPO. Under the UK approach, while the invention had a technical character, no technical contribution was seen (other than that provided by a conventional computer which, according to the Fujitsu decision, had to be excluded from consideration). The application should therefore be rejected as being no more than a method of doing business, as well as directed to a computer program as such.

Then, applying the EPO approach, it was first noted that, in *Hitachi*, the application had been rejected for lack of inventive step, because it had been held (as in *T* 931/95, *supra*) that, in assessing inventive step, the non-technical features of the claims had to be stripped out. When this was done, no inventive step could be found. Thus, both approaches led to the same result, and the decisions had the same effect and were consistent with each other within the terms of section 130(7).

Further decisions rejecting inventions under subsection (2)(c) are: *Dell USA's* Application No. 9919949.9 (BL O/432/01, *noted* [2001] *CIPA* 576) in which the (very successful) web-based online user interface provided by Dell Corporation to enable users to custom configure a computer system for purchase was seen to be a computerised version of a salesman advising a client on the ordering of a suitable system and hence a "method of doing business" and unpatentable; and *Bilgrey Samson's Application* (BL O/577/01) in which claims to the operation of a "fruit machine" type apparatus were held not to involve a technical contribution and to relate to a scheme, etc., for doing business.

A further application by Dell was refused on the same basis (*Dell USA's* Application No. 0005904.8 (BL O/177/02)) and on the basis that the specification was silent with respect to the technical detail of the process, so that it offered no technical contribution to the art. This decision considered the UK, EPO and German case law in coming to this conclusion. An argument that the Dell website was able to offer a variety of choice amounting to 70 million options, more than a salesperson could handle, did not succeed because the specification imposed no limit on the complexity of the system; it could be set up to deal with fewer combinations. In any event, even with a large number of combinations, the computer was doing no more than its familiar function of performing a large number of iterations quickly.

A Divisional out of the first application No. 9919949.9 was considered in a further decision (*Dell USA's* Application No. 0127329.1, BL O/377/02) but rejected on the same basis, the Hearing Officer concluding that although the form and content of the claims had been changed, the substance of the invention claimed remained "an interaction between a user and a computer, which … replicates what a customer may do in a store, by telephone or in writing".

An application directed to an internet betting system was refused as relating to a method of doing business in *Sporting Exchange's Application* (BL O/280/02).

The conclusion of the British Government consultation process (see § 1.15) in relation to business methods is that "those who favour some form of patentability for business methods have not provided the necessary evidence that it would be likely to increase innovation." Accordingly "ways of doing business should remain unpatentable". A notice in the O.J. of April 17, 2002 states that applications directed to business methods as such will continue to be rejected before any search is conducted as it is not seen that a search would serve any useful purpose. Applications for "pure business methods" have "no prospect of maturing into valid UK patents." However a further notice in the O.J. of April 24, 2002 ([2002] RPC 774) announced a new policy of the Patent Office that inventions *which involve a technical contribution* will not be refused a patent merely because they relate to business methods or mental acts. It is stated that this position will be consistent with the Office's existing practice on computer programs, and will align more nearly with practice under the corresponding provisions of the European Patent Convention.

The result of the European Commission's own consultation process on the protection of computer implemented inventions (also see § 1.15) indicates that there will be no change in the existing law in relation to business methods. The Commission says that although the consultation did not deal directly with business methods, the responses indicated "general satisfaction" with the current situation where "pure" business methods are not patentable. This means that there will remain a divergence between European and United States law in this area. See also the articles by A. Laakkonen and R. Whaite "The EPO leads the way, but where to?" ([2001] EIPR 244), and M. Likhovski "Fighting the Patent Wars" ([2001] EIPR 267).

1.15 —*Computer programs (subs. (2)(c) in part)*

The book *Patenting Software under the* European Patent Convention by

K.R.L. Beresford (Sweet & Maxwell, 2000) provides a comprehensive discussion of the history of patenting software-related inventions and a detailed discussion of decisions thereon before 2000.

In *Minnesota Mining's Application* (BL O/259/00), a computer program designed to provide a screen display of noise levels in a workplace was not regarded as itself providing a technical effect. The possibility that the screen display could lead to action to control undue noise was seen as a collocation. The application also failed as being analogous to a mental act, see § 1.12.

Hutchins' Application ([2002] RPC 264) was rejected following *Pintos Global Services' Application* (BL O/171/01) (see § 1.14), as being a computer program as such, the invention not providing any technical effect. *EPO Decision T 931/95, PBS PARTNERSHIP/ Controlling pension benefits system* ([2002] EPOR 522) was referred to but seen as exalting form over substance. The Hearing Officer commented that under the Patents Act 1977 "there does not appear to be any basis for determining the *patentability* of an invention by considering the *form* in which it is claimed."

International Business Machines' Applications (BL O/390/01 and O/399/01) (see § 1.12) failed also as being directed to computer programs as well as methods of performing mental acts.

In *Fujitsu's* Application No. 9720151.1 (BL O/459/02) an invention comprising a method of designing and developing software using a computer was seen as nothing more than a program written to perform a particular function and therefore refused as relating to a computer program as such, although it was held not subject to objection as a method for performing a mental act or doing business.

The EPO in *EPO Decision T 204/93, AT&T/Computer system* ([2001] EPOR 39) held that as well as computer programs as such being excluded from patentability by EPCa. 52(2)(c), a programmer's activity of writing a computer program is also excluded, because it requires performing mental acts as such. Making use of a "system" comprising software and hardware which caused the computer to implement the programmer's activity did not cause the computer to work in a new way from a technical point of view so the claim was excluded from patentability.

The results of a consultation process initiated by the British Government via the Patent Office on whether patents should be granted for computer software and ways of doing business were published in March 2001 and made available on the Patent Office website (www.patent.gov.uk). The Government's conclusion in relation to software is to reaffirm the principle that patents are for technological innovations. Software should not be patentable where there is no technological innovation, and technological innovations should not cease to be patentable merely because the innovation lies in software. However, the Government agreed with respondents who said that at present the law is not clear enough, in relation to the boundary determining when software is, and is not, part of a technological innovation, so that what is patentable will be clear in specific cases.

On February 20, 2002 the European Commission published the results of its own consultation process on the protection of computer-implemented inventions. Broadly, the conclusion is that the *status quo* should be maintained (in particular the requirement for a technical contribution for patentability) but the Commission wishes a change in practice in relation to patents for computer programs "on their own, *i.e.* in isolation from a machine on which they may be run". The proposal is for a Directive which would require Member States to bring their laws into line with it and to co-operate in any necessary amendments to the EPC. The new regime is likely therefore to overturn the 1999 *IBM* decisions referred to in the Main Work in so far as they permit the patenting of computer programs on discs or other carriers or as a signal transmissible over the internet. In the meantime it is perhaps unlikely that the United Kingdom courts will relax their more restrictive approach as exemplified in *Gale's Application* ([1991] RPC 304). See also the article by A. Laakkonen and R. Whaite " *The EPO leads the way, but where to?* " ([2001] EIPR 244).

The proposed Directive on the patentability of computer-implemented inventions (COD/2002/0047) has seen both strong support and opposition from different interests, and the legislative process is still ongoing. There has been tension between the Commission and the European Parliament, which has proposed many amendments to the directive not acceptable to the Commission.

1.16 *—Presentation of information (subs. (2)(d))*

The EPO has held that a record carrier having functional data recorded thereon is not a "presentation of information" as such (*EPO Decision T* 1194/97, *PHILIPS/Data structure product* (OJEPO 2000, 525; [2001] EPOR 193), thereby extending the ruling in *EPO Decision T* 163/85, *BBC/Television signal*, cited in the Main Work.

Specific exclusions from patentability despite being inventions (subs. (3))

1.19 *—Exclusion on grounds of public policy (subss. (3)(a) and (4))*

A challenge to the EU Biotechnology Directive by the Dutch Government on the grounds that the patentability of living organisms offended against principles of morality failed before the European Court of Justice (*Kingdom of the Netherlands v. European Parliament* (Case C–377/98) ([2002] FSR 574; OJEPO 2002, 231; [2002] IP&T 121).

The decision of the Opposition Division in *HARVARD/Onco-mouse* referred to in the Main Work has been published (OJEPO 2003, 473). The oppositions were rejected subject to the claims being limited to the creation of transgenic rodents. It is understood that the decision has been appealed. See the article by A. Sharples and D. Curley [2002/2003] 1 BSLR 26 for further comment on this case. The EPO Opposition Division has issued a decision in *European Patent No. 069535, UNIVERSITY OF EDINBURGH/Stem Cells* that claims directed to or embracing human embryonic stem cells are unpatentable as contrary to *Ordre Public* and morality under EPCa. 54 in light of Rule 23d(c), which specifically prohibits patents for human embryos for industrial or commercial purposes. In any event, the description in relation to human embryonic stem cells was held to lack sufficiency under EPCa. 83 in view of post-priority publications describing difficulties in producing such cells. However, claims to isolated animal stem cells (including human) other than embryonic stem cells could be allowed and were sufficiently supported by data on mouse stem cells. Such claims were not excluded from patentability because they are an element isolated from the human body or otherwise produced by a technical process. They are therefore patentable under Rule 23e(2) EPC, and are not excluded under Rule 23d(c) in view of the exclusion of embryonic stem cells from the ambit of the claims.

1.20 *—Exclusion for plant and animal varieties (subs. (3)(b))*

EPO (Opposition Division) Decision *LELAND STANFORD/Modified Animal* ([2002] EPOR 16) has held that an immuno-compromised mouse implanted with human tissue may be patented, the claims being directed to a taxonomic group higher than an animal variety, such claims being allowable in accordance with the EU Biotechnology directive and *EPO Decision G* 01/98, *NOVARTIS/Transgenic plant* ([2000] EPOR 303). This is thought to be the first decision on patenting of animals since *EPO Decision T* 19/90 *HARVARD/Onco-mouse* ([1990] EPOR 501). The patenting of living matter under the terms of the Biotechnology Directive has been upheld by the ECJ in *Kingdom of the Netherlands v. European Parliament* (Case C–377/98) ([2002] FSR 574; OJEPO 2002, 231; [2002] IP&T 121).

The decision of the Opposition Division in *HARVARD/Onco-mouse* referred to in the Main Work has been published (OJEPO 2003, 473). The oppositions were rejected subject to the claims being limited to the creation of transgenic rodents. The Board of Appeal set aside the decision of the Opposition Division and remitted the case to them with an order to maintain the patent subject to the claims being further limited to the creation of transgenic mice. See the article by A. Sharples and D. Curley [2002/2003] 1 BSLR 26 for further comment on this case.

Plant breeders' rights   **1.21**

The Patents and Plant Variety Rights (Compulsory Licensing) Regulations (S.I. 2002 No. 247) came into force on March 1, 2002 (to complete the implementation of Art. 12 of the Biotechnology Directive), and provide that, where a person cannot acquire or exploit plant breeders' rights without infringing a prior patent, he may apply to the Comptroller for a licence under the patent. A licence is only available where the new plant variety constitutes significant technical progress of considerable economic interest in relation to the invention. Further, where a proprietor of a patent for a biotechnological invention cannot exploit the invention without infringing prior plant breeders' rights, he may apply to the Controller of Plant Variety Rights for a licence under such rights, but only where the biotechnological invention protected by the patent constitutes significant technical progress of considerable economic interest in relation to the plant variety. It is thought that the Regulations may for this reason find application only in rare circumstances and they are not reproduced in this Supplement; see also § 48.04.

SECTION 2—Novelty   **2.01**

The Patents Act 2004 (c. 16, Scheds. 2(2) and 3) prospectively removed subsection 2(6). This amendment will be brought into effect when the EPC revisions agreed in 2000 come into force. The provisions of subsection 2(6) will then be found, with additional effect, in new subsections 4A(3) and (4), for which see § 4A.02 *infra*.

COMMENTARY ON SECTION 2

Scope of the section   **2.03**

The Court of Appeal decision in *American Home Products v. Novartis*, cited in the Main Work as BL C/31/00, has been published ([2001] RPC 159).

Novelty destroyed by the state of the art (subss. (1) and (2))

—*Anticipatory disclosures must be made available "to the public"*   **2.05**

The German Supreme Court has held that there has been no disclosure to the public, as such, when others collaborate in manufacturing and animal trials (*S.B. v. S.J.M.* [Germany] [2000] ENPR 177).

In *EPO Decision T* 348/94, *SUMITOMO/Superconductive film* ([2001] EPOR 161) it was held that there was no presumption that conference proceedings published 10 months afterwards were an accurate record of those proceedings. There was a burden of proof on the opponent to show this, in the absence of which the disclosures in the document (which had been published after the priority date) did not form part of the state of the art.

—*Date when material is made available to the public*   **2.06**

In *Vericore's Patent* (BL O/125/02) evidence given as to the likelihood that a thesis would have been put on the shelves of a library earlier than the catalogue date would have indicated was not found sufficient to prove that the thesis had been made available to the public before the relevant date. However, evidence from the author that he supplied copies to colleagues without confidentiality restriction before the relevant date was accepted. The Comptroller's decision was upheld on appeal to the court (BL C/4/03, *noted* IPD 26026).

2.09   *—Lack of novelty arising from the inevitable result of a described operation*

The decision of lack of novelty in *Rocky Mountain Traders v. Hewlett Packard*, cited in the Main Work, was reversed on appeal ([2002] FSR 1) because the directions in the prior art document could be carried out in a variety of ways and thus had not unambiguously described "planting the flag" in the same way as the claim required.

In *Inhale Therapeutics v. Quadrant* ([2002] RPC 419) it was held that a disclosure which is capable of being carried out in a manner which does not fall within the claim does not anticipate, although it may be the basis of an obviousness attack.

In revocation proceedings by Synthon against *SmithKline Beecham's* [PMS] *Patent (No. 2)* ([2003] RPC 607) it was held that there had been anticipation by an earlier application forming part of the state of the art under section 2(3) (and therefore effective only against novelty), which had disclosed a method of making paroxetine methanesulphonate (PMS) in crystalline form. Although there were found to be difficulties in reproducing the method of the earlier application so as to obtain crystals, and some obscurities in the background to the data contained in the earlier application, the judge found on the balance of probabilities that there was only one crystalline form of PMS and that this was what Synthon had made and described in their prior patent application. However, the decision was reversed on appeal ([2003] RPC 769), it being held that the example given in the Synthon application could not be made to work without modification and therefore there were no clear and unmistakeable directions to make the claimed form of PMS. Accordingly, the prior disclosure did not make the PMS claimed in the patent available to the public (see also § 2.24 *infra*). The House of Lords was scheduled to hear a final appeal in May 2005.

In *SmithKline Beecham's* [Paroxetine Anhydrate] *Patent* (BL C/28/02, *noted* IPD 25083), the court stated the principle as being that "if the prior disclosure does not contain a teaching which is of equal utility to the teaching of the patent, it may nevertheless anticipate if [in]carrying out its directions the skilled man carries out a process or makes a product falling within the claim." In this case the claims referred to the paroxetine anhydrate as free from bound propan-2-ol, which was the solvent used in its preparation. The prior art process used a different solvent in the process such that propan-2-ol could not be present in the end product. The patentee contended that the claim should be read as requiring the product to be free of any bound organic solvent used in its production, and not just free of propan-2-ol, in order to give fair protection to the patentee. The court found the claims invalid for lack of novelty and the Court of Appeal ([2003] RPC 855; [2004] IP&T 846) agreed, holding that the suggestion that the word "propan-2-ol" should be read as "organic solvent" was a deviation from the ordinary rules of construction and would do violence to the language, which was a result to be avoided unless no other reasonable construction was possible. The judge had accordingly been entitled to reach the conclusion that the claims were invalid. His decision to uphold certain other claims as valid was also upheld.

2.10   *—The "planting the flag" test*

Monsanto v. Merck, cited in the Main Work, was published [2002] RPC 709; the decision on appeal is *Pharmacia v. Merck* ([2002] RPC 775; [2002] IP&T 828).

2.11   *—Construction of the prior art document*

Where a device illustrated in the prior art is reconstructed with a view to experiments being carried out to demonstrate that that device works in the same way as a later claimed device, it is important that such reconstruction be carried out on the same scale and without use of any later information, particularly that derived from the alleged infringement, see *Dyson v. Hoover* ([2001] RPC 473).

In *Hewlett Packard v. Waters* (BL C/42/01; [2002] IP&T 5) the court accepted the correctness of a submission that it is its task to determine what the prior art "clearly and distinctly taught the skilled person at the priority date, not what can be read out of [it] by the application of hermeneutical stress", which "admirable phrase" was said to concisely describe "the process of squeezing a document to extract every last drop of meaning". The decision on novelty was upheld on appeal (BL C/18/02; [2003] IP&T 143, *noted* IPD 25044).

The Court of Appeal decision in *Bristol-Myers Squibb v. Baker Norton*, cited in the Main Work, has now been reported at [2001] RPC 1.

The requirement for a novelty-destroying disclosure to have an "enabling" character   **2.12**

In *McGhan Medical v. Nagor* (BL C/6/01) there was evidence that samples of the claimant's product (breast implants) had been given away to members of the public before the priority date, apparently for use as paperweights [*sic*] and for other reasons. The court held that it was in the highest degree improbable that such persons would be remotely interested in the details of the process whereby the products were manufactured and so the objection of lack of novelty failed.

EPO Decision T 977/93, AMERICAN HOME PRODUCTS/Canine coronavirus ([2001] EPOR 274) confirms that the properties of a product are considered not to have been made available to the public if the skilled person has no means of establishing the composition or the internal structure of the product and was not able to reproduce it, in spite of the product being in the hands of the public before the priority date of the patent.

In *SmithKline Beecham's* [PMS] *Patent (No. 2)* ([2003] RPC 607), the disclosure of the earlier application was held to be sufficiently enabling since any problems in making PMS in crystalline form could be overcome by the person skilled in the art and had indeed been overcome by the experimenters instructed in the litigation—albeit with some difficulty, see § 61.59 *infra*. However, this decision was reversed on appeal ([2003] RPC 769) because the applicable test under section 2(3) was a strict one of lack of novelty—see §§ 2.09 and 2.24.

In *Vericore's Patent* (BL O/125/02) there was a speculative disclosure in one of the prior art that synthetic pyrethroids might be used in the invention as well as natural pyrethrum. This was rejected as non-enabling, nor as giving clear and unmistakeable directions. However, a lack of novelty was found based on other prior art which described the use of "pyrethroids" generally, which was held to be broad enough to cover both the natural and synthetic compounds. Had this interpretation been wrong, the same conclusion would be reached on the basis of lack of inventive step—see § 3.11. The Comptroller's decision was upheld on appeal to the court (BL C/4/03, *noted* IPD 26026).

—Mere novelty of purpose   **2.13**

The Court of Appeal decision in *Bristol-Myers Squibb v. Baker Norton*, cited in the Main Work, has now been reported at [2001] RPC 1.

EPO decisions concerning prior art teaching when addressing novelty

—The total information content of a prior art document   **2.17**

Monsanto v. Merck, cited in the Main Work, was published [2002] RPC 709; the decision on appeal is *Pharmacia v. Merck* ([2002] RPC 775; [2002] IP&T 828).

11

2.18   *—Apparent disclosures which are not regarded as such*

In *Inhale Therapeutics v. Quadrant* ([2002] RPC 419), it was also held that, if a piece of prior art describes clearly a process or product, it is not enough for the patentee to hint that it might not work or have the properties asserted for it. If the assertion is that the prior art is in error in its description of what it has produced, it is for the party asserting the error to prove it. In relation to another piece of prior art the judge said "Just as it is no defence to infringement for the infringer to say he did not know that he had the features of the claim in his product, so it is no answer to an allegation of anticipation that no-one would have realised that the article or process described in, or obtained from, the prior art had the features of the claim".

2.20   *—The EPO approach to selection inventions*

The *HOECHST/Thiochloroformates* decision, erroneously cited in the Main Work as *EPO Decision T* 98/85, is *EPO Decision T* 198/84.

EPO Decision T 1046/97, *ZENECA/Enantiomer* ([2002] EPOR 325) held that it was not sufficient for lack of novelty that the claimed enantiomer belonged conceptually to the group of possible optically-active forms mentioned in the prior art unless there was a pointer to the individual member of the group at stake. Although the skilled man would be expected to combine the disclosure of the specific example with the general teaching in the patent as to optically active forms, this could not be equated to the disclosure of a specific enantiomer.

Anticipation by prior use

2.21   *—Pleading and proof*

Former CPR 49EPD 7.4 and 49EPD 12.3 have been respectively replaced by CPR 63PD 11.3(1) and 11.4(2), for which see § F63PD.11 *infra*. CPR 63PD 11.4(1) applies to allegations of lack of novelty arising from prior written description and CPR 63PD 11.5 provides for inspection of machinery or apparatus alleged to have been used before the priority date.

The reference in this section to the first instance decision in *Leggatt v. Hood* should refer to (1950) 67 RPC 134 at 141, with a corresponding amendment to the Table of Cases.

2.23   *—Consideration of prior use by the EPO*

EPO Decision T 472/92, *SEKISUI/shrinkable sheet*, cited in the Main Work as indicating that the EPO requires a prior use to be proved "up to the hilt", has been explained (*EPO Decision T* 254/98 *MINGATI/Vertical lathe*, [2003] EPOR 316) as only applying to an alleged prior use made by the opponent: where the alleged prior use was by a third party, proof on the balance of probabilities suffices. In *Kavanagh Balloons v Cameron Balloons* [2004] RPC 87, the judge of the Patents County Court commented that the requirement for a higher standard of proof in the EPO stemmed from the procedural limitation of the board in oppositions, where effective cross-examination is in practice unavailable. Therefore he declined to follow the "up to the hilt" approach in the circumstances of this case.

In *EPO Decision T* 494/96, *HOYA/Intraocular lens* ([2002] EPOR 131), prior use was not found where artificial intra-ocular lenses had been supplied (by the opponent) to a hospital for surgeons to use in clinical trials. The hospital paid for the lenses and billed the patients for them but the patients could not examine the lenses and there was no evidence that the surgeons (apart from their being under an obligation of confidence) had any clear knowledge of the composition of the lenses, so the question of a patient's ability to gain such information from the surgeon was "hypothetical".

Another decision showing the requirements for proving prior use before the EPO is *EPO Decision T 37/96, BELOIT/Digester* ([2002] EPOR 308) in which prior use was held not sufficiently established on the evidence and it could not be assumed that certain company-generated leaflets would automatically have made their way to the public.

Effect of prior concurrent application (Subs.(3))

—Effect of the subsection   **2.24**

In considering a preliminary point in *SmithKline Beecham's [PMS] Patent* (BL C/24/02 and [2003] RPC 114) the court held that evidence of experiments to prove that a method described in the earlier application cited under s. 2(3) was admissible. The Court of Appeal agreed holding that the word "content" in Article 54(3) EPC referred to what was taught by the document. If the earlier application taught a process which inevitably produced the product claimed, that product was also taught, was part of the content of the application, and was therefore matter part of the state of the art by virtue of section 2(3). The quality of such matter must be the same whether the document was prior published or taken to be part of the state of the art under section 2(3). The judge was right to conclude that the tests in sections 2(2) and 2(3) of the Act were the same. In reaching this conclusion the Court of Appeal considered EPO decisions including *EPO Opinion G 2/98, Requirement for claiming priority of the "same invention"* (OJEPO 2001, 413, [2002] EPOR 167), in which it was held that for a valid priority claim the skilled person must be able to derive the subject matter "directly and unambiguously" from the priority document. In this case it was assumed that the process in the prior application can be carried out and the application would provide proper support for a claim to the process. If so, the product produced by the process must be directly and unambiguously derived from the prior application. Evidence to enable the features of that product to be characterised would be admissible.

In the subsequent substantive revocation proceedings (*SmithKline Beecham's [PMS] Patent (No. 2)* [2003] RPC 607), it was held at first instance that there had indeed been anticipation by the earlier application, but on appeal ([2003] RPC 769) it was held that because it was not possible to repeat the example of the prior art without modification there were no clear and unmistakeable directions to make the claimed compound; therefore the claim could not be invalid for lack of novelty—see § 2.09.

In *Koninkijke Philips v. Princo Digital* ([2003] EWHC 1598 (Ch), BL C/24/03), the disclosures of the alleged anticipating documents were also capable of different interpretations, so that the patent could not be invalid for lack of novelty (the relevant citations again being under s. 2(3) only).

Effect of a withdrawn, but published, application under subsection (3)   **2.26**

In *Zbinden's Application* ([2002] RPC 310) an application had been withdrawn too late to prevent publication and was held to be novelty destroying prior art against a subsequent application by the same applicant which was filed after the first had been withdrawn and before it was published. The Comptroller affirmed the principle that prior withdrawal of an application did not prevent section 2(3) from applying if the application was in due course published. In the Comptroller's view, the fact that the EPO followed a different practice was based not on the provisions of the EPC itself but on an *obiter* statement of a Board of Appeal, and could not be given effect in the United Kingdom without an amendment to section 2(3). The same result was reached in *Woolard's Application* (BL O/513/01). However, the Court, on hearing the appeal in the latter application ([2002] RPC 767; [2002] IP&T 897), held that the object of section 2(3) (required to have the same effect as

Art. 54(3)) was to avoid double patenting. Accordingly it was held that the publication of an application withdrawn before the date of publication did *not* make that application part of the state of the art. The Court said that "It is desirable, where possible, to adopt an interpretation of the EPC which is consistent with the interpretation applied in the EPO…". Thus the decision in *Zbinden* has been overruled.

2.29 *Excepted disclosures*

The United Kingdom Patent Office initiated a consultation process on "grace periods" in early 2002. The results of the consultation indicated support for a limited grace period provided there is a strong burden of proof on the applicant to show entitlement to it.

2.30 *—Scope of subsections (4) and (5)*

In *EPO Decision G* 3/98, *UNIVERSITY PATENTS/Six-month period* (OJEPO 2001, 62; [2001] EPOR 249), the EPO Enlarged Board of Appeal decided that the six months grace period under the equivalent EPC provision to subsection (4) applies in respect of the date of filing of the application in the EPO, and not from the priority date, thereby over-ruling the first instance EPO decision in *PASSONI/Stand structure* ([1992] EPOR 79).

2.33 | *Patents for the first medical indication (subs. (6))*

When the prospective repeal of subsection (6) takes effect (for which see § 2.01 *supra*), the subject matter dealt with under this heading will continue to have effect under new subsection 4A(3), for which see § 4A.02 *infra*.

2.34 *—Patents for the protection of the second (or further) medical indications*

Monsanto v. Merck, cited in the Main Work, was published ([2002] RPC 709); the decision on appeal is *Pharmacia v. Merck* ([2002] RPC 775). *Pharmaceutical Management v. Commissioner of Patents [New Zealand]*, also cited in the Main Work, has been additionally published ([2000] RPC 857); the Court of Appeal decision in *American Home Products v. Novartis*, cited in the Main Work as BL C/31/00, has been published ([2001] RPC 159); and the Court of Appeal decision in *Bristol-Myers Squibb v. Baker Norton*, cited in the Main Work, has been reported at [2001] RPC 1.

The specified further indication should be one different from that of the prior art. Thus, in *EPO Decision T* 315/98, *"STERLING/S(+)ibuprofen* ([2000] EPOR 401), it was doubted whether the recitation of hastened onset of analgesia could be regarded as a different indication from the known analgesic use of the specified compound.

Claims to a medicament for use in a particular dosage regime were rejected in *Merck's Patents [Alendronate product]* ([2003] FSR 498) following *Bristol-Myers Squibb v. Baker Norton (supra)*, it being held that in view of the availability of the relevant active ingredient in tablet form at the priority date the only point of novelty was the requirement for something different to be written on the bottle. The judge commented that "the patent system does not confer monopolies on those who develop obvious or old products, even if they have never been exploited. A workable system for that might be a good idea, particularly in the field of medicine and analogous fields". The decision was upheld on appeal ([2004] FSR 330). See the case comment by Kirstie Sloper (*Patent World*, April 2003 (No. 151) page 12).

When the prospective repeal of subsection (6) takes effect (for which see § 2.01 *supra*), the subject matter dealt with under this heading will continue to have effect under new subsection 4A(4), for which see § 4A.02 *infra*. This new provision gives formal effect to the patentability of the "Swiss form" of claim as a further expansion of the concept of the law of novelty previously provided by this subsection (6).

SECTION 3—Inventive step

COMMENTARY ON SECTION 3

Scope of the section   **3.02**

The decision of the Court of Appeal in *Wheatley v. Drillsafe*, cited in the Main Work, has been published ([2001] RPC 133); and *Instance v. Denny Bros* has been published ([2000] FSR 869), a decision upheld on appeal ([2002] RPC 321). In the light of these judgements, and for the reasons set out in § 3.04, it is now difficult to reverse an initial finding in relation to obviousness by a court which has determined the issue based on the facts and evidence presented to it, except where it can be shown that the trial judge had made an "error of principle", which presumably includes an error in the basic law which it has been applied. It should be remembered that it is only the initial trial court which has the benefit of hearing the witnesses and their reaction to cross-examination, assessing their demeanour, etc., whereas the appeal court must proceed only on the basis of the transcripts of the first instance judgment.

In *Hewlett Packard v. Waters* (BL C/42/01; [2002] IP&T 5, *noted* IPD 24071) the disclosure represented by an obscure item of prior art (referred to further in § 3.04 *infra*) was held to be of the "kind often called 'anticipation or nothing'". There was insufficient general teaching to find a convincing argument of obviousness. The decision on obviousness was upheld on appeal (BL C/18/02; [2003] IP&T 143, *noted* IPD 25044).

The Windsurfing approach   **3.04**

In *Spring Form v. World's Apart* (BL C/22/01) the court found that a *"Gillette* defence" approach could be helpful in addressing the third and fourth *Windsurfing* questions: in what regard does the alleged infringement differ from the prior art relied on? Was it obvious to take that step?

In *Instance v. Denny Bros.* ([2002] RPC 321) the Court of Appeal rejected an appeal against a finding of obviousness on the basis that, as held by the House of Lords in *Designer's Guild v. Russell Williams* ([2001] FSR 113 at 122; [2001] IP&T 277), and see also *Biogen v. Medeva* ([1997] RPC 1 (HL)), an appeal court should only reverse a decision based on the facts and evidence if satisfied that the trial judge had made an error of principle. In the *Instance* case, the error of principle was alleged for this purpose to be that the judge had not, in his finding of obviousness, used the structured approach required by the *Windsurfing* judgment. The Court of Appeal held that this approach was not essential, provided the judge had asked the right questions, which he had done.

In *Hewlett Packard v. Waters* (BL C/42/01; [2002] IP&T 5, *noted* IPD 24071) the judge held that the application of the *Windsurfing* test in relation to obviousness over an obscurely worded prior art document was inappropriate because it was not possible to identify a clear disclosure which could be used as the basis of the assessment. Rather the question was whether the "ambiguities and obscurities" of the prior art disclosure would be resolved by the skilled man in such a way that he came up with something falling within the claim without the exercise of inventive ingenuity. The decision on obviousness was upheld on appeal (BL C/18/02; [2003] IP&T 143, *noted* IPD 25044).

—The background of the "common general knowledge" in the art   **3.06**

The decision of the Court of Appeal in *Wheatley v. Drillsafe* cited in the Main Work, has been published ([2001] RPC 133).

A party who chooses not to present evidence of the common general knowledge in the art, although clearly able to do so, is likely to be disadvantaged in pursuing his case under the section, see *Dyson v. Hoover* ([2001] RPC 473).

In *Tickner v. Honda* (BL C/68/01, *noted* IPD 25020) the court said that it would be desirable in future cases if the experts could specifically address the items of agreed common general knowledge separately.

In *Storage Computer v. Hitachi* ([2003] EWCA Civ. 1155; BL O/4103), the Court of Appeal upheld the decision at first instance that prior art acknowledged in the patent was part of the common general knowledge and could be used as the basis of a finding of obviousness, being at least an admission made against the patentee's interest. If the patentee had wished to contend that the statement in the patent did not provide an adequate statement of what was disclosed in the prior art, then it was for them to lead the appropriate evidence, which they had not done.

3.08   —*Does the difference between the prior art and the claimed invention involve an inventive step?*

Kimberley-Clark v. Procter & Gamble (No. 2) BL C/25/00, *noted* IPD 23087) has been reported ([2001] FSR 339).

The difference between the prior art and the claimed invention must be judged through the eyes of the addressee of the specification, as discussed in § 3.18 in the Main Work and *infra*.

In *Inhale Therapeutics v. Quadrant* ([2002] RPC 419) although allegations of anticipation over certain prior art did not succeed, the patent lacked inventive step because it was found to be "extremely likely" that a particular parameter of the claim would have resulted from carrying out the teaching of the prior art.

The sub-tests for (un)obviousness used by United Kingdom courts

3.09   —*The "right to work" test*

In *Ancare's Patent [New Zealand]* ([2003] RPC 139) the invention was a preparation containing two ingredients for treatment of roundworms and tapeworms in sheep. The patentee said that it was not obvious to include a tapeworm agent at all because scientific opinion considered it unnecessary to treat tapeworms in sheep. However, the evidence was that, at the priority date, most New Zealand farmers did treat their sheep for tapeworms. The Privy Council (on appeal from the Court of Appeal of New Zealand) held that the fact that scientific opinion thought that something was useless did not mean that practising it, or having the idea of making a preparation to do it, was an inventive step. Otherwise, anyone who adopted an obvious method for doing something which was widely practised but which the best scientific opinion thought was pointless could obtain a patent. It was held also that the specification as filed taught in terms of a preparation for treating both types of worms. It was not drafted in terms of an unrecognised need for treating one type of worm.

3.10   —*The "lying in the road" test*

Monsanto v. Merck, cited in the Main Work, was published [2002] RPC 709; and the Court of Appeal decision in *Bristol-Myers Squibb v. Baker Norton*, cited in the Main Work, has also been reported at [2001] RPC 1. *Stoves v. Baumatic* (BL C/27/00), likewise cited, has been noted (IPD 23086).

Asahi Medical v. Macapharma (BL C/46/00 and C/15/02; [2002] IP&T 709, *noted* IPD 25037), and *Amersham v. Amicon* (BL C/49/00, *noted* IPD 24011 and BL C/32/01, *noted* IPD 24078) are other decisions where an inventive step was denied because the claims were seen to be directed to a mere workshop variation of prior art. In the case of *Asahi*, this art was rather ancient, but the court held the skilled person must be assumed to have read this and be interested in its contents. The Court of Appeal upheld this view.

Another such case is *Sapey v. Trianco Redfyre* (*unreported*, July 31, 2001) in which the court held that it would have been obvious to alter the prior art boiler in the manner described in the patent, this being "pre-eminently the kind of alteration to an existing design which a patent should not prevent" and "the sort of thing that any designer, however uninventive, would consider as a possibility to be accepted or rejected depending on the other constraints placed upon him".

—The obvious to try test   **3.11**

Monsanto v. Merck, cited in the Main Work, was published [2002] RPC 709. In similar vein to that decision, *Pfizer's Patent* ([2001] FSR 201) indicates that the "obvious to try" test is being used with little attention paid to whether there was an expectation of success. In this case, the incentive to seek an oral treatment for impotence was seen to be so great as to make any indicated approach to be worth trying, even to the extent of carrying out a literature search to ascertain compounds stated to act as inhibitors of a certain enzyme which prior art documents had suggested played a role in a multi-stage physiological pathway.

The approach of the High Court in *Pfizer's Patent* was upheld by the Court of Appeal (BL C/2/02; [2002] IP&T 244, *noted* IPD 25022, see § 3.11) which held that even though there were reasons for doubting the ability to orally administer a drug to treat erectile dysfunction, that did not mean it was inventive to decide to do so. "If it was obvious to try, it seems that success was within the reach of the skilled person carrying out routine procedures"—thus the court appears to disregard the requirement for a reasonable expectation of success.

This approach was followed by the Court of Appeal in the appeal in *Monsanto v. Merck* (cited as *Pharmacia v. Merck*, [2002] RPC 775; [2002] IP&T 828), the court saying that whether or not there is a reason for taking the step from the prior art may be an important consideration but it is not an essential requirement for a conclusion of obviousness. Compare however *EPO Decision T 202/95, FUJISAWA/Alpha-human ANP* ([2002] EPOR 34) in which reasonable prospects of success formed part of the EPO's decision to hold certain broad claims obvious and *EPO Decision T 425/96, MONSANTO/Insect-resistant tomato plants* ([2002] EPOR 45) in which obviousness was not found where, although the prior art would have convinced the skilled person that the claimed method was feasible, there was no reasonable expectation that the method would give the desired result so that the skilled person would have chosen an alternative method with a reasonable expectation of success and not the method claimed.

In *Glaxo Group's Patent* ([2004] RPC 843), the judge stated that "if it is obvious to try that thing for other reasons, there need be no superadded requirement that there should also be some expectation of success". He saw this approach as in line with that adopted by the EPO and saw "no basis for the suggestion that UK law is out of step with the principles applied in the EPO". In relation to synergistic effects, the judge said that if such an effect is to be relied on, it must be described in the specification.

In *DSM's Patent* ([2001] RPC 675), it was (unsuccessfully) alleged that the skilled worker would have disbelieved the statement in a prior art paper that an enzyme had been purified (to enable its structure to be determined), it then being held that the methodology of this paper would probably have been followed leading to the elucidation of that structure.

In *Stannah Stairlifts v. Freelift* (PCC July 4, 2002) the court held that the use of an electronic seat levelling mechanism instead of a mechanical one would have presented itself to the skilled addressee as being technically worth investigating and as presenting no inherent problems in its implementation, and the claim to it was therefore held obvious.

In *Vericore's Patent* (BL O/125/02) it was held that the skilled person would have thought of using a synthetic pyrethroid instead of pyrethrum with a reasonable expectation of success, leading to a finding of lack of inventive step, even if (contrary to the Hearing Officer's preferred view) the word "pyrethroid" in the claims was to be given a narrow meaning restricted to synthetic pyrethroids. See also § 2.12. The Comptroller's decision was upheld on appeal to the court (BL C/4/03, *noted* IPD 26026), the judge considering the Comptroller's decision as a model one which could not be faulted, but in deference to the arguments raised he considered the arguments in detail and explained why the decision was correct.

3.12   *The "would", not "could", test*

Nutrinova v. Scanchem, cited in the Main Work, has been published ([2001] FSR 797).

Where the commercial prospects can be seen to be very great, it appears that the "could" and "would" tests are likely to be seen as synonymous, see *Pfizer's Patent* ([2001] FSR 201 and BL C/2/02; [2002] IP&T 244).

3.13   *—The question "If obvious, why was it not done before?"*

The decision on obviousness in *Rocky Mountain Traders v. Hewlett Packard*, cited in the Main Work, was upheld on appeal ([2002] FSR 1), it being stated: "any member of the public is entitled, without fear of patent infringement, to take a prior art device and improve it in an obvious way"; and "a product can be satisfactory, but that does not mean that a modification of that product was not obvious".

Instance v. Denny Bros, cited in the Main Work, has been reported ([2000] FSR 869), with subsequent appeal ([2002] RPC 321).

In the Court of Appeal decision in *Dyson v. Hoover* ([2002] RPC 465) there was some discussion of the mantle of the skilled person "including all the attitudes and perceptions of such a person". In the relevant art there was seen to be a "mindset" against bagless vacuum cleaners which "played a part in setting the notional addressee's mental horizon, making a true inventor of the individual who was able to lift his eyes above the horizon and see a bag-free machine". It was seen as "one of the ironies of the case" that the defendant, which had "a pre-eminent reputation" in domestic vacuum cleaners, had in fact rejected the invention when offered to it, but then claimed that the judge was wrongly influenced by the existence of that mindset in coming to his decision that the invention was not obvious.

The idea of "mindset" also played a part in the Court of Appeal's decision in *Panduit v. Band-It* ([2003] FSR 127) in which the first instance decision of a Patents County Court deputy judge (BL C/11/01) finding the invention obvious was reversed. The patent concerned partially coated cable ties, and the Court of Appeal found that there was secondary evidence that there had been a mindset in the field that partially coated ties could not be used because the exposed metal was a disadvantage in cold weather and for other reasons. The "whole idea of coating was seen as being to coat the tie as a whole". The fourth *Windsurfing* step required the court to consider whether the differences were obvious without having in mind the invention. The judge's reasoning involved *ex post facto* analysis without recourse to the evidence. He had moved to the claimed invention by two steps, neither of which were established by the primary evidence to be obvious, "because the destination, the invention, was known to him".

3.14   *—Relevance of commercial success*

Former CPR 49EPD 7.6 has been subsumed into the general CPR which require a case to be fully pleaded. CPR 49EPD 9.2 and 9.3 have been replaced by CPR 63PD 5.2 (reprinted *infra* in § F63PD.5).

It is not possible to circumvent the disclosure requirements for a plea of commercial success (for which see § 3.44 in the Main Work) by a plea of "technical acclaim", see *Dyson v. Hoover* ([2001] RPC 473).

In *SABAF v. MFI and Meneghetti* (BL C/37/01, *noted* IPD 24059) the argument of commercial success did not help save the patent at first instance where it was asserted that a significant number of manufacturers had taken licences under the patent but where the royalty rates charged were so low that it would have made little sense for anyone to refuse the offer of a licence and to have litigated instead. On appeal ([2003] RPC 264) the finding of obviousness was reversed on other grounds and then restored by the House of Lords ([2005] RPC 209), but the aspect of commercial success was not argued.

Ex post *facto analysis*   **3.15**

The Court of Appeal decision in *Cartonneries de Thulin v. CTP White Knight*, cited in the Main Work, has been reported ([2001] RPC 107).

In *SABAF v. MFI and Meneghetti* ([2003] RPC 264), the Court of Appeal commented that "the dangers of hindsight are notorious" in holding that "it would be easy to assume from the fact that there are disclosures in the prior art that which has to be established, that is to say that the skilled man using his common general knowledge would put together what had hitherto not been combined". However, in the House of Lords ([2005] RPC 209), Lord Hoffmann looked at the problem as one of identifying the separate inventions in the patent and applying the Windsurfing tests to each. If both are obvious, and they do not interact to produce some new or improved result, then the resulting collocation will also be obvious and unpatentable. See § 3.16.

In *Koninkijke Philips v. Princo Digital* ([2003] EWHC 1598 (Ch), BL C/24/03) (referred to in § 2.24 as regards novelty citations under s. 2(3)), it was asserted that the skilled person would have taken a number of steps to proceed from another piece of prior art to reach the claimed invention, but it was held to be unfair to the inventor to dissect a combination into its component parts and then demonstrate that each of those parts is or may be obvious, this being an impermissible hindsight approach. The skilled team would not have made the invention without the insight of the inventors.

—Collocations   **3.16**

In *SABAF v. MFI and Meneghetti* (BL C/37/01, *noted* IPD 24059) the judge quoted with approval the statement from EPO Guideline C-IV, Annex 2.1 that an invention will be considered obvious and consequently non-inventive if "the invention consists merely in the juxtaposition or association of known devices or processes functioning in their normal way and not producing any non-obvious working inter-relationship" and which quotes as an example a sausage machine consisting of a known mincing machine and a known filling machine disposed side by side. However, the Court of Appeal ([2003] RPC 264) held that there is no "separate law of collocation" applied the *Windsurfing* test and concluded that the patent was valid. When the matter came before the House of Lords ([2005] RPC 209), it was explained by Lord Hoffmann that "before you can apply section 3 and ask whether the invention involves an inventive step, you first have to decide what the invention is. In particular ... whether you are dealing with one invention or two or more inventions". He went on to say that: "Two inventions do not become one invention because they are included in the same hardware. A compact motor car may contain many inventions, each operating independently of each other but all designed to contribute to the overall goal of having a compact car. That does not make the car a single invention". He noted that the judge had applied the test for obviousness to each of the features alleged to constitute the invention and found each to be obvious and the patent accordingly invalid. His approach was correct and in accordance with the *Windsurfing* test, and was to be preferred to the Court of Appeal's approach, which involved combining separate inventions and then asking whether the combination would have been obvious.

In *EPO Decision T* 362/86, *DISCOVISION/Rotation apparatus for information storage* [2002] EPOR 90, the relevant improvements were disclosed in three different prior art documents, but it was held that the combined application of each of the improvements would have been obvious to a skilled person.

3.18   *The person skilled in the art*

The modern principles which apply to the assessment of obviousness in relation to the skilled addressee of the specification were set out by Laddie J. in *Pfizer's Patent* ([2001] FSR 201) in the following terms:

> "The question of obviousness has to be assessed through the eyes of the skilled but non-inventive man in the art. This is not a real person. He is a legal creation. He is supposed to offer an objective test of whether a particular development can be protected by a patent. He is deemed to have looked at and read publicly available documents and to know of public uses in the prior art. He understands all languages and dialects. He never misses the obvious nor stumbles on the inventive. He has no private idiosyncratic preferences or dislikes. He never thinks laterally. He differs from all real people in one or more of these characteristics. A real worker in the field may never look at a piece of prior art—for example he may never look at the contents of a particular public library—or he may be put off because it is in a language he does not know. But the notional addressee is taken to have done so. This is a reflection of part of the policy underlying the law of obviousness. Anything which is obvious over what is available to the public cannot subsequently be the subject of valid patent protection even if, in practice, few would have bothered looking through the prior art or would have found the particular items relied upon. Patents are not granted for the discovery and wider dissemination of public material and what is obvious over it, but only for making new inventions. A worker who finds, is given or stumbles upon any piece of prior art must realise that that art and anything obvious over it cannot be monopolised by him and he is reassured that it cannot be monopolised by anyone else."

The decision was upheld on appeal (BL C/2/02; [2002] IP&T 244, *noted* IPD 25022, see § 3.11).

Also, in *Minnesota Mining v. ATI Atlas* ([2001] FSR 514; [2001] IP&T 535), it was noted, as a matter of principle, that invention cannot lie in bringing into a notional team working on a particular problem a new notional member with different skills from those of the existing notional team.

In *Inhale Therapeutics v. Quadrant* ([2002] RPC 419) it was held that where a claim covers a wide field, parts of it may be obvious to a notional skilled person in one field and other parts may be obvious to the notional skilled person in another. This is not unfair to the patentee, but simply a reflection of the fact that the scope of protection is wide. Thus an argument that the claim fell to be construed by an expert in freeze drying, although the claims also covered other techniques such as spray drying (as used by the defendant), was held to be misconceived.

3.19   *Obviousness in United Kingdom biotechnology cases*

DSM's Patent ([2001] RPC 675) is conceptually similar to *Genentech's Patent*, cited in the Main Work, in that it claimed the sequence of a known biological material. The court saw difficulty in identifying any inventive step over the common general knowledge in that, by the priority date, the sequencing methodology had become routine once a pure sample of the material had been obtained. It was contended that this problem had been solved by the use of a particular purifying technique when other known techniques had failed, but the technique used successfully was a well-known one, simple to use and involving apparatus commercially available, even though this technique may not have been that of first choice. This led to a finding of obviousness over the common general knowledge. Obviousness was also found over a prior art paper, see § 3.11.

The EPO problem and solution approach to consideration of inventive step

3.22   *—EPO decisions indicating the philosophy for assessment of inventive step*

The contents of a cited document must be considered in their entirety and its teaching must not be influenced by the problem solved by the invention (*EPO Decision T* 554/98, *TECNICA/Ski boot lining* [2000] EPOR 475).

The nature of the prior art to be considered

—The relevant prior art   **3.23**

In *EPO Decision T 79/96, APV ANHYDRO/Granulation by spray drying* ([2001] EPOR 309), the EPO said that if there are several prior art documents disclosing subject matter about equally close to that of the patent, the most recent should be regarded as the closest prior art.

—Age of the prior reference   **3.25**

In *EPO Decision T 345/96, DU PONT/Fibre-filled elastomer* ([2001] EPOR 345), one piece of prior art was discounted as being dated over 10 years before the priority date, the relevant field being one which was closely worked; see § 3.23 *supra* with regard to the remarks of the EPO that the most recent of several relevant references should be regarded as the closest prior art.

Assessment of the solution

—The "obvious to try" test   **3.33**

The teaching of a document must not be influenced by the problem solved by the invention, *e.g.* where the skilled person had no reason for manufacturing the article described in the prior art according to the particular sequence of steps specified in the claim (*EPO Decision T 554/98, TECNICA/Ski boot lining* [2000] EPOR 475).

Where modified egg yolk had been described as an alternative to egg yolk, it was obvious to use the modified, instead of the unmodified, material in a prior art process (*EPO Decision T 384/94, UNILEVER/Emulsions* [2000] EPOR 469).

It was held not obvious to adopt a construction which appeared more complicated than the prior art or by use of a more expensive material that shown in the prior art in *EPO Decision T 411/98, KIMBERLY-CLARK/Training pant* ([2002] EPOR 331). Nor was it obvious to look at prior art relating to articles of a different type or construction.

—Probability of attainment of solution   **3.34**

In *EPO Decision T 922/94, MITSUI/Photocurable resin composition* ([2002] EPOR 208), inventive step was upheld where the problem was a general one and there was a wide field of variation open to the skilled person such that hindsight was needed to come to the conclusion that the patentee's solution was obvious.

Chemical compounds

—Structural obviousness   **3.36**

In *Pharmacia v. Merck* ([2002] RPC 775; [2002] IP&T 828) the Court of Appeal held that the identification of a previously unmade class of chemical compounds was not itself patentable. Patentability required there to be a technical contribution. There was no technical contribution in a list of compounds which a skilled person would have known how to make at the priority date. In this case the court identified the technical contribution as relating to a particular property (Cox II selectivity) which was referred to in the description but not in the claims. The patentability of "compound *per se* " claims in chemical and pharmaceutical cases was the subject of an article by A.W. White ([2002] *CIPA* 89 and

134 and [2000/2001] 6 BSLR 237). This has provoked some comment, see for example letters by S. Crespi and R.P. Lloyd at [2002] *CIPA* 225.

PRACTICE UNDER SECTION 3

3.44 *Pleading of commercial success*

Former CPR 49EPD 7.6 has been subsumed into the general CPR which require a case to be fully pleaded. CPR 49EPD 9.2 and 9.3 have been replaced by CPR 63PD 5.2 (reprinted *infra* in § F63PD.5).

4.01

SECTION 4—Industrial application

The Patents Act 2004 (c. 16, Scheds. 2(3) and 3) prospectively removed from subsection 4(1) the words "Subject to subsection (2) below" and deleted subsections (2) and (3), relocating these in new subsections 4A(1) and (2), for which see § 4A.02 *infra*.

COMMENTARY ON SECTION 4

4.03 *Definition of "industrial application" (subs. (1))*

For rejection of an application as directed to subject-matter inconsistent with Newton's Third Law of Motion, see *Richardson's Application* (BL O/368/00). For rejection of an application in which the claims "did not make technical sense" see *American Photo Booth's Patent* (BL O/457/02).

In *EPO Decision T* 1165/97, *ULTRAFEM/Feminine hygiene device* ([2002] EPOR 384) the claimed method of using a vaginal discharge collector was held not to relate to a service satisfying only the strictly personal needs of the woman in question, as in *EPO Decision T* 74/93 referred to in the Main Work as it was capable of being used by an enterprise of which the object is to assist women in collecting a sample of their vaginal discharge for subsequent examination or other purposes. It was said that "whether such enterprises actually exist is not relevant for the purposes of Art. 57 EPC; what counts is the possibility that such a service may be offered by an enterprise". See also § 4.05 for whether such a method would be excluded in any event as a diagnostic method.

4.04 *Unpatentability of medical and veterinary treatment (subss. (2) and (3))*

Although a prohibition against patents for medical and veterinary treatment is permitted under the TRIPS Agreement, this increasingly appears as an anachronism, see the decisions permitting such claims in Australia under the former "manner of new manufacture" test, *Anaesthetic Supplies v. Rescare [Australia]* ((1994) 28 IPR 383), discussed by D. Kell ([1995] EIPR 202), and *Bristol-Myers Squibb v. Faulding [Australia]* ((1999–2000) 46 IPR 553), in which the judgment of Finkelstein J. (at p. 586) reviewed the worldwide history of the allowability of this type of patent protection, particularly in the United States, and discussed the ethical questions involved. A similar position has been taken in New Zealand (*Pharmaceutical Management v. Commissioner of Patents [New Zealand]* ([2000] RPC 857), for which see § 2.34. For further discussion on the patentability of methods of medical treatment and of second medical uses, see Audrey Horton (*Patent World*, 124 (August 2000), 9); and on *Bristol-Myers Squibb v. Baker Norton* ([1999] RPC 253 and the Court of Appeal decision (noted in the Main Work as BL C/23/00 but now published at [2001] RPC 1), see the paper by J. Williams ([2000] BSLR 238).

Claims to a medicament for use in a particular dosage regime were rejected in *Merck's Patents [Alendronate product]* ([2003] FSR 498 and [2004] FSR 330), following *Bristol-Myers Squibb v. Baker Norton* (*supra*), see also § 2.34.

In *EPO Decision T* 04/98, *SEQUUS/Liposome composition* ([2002] EPOR 371) claims to a composition for intravenous administration defined as containing a liposome composition in an amount of at least three times its therapeutically effective amount were rejected as failing to provide any indication of the disease to be treated, the nature of the therapeutic compound used or the subject to be treated. They were accordingly not permissible "Swiss form" claims and as process claims for a method of making liposome compositions were.rejected as lacking inventive step over the relevant prior art.

Claims to a known compound for a known therapeutic purpose on accordance with a dosage regime claimed to be novel were rejected in *Teva Pharmaceutical v. Instituto Gentili* (Jacob, J., January 21, 2003).

—The meaning of treatment practised on the human or animal body   **4.05**

EPO Decision T 35/99, *GEORGETOWN UNIVERSITY/Pericardial access* (OJEPO 2000, 447) held that "In contrast to procedures whose end result is the death of the living being 'under treatment', either deliberately or incidentally (*e.g.* the slaughter of animals or methods for measuring biological functions of an animal which comprise the sacrificing of said animal), those physical interventions on a human or animal body which, whatever their specific purpose, give priority to maintaining the life or health of the body on which they are performed, are 'in their nature' methods of treatment by surgery." Also, "the exclusion from patentability of such methods encompasses any surgical activity, irrespective of whether it is carried out alone or in combination with other medical or non-medical measures".

In *EPO Decision T* 1165/97, *ULTRAFEM/Feminine hygiene device* ([2002] EPOR 384) the claimed method of using a vaginal discharge collector was held not to relate to a method of treatment by surgery or therapy, because there was no curative or preventative treatment involved nor was any medical skill required for the use of the device. Nor was it deemed to be a method of diagnosis because the steps of providing and placing the collector and the use and disposal thereof as claimed did not involve all the steps involved in reaching a medical diagnosis. See also § 4.03.

—The meaning of "surgery"   **4.07**

In *EPO Decision T* 775/97, *EXPANDABLE GRAFTS/Surgical Device* ([2002] EPOR 24) claims in the "Swiss-style" form were refused where directed to a method by which tubular members were assembled inside the body of a patient, such that the final construction of the product was only arrived at in the body following a surgical procedure. This was held to be a method of treatment by surgery and therefore unpatentable under EPCa. 52(4).

—The meaning of "diagnosis"   **4.08**

EPO Decision T 964/99, *CYGNUS/Surgical Device* (OJEPO 2002, 4; [2002] EPOR 272) would appear to change the position as stated in the Main Work (that EPCa. 52(4) should be construed narrowly in relation to methods of diagnosis) in that it holds that all methods practised on the human or animal body which relate to diagnosis or are of value for the purpose of diagnosis should be excluded from patentability. This decision would appear to overturn previous case law (*e.g.* *T* 385/86) and the position as stated in EPO Guideline C–IV, 4.3. However, this controversy has been referred to the Enlarged Board of Appeal as *Reference G* 1/04, which factually distinguished this case from the likes of *T* 385/86 and remitted the case for further examination on the basis of the third auxiliary request of the applicant, limited to device claims only.

4A.01

SECTION 4A [ADDED]—Methods of treatment or diagnosis

4A.—(1) A patent shall not be granted for the invention of—

    (a) a method of treatment of the human or animal body by surgery or therapy, or

    (b) a method of diagnosis practiced on the human or animal body.

(2) Subsection (1) above does not apply to an invention consisting of a substance or composition for use in any such method.

(3) In the case of an invention consisting of a substance or composition for use in any such method, the fact that the substance or composition forms part of the state of the art shall not prevent the invention from being taken to be new if the use of the substance or composition in any such method does not form part of the state of the art.

(4) In the case of an invention consisting of a substance or composition for a specific use in any such method, the fact that the substance or composition forms part of the state of the art shall not prevent the invention from being taken to be new if that specific use does not form part of the state of the art.

Note. This new section was prospectively added to the Act by the Patents Act 2004 (c. 16, s. 1), to give effect to EPCaa. 53(c), 54(4) and 54(5) of the revised EPC as agreed in 2000. The new section will be brought into effect when these EPC revisions come into force.

Commentary on Section 4A

4A.02   *Scope of the section*

In this new section 4A, which corresponds to revised EPCa. 53(c), subsections 4A(1) and (2) replace former subsections 4(2) and (3) because the unpatentability of methods of human or animal medical treatment or diagnosis is now to be based on the interests of public health, rather than, as previously, on a lack of industrial applicability. Thus, it is only the foundation of the law, not the law itself, which will be changed when this statute amendment takes effect. The contents of §§ 4.04 – 4.08 in the Main Work and in this Supplement will, therefore, remain applicable.

Subsection 4A(3) replaces former subsection 2(6) to continue to permit inventions of the first medicinal utility of a known substance to be protected by a use-bound product claim, as discussed in § 2.33 *supra*. New subsection 4A(4) extends the same principle to an invention of a new medicinal utility of a substance already known to have a different medicinal utility. When brought into force, it will no longer be necessary to claim this type of invention by a "Swiss form" of claim expressed as "Use of X for the production of a medicament for use in the medical treatment of Y", but rather a claim will alternatively be permitted in the form "Substance X for use in the treatment of disease Y". With the addition of this flexibility of claim wording, § 2.34 in the Main Work and in this Supplement will continue to apply to new subsection (4). However, the relaxation of the law of lack of novelty under the provisions of subsections (3) and (4) continues to apply only where the actual use envisaged is one which cannot be patented as such under subsection 4A(1).

5.01

SECTION 5—Priority date

Subsection 5(2) was amended by the RRO (a. 3) so that lines 5–7 thereof (as printed in the Main Work) now read:

"applicant or a predecessor in title of his and [*each having a date of filing... the application in suit*] **the application in suit has a date of filing during the period allowed under subsection (2A)(a) or (b) below, then**—."

The Order also inserted new subsections (2A)–(2C) reading:

(2A) The periods are—
    (a) the period of twelve months immediately following the date of filing of the earlier specified relevant application, or if there is more than one, of the earliest of them; and
    (b) where the comptroller has given permission under subsection (2B) below for a late declaration to be made under subsection (2) above, the period commencing immediately after the end of the period allowed under paragraph (a) above and ending at the end of the prescribed period.
(2B) The applicant may make a request to the comptroller for permission to make a late declaration under subsection (2) above.
(2C) The comptroller shall grant a request made under subsection (2B) above if, and only if—
    (a) the request complies with the relevant requirements of rules; and
    (b) the comptroller is satisfied that the applicant's failure to file the application in suit within the period allowed under subsection (2A)(a) above was unintentional.

Note. These amendments took effect from January 1, 2005, the RRO Commencement Date. However, as explained in Note 3 to § 15.01 *infra*, the previous version of the section continues to apply to applications which were pending on January 1, 2005.

The added subsection (6) has been applied to the Isle of Man (S.I. 2003 No. 1249).

RELEVANT RULE—RULE 6

Rule 6—Declaration of priority for the purposes of section 5(2)

5.02

Rule 6 was replaced with effect from January 1, 2005 (S.I. 2004 No. 2358).

6.—(1) Subject to paragraph (2) and rule 6A(4), a declaration for the purposes of section 5(2) shall be made at the time of filing the application for a patent.

(2) Subject to rule 6A(4), a declaration for the purposes of section 5(2) may only be made after the date of filing where—
    (a) it is made on Patents Form 3/77;
    (b) it is made before the end of the period of sixteen months starting immediately following the date of filing of the earlier relevant application (or if there is more than one, the earliest of them) set out in that declaration; and
    (c) the condition in paragraph (3) is met.

(3) The condition is that—
    (a) the applicant has not made a request under section 16(1) to publish the application during the period prescribed for the purposes of that section; or
    (b) any request made was withdrawn before the preparations for the publication of the application by the Patent Office had been completed.

(4) A declaration for the purposes of section 5(2) shall specify—
    (a) the date of filing of each earlier relevant application; and
    (b) the country in or for which it was made.

(5) In the case of a new application to which section 15(9) applies, no declara-

tion shall be made which has not also been made in or in connection with the earlier application.

(6) For the purposes of rules 6B and 6C, "priority application" means an earlier relevant application specified in the declaration.

5.02A | **Rule 6A [Added]—Request to the comptroller for permission to make a late declaration under section 5(2B)**

6A.—(1) The period prescribed for the purposes of section 5(2A)(b) shall be the period of two months.

(2) A request under section 5(2B) may only be made where—

(a) it is made on Form 3/77;

(b) it is made before the end of the period allowed under section 5(2A)(b);

(c) it is supported by evidence of why the application in suit was not filed before the end of the period allowed under section 5(2A)(a); and

(d) the condition in paragraph (3) is met.

(3) The condition is met where—

(a) the applicant has not made a request under section 16(1) to publish the application during the period prescribed for the purposes of that section; or

(b) any request made was withdrawn before the preparations for the publication of the application by the Patent Office had been completed.

(4) Where an applicant makes a request under section 5(2B), he shall make the declaration for the purposes of section 5(2) at the same time as making that request.

Rule 6A was added by S.I. 2004 No. 2358 with effect from January 1, 2005.

5.02B | **Rule 6B—Filing of priority documents to support a declaration under section 5(2)**

6B.—(1) In respect of each priority application to which this paragraph applies the applicant shall, before the end of the period of sixteen months starting on the declared priority date, furnish to the Patent Office the file number of that application; otherwise the declaration made for the purposes of section 5(2), in so far as it relates to the priority application, shall be disregarded.

(2) In respect of each priority application to which this paragraph applies the applicant shall, before the end of the period of sixteen months starting on the declared priority date, furnish to the Patent Office a copy of that application duly certified by the authority with which it was filed or otherwise verified to the satisfaction of the comptroller; otherwise the declaration made for the purposes of section 5(2), in so far as it relates to the priority application, shall be disregarded.

(3) Paragraph (1) applies to every priority application except where—

(a) the application in suit is treated as an application for a patent under the Act, by reason of a direction given under section 81, and the file number of the priority application was filed in compliance with rule 38(2) of the Implementing Regulations to the European Patent Convention; or

(b) the application in suit is an international application for a patent (UK) and the file number of the priority application was indicated in compliance with rule 4.10(a) and (b) of the Regulations made under the Patent Co-operation Treaty.

(4) Paragraph (2) applies to every priority application except where—

 (a) the application in suit is treated as an application for a patent under the Act, by reason of a direction given under section 81, and a certified copy of the priority application was filed in compliance with rule 38(3) of the Implementing Regulations to the European Patent Convention;

 (b) the application in suit is an international application for a patent (UK) and a certified copy of the priority application was filed in compliance with rule 17.1 of the Regulations made under the Patent Co-operation Treaty; or

 (c) the priority application or a copy of the priority application is kept at the Patent Office.

Rule 6B was added by S.I. 2004 No. 2358 with effect from January 1, 2005.

Rule 6C—Translation of priority documents

5.02C

6C.—(1) The comptroller may direct the applicant to comply with the requirements of paragraph (4), if—

 (a) a copy of the priority application—

  (i) was furnished in accordance with rule 6B(2);

  (ii) was filed in compliance with rule 38(3) of the Implementing Regulations to the European Patent Convention;

  (iii) was filed in compliance with rule 17.1 of the Regulations made under the Patent Co operation Treaty; or

  (iv) has been made by the comptroller in accordance with rule 112A(2).

 (b) that copy is in a language other than English; and

 (c) the matters disclosed in the priority application are relevant to the determination of whether or not an invention, to which the application in suit relates, involves an inventive step.

(2) In his direction under paragraph (1), the comptroller shall specify a period within which the applicant must comply with the requirements of paragraph (4).

(3) The comptroller shall not specify a period under paragraph (2) that ends after the grant of the patent.

(4) Where the comptroller has given a direction under paragraph (1), the applicant shall, before the end of the period specified by the comptroller, file—

 (a) an English translation of the priority application; or

 (b) a declaration that the application in suit is a complete translation into English of the priority application,

otherwise the declaration made for the purposes of section 5(2), in so far as it relates to the priority application, shall be disregarded.

Rule 6C was added by S.I. 2004 No. 2358 with effect from January 1, 2005.

COMMENTARY ON SECTION 5

Scope of the section

5.03

The amendments to section 5 deal with two situations, *viz.*: (1) where an application is filed within 12 months of the earliest priority date which is to be sought to be declared (subs. (2A)(a)), where it is possible as of right to file a priority declaration up to 16 months after the earliest priority date to be declared; and (2) where it is sought to file a priority declaration for an earlier application which bears a date more than 12 months before the filing date of the application (subs. (2A)(b)), where it is possible to seek leave from the Comptroller to make a late declaration and still retain the desired priority date. The relevant rules are the replaced rule 6 and new rules 6A, 6B and 6C (reprinted respectively in §§ 5.02 – 5.02C *supra*).

Normally, a priority declaration will be filed at the same time as the application is filed, *i.e.* within the normal period of 12 months starting from the filing of the earliest priority application: replaced rule 6(1) so states. However (under subs. (2A)(a) and replaced r. 6(2), as discussed in § 5.07 *infra*), it is possible for the priority declaration on such an application to be filed after this normal period up to a date no later than 16 months after the earliest priority date to be declared, as discussed in § 5.07 *infra*.

Where the application has a filing date which is not more than 14 months after the first priority date to be declared, it is still possible (under subs. (2A)(b)) to file a priority declaration in respect of that priority date if the Comptroller grants leave for this filing, see new rule 6A as discussed in § 5.07A *infra*. A request for permission to make a late declaration (under subs, (2A)(b)) must be sought by making of a "request" to the Comptroller (subs. (2B)). Such request can only be granted if the Comptroller is satisfied that the failure to file the declaration within the normal 12 months period was "unintentional" and provided that the request has complied with the relevant requirements of the rules (subs. (2C)), as discussed in § 5.07A *infra*. These include the further payment of the same fee as would be paid for late filing under subsection 5(2A)(b)).

The periods under rules 6 and 6A may not be extended (see rule 110 and Part 1 of Schedule 4A to the Rules, reprinted in §§ 123.09 and 123.09A *infra*).

The possibility of making a late declaration of priority (under subs. (2A)(b)) mirrors a similar provision which remains to be introduced into the EPC by the revisions agreed in 2000. This is recognised by a prospective amendment to section 78(3)(b), see §§ 78.01 and 78.03 *infra*.

5.04   *Conformity of sections 5 and 6 with the EPC and PCT*

In the sub-paragraph (3) under EPCa. 88 "covered in the application" should read "included in the application".

In *Unilin Beheer v. Berry Floor* ([2005] FSR 56), the court focussed on the wording of EPC Article 87 (as interpreted by *EPO Decision G 2/98, Same invention*), as well as Articles 4A, B and F of the Paris Convention, rather than the way in which these principles had been incorporated into section 5 of the 1977 Act.

5.07   *The necessity for a valid declaration of priority*

In line 6 of the first complete paragraph on page 137 "withdrawn after" should read "withdrawn before".

The amendments made to section 5 and the new form of rule 6 (together with new rules 6A–6C) (for which see §§ 5.01 and 5.02 *supra*) maintain (under new subsection (2A)(a)) that a declaration of priority should be made within 12 months immediately following the date of filing of the earlier specified relevant application, or if there is more than one, of the earliest of them. This may conveniently be called "the normal period" and no fee is required at this stage, (see § 14.08 *infra*). However, where the application was filed within the normal 12 months period, it is still possible to file a priority declaration after that date, provided that this is done by filing new PF 3/77 (with its attendant fee, for which see § 142.02 *infra*) no later than 16 months after the earliest priority date to be declared and provided that, when PF 3/77 is filed, no application (unless by then this has been withdrawn) has been made for early publication of the application under section 16 (r. 6(2) and (3)).

Revised rule 6(4) continues to require (as did former rule 6(1)) that the priority declaration shall specify the date of filing of each earlier application (now termed a "priority application", see r. 6(6)) and the country in which it was filed. In the case of a divisional application or "replacement application" (each as filed on the basis of an earlier application under new s. 15(9), replacing former s. 15(4)), no priority declaration may be made that has not also been made in, or in connection with, that earlier application (replaced r. 6(5)). Where this information has not been provided at the date of filing the application, an extension is permitted under rules 110(3) or (4) (Rules, Schedule 4A, Part 3, reprinted at § 123.09C *infra*), but revised rule 6(2)(b) requires that the declaration be completed within the period of 16 months from the earliest date of filing of the priority applications the subject of the priority declaration and provided that a request for early publication has not been made or (if made) has been withdrawn (r. 6(3)). This 12 months period (under r. 6(2)(b)) is inextensible (Rules, Schedule 4A, Part 1, reprinted in § 123.09A *infra*)).

The file number of a priority application (as well as a certified copy of that application, as discussed in § 5.18 *infra*) must also be furnished to the Patent Office within 16 months from the declared priority date (r. 6B(1) and (2)), although these periods are also extensible under rules 110(3) or (4) (Rules, Schedule 4A, Part 3).

Late filing of priority declaration under subsection (2A)(b) and rule 6A   **5.07A**

As compared to the situation under subsection (2A)(a) (discussed in § 5.07 *supra*), where a priority declaration may be filed late in respect of an application which was filed within the normal period of 12 months after the earliest priority date, subsection (2A)(b) can be used to permit a late filing of a priority declaration where the date of filing of the application in suit is more than 12 months after the earliest priority date to be declared. New rule 6A (reprinted in § 5.02A *supra*) is then applicable.

This requires making a request for permission to file a late declaration on new form PF 3/77, with its attendant fee (for which see § 142.02 *infra*), this being higher than that prescribed when PF 3/77 is filed under subsection (2A)(a) and is filed within a period of two months after the end of the normal period (r. 6A(1)), With PF 3/77 supporting evidence must also be filed explaining why the application in suit was not filed before the end of normal 12 months period allowed under subsection (2A)(a); and, at the same time, there must be filed the declaration which it is desired to file if leave is granted (r. 6A(4)). This requires also paying the same fee as would be required when filing PF 3/77 for a late declaration made under section 5(2A)(b) and rule 6. The declaration must state the date of filing of each "priority application" and the country in or which it was made (r. 6(4)). However, no such request can be accepted if the applicant has made a request for early publication of the application under section 16 unless this had been withdrawn before the preparations for such publication had been completed (rule 6A(3)).

The period specified in rule 6A(1) is inextensible (Rules, Schedule 4A, Part 1, reprinted in § 123.09A *infra*).

The required supporting evidence must establish, to the satisfaction of the Comptroller, that the omission to file the application within the normal period was "unintentional". Any indication that that applicant had had a change of mind, from an original intention not to file the application or to file it without a priority declaration, is likely to be fatal to an application under subsection (2A)(b) and rule 6A. Case law will elaborate the circumstances which can be regarded as "unintentional", but paramount will be a lack of evidence of any change of mind of the applicant. However, often the failure to file timely the required declaration will have arisen from a clerical error and the intention to make the declaration should then be apparent from the records of the applicant or his agent. There is here a parallel with new section 20A, under which an application which has been terminated for non compliance with a time limit, can be reinstated if the Comptroller can be satisfied that this non compliance had been unintentional, for which see § 20A.03 *infra*.

Test of "supported by the matter disclosed" (subs. (2)(a))   **5.10**

Monsanto v. Merck, cited in the Main Work, was published ([2002] RPC 709). The

Court of Appeal in that case (cited as *Pharmacia v. Merck* ([2002] RPC 775)) upheld the finding of lack of priority, holding (following Lord Hoffmann in *Biogen v. Medeva*, [1997] RPC 1) that if the technical contribution to the art which had been disclosed in the priority document did not justify a claim to a monopoly of the width of the claim of the patent, the claim was not entitled to the priority date. "The priority document must contain sufficient disclosure to constitute the enabling disclosure of the claim." This approach was held to be consistent with the opinion of the Enlarged Board of Appeal in *EPO Opinion G* 2/98—see § 5.13 *infra*.

Balmoral Group v. CRP, also so cited, was published ([2000] FSR 860.

In *Unilin Beheer v. Berry Floor* ([2005] FSR 56) the proper test was seen to be: "Is there enough in the priority document to give the skilled man essentially the same information as forms the subject of the claim and enables him to work the invention in accordance with that claim".

5.13   *Relevant EPO decisions*

EPO Opinion G 2/98, *Requirement for claiming priority of the "same invention"* (OJEPO 2001, 413, [2002] EPOR 167), followed a request for clarification of the apparently inconsistent approaches in *EPO Decision T* 73/88, *Howard/Snackfood* and *EPO Decision T* 77/97, *RHÔONE-POULENC/Taxoids* referred to in the Main Work. The Enlarged Board generally accepted the *Taxoids* decision, but modified it such that "priority is to be acknowledged only if the skilled person can derive the subject matter of the claim directly and unambiguously, using common general knowledge, from the previous application as a whole". This appears to discredit the *Snackfoods* approach whilst allowing room for implicit as well as explicit disclosures to be taken into account. A case comment by Stephanie Michiels on the Enlarged Board's decision and its implications for the pharmaceutical and biotechnology industries was published at [2001/2002] 2 BSLR 51.

5.15   *"Relevant application" (subss. (5) and (6))*

In relation to the comment on United States provisional applications in the penultimate paragraph, it is understood that US law changed in 1999 such that a provisional application can now be converted into a full US patent application within one year of filing.

PRACTICE UNDER SECTION 5

5.16   *Claim drafting*

The cross-reference at the end of this section should be to § 125.28.

5.17   *Filing of declaration of priority*

For the effect of the revisions to rule 6 on the filing of a declaration of priority, see §§ 5.07 and 5.07A *supra*.

5.18   *Filing of certified copy of priority application*

The furnishing to the Patent Office of the file number of a priority application and the filing of certified copies of priority documents is now covered by new rule 6B(1) and(2) (reprinted in § 5.02) *supra*, the periods for each of these requirements remaining at 16 months from the declared priority date (r. 6B(2)) but extensible under rules 110(3) or (4) (Rules Schedule 4A, Part 3, reprinted at § 123.09C *infra*), as discussed in §§ 123.33 and 123.34 *infra*. Failure to comply with these requirements results in the priority declaration being disregarded. Exceptions to these provisions exist where a copy of the priority document is already on file in the Patent Office; or where the application is one proceeding as a result of a direction under section 81, or is an international application for a patent (UK), in each case such copy having previously been provided to the Patent Office by the EPO or WIPO (r. 6B(3), (4)). In those situations, the Patent Office will itself prepare the necessary copy (r. 112A, reprinted at § 123.10A *infra*).

Supply of translation of certified copy of priority application (r. 6(6))   **5.19**

New rule 6C (reprinted in § 5.02 *supra*) now absolves an applicant from automatically being required to file a translation of a priority document. Such is now only required where the Comptroller has, in the exercise of his discretion, provided a direction for such supply, which he may only do where it is considered that the validity of the priority claimed is relevant to the determination of whether or not an invention involves an inventive step (r. 6C(1)(c)). It is surprising that this power to require the filing of a translation of a priority document is not apparently available where it would be relevant to an assessment of novelty (*e.g.* under s. 2(3)), However, rule 6C does not apply to applications filed before January 1, 2005 (the RRO Commencement Date), see Note 3 to § 15.01 *infra*.

Where such a direction is given, and the priority application is not in English, a translation thereof is required to be filed, or a declaration given that the application in suit is a complete translation thereof into English. This is to be done within a period of two months from the date of that direction, or the period of 16 months from the filing date of the priority application, whichever is the later (r. 6C(3)), failing which the declaration made under section 5(2) is to be disregarded as regards that priority application. This period is extensible under revised rule 110(1).

SECTION 8—Determination before grant of questions about entitlement to patents, etc.   **8.01**

The Patents Act 2004 (c. 16, s. 6) amended subsection 8(3)(c) by replacing the words "but after publication of the application" by "(whether the application is refused or withdrawn before or after its publication)", this taking effect from January 1, 2005, but without effect on a reference made before that date (S.I. 2004 No. 3202, aa. 2(b) and 9(2)).

RELEVANT RULES—RULES 7–11

Rule 9—Orders under section 8 or 12   **8.04**

9.—(1) Where an order is made under section 8 or 12—
  (a) that an application for a patent shall proceed in the name of one or more persons none of whom was an original applicant; or
  (b) that a new application for a patent may be made,
the comptroller shall give notice of the making of the order to the original applicant or applicants, and to any of their licensees of whom he is aware.

(2) A person who makes a request under section 11(3) or (3A) must do so before the end of the relevant period.

(3) The relevant period is
  (a) where the request is made by an original applicant, the period of two months starting on the date the notice is sent to him;
  (b) where the request is made by a licensee, the period of four months starting on the date the notice is sent to him.

(4) In this rule, a reference to section 11 includes a reference to that section as applied by section 12(5).

Note. This rule replaced its former form with effect from January 1, 2005, but the former form continues to apply to a reference made before that date (S.I. 2004 No. 3202, aa. 4 and 9(2)).

COMMENTARY ON SECTION 8

8.09 *Nature of the invention to be considered under section 8*

Collag v. Merck ([2003] FSR 263) was a case in which a number of inventive concepts were contained in the application, and the court held that this had to be assessed from the application as a whole, not just the claims. Different inventive concepts involved different contributions from the parties.

Relief under section 8

8.11 *—Filing of new application (subs. (3))*

The revision of subsection 8(3)(c), noted in § 8.01 *supra*, allows a replacement application, which is permitted under subsection (3) to be filed, to be back dated to the date of filing of the original application, irrespective of whether the original application has been published. This means that, where the original application was never published, but its contents had been disclosed after its filing, the novelty of the replacement application is no longer impugned. The provisions of section 2(4) should also be applicable to the replacement application. A corresponding amendment is to been made to section 12, see § 12.01 *infra*. Rule 9 has been re-written accordingly (see § 8.04 *supra*).

In *Young and Chatwin's Application* (BL O/174/01) the Comptroller had in an earlier decision (BL O/70/01) determined that the claimant was entitled to part of the subject matter included in the patent application in dispute. He accordingly made an order allowing the claimant to make a new application under section 8(3) limited to that subject matter only. Even though this was an unusual order, the Hearing Officer commented that orders under section 8(3) are uncommon, and when they have been made, they have usually been in respect of the whole contents of the patent application in question.

In *Stafford Rubber Company's Application* (BL O/255/02) the claimant was allowed to file a new application under s. 8(3) taking the date of the defendant's earlier application, but the order was made subject to third party terms analogous to those employed in section 28A for revocation actions, because of the perceived risk that a third party may have begun working the invention in reliance on the lapsing of the earlier application, at least in respect of matter common to the two applications. It was accepted as likely that such terms would be academic, but in the event that they were invoked, the Hearing Officer thought that the claimant might have a case for damages against the defendant.

In *University College London's Application* (BL O/381/02) the relevant application had been withdrawn before publication but following *Szucs' Application* (cited in the Main Work) a declaration was made that the applicant was the inventor and entitled to the invention. The invention was the subject of a corresponding international application, so a declaration was also made under s. 12 (see § 12.04 *infra*).

8.14 *Filing of new application under section 8(3), 12(6) or 37(4)*

Rule 9 (reprinted at § 8.04 *supra*) now applies also to an order where the Comptroller permits a replacement application to be filed.

SECTION 11—Effect of transfer under section 8 or 10 | **11.01**

The Patents Act 2004 (c. 16, s. 6) added new subsection 11(3A), and amended subsections (4) and (5), as follows:

New subsection (3A) reads:

(3A) If, before registration of a reference under section 8 above resulting in the making of an order under subsection (3) of that section, the condition in subsection (3)(a) or (b) above is met, the original applicant or any of the applicants or the licensee shall, on making a request within the prescribed period to the new applicant, be entitled to be granted a licence (but not an exclusive licence) to continue working or, as the case may be, to work the invention so far as it is the subject of the new application.

In subsection (4), the words "Any such licence" have been replaced by "A licence under subsection (3) or (3A) above".

In subsection (5), after "(2)" there is inserted "or (3A)"; and after "proceed", there is inserted "or, as the case may be, who makes the new application".

These amendments had effect from January 1, 2005, except for a reference made before that date (S.I. 2004 No. 3205, aa. 2(b) and 9(2)).

RELEVANT RULE—RULE 13

Rule 13—Reference to the comptroller under section 11(5) | **11.02**

13.—(1) A reference under section 11(5) shall be made on Patents Form 2/77 and shall be accompanied by a copy and by a statement in duplicate setting out fully—

    (a) the question referred;

    (b) the facts upon which the person making the reference relies; and

    (c) the period or terms of the licence which he is prepared to accept or grant.

(2) The comptroller shall send, except to the person who made the reference, a copy of the reference and statement to—

    (a) every person in whose name the application is to proceed or, as the case may be, who makes the new application; and

    (b) every person claiming to be entitled to be granted a licence,

and any such person who receives a copy of the reference and statement may, before the end of the period of six weeks starting on the date the copies were sent to him, file a counter statement (which must be in duplicate) setting out fully his grounds of objection.

(3) The comptroller shall send a copy of the counter-statement to the person who made the reference.

(4) The comptroller may give such directions as he thinks fit with regard to the subsequent procedure.

(5) In this rule, a reference to section 11 includes a reference to that section as applied by section 12(5).

Note. This rule replaced its former form with effect from January 1, 2005, but the former form continues to apply to a reference made before that date (S.I. 2004 No. 3205, aa. 5 and 9(2)).

Commentary On Section 11

11.04 *Effect of transfer of application under section 8 or 10*

The amendments set out in § 11.01 *supra*, particularly the insertion of new subsection (3A), provide that, where a replacement application is permitted to be filed, the original applicant and any existing licensees can acquire a non-exclusive licence under the replacement application and under the provisions of subsections (3) and (4), but only provided that such a person had already begun to work the invention in good faith. Section 38 has also been correspondingly amended, see §§ 38.01 and 38.04 *infra*. The procedure is now governed by a new version of rule 13 (reprinted at § 11.02 *supra*).

11.06 Practice under Section 11

Rule 13 has been amended (see § 11.02 *supra*), but the procedure seems essentially to be unchanged.

12.01 **SECTION 12—Determination of questions about entitlement to foreign and convention patents, etc.**

The Patents Act 2004 (c. 16, Sched. 2(5)) amended subsection 12(6) by: in paragraph (a) after the words "application is withdrawn" inserting the words "whether before or"; and, in paragraph (c) for the words "but after" substituting the words "or the". These amendments took effect from January 1 2005, except for a reference made before that date (S.I 2004 No. 3205, aa. 2(f)(k) and 9(2)).

Commentary On Section 12

12.03 *Scope of the section*

No relief can be granted under section 12 where the foreign application has already proceeded to grant, see *Magill's Application* (BL O/256/00).

12.04 *Application of section 12 in practice*

In *British Telecommunications' Applications* (BL O/402/01), the inventor had left the applicant (BT) after the priority application had been filed and could not be traced. An application for an international application designating the USA and Canada had been rejected by the United Kingdom Patent Office (acting as receiving office) because the power of attorney for the United States application had not been signed by the inventor. The Comptroller was satisfied that BT was entitled to the invention under section 39 for the purposes of the United States and Canadian applications and therefore BT's head of IP was authorised to sign the power of attorney and to execute assignments of the inventor's rights to BT.

In *University College London's Application* (BL O/381/02 —see § 8.11 *supra*), although the UK application had been withdrawn before publication, a declaration was made under section 12 so that it could be used by the applicant in support of any request to the International Bureau or to national or regional authorities in connection with the corresponding international application or any national or regional applications deriving from it.

12.05 *New application under subsection (6)*

In *Bradford Hospital's Application* (BL O/85/01), the filing of a replacement application under subsection (6) was allowed, in accordance with *EPO Decision G* 3/92, cited in the Main Work, following a decision as to entitlement on European and international applications which had been allowed to lapse by the original applicant, for which see § 39.08 *infra*.

The amendments to be made to subsection (6) echo those made to section 8(3)(c), for the effect of which see § 8.11 *supra*.

SECTION 13—Mention of inventor

RELEVANT RULES—RULES 14 AND 15

Rule 14—Mention of inventor under section 13 **13.02**

In the re-printing of rule 14(1) in the Main Work, the first three lines should read:

(1) An application to the comptroller under section 13(1) or (3) by any person who alleges—
(a) that **any person** [*he*] ought to have been mentioned …".

Rule 15—Procedure where applicant is not the inventor or sole inventor **13.03**

S.I. 2004 No. 2358 amended rule 15, with effect from January 1, 2005, as follows: Paragraph (1) was replaced by:

15.—(1) Subject to rules 26, 81(3), 82(3), 85(7) and 85(7A)(a), the period prescribed for the purposes of section 13(2) shall be—
(a) where there is no declared priority date, the period of sixteen months starting on the date of filing the application;
(b) where there is a declared priority date, the period of sixteen months starting on that date.

New paragraph (1A) was inserted, reading:

(1A) A statement filed under section 13(2) shall be made on Patents Form 7/77.

Paragraphs (3) and (4) were deleted.

Note. These changes seem to be semantic in nature and not to change the essential effect of the rule.

COMMENTARY ON SECTION 13

Scope of the section **13.04**

The prospective amendment of section 123(2)(i) (for which see §§ 123.01 and 123.41 *infra*) provides for rules to be made setting out the ways in which an inventor may waive his rights to be mentioned as such in a patent or application therefor. Consequential amendments have also been prospectively made in sections 16(1) and 24(3), for which see §§ 16.03, 16.07 and 24.08 *infra* where the reason for providing this facility is explained.

In *University of Southampton's Applications* ([2004] EWHC 2107 (Pat), [2005] RPC 220), it was held that to identify an inventor it is necessary to identify the inventive concept in issue, and then to identify the person or persons who had come up with it. A person is not an inventor merely because he has contributed to the work embodied in a patent claim. The contribution must be to the inventive concept.

Time for filing PF 7/77 **13.06**

The automatic extension of time for filing PF 7/77 available under revised rule 110(3) is now two months, with a further extension available with discretion under rule 110(4) not exceeding two months (r. 110(8) and (10)), see § 123.33 *infra*.

PRACTICE UNDER SECTION 13

13.11 *Filing of declaration of inventorship on PF 7/77*

The passage in the final two lines of sub-paragraph (2) on page 191 should read as follows:

"… the number required is one more than the number of named non-applicant inventor(s); thus, two for one such inventor, three for two such inventors, etc."

14.01   **SECTION 14—Making of application**

The RRO (a. 4) amended section 14 so that subsection (1)(b) and the word "and" immediately before then ceased to have effect; and new subsections (1A) and (10) were inserted, respectively reading:

(1A) Where an application for a patent is made, the fee prescribed for the purposes of this subsection ("the application fee") shall be paid not later than the end of the period prescribed for the purposes of section 15(10)(c) below.

(10) Subsection (9) above does not affect the power of the comptroller under section 117(1) below to correct an error or mistake in a withdrawal of an application for a patent.

Although these amendments took effect on January 1, 2005, the previous form of subsection (1)(b) continues to apply to applications then "pending", a term defined in Note 3 to § 15.01 *infra*, with subsection (1A) then having no effect.

RELEVANT RULES—RULES 16, 18–20 AND 22

14.02 Rule 16—Applications for the grant of patents under sections 14 and 15

Paragraph (2) was amended (by S.I. 2003 No. 513, with effect from April 1, 2003) by the addition of the words:

"but, where the application is delivered in electronic form or using electronic communications, that order shall not apply to the extent that it has been removed or varied by the comptroller in directions made under section 124A and the specification shall comply with such directions.

Further, new paragraphs (1B), (1C), (5) and (6) to rule 16 were added (by S.I. 2004 No. 2358), with effect from January 1, 2005, as follows:

(1A) Where the documents filed at the Patent Office to initiate an application for a patent did not include the applicant's name and address the comptroller shall notify the applicant that his name and address are required.

(1B) Where the applicant has been notified under paragraph (1A), he shall, before the end of the period of two months starting on the date of the notification, file his name and address; otherwise the comptroller may refuse his application.

(5) Where—

(a) the documents filed at the Patent Office to initiate an application for a patent include something which is or appears to be a description of the invention in a language other than English; and

(b) the applicant has not filed—
    (i) a translation into English of that thing; or
    (ii) a description in English, with a declaration that it is a complete
        and accurate translation into English of that thing,

the comptroller shall notify the applicant that a translation satisfying either paragraph (i) or (ii) is required.

(6) Where the applicant has been notified under paragraph (5), he shall, before the end of the period of two months starting on the date of the notification, file either a translation or a description with a declaration; otherwise the comptroller may refuse his application.

Rule 18—Drawings
14.03

A new paragraph (4) was inserted (by S.I. 2003 No. 513, with effect from April 1, 2003) reading:

(4) Where the application for a patent is delivered in electronic form or using electronic communications, paragraphs (1) and (2) shall not apply to the extent that they have been removed or varied by the comptroller in directions made under section 124A and drawings forming part of that application shall comply with such directions.

Rule 20—Size and presentation of documents
14.05

A new paragraph (16) was inserted (by S.I. 2003 No. 513, with effect from April 1, 2003) reading:

(16) Where the application for a patent is delivered in electronic form or using electronic communications, paragraphs (2) to (10), (13) and (15) shall not apply to the extent that they have been removed or varied by the comptroller in directions made under section 124A and the application shall comply with such directions.

COMMENTARY ON SECTION 14

Filing of application (subss. (1), (1A) and (2))
14.08

The amendment to subsection (1) (noted in § 14.01 *supra*) abolished the former "filing fee" which, anyway, had been set at zero, but new subsection (1A) replaces this with a requirement to pay an "application fee" (defined in an addition made to s.130(1), as noted in § 130.01 *infra*). For the amount of this, see the final section of the amended Schedule to the Patent (Fees) Rules 1998 as noted in § 142.02 *infra*.

The "application fee" is the fee to cover the "preliminary examination" under new section 15A and, for a normal domestic application, this was set for January 1, 2005 at £30.00 with a consequent reduction of the former fee for the search on such an application from £180.00 to £150.00, see § 142.02 *infra*.

The application fee is to be paid within the "relevant period" as now defined in rule 25(2), (4) and (5) in relation to section 15(10)(c) (reprinted respectively in §§ 15.04 and 15.01 *infra*). This period is 12 months from the date of filing the application where there is no declared priority date; but, where there is such a date, the period is the later of 12 months starting from that date or two months from the date of filing the application. The application fee may be paid in conjunction with the filing of PF 1/77 or with the filing of PF 9A/77 (together with the search fee required thereon, for which see § 142.02 *infra*). If the application fee is not paid with either of these forms, the informal Form AF1 may conveniently be used when paying this fee.

Under replaced section 15(1), an application can be "initiated" merely by furnishing to the Patent Office documents which indicate that a patent is sought, identifying the intended applicant and either something which appears to be a description of the invention for which a patent is sought or contains a reference to an earlier application, the description of which is intended to form the description of the application now being made, as discussed in § 15.08 *infra*.

New sub-rules 16(1A) and (1B) (noted in § 14.02 *supra*) provide that, where the documents initially filed omit the name and address of the applicant, the Comptroller is required to notify the applicant of the deficiency and, if this is not rectified within two months of that notification, the application may be refused. Presumably, this supposes that the initial documents were not filed wholly anonymously, but were perhaps filed by an agent seen to be acting for an undisclosed principal. This period nay be extended (under r. 110(1) by discretion, but this must be requested within this two months period (r. 110(4)) and may not exceed two months (r. 110(8) and Rules, Schedule 4A, Part 4), see § 123.36 *infra*).

New sub rules 16(5) and (6) likewise provide that, where a document initially filed is not in English and no English translation has been filed, the Comptroller is required to notify the applicant of the deficiency in not providing a translation and requiring to be filed within two months of the notification either a translation thereof or a description of the invention together with a declaration that that description is a complete and accurate translation of the document initially filed. If this is not done, the application may likewise be refused.

As rule 16 is not mentioned in Schedule 4A of the Rules (reprinted in §§ 123.09B-123.09D *infra*), it appears that each of these two month periods could be extended by exercise of the Comptroller's discretion, but this would require explanation of the reason for failure to meet the requisite obligation.

The Request (subs. (2)(a))

14.09   *—General*

Because an application may now be initiated merely by furnishing to the Patent Office minimal information (as discussed in § 14.08 *supra* and § 15.08 *infra*), the "Request Form" (PF 1/77) has been revised.

The revision of rule 16(2) (noted in § 14.02 *supra*) enables an application to be filed in electronic form or by way of an electronic communication. Such filing is now permitted under the Directions reprinted at § 124A.02 *infra*, see also § 124A.03 *infra*.

14.12   *Documents and language*

Note that the Patent Office appears to believe that it would be obliged to accept a patent application filed in Welsh under the provisions of the Welsh Language Act 1994 (c. 38).

The specification (subs. (2)(b))

14.13   *—General*

The "Code of Practice for patent applicant and agents" (which is available on the Patent Office web site www.patent.gov.uk) should be consulted for general information about the content of the specification, see also § 14.22 *infra*.

—The description   **14.14**

As indicated in § 14.05 *supra*, the provisions of rule 20 have been extensively altered, but only for application of the rule to any permitted filing of an application in electronic form or by way of an electronic communication.

—The drawings   **14.15**

As indicated in § 14.03 *supra*, paragraphs (1) and (2) of rule 18 will not apply, or only apply in modified form, to any permitted filing of an application in electronic form or by way of an electronic communication under a direction given by the Comptroller, for which see § 124A.02 *infra*.

Sufficiency of description (subs. (3))

—Relationship between extent of sufficiency and scope of the claims   **14.17**

In *DSM's Patent* ([2001] RPC 675), claims extending to hybridized DNA sequences were, if construed literally, held invalid as covering unworkable embodiments; and, if (as the patentee contended) were construed to include an implied functional limitation, there was no supporting teaching as to the conditions to be applied (other than trial and error) to achieve that result; the claims were invalid for insufficiency in either situation, see also § 125A.25 *infra*.

In *Kirin-Amgen v. Roche Diagnostics* ([2002] RPC 1), the court at first instance observed that there were two kinds of insufficiency. "Classic" insufficiency is where the teaching of the patent does not support that which it specifically purports to deliver. " *Biogen* " insufficiency (based on *Biogen v. Medeva* [1997] RPC 1 (HL)) is where the claim is cast more widely than the teaching of the patent enables. The test for *Biogen* insufficiency may perhaps be summed up as whether or not the patent describes some principle of general application (Lord Hoffmann in *Biogen* having said that one way in which the breadth of claim might be cast too widely is where it enables only one product out of a class and discloses no "principle" which would enable others to be made). In *Kirin-Amgen* the court, whilst adopting that test, said that the word "principle" should not be interpreted too strictly, such that it was possible to describe the disclosure of the patent as being how to make recombinant erythropoietin (epo) using its gene sequence without this giving rise to an objection of insufficiency. However, on appeal (*Kirin-Amgen v. Transkaryotic Therapies* [2003] RPC 31) it was held that it was wrong to say that there were two types of insufficiency. Section 72(1)(c) provides just one ground of invalidity. Prior to *Biogen* it was thought that the invention was sufficiently disclosed in the specification if it enabled performance of a single embodiment. That was held to be wrong by the House of Lords in that case, in which they held that the specification must enable the invention to be performed to the full extent of the monopoly claimed. The Court of Appeal was satisfied that the specification here disclosed a principle capable of general application and the patentee was therefore entitled to a claim in correspondingly general terms. See the case comment by H. Sheraton and A. Sharples, [2002] EIPR 596. When the case came before the House of Lords ([2005] RPC 169), however, Lord Hoffmann said that "the first step was to identify the invention and decide what it claims to enable the skilled man to do. Then one can ask whether the specification enables him to do it". On the facts of this case he held that the judge had been right to reach the conclusion that the specification, in not giving sufficient information about the methods of preparation of the product, did not sufficiently enable the relevant claim. The judge's decision was therefore restored and the claim was held invalid on this ground. No mention was made by the House of Lords of any distinction between "Biogen" and "classic" insufficiency, so the decision of the Court of Appeal must be taken to be correct on this point.

In *Pharmacia v. Merck* ([2002] RPC 775) the Court of Appeal held that the specification must enable the invention to be performed to the full extent of the monopoly claimed. If the invention is a selection of certain compounds having a particular characteristic, the specification must contain sufficient information on how to make the compounds having that characteristic and the compounds of the claim must all have that characteristic. If certain subclasses of the claimed class did not have the characteristic asserted, the extent of the monopoly exceeded the technical contribution. This would not necessarily be rebutted if one compound in a subclass showed some activity. The evidence must be considered as a whole, and any evidence of activity weighed against the rest of the evidence.

In *Tickner v. Honda* (BL C/68/01 *noted* IPD 25020) the court said that it was not an objection to an insufficiency attack to say that it could have been an attack of lack of fair basis in the past. "You just ask the statutory question ... Whether it overlaps with the "fair basis" attack of the past is neither here nor there".

EPO Decision T 612/92, *RIJKSUNIVERSITEIT LEIDEN/Monocotyledonous plants*, mentioned in the Main Work, has been reported at [2002] EPOR 79.

A further case following *EPO Decisions T* 612/92 and 694/92 cited in the main work is *EPO Decision T* 187/93, *GENENTECH/Vaccines* ([2002] EPOR 221) which held the technical effect relied on to demonstrate that the claimed subject matter involved an inventive step could not be achieved by the skilled person without undue burden within the whole range of application claimed, so that claims of broad scope were not allowable under Arts. 83 and 84 EPC.

14.19   *—Addressee as a person skilled in the art*

In *Kirin-Amgen v. Roche Diagnostics* ([2002] RPC 1), it was held that the court should be careful before it ascribed to the skilled addressee information outside his common general knowledge as this would be "entering into a field of uncertainty". However it might not be impossible for the skilled man to consult someone else when trying to implement the teaching of the patent. The court should not adopt a rigid approach. If a document was referred to on one point it did not necessarily follow that the addressee should be taken to be aware of information contained in it relating to another point which may have been relevant to the teaching of the patent. This would depend on the facts.

14.20   *—Comparison with requirement of sufficiency under the 1949 Act*

Kimberly-Clark v. Procter & Gamble (No. 2) (BL C/25/00, *noted* IPD 23087) has been reported ([2001] FSR 339).

14.21   *—EPO decisions on insufficiency*

In *EPO Decision T* 727/95, *WEYERSHAEUSER/Cellulose* ([2001] EPOR 35) it was held that there was an undue burden on a person skilled in the art in respect of the isolation of relevant micro-organisms because the reproducibility of the exercise depended on chance. Reliance on chance was unsatisfactory unless there was evidence that the probability of the chance events occurring was sufficiently high to guarantee success.

But it is no objection to the sufficiency of the description of the invention for the skilled person to be obliged to carry out tedious experimentation execute it where this is nothing out of the ordinary in the relevant filed and would involve only routine trials (EPO Decision T 391/91, *UNIVERSITY OF CALIFORNIA/Ice nucleating*, [2002] EPOR 70).

The Claims (subs. (5))

—*Purpose and requirements of claims*   **14.22**

The Patent Office has published a "Code of Practice for patent applicants and agents" (available on the Patent Office web site www.patent.gov.uk) which summarises some of the sections from the Manual of Patent Practice. This states that claims as filed should be structured to have:

(a) One independent claim defining all the technical features essential to the invention or inventive concept. This should include the core integers as well as sufficient details of interrelationship, operation or utility to establish that the invention achieves the intended objectives; and

(b) Dependent claims incorporating all the features of the independent claim and characterised by additional non-essential features.

(c) Further independent claims are only justified where the inventive concept covers more than one category, *e.g.* apparatus, use, process, product; complementary versions within one category, *e.g.* plug and socket, transmitter and receiver, which work only together, or distinct medical uses of a substance or composition.

Therefore claims as filed should not, where it might have been avoided, contain:

(d) Multiple unrelated inventions that would clearly give rise to a plurality objection.

(e) Multiple independent claims in any one category, even if only one inventive concept is present.

(f) Claims of a total number or complexity not justified by the nature of the invention.

(g) Claims which are in principle unsearchable by reason of the number of alternatives embraced, or the choice of characterising parameters or *desiderata*.

(h) Dependent claims that are not fully limited by the terms of the preceding independent claim, *e.g.* dependent claims which omit, modify or substitute a feature of an independent claim.

Further, the claims as filed should not, where it might have been avoided, define an invention which is clearly excluded from being patentable under the Act.

—*Categories of claims*   **14.23**

In *Kirin-Amgen v. Roche Diagnostics* ([2002] RPC 1), the court had held that, as a matter of ordinary language, a claim to a product obtained or produced by a specific process (a product-by-process claim) could not extend to any product other than one produced by that process, and the court declined to follow a line of decisions of the EPO Boards of Appeal, *e.g. EPO Decision T* 219/83, BASF/Zeolites (OJEPO 1986, 211) which hold that product-by-process claims "have to be interpreted in an absolute sense, *i.e.* independently of the process"; see § 14.27 *infra*. The previous edition of this supplement discussed why this reasoning was upheld by the Court of Appeal (*Kirin-Amgen v. Transkaryotic Therapies* [2003] RPC 31). However, when the case reached the House of Lords ([2005] RPC 169), Lord Hoffmann reassessed this aspect of UK patent law and commented that it was important that the United Kingdom should apply the same law as the EPO and the other member states when deciding what counts as new for the purposes of the EPC. He held that, since article 64(2) extends the protection afforded by a process claim to a product directly made by that process, it makes it "uneccessary to claim the product defined by reference to the process". This overturns many years of practice in the UK and means that "product by process claims" will not be valid, and should not in future be accepted by the Patent Office, except in the circumstances permitted under the EPO's Guidelines, *i.e.* where the product cannot satisfactorily be defined by other parameters. In that case, however, the claim will be interpreted as covering the product however made (*cf. T* 219/83, *supra*), and hence will be anticipated if the product has been disclosed in the prior art, but made by a different process. [*Editor's Note*: this decision would appear to have wider implications; for example, will claims to biotechnology products be allowable with disclaimers to the product when isolated from a natural source?]

14.25   —*Claims of a functional nature*

A modern example of a functional claim being upheld on the basis of performance by one of its embodiments, despite evidence that performance failed with other constructions, is *EPO Decision T 524/98, IMPERIAL TOBACCO/Smoking article* ([2000] EPOR 412).

14.27   —*EPC requirements as to claims*

In the Main Work, the case law of the EPO Boards of Appeal summed up in *EPO Decision T 124/93, AMOCO/Olefin Catalyst* ([1996] EPOR 624) in which the Board referred to its previous decisions as establishing that "Product-by-process claims give protection for the products themselves, independent from the process by which they were made" was described as a "doubtful proposition" under English law. In *Kirin-Amgen v. Roche Diagnostics* ([2002] RPC 1) and *Kirin-Amgen v. Transkaryotic Therapies* ([2003] RPC 31), the English Patents Court and Court of Appeal declined to follow the EPO on this point. However, the House of Lords ([2005] RPC 169), determined that the EPO practice should now be followed, meaning that product-by-process claims will no longer be generally allowable; see § 14.23 *supra*.

In *EPO Decision T 73/92, BALFOUR/Feedstuff* ([2004] EPOR 73), the Board held that a known product does not necessarily acquire novely by reason that it is made by a new or modified process unless the parameters of that process necessarily result in a process inherently having novel distinctive features, and there is no other information available in the specification for a more satisfactory definition on the basis of composition, structure or some other testable parameter. In *EPO Decision T 20/94, ENICHEM/Amorphous TPM* ([2003] EPOR 56), the EPO applied its previous decisions on the interpretation of product-by-process claims in holding that an amendment of a process claim to claim a product "directly obtained" by the process extended the scope of protection because the product-by-process claim was a claim to the product itself. This principle should now be applied in the UK following the House of Lords decision in *Kirin-Amgen, supra*.

The controversy as to the meaning and effect of product-by-process claims between practice in the EPO and that in the UK has been discussed at a "Judges Symposium", see the papers by R.J. Young, M. Fysh and M. Scuffi reprinted in OJEPO (Special Edition No. 2) 2003, 20, 44 and 60, although this was published before the House of Lords decision in *Kirin-Amgen*.

14.28   —*Claims to be clear and concise (subs. (5)(b))*

The EPO has held that a "Swiss form" of claim directed to "a medicament for treating a mammal suffering from or susceptible to a condition which can be improved or prevented by selective occupation of a [defined] receptor" lacked clarity as regards its scope, especially as some of the conditions indicated to be treated by such a medicament were held already to have been part of the prior art (*EPO Decision T 241/95, ELI LILLY/Serotonin receptor* OJEPO 2001, 103; [2001] EPOR 292).

The EPO has held that, where a trade mark is used as a definition of an element in a claim, it is inherently lacking in clarity and an attempt to replace the mark by a description of the product as it was sold under that mark at the priority date was rejected as impermissibly adding subject-matter (*EPO Decision T 480/98, CIUFFO GATTO/Trade mark* [2000] EPOR 494).

In *EPO Decision T 1129/97, GALDERMA/Benzimidazole derivatives*, (OJEPO 2001, 273, [2001] EPOR 478) the applicant was required to amend the claims to include the definition of "lower alkyl" from the description. Explicit disclosure of the meaning of the term in the description and not in the claims was not sufficient. Although Article EPCa. 69(1) stated that the description was to be used to interpret the claims, that article was only concerned with determining the extent of protection (*e.g.* when that had to be determined for the benefit of third parties), and not with defining the matter for which protection was sought by means of a claim, as required by Article 84.

In *Bilgrey Samson's Application* (BL O/577/01) claims to the operation of a "fruit machine" type apparatus were held to lack clarity because a claim limited to tax thresholds prevailing at a given time may result in apparatus not originally an infringement becoming so upon a change in the law, and because reference to a "dark and uninviting corner" of an amusement arcade was too subjective to provide a sufficiently clear description of the invention.

Claims to be supported by the description (subs. (5)(c))   **14.29**

Monsanto v. Merck, cited in the Main Work, was published [2002] RPC 709, and was upheld on this point on appeal (cited as *Pharmacia v. Merck* ([2002] RPC 775)) see § 14.17 *supra*. The Court of Appeal decision in *American Home Products v. Novartis*, cited in the Main Work as BL C/31/00, has been published ([2001] RPC 159).

In *EPO Decision T* 1173/00, *ABB PATENT/Transformer* (OJEPO 2004, 16), the invention could not be practised as described and the promised result could only by achieved by use of a different principle of operation; the application was refused because of an insufficient description.

Unity of invention (subss. (5)(d) and (6))   **14.31**

EPO Decision W 11/99, cited in the Main Work, has also been reported ([2000] EPOR 515).

Withdrawal (subs. (9))   **14.34**

Section 117 has been amended to allow an application to be resuscitated when the withdrawal was made in error or by mistake, see §§ 117.01 and 117.03 *infra*. New subsection (10) gives effect to such resuscitation which has the effect set out in new section 117A, see §§ 117A.01 and 117A.02 *infra*.

PRACTICE UNDER SECTION 14

Voluntary Withdrawal   **14.43**

By directions given under section 124A, and since July 8, 2003, it is possible to effect a withdrawal of a patent application by sending an e-mail to withdraw@patent.gov.uk entitled: "Withdrawal of patent application number GBYYXXXXX.X" stating, "I withdraw patent application number GBYYXXXXX.X" and identifying the sender as the applicant or appointed agent. For the format of such an e-mail see § 27.15 *infra*. An e-mail reply will be sent and it should not be assumed that the withdrawal has had effect until this is received. This will be followed by written confirmation from the Patent Office. The e-mail will be given the time and date when it enters the Patent Office internal e-mail system which may be later than the time of actual receipt. To ensure withdrawal before publication of an application, such an e-mail must be received not later than 23.59 on the day before preparations for publication are deemed to be complete: otherwise publication will occur (see O.J. May 7, 2003).

15.01

SECTION 15 [REPLACED]—Date of filing application

The RRO (a. 5) replaced section 15 by the following new version:

15.—(1) Subject to the following provisions of this Act, the date of filing an application for a patent shall be taken to be the earliest date on which documents filed at the Patent Office to initiate the application satisfy the following conditions—

(a) the documents indicate that a patent is sought;

(b) the documents identify the person applying for a patent or contain information sufficient to enable that person to be contacted by the Patent Office; and

(c) the documents contain either—

(i) something which is or appears to be a description of the invention for which a patent is sought; or

(ii) a reference, complying with the relevant requirements of rules, to an earlier relevant application made by the applicant or a predecessor in title of his.

(2) It is immaterial for the purposes of subsection (1)(c)(i) above—

(a) whether the thing is in, or is accompanied by a translation into, a language accepted by the Patent Office in accordance with rules;

(b) whether the thing otherwise complies with the other provisions of this Act and with any relevant rules.

(3) Where documents filed at the Patent Office to initiate an application for a patent satisfy one or more of the conditions specified in subsection (1) above, but do not satisfy all those conditions, the comptroller shall as soon as practicable after the filing of those documents notify the applicant of what else must be filed in order for the application to have a date of filing.

(4) Where documents filed at the Patent Office to initiate an application for a patent satisfy all the conditions specified in subsection (1) above, the comptroller shall as soon as practicable after the filing of the last of those documents notify the applicant of—

(a) the date of filing the application, and

(b) the requirements that must be complied with, and the periods within which they are required by this Act or rules to be complied with, if the application is not to be treated as having been withdrawn.

(5) Subsection (6) below applies where—

(a) an application has a date of filing by virtue of subsection (1) above;

(b) within the prescribed period the applicant files at the Patent Office

(i) a drawing, or

(ii) part of the description of the invention for which a patent is sought, and

(6) Unless the applicant withdraws the drawing or the part of the description filed under subsection (5)(b) above ("the missing part") before the end of the prescribed period—

(a) the missing part shall be treated as included in the application; and

(b) the date of filing the application shall be the date on which the missing part is filed at the Patent Office.

(7) Subsection (6)(b) above does not apply if—

(a) on or before the date which is the date of filing the application by virtue of subsection (1) above a declaration is made under section 5(2) above in or in connection with the application;

(b) the applicant makes a request for subsection (6)(b) above not to apply; and

(c) the request complies with the relevant requirements of rules and is made within the prescribed period.

(8) Subsections (6) and (7) above do not affect the power of the comptroller under section 117(1) below to correct an error or mistake.

(9) Where, after an application for a patent has been filed and before the patent is granted—

(a) a new application is filed by the original applicant or his successor in title in accordance with rules in respect of any part of the matter contained in the earlier application, and

(b) the conditions mentioned in subsection (1) above are satisfied in relation to the new application (without the new application contravening section 76 below),

the new application shall be treated as having, as its date of filing, the date of filing the earlier application.

(10) Where an application has a date of filing by virtue of this section, the application shall be treated as having been withdrawn if any of the following applies—

(a) the applicant fails to file at the Patent Office, before the end of the prescribed period, one or more claims and the abstract;

(b) where a reference to an earlier relevant application has been filed as mentioned in subsection (1)(c)(ii) above)—

   (i) the applicant fails to file at the Patent Office, before the end of the prescribed period, a description of the invention for which a patent is sought,

   (ii) the applicant fails to file at the Patent Office, before the end of the prescribed period, a copy of the application referred to, complying with the relevant requirements of rules;

(c) the applicant fails to pay the application fee before the end of the prescribed period;

(d) the applicant fails, before the end of the prescribed period, to make a request for a search under section 17 below and pay the search fee.

(11) In this section "relevant application" has the meaning given by section 5(5) above.

Notes.

1. The provisions formerly present in section 15 relating to Preliminary Examination are now to be found in new section 15A (reprinted in § 15A.01 *infra*). This section 15A now also contains part of the matter formerly present in section 17 which becomes limited to the "search" aspect of the preliminary examination.

2. Under S.I. 2004 No. 2357, this new form of section 15 took effect from January 1, 2005, the RRO Commencement Date, when new rule 22A (reprinted at § 15.01A *infra*) also took effect.

3. 3. However (under Arts. 20–22 of the RRO, not reprinted herein), the previous version of section 15 (as well as the provisions of sections 5, 14(1)(b), 17, 18, 72, 76, 78 and 130(1)) continue to apply to:

   a. an application (under the 1977 Act) which had been "initiated by" the filing at the Patent Office before January 1, 2005 of a document containing information such as is mentioned in any of paragraphs (a) to (c) of Section 15(1) (as applied to the form of s. 15(1) as it existed before this date);

b. an application which is treated as an application under section 81 by reason of a direction given under section 81(1) before January 1, 2005, to which the other provisions of section 81 also continue to apply; and

c. an international application for a patent (UK) which had entered the national UK phase (as defined in s. 89A(3)) before January 1, 2005,

and the provisions of new sections 14(1A) and 15 do **not** apply to such applications (RRO, a. 20–22).

For such applications, the forms of the rules existing immediately before January 1, 2005 continue to apply, see S.I. 2004 No. 2358, rule 20.

Relevant Rules—Rules 22A and 23–26

15.01A

Rule 22A [Added]—References under section 15(1)(ii)

22A.—(1) A reference made under section 15(1)(c)(ii) shall include—

(a) the date of filing of the earlier relevant application;

(b) its application number; and

(c) the country in or for which it was made.

(2) Subject to paragraph (3), the copy of the application provided under section 15(10)(b)(ii) shall—

(a) be duly certified by the authority with which it was filed; and

(b) where it is in a language other than English, be accompanied by—

(i) a translation into English of that application; or

(ii) a declaration that the description filed under sub-paragraph (i) of section 15(10)(b) is a complete and accurate translation into English of the description contained in the application provided under sub-paragraph (ii) of that provision.

(3) Where the application or a copy of the application is kept at the Patent Office it shall, for the purposes of section 15(10)(b)(ii), be treated as having been filed in accordance with rules.

Note. Rule 22A was inserted (by S.I. 2004 No. 2358) with effect from January 1, 2005.

15.02

Rule 23 [Replaced]—Missing parts

Rule 23 was replaced (by S.I. 2004 No. 2358) with effect from January 1, 2005, to read:

23.—(1) Subject to paragraph (2), the period prescribed for the purposes of section 15(5)(b) and (6) shall be the period starting on the date of filing of the application for a patent and ending on the date of the preliminary examination.

(2) Where the applicant is notified under section 15A(9) that a drawing or part of the description of the invention has been found to be missing, the period prescribed for the purposes of section 15(5)(b) and (6) shall be the period of two months starting on the date of the notification.

(3) An applicant may only withdraw a missing part by giving written notice to the comptroller.

(4) A request made under section 15(7)(b) shall be made in writing and shall—

(a) include sufficient information to identify where in the earlier relevant application the contents of the document filed under section 15(5)(b) were included; and

(b) be made before the end of the period prescribed for the purpose of section 15(5)(b).

(5) Any request under section 15(7)(b) shall be considered never to have been made where—

(a) the earlier relevant application does not contain every missing part filed under section 15(5);

(b) the applicant fails to furnish to the Patent Office copies of all earlier relevant applications, duly certified by the authority with which they were filed, before the end of the relevant period.

(6) Paragraph (5)(b) does not apply in respect of an earlier relevant application where that application or a copy of the application is kept at the Patent Office.

(7) The relevant period is the first to expire of—

(a) the period of sixteen months starting on the declared priority date; or

(b) the period of four months starting on the date the request was made under section 15(7)(b).

Rule 24—New applications under section 15(9) | 15.03

In the title to this rule, and in sub-rule (1), the references to "section 15(4)" were each changed (by S.I. 2004 No. 2358) to "section 15(9)" as a consequence of the new form of section 15 enacted under the RRO.

Rule 25 [Replaced]—Periods prescribed for the purposes of section 15(10) and 17(1) | 15.04

Rule 25 was replaced (by S.I. 2004 No. 2358) by:

25.—(1) Subject to paragraph (4), the period prescribed for the purposes of section 15(10) (a) and (b)(i) shall be the relevant period.

(2) Subject to paragraph (4) and rules 81(3), 82(3), 85(7) and 85(7A)(b), the period prescribed for the purposes of section 15(10)(c) and (d) and section 17(1) shall be the relevant period.

(3) Subject to paragraph (4), the period prescribed for the purpose of section 15(10)(b)(ii) shall be the period of four months starting on the date of filing.

(4) Where a new application is filed under section 8(3), 12(6), 15(9) or 37(4) after the relevant period has expired—

(a) subject to sub-paragraph (b), the period prescribed for the purposes of section 15(10)(a) to (d) and section 17(1) shall be the period of two months starting on the initiation date; or

(b) where it is filed less than six months before the period prescribed by rule 34 is due to expire (including the expiry of any extension of that period), the period prescribed for the purposes of section 15(10) (a) to (d) and section 17(1) shall end on the initiation date.

(5) The relevant period is—

(a) where there is no declared priority date, the period of twelve months starting on its date of filing of the application; or

(b) where the there is a declared priority date, the last to expire of—

(i) the period of twelve months starting on the declared priority date; or

(ii) the period of two months starting on the date of filing of the application.

Note. This replaced rule had effect from January 1, 2005, but the former rule 25 may continue to apply, see Note 3 to § 15.01 *supra*, as to which, in old rule 25(2), "85(7)(a)" had been replaced by "85(7)" (S.I. 2002 No. 529); and, in the reprinting of rule 25(4) in the Main Work, the word "of" should have appeared in the penultimate line after the word "filing".

15.05 | **Rule 26 [Replaced]—Extensions for new applications**

Rule 26 was replaced (by S.I. 2004 No. 2358) by:

26. Where a new application is filed under section 8(3), 12(6), 15(9) or 37(4) after the expiry of the periods prescribed in rule 6B or rule 15(1) (or after the expiry of any extensions of those periods)—

(a) the requirements of rules 6 to 6B and rule 15 shall be complied with on the initiation date;

(b) the requirements of paragraph 1(2)(a)(ii), 1(2)(a)(iii) and 1(3) of Schedule 2 shall be complied with at the initiation date (or, if later, the expiry of the relevant period ascertained under paragraph 1(3) of that Schedule.

Note. This replaced rule had effect from January 1, 2005, but the former rule 26 may continue to apply, see Note 3 to § 15.01 *supra*, as to which, in old rule 26(1)(b), there had been added (by S.I. 2002 No. 529), "1(2)(a)(iii)" after "1(2)(a)(ii)".

COMMENTARY ON SECTION 15

15.06 | *Scope of the section*

The replaced section 15 concerns only the means of "initiating" the filing of an application. New Section 15A then provides that there should be a "preliminary examination" to identify any deficiency in the documents initially submitted for this purpose and section 17 now deals only with the request for a patentability search on an application which has survived the preliminary examination carried out under section 15A.

In the replaced section 15: the subject matter of old subsection (1) is dealt with in new subsections (1)–(4); of old subsections (2)–(3A) in new subsections (5)–(8); and of old subsection (4) in new subsection (9). New subsection (10) deals with deemed withdrawal of an application for non compliance with the previous subsections and new subsection (11) provides that the term "relevant application" has the same meaning as that given in section 5(5) (for which see § 5.15 in the Main Work and *supra*) and embraces an international application for a patent (UK).

Date of filing

15.08 | *—Documents necessary to establish a date of filing (new subss. (1)–(4))*

Under the replaced section 15, a date of filing can now be established in a far more informal manner than previously. Under subsection (1) the date of filing is the earliest date when documents are filed at the Patent Office indicating: (a) that a patent is sought; (b) identifying the identity of the applicant sufficient to enable that person/entity to be contacted by the Patent Office; and (c) either (i) something which at least appears to be a description of an invention; or (ii) is an earlier relevant application made by the applicant or a predecessor in title thereof and identified with reference to its date of filing, its application number and the country in or for which it was made (see r. 22A, reprinted in § 15.01A *supra*). Compliance with any of the requirements of (a)–(c) is sufficient for the application to be "initiated" on the date when this is filed at the Patent Office. This date is then called the "initiation date" (as defined in amended r. 2, reprinted in § 123.02 *infra*) and some of "prescribed periods" run from that date, see § 15.10 *infra*.

Where the documents filed initially meet some, but not all, of the requirements of subsection (1), the application becomes "initiated" and subsection (3) requires the Comptroller, as soon as practicable, to notify the applicant of what else needs to be filed to establish a formal "date of filing". When these conditions are met, the Comptroller is required to notify the applicant of the date of filing which he has accorded and of the requirements which must be complied with, within the time limits specified, if the application is not to be treated as withdrawn (subs. (4)).

Accordingly, no form or fee is required for an application to be "initiated", nor need a formal specification be filed and the documents filed need not be in the English language, see subsection (2). Nevertheless, rule 16(1) does require that PF 1/77 is filed at some time, but its format has been changed to encompass the new provisions for informal "initiation" of an application, see § 140.01 *infra*. Although a "date of filing" is accorded to such an informal filing as that when the requirements of subsection (1) have been met, there will be a deemed withdrawal of the application if further conditions are not met within the prescribed periods, see subsection (10) as discussed in § 15.10 *infra*.

Thus, a date of filing can be obtained without filing a description as such, but instead by making a reference to an earlier "relevant application" (filed in the UK or in another country, for which see s. 5(5) and (6)) in circumstances where the description of the application is intended to be identical with that of an earlier application from which priority (under s. 5(2)) is claimed or intended to be claimed (for which see § 5.02 *supra*). Where reference is so made to an earlier "relevant application" (as defined in subs. (11) with reference back to s. 5(5)) and so is used to establish the "date of filing", rule 22A(2) requires that (in due course, but within the period prescribed under subs. (10)(b) which (under r. 25(3) is four months starting on the date of filing) there shall be filed: a certified copy of that application; and, if not in the English language, a translation into English thereof, or a declaration that the description filed is a complete and accurate translation of such. But, such a document is not required if the application, or a copy thereof, is kept at the Patent Office (r. 22A(3)), when the Patent Office will itself prepare the necessary copy under rule 112A (reprinted at § 123.10A *infra*). If the description subsequently filed under subsection (10)(b)(i) contains "additional matter", *i.e.* "matter extending beyond that disclosed in the earlier relevant application", the application is not to be allowed to proceed until it is amended to exclude that additional matter, see new subsection 76(1A), reprinted in § 76.01 *infra*.

—Missing documents (new subsections (5)–(8))   **15.09**

Old subsections (2)–(3A) dealt only with drawings missing from the application documents initially filed. However, new subsection (5) expands the former provisions so as to deal also with a failure to include in the initially filed description a part thereof, although this provision only comes into effect once a date of filing has been established under subsection (1) and where a drawing, or part of the description, was missing from the documents (as defined in subs. (1)(c)) which were filed to obtain that date, and is subsequently filed. New rule 23 (reprinted in § 15.02 *supra*) is therefore now entitled "Missing parts".

To try to include a "missing part" (either a drawing or part of the description) in the total description, an application must be made before the "date of the preliminary examination" (presumably when this actually takes place rather than merely the date of referral therefor under s. 15A(1)) or within two months after the Comptroller has notified the applicant (under s. 15A(9)) that a drawing or part of the description appears to be missing (r. 23(1), (2)).

In these circumstances, subsection (6) provides that, unless the "missing part" is withdrawn (for which a written request is required by r. 23(3)): (a) the missing part is to be treated as part of the application, but (b) with the date of filing changed to the actual date of filing thereof.

However, where the missing part is contained in a priority document, subsection (7)(b) makes it is possible for the original date of filing to be maintained by the applicant making a request for subsection (6)(b) not to apply (*i.e.* for the original date of filing to be maintained) provided that a priority declaration (under s. 5(2)) has been made on or before the date designated as the "date of filing". Such a request must comply with the requirements of rules 23(4)–(7), *i.e.* that the request is in writing and is made within 16 months of the declared priority date or (if earlier) four months from the date of that request (r. 23(7)). Sufficient information has to be provided to identify where there is to be found in the earlier relevant application the contents of the document filed (under s. 15(5)(b)) to identify the missing part; and a certified copy of the earlier relevant application is required (unless at least a copy thereof is already on file in the Patent Office) (r. 23(4), (6)), when the Patent Office will itself prepare the necessary copy (under r. 112A, reprinted in § 123.10A *infra*). If a required certified copy is not provided, or it is found that the earlier relevant application does not contain "every missing part" as identified in the request, this is to be considered as never having been made (r. 23(5)).

Limited extensions of the times specified in rule 23 remain available under rule 110(3) and (4), as discussed in § 123.33 *infra*.

15.10 | *Times for filing claims, abstract and paying application fee (subs. (10))*

The search fee is now normally to be paid by filing new PF 9A/77, which is now only a request for a search whereas old PF 9/77 was a combined request for preliminary examination and search. However old PF 9/77 is still required where the application in suit was a pending one at the RRO Commencement Date of January 1, 2005, see Note 3 to § 15.01 *supra*.

New subsection (10) provides that an application is to be deemed withdrawn if certain actions have not been done before the end of the prescribed period. These actions are:

(a) the filing of claims and abstract (*q.v.* § 15.17 in the Main Work);

(b) in a case where the description initially filed was merely a reference to an earlier relevant application (as permitted by subs. (1)(c)(ii)), the filing of a full description and a copy of the earlier application referred to (which itself complies with the relevant requirements of the rules) (*q.v.* § 5.08 *supra*);

(c) the required "application fee" fee is paid (*q.v.* § 14.08 *supra*); and

(d) a request is made for a search (under s. 17(1)), and the search fee is paid (*q.v.* § 17.07 in the Main Work).

For each of the matters set out in (a), (b)(i), (c) and (d) above (unless the application is a "divisional" or "replacement" application), the "prescribed period" is 12 months from the declared priority date or (if later) two months from the date of filing the application; or (if there is no declared priority date) 12 months from the date of filing (r. 25(5)); but, in a case falling within (b)(ii) above, the prior is four months from the date of filing.

For the position where the application is a "divisional" or "replacement" application, see §§ 15.15 and 15.23 *infra*.

15.11 | *Extension of time for compliance with new subsection (10)*

Subsection (10) has replaced former subsection (5); and rule 110 has been recast (as amplified with introduction of Rules Schedule 4A, Parts 1, 2 and 4), all as reprinted in §§ 123.09–123.09B and 123.09D *infra*.

Under these provisions, the periods prescribed for the filing, or late filing, of a priority declaration (under rr. 6(2)(b) and 6A(1), and under r. 26 insofar as this relates thereto) remain inextensible (Rules, Sched. 4A, Part 1). However, automatic extensions of two months are available (under r. 110(3)), with further extension possible (under r. 110(4)) if discretion therefore can be exercised (Rules, Schedule 4A, Part 3) of the periods prescribed for:

    (a) furnishing the file number and certified copies of priority documents under rule 6B;

    (b) complying with rule 23(1) and (2) relating to missing parts of a description or drawings;

    (c) filing claims and requesting preliminary examination and search as prescribed under rules 25(1), (2) and (4)(a), but not as regards the periods specified under rule 25(4)(b);

    (d) compliance with rule 26 for new applications, but not as regards the filing of priority declarations under rules 6 and 6A.

However (by Rules, Schedule 4A, Part 4), the availability of these extensions in relation to rules 25 and 26 is limited to a two month extension only, and no such extension can be granted after the expiry of a two months period starting immediately the period of time (or extended period of time) prescribed by these rules (r. 110(8) and (10)).

Divisional applications (subs. (9))

—Time for filing

15.13

In the new form of section 15 (as set out in § 15.01 *supra*), former subsection (4) has become subsection (9) with a consequent change in rule 24, but without change except that a divisional application (with the same effect as under former s. 15(4)) can now be initiated merely by compliance with the requirements of subsection (1) (for which see § 15.08 *supra*), with the facility for filing the other required documents at a later date, as discussed in see §§ 15.15 *infra*.

Central Research Laboratories' Application (BL O/419/00) is another example of discretion being refused to permit late filing of a divisional application: there were indications of a change of mind and insufficient diligence in the period before the application was filed.

In *Anderson's Application* (BL O/297/02) the applicant filed a divisional application out of time but an extension under rule 110(1) was refused because the applicant had not been sufficiently diligent in prosecuting his application. An argument under the Human Rights Act 1998 (c.42) failed.

—Content of divisional applications

15.14

There appears to be no objection to a divisional application having an independent claim which includes all the features of a claim in the parent application together with an additional feature (*EPO Decision T 587/98, KOMAG/Divisional claim conflicting with parent* OJEPO 2000, 497).

Time limits for filing other documents on divisional applications

—The applicable rules

15.15

Under the changes made as a result of the RRO, the applicable rules as to time limits for filing documents to support a divisional application are now to be found in new rules 25(4) and 26 (reprinted respectively in §§ 15.04 and *supra*). Under this rule 25(4), each of the requirements of section 15(10) need to be met within the period of two months starting on the "initiation date", for which see § 15.08 *supra*, but, where the divisional application has been filed after the "relevant period" required by subsection (10) has expired, the requirements thereof can be satisfied within two months of this "initiation date", except where the divisional application is filed less than six months before the end of the rule 34 period (for placing the application in order, as discussed in § 18.10 in the Main Work and *infra*), when all of these requirements must have been met by that "initiation date" (r. 25(4)(b)).

Apart from the references to "initiation date", instead of the previous references to "filing date", the time periods discussed in §§ 15.16–15.21 appear to be essentially unchanged as to the dates when the various requirements for filing documents must be filed to avoid the application being deemed to have been withdrawn.

As to whether an extension of any of these prescribed periods is possible and (if so) on what basis and for how long, see § 15.11 *supra*.

15.23 | *Replacement application under sections 8(3), 12(6) and 37(4))*

The requirements for filing a "replacement application", when permitted under any of sections 8(3), 12(6) and 37(4), remain essentially the same as for divisional applications, for which see § 15.15, with the possibility of time extensions having been discussed in § 15.11, each *supra*.

Practice under Section 15

15.24 | *Filing of initial application*

As described in § 15.08 *supra*, an application can be "initiated" merely by fulfilling certain fairly basic requirements as set out in replaced subsection (1). If these are not met, a "date of filing" is not accorded until the deficiencies have been rectified. However, many of the formal requirements to establish an application can now be filed at a later date, see § 15.10 *supra*. Once a date of filing has been accorded, a preliminary examination takes place under new section 15A. This will lead to a report of any deficiencies in the specified formal requirements which, if not rectified within the prescribed period, will lead to a deemed withdrawal of the application. Only after this preliminary examination has been concluded will the application proceed to a search (under s. 17) and then a substantive examination (under s. 18).

Divisional applications

15.29 | *—Documents required for filing*

Contrary to the statement in the Main Work, it is understood that, where it is clear that no additional search is likely to be required under section 17(8), a refund of the search fee can be made before grant.

15.32 | *—Applicant for divisional application*

In EPO Decision J 17–18/97, SULZERMEDICA/Identity of applicant [2004] EPOR 8 correction of the identity of the applicant was not allowed under EPCr. 88 where a divisional aplication had been filed in the name of an assignee, not the original applicant.

15A.01 | **SECTION 15A [ADDED]—Preliminary examination**

The RRO (a. 5) introduced new section 15A to replace the provisions relating to Preliminary Examination contained in the former version of section 17. Section 15A reads:

15A.—(1) The comptroller shall refer an application for a patent to an examiner for a preliminary examination if—

    (a) the application has a date of filing;

    (b) the application has not been withdrawn or treated as withdrawn; and

    (c) the application fee has been paid.

  (2) a preliminary examination of an application the examiner shall

    (a) determine whether the application complies with those requirements of this Act and the rules which are designated by the rules as formal requirements for the purposes of this Act; and

    (b) determine whether any requirements under section 13(2) or 15(10) above remain to be complied with.

  (3) The examiner shall report to the comptroller his determinations under subsection (2) above.

  (4) If on the preliminary examination of an application it is found that—

    (a) any drawing referred to in the application, or

    (b) part of the description of the invention for which the patent is sought,

is missing from the application, then the examiner shall include this finding in his report under subsection (3) above.

  (5) Subsections (6) to (8) below apply if a report is made to the comptroller under subsection (3) above that not all the formal requirements have been complied with.

  (6) The comptroller shall specify a period during which the applicant shall have the opportunity

    (a) to make observations on the report, and

    (b) to amend the application so as to comply with those requirements (subject to section 76 below).

  (7) The comptroller may refuse the application if the applicant fails to amend the application as mentioned in subsection (6)(b) above before the end of the period specified by the comptroller under that subsection.

  (8) Subsection (7) above does not apply if—

    (a) the applicant makes observations as mentioned in subsection (6)(a) above before the end of the period specified by the comptroller under that subsection, and

    (b) as a result of the observations, the comptroller is satisfied that the formal requirements have been complied with.

  (9) If a report is made to the comptroller under subsection (3) above—

    (a) that any requirement of section 13(2) or 15(10) above has not been complied with; or

    (b) that a drawing or part of the description of the invention has been found to be missing,

then the comptroller shall notify the applicant accordingly.

Note. Although these amendments took effect on January 1, 2005, they do not apply to applications which were then "pending", a term defined in Note 3 to § 15.01 *supra.* For these applications, the former version of section 15 continues to have effect and section 15A has no effect.

15A.02 | **Rule 28 [Replaced]—Preliminary examination under section 15A**

(1) On a preliminary examination the examiner shall determine whether the application complies with the requirements of rules 6 to 6C.

(2) The examiner shall report to the comptroller his determinations under paragraph (1) and the comptroller shall notify the applicant accordingly.

Note. The subject matter of former rule 28 (reprinted in the Main Work at § 17.02) has been split (by S.I. 2004 No. 2358) into replaced rule 28 for the "preliminary examination" (under s. 15A) and new rule 28A (reprinted at § 17.02 *infra*) for the "search" (under s. 17). These divided rules took effect from January 1, 2005, but not as regards applications which were then "pending" to which the old rules remained applicable, see Note 3 to § 15.01 *supra*.

COMMENTARY ON SECTION 15A

15A.03 | *Scope of the section*

This new section 15A provides for a "preliminary examination" of an application by an examiner before it proceeds to a search under revised section 17. However (by subs. (1)), an application only proceeds to this examination if: it has a date of filing; has not been withdrawn or treated as withdrawn; and the application fee has been paid (for which see § 14.08 *supra*).

The examiner then determines whether the application complies with the "formal requirements" designated as such by the Act and Rules, for which see rule 31 (reprinted in the Main Work at § 17.04, as amended as noted in § 17.04 *infra*). In particular, the examiner is required (by subs. (2)) to determine whether the requirements of sections 13(2) and 15(10) have been met, for which see respectively §§ 13.04–13.08 in the Main Work and § 15.10 *supra*. This is followed by a preliminary examination report to be made to the Comptroller (subs. (3)). Also, if the examiner finds that a drawing, or part of the description, is apparently missing from the application, notice of this is to be included in this report (subs. 4)). In turn, the Comptroller must then notify the applicant accordingly (subs. (9)).

Where the examiner's report to the Comptroller identifies formal requirements that have not been complied with, the Comptroller is required to specify a period during which the applicant has the opportunity to contest the report by making observations or make rectifying amendments, which must, of course, comply with section 76 (subs. (6)). If satisfactory amendments are not made within the specified period, or the observations are not accepted, the application may be refused (subss. (7) and (8)).

These aspects of procedure were formerly part of section 17. Consequently, besides replaced rule 28, rules 29 and 31, as well as commentary thereon and practice thereunder, should now be considered under section 15A. Thus, §§ 17.03, 17.04 and 17.07–17.09 in the Main Work and below should be considered instead as part of the Commentary on Section 15A.

16.01 | **SECTION 16—Publication of application**

The Patents Act 2004 (c. 16, Sched. 2(6)) prospectively amended subsection 16(1) by, after the words "Subject to section 22 below", adding the words "and to any prescribed restrictions".

Scope of the section   16.03

The amendment to subsection (1) would, when implemented, allow for rules to be made which would permit an inventor's name and address to be withheld from the application/ patent file open to publication.

This may be desirable in a situation where activists may seek to harass an inventor because of his involvement in the research leading to the invention.

Creation of entry in the register

—Avoiding publication by withdrawal   16.06

It is now no longer possible to prevent publication once the preparations therefor are complete. A letter of intended publication will be sent to the applicant giving three days notice of the intended publication of an application (A-series), and notice of withdrawal must be received before that date to avoid publication. Such notice may now be sent by email to the dedicated address withdraw@patent.gov.uk —see OJ July 2, 2003 and § 14.43 *supra*. For granted patents (B-series), notice of withdrawal would have to be received before issue of the letter of intention to grant a patent under s. 24. Enquiries concerning publication should be made to the Publication Liaison Officer on 01633 814089.

PRACTICE UNDER SECTION 16

Form of front page of the published application   16.07

The amendment to subsection (1) would permit a rule to be made enabling the name of an inventor to be withheld from the bibliographic data published on the front page of an A specification, *e.g.* for the reason indicated in § 16.03 *supra*.

SECTION 17—Search   17.01

The RRO (a. 6) changed: the title of section 17 to "Search"; replaced subsection (1) as follows, with subsections (2) and (3) then ceasing to have effect because the subject matter thereof has been relocated to new section 15A, see § 15A.03 *supra*.

(1) The comptroller shall refer an application for a patent to an examiner for a search if, and only if—
  (a) the comptroller has referred the application to an examiner for a preliminary examination under section 15A(1) above;
  (b) the application has not been withdrawn or treated as withdrawn;
  (c) before the end of the prescribed period—
      (i) the applicant makes a request to the Patent Office in the prescribed form for a search; and
      (ii) the fee prescribed for the search ("the search fee") is paid;
  (d) the application includes—
      (i) a description of the invention for which a patent is sought; and
      (ii) one or more claims; and
  (e) the description and each of the claims comply with the requirements of rules as to language.

Note. Although these amendments took effect on January 1, 2005, they do not apply to applications then "pending", a term defined in Note 3 to § 15.01 *supra*.

RELEVANT RULES—RULES 28, 29, 31 AND 32

17.02 | **Rule 28A [Added]—Search under section 17**

(1) A request under section 17(1)(c)(i) for a search shall be made on Patents Form 9A/77.

(2) The comptroller may, if he thinks fit, send to the applicant a copy of any document (or any part thereof) referred to in the examiner's report made under section 17(5).

Note. Former rule 28 has been split into two rules dealing respectively with preliminary examination under section 15A (for which see § 15A.02 *supra*) and rule 28A as presented above (see S.I. 2004 No. 2358). These divided rules took effect from January 1, 2005, but not as regards applications which were then "pending" to which the old rules remained applicable, see Note 3 to § 15.01 *supra*.

17.03 | **Rule 29 [Added]—Procedure where earlier application made**

(1) Where, on a preliminary examination, the examiner finds that a declaration made for the purposes of section 5(2) specifies a date of filing for an earlier relevant application—

(a) more than twelve months before the date of filing the application in suit; or

(b) where the comptroller has given permission for a late declaration to be made under section 5(2), more than fourteen months before the date of filing of the application in suit,

he shall report this finding to the comptroller and the comptroller shall notify the applicant accordingly.

(2) Where the comptroller has notified the applicant under paragraph (1), the applicant shall, before the end of the relevant period, provide the comptroller with a corrected date; otherwise the declaration, in so far as it relates to the earlier relevant application, shall be disregarded.

(3) The relevant period is the period of two months starting on the date of the notification under paragraph (2).

(4) For the purposes of paragraph (2), "corrected date" means a date that would not have been reported by the examiner under paragraph (1).

Note. This replacement rule (made by S.I. 2004 No. 2358) more accurately relates to the preliminary examination now covered by new section 15A. It took effect from January 1, 2005, but not as regards applications which were then "pending" to which the old rules remained applicable, see Note 3 to § 15.01 *supra*.

17.04 | **Rule 31—Formal requirements**

A new paragraph (1A) was inserted (by S.I. 2003 No. 513, with effect from April 1, 2003) reading:

(1A) Where any of the requirements referred to in paragraph (1) do not apply by virtue of rule 18(4) or rule 20(16), the formal requirements for the purposes of the Act shall include the requirements of so much of any directions given by the comptroller under section 124A as replace those requirements.

Rule 32—Searches under section 17(6) and (8)

17.05

In rule 32(3), "Form 9/77" has been replaced by "Form 9A/77", with effect from January 1, 2005, except for applications then pending (S.I. 2004 No. 2358, r. 20 and Sched. 2(4)).

COMMENTARY ON SECTION 17

Scope of the section

17.06

By the amendments set out in §§ 17.01 *supra*, section 17 now deals only with the search which is to follow the "preliminary examination", the provisions for which are now contained in new section 15A, see §§ 15A.01–15A.03 *supra*. Thus, rules 29 and 31 (although reprinted respectively under §§ 17.03 and 17.04 *supra*) need to be considered as relating to section 15A, as also do the contents of §§ 17.07–17.09 and 17.14–17.18 in the Main Work and *infra*.

Preliminary examinations (subss. (1)–(3))

—Scope and definitions

17.07

New rule 28A is now the operative rule for making the necessary request for a search. This to be done on new PF 9A/77, which replaces PF 9/77 (for which see §§ 140.09 and 104.09A *infra*). Old form PF 9/77 is now only required for applications which were pending on January 1, 2005, for which see Note 3 to § 15.01 *supra*.

—Meeting of formal requirements (r. 31)

17.08

In the third paragraph under this heading on page 259, the reference in the first line to r. 20(15) should be to r. 20(14) and in the second line the reference to r. 20(13) should be to r. 20(12).

New rule 31(1A) (for which see § 17.04 *supra*) provides that rule 31 may be varied by direction of the Comptroller in relation to any permitted filing in electronic form or by way of electronic communication, but no such direction has yet been made.

—Declaration of priority

17.09

Rule 29 has been amended to accommodate the possibility of a late declaration of priority being made and accepted under added sections 5(2A)-(2C) leading to the replacement of rule 6 and the addition of new rules 6A-6C, for which see §§ 5.01–5.03 and 15.08 *supra*. Accordingly, rule 29 now requires a corrected date to be given if the priority declaration refers to a date more than 12 moths before the "date of filing" (as defined in s. 15(1), for which see § 15.08 *supra*), or 14 months before that date where a late declaration has been permitted to be filed.

Practice under Section 17

Time limits

17.15 *—Minimum requirements on filing*

The minimum requirements before a "date of filing" can be accorded to an application have been much relaxed by the RRO as explained in § 15.08 *supra* which should be read in place of § 17.15 in the Main Work.

17.18 *Preliminary examination*

In the fourth complete paragraph on page 266, the sentence starting in line 5 should read "Meanwhile the application can, but usually will not, proceed to publication under section 16 (see § 16.04), and in lines 9 and 10 of that paragraph, the statement "although a limited extension of time may be possible" should be deleted.

The Practice Notice of April 17, 2002 (see § 1.14 *supra*) states that applications directed to business methods as such will continue to be rejected before any search is conducted.

17.19 *The extent of the search*

A notice "New examination procedures: disclosure of search results" appeared in the OJ of March 31, 2004 setting out a new procedure for the processing of patent applications. The search examiner will make a disclosure request at the time of issuing the search report on each application. The request will relate to official search reports produced by other patent offices on corresponding applications and can be fulfilled either by filing a copy of the search report, or by emailing the details of the citations made. The request is active up to the time of responding to the first examination report under section 18, whether under section 18(3) or 18(4). If a section 18(4) report is not responded to, the cut-off date is two months after issue of the report. Search results can be provided at any time before then, but the notice says that it is helpful if, when requesting substantive examination, search results available at that time are disclosed. Search reports do not need to be provided if they show a nil response, they have been published by WIPO or EPO or they have been provided on a parent application. Disclosure requests will start to be included in letters accompanying search reports issued from July 1, 2004.

18.01 **SECTION 18—Substantive examination and grant or refusal of patent**

The RRO (a. 7) amended section 18 by:
(1) in subsection (1), omitting (in line 2 of the Main Work reprint thereof) the words "preliminary examination and";
(2) in subsection (2), inserting after the words "any examination" (in line 2 of the Main Work reprint thereof) the words "carried out under section 15A above"; and
(3) in subsection (4), substituting for the words "section 17" (in line 2 of the Main Work reprint thereof) the words "section 15A".

Note. Although these amendments took effect on January 1, 2005, they do not apply to applications then "pending", a term defined in Note 3 to § 15.01 *supra*.

Relevant Rules—Rules 33 and 34

18.02 **Rule 33—Request for substantive examination under section 18**

Consequent upon the amendment of rule 85 (noted in § 89A.02 *infra*), rule 33(2) has been amended by replacing "85(7)(a)" by "85(7)" (S.I. 2002 No. 529).

Also, consequent to the replacement of old section 15(4) by new section 15(9), the references in rule 33(3) and (5) to "15(4)" have each been replaced by "15(9)" (S.I. 2004 No. 2358).

Rule 34—Period for putting application in order

18.03

Consequent to the replacement of old section 15(4) by new section 15(9), the reference in rule 34(1)(c) to "15(4)" has been replaced by "15(9)" (S.I. 2004 No. 2358).

COMMENTARY ON SECTION 18

Scope of the section

18.04

The topics of preliminary examination and search have now been separated into sections 15A and 17 respectively and the changes made to the Act and rules as a consequence are dealt with in the commentaries on these sections above. The amendments to section 18 (set out in § 18.01 *supra*) are a further consequence of these changes.

Request for substantive examination

18.05

The automatic extension of time for filing the request for substantive examination (PF 10/77) which is available under revised rule 110(3) is now two months, with a further extension available with discretion under rule 110(4) not exceeding two months (r. 110(8) and (10)), see § 123.33 *infra*.

Substantive examination (subss. (2) and (3))

18.07

A notice in the OJ of March 31, 2004 entitled "New examination procedures: examination opinions" details new procedures to be employed from April 1, 2004 where the search reveals major issues that will have to be addressed at substantive examination, such as where the scope of the independent claim is so wide that numerous anticipating documents exist. The examiner will now provide early warning of such issues in an "examination opinion" to encourage early amendment before examination. If the applicant does not amend, the first substantive examination report under section 18 will be similar in content to the examination opinion and specify a two month period for response.

Time for complying with Act and Rules

18.10

The automatic extension of time for putting the application in order for acceptance under rule 34 which is available under revised rule 110(3) is now two months, with a further extension available with discretion under rule 110(4) not exceeding two months (r. 110(8) and (10)), see § 123.33 *infra*.

PRACTICE UNDER SECTION 18

Plurality of invention

18.13

The references in the Main Work to rule 24 are outdated and § 15.13 therein should be consulted for details of the times permitted for filing a divisional application.

Substantive examination

—Extension of time for response

18.15

In *Lionweld Kennedy's Application* (BL O/258/00), a request for response time extension, based on changes in the management organisation of the applicant company which had made it difficult to obtain material and meaningful instructions, was not regarded as the required "exceptional circumstances". A subsidiary factor in refusing extension was that an extension request had not been made earlier.

In *Smart Card Solutions' Application* ([2004] RPC 273) an extension was requested to the time set under section 18(3) for responding to the substantive examination report to give the agent time to study the International Search Report before responding. Although the agent indicated that this had been his common practice and that similar requests had been granted previously, the application for extension was refused. Following *Jaskowski's Application* ([1981] RPC 197) cited in the Main Work, there must be a reason for exercising the discretion to extend "which is peculiar to the particular applicant or application in suit" and in *MacDonald's Application* (BL O/71/96) also referred to in the Main Work, awaiting results of searches from other countries had not been accepted as an excuse for an extension.

New section 117B (reprinted at § 117B.01 *infra*) deals with extensions of time of periods which have been specified by the Comptroller, rather than specified in the Act or Rules, and hence concerns time extensions of the period set for response to a substantive examination report. As explained in § 117B.03 *infra*, an initial extension of two months is available upon written request therefor, but such an extension is terminated at the end of the period for placing the application in order under section 20. Under section 117B(4), a further extension of an initial extension may be possible, but such may be granted subject to such conditions as the Comptroller may think fit.

SECTION 19—General power to amend application before grant

PRACTICE UNDER SECTION 19

19.12 *Amendment of the request (PF 1/77)*

In the final paragraph on page 288, the reference in the first line to §§ 18.02 and 32.05 should be to §§ 19.02 and 32.04.

SECTION 20—Failure of application

COMMENTARY ON SECTION 20

Appeal from refusal

20.05 *—Time for appeal*

Under CPR 63.17 (reprinted *infra* at § F63.17), the procedure in appeals from the Comptroller is now governed by the general rules for appeals set out in CPR Part 20, the main parts of which are reprinted in §§ E52.1–E52PD.21 in the Main Work. Under CPR 52.4, the "lower court" (here the Comptroller) sets the time for appeal, which time can, apparently, only be extended by the appellate body (here the Patents Court), see CPR 52.6. For the procedure, see § 97.12 (in the Main Work and *infra*).

In *Degussa-Hüls' Application* (BL O/180/04), it was noted that, under s. 20(2) the rule 34 period for placing the application in order for acceptance is automatically extended to the end of the appeal period of 28 days; and it was pointed out that this extension runs concurrently with any extension under rule 110(3) and not consecutively (reference being made to paragraph 20.10 of the *Manual of Patent Practice*).

20.07 *Effect of failing to comply with Act and Rules within prescribed period*

In *Duncan and Harcombe's Applications* (BL O/426/01) a series of errors had been made by private applicants who now sought an extension of time for putting an application in order despite the expiry of the rule 34 period. The Comptroller remarked that "Confusion and ignorance of patent law are not grounds for exercising discretion for time extensions. An applicant must demonstrate a continuing underlying intention to pursue the application".

SECTION 20A [ADDED]—Reinstatement of applications

20A.01

The RRO (a. 8), with effect from January 1, 2005 the Commencement Date of S.I. 2004 No. 2358, introduced new section 20A, reading:

20A.—(1) Subsection (2) below applies where an application for a patent is refused, or is treated as having been refused or withdrawn, as a direct consequence of a failure by the applicant to comply with a requirement of this Act or rules within a period which is—

(a) set out in this Act or rules, or

(b) specified by the comptroller.

(2) Subject to subsection (3) below, the comptroller shall reinstate the application if, and only if—

(a) the applicant requests him to do so;

(b) the request complies with the relevant requirements of rules; and

(c) he is satisfied that the failure to comply referred to in subsection (1) above was unintentional.

(3) The comptroller shall not reinstate the application if—

(a) an extension remains available under this Act or rules for the period referred to in subsection (1) above; or

(b) the period referred to in subsection (1) above is set out or specified—

(i) in relation to any proceedings before the comptroller;

(ii) for the purposes of section 5(2A)(b) above; or

(iii) for the purposes of a request under this section or section 117B below.

(4) Where the application was made by two or more persons jointly, a request under subsection (2) above may, with the leave of the comptroller, be made by one or more of those persons without joining the others.

(5) If the application has been published under section 16 above, then the comptroller shall publish notice of a request under subsection (2) above in the prescribed manner.

(6) The reinstatement of an application under this section shall be by order.

(7) If an application is reinstated under this section the applicant shall comply with the requirement referred to in subsection (1) above within the further period specified by the comptroller in the order reinstating the application.

(8) The further period specified under subsection (7) above shall not be less than two months.

(9) If the applicant fails to comply with subsection (7) above the application shall be treated as having been withdrawn on the expiry of the period specified under that subsection.

Relevant Rule—Rule 36A

20A.02 | **Rule 36A [Added]—Reinstatement of application under section 20A**

36A.—(1) Any request under section 20A for the reinstatement of an application shall be made before the end of the relevant period.

(2) The relevant period shall be the first to expire of—

(a) the period of twelve months starting on the date on which the application was terminated, or

(b) the period of two months starting on the date on which the removal of the cause of non-compliance occurred.

(3) The request shall be made on Patents Form 14/77 supported by evidence of the statements made in it.

(4) Where the comptroller is required to publish a notice under section 20A(5), it shall be published in the Journal.

(5) Where, upon consideration of the evidence provided in accordance with paragraph (3), the comptroller is not satisfied that a case for an order under section 20A has been made out, he shall notify the applicant accordingly.

(6) Where the comptroller has notified the applicant under paragraph (5), the applicant may, before the end of the period of one month starting on the date of the notification, request to be heard by the comptroller.

(7) Where the applicant requests a hearing under paragraph (6), the comptroller shall give the applicant an opportunity to be heard, after which he shall determine whether the request under section 20A shall be allowed or refused.

(8) Where the comptroller reinstates the application after a notice was published under paragraph (4), he shall advertise in the Journal the fact that he has reinstated the application.

(9) In determining the date on which the removal of the cause of non-compliance occurred, the comptroller shall have regard to any relevant principles applicable under the European Patent Convention.

Note. New rule 36A was added by S.I. 2004 No. 2358, with effect from January 1, 2005.

Commentary on Section 20A

20A.03 | *Scope of the section*

New section 20A, to be read in conjunction with new rule 36A (reprinted respectively in §§ 20A.01 and 20A.02 *supra*), provides for reinstatement of an application which has been refused, or treated as refused or withdrawn as a direct consequence of the applicant failing to comply with a requirement of the Act or any rules within a period which is set out in the Act or Rules, or is one as specified by the Comptroller (subs. (1)). However, reinstatement can only be allowed when the applicant so requests in compliance with the relevant requirements of the Rules and only when he satisfies the Comptroller that this failure to comply was "unintentional" (subs. (2)).

Nevertheless (under subs. (3)), the Comptroller may **not** order a reinstatement if: (a) an extension of time remains available for the period for which there was non compliance; or (b) if the period is one set out or specified (i) in relation to any proceedings before the Comptroller; or (ii) is one for the purpose of section 5(2)(a) re. a declaration of priority; or (iii) is one for the purpose of making a request for reinstatement under the section or is one for an extension (or further extension) of a time limit specified by the Comptroller under new section 117B (for which see § 117B.02 *infra*).

Where there are joint applicants, one or some of the applicants may be made without joining the others, provided that the Comptroller so permits (subs. (4)).

Where the application has already been published under section 16, notice of a reinstatement request is to be published in the O.J. (subs. (5) and r. 36A(4)); and if reinstatement is to be permitted it is to be made by order (subs. 6)) which is also to be advertised in the O.J. (r. 36A(8)).

A request for reinstatement under the section must be made before the expiry of either 12 months from the date when the application was terminated; or two months from the date on which the removal of the cause of non compliance occurred, whichever is the earlier (r. 36A(1) and (2)). This period is inextensible (Rules, Sched. 4A, Part 1, reprinted at § 123.09A *infra*). The request is to be made on new PF 14/77 with its attendant fee (for which see § 142.02 *infra*); and evidence must be filed sufficient to support the request, in particular to establish to the satisfaction of the Comptroller that the non compliance was "unintentional" (r. 36A3)). This evidence must be filed within 14 days of making the request (as noted in §§ 72.09 and 72.33 *infra* re revised rule 107), but this period is extensible with discretion exercised under rule 110(1).

There is here a parallel with new section 5(2C), under which the late filing of a priority declaration can be allowed if, likewise, the Comptroller can be satisfied that the timely failure to make the declaration had been unintentional, as to which see § 5.07A *supra*.

If the Comptroller is not satisfied that the request should be accepted, the applicant is to be notified, whereupon the applicant can (within one month of the date of notification) request a hearing. The Comptroller must then provide an opportunity for the applicant to be heard, after which he is to determine whether the request should be allowed or refused (r. 36A(6)–(8)).

In this determination, the Comptroller is required to "have regard to any relevant principles applicable under the European Patent Convention" (r. 36A(9)). This presumably means that the Comptroller should take judicial notice of the EPC Implementing Regulations and of decisions of the EPO Boards of Appeal and endeavor to reach an analogous conclusion in relation to the reinstatement of a European application which has been terminated for non-compliance with a specified time limit.

When an order is made under the section for reinstatement of a terminated application under the Act and Rules, it will specify the period (of not less than two months) within which compliance is to take place; and, if this is not done, the application is to be treated as having been withdrawn on the expiry of the period referred to in subsection (1), *i.e.* that which caused the original termination (subs. (7)–(9)).

The effect of reinstatement is as set out in new section 20B, for which see §§ 20B.01 and 20B.02 *supra*.

SECTION 20B [ADDED]—Effect of reinstatement under section 20A | 20B.01

The RRO (a. 8) added new section 20B into which subsection (6A) was incorporated by the Patents Act 2004 (c. 16, Sched. 2(7)), all having effect from January 1, 2005 the Commencement Date of the RRO. Section 20B, as so amended, reads:

20B.—(1) The effect of reinstatement under section 20A of an application for a patent is as follows.

(2) Anything done under or in relation to the application during the period between termination and reinstatement shall be treated as valid.

(3) If the application has been published under section 16 above before its termination anything done during that period which would have constituted an infringement of the rights conferred by publication of the application if the termination had not occurred shall be treated as an infringement of those rights—

    (a) if done at a time when it was possible for the period referred to in section 20A(1) above to be extended, or

   (b) if it was a continuation or repetition of an earlier act infringing those rights.

   (4) If the application has been published under section 16 above before its termination and, after the termination and before publication of notice of the request for its reinstatement, a person—

   (a) began in good faith to do an act which would have constituted an infringement of the rights conferred by publication of the application if the termination had not taken place, or

   (b) made in good faith effective and serious preparations to do such an act,

he has the right to continue to do the act or, as the case may be, to do the act, notwithstanding the reinstatement of the application and the grant of the patent; but this right does not extend to granting a licence to another person to do the act.

   (5) If the act was done, or the preparations were made, in the course of a business, the person entitled to the right conferred by subsection (4) above may—

   (a) authorise the doing of that act by any partners of his for the time being in that business, and

   (b) assign that right, or transmit it on death (or in the case of a body corporate on its dissolution), to any person who acquires that part of the business in the course of which the act was done or the preparations were made.

   (6) Where a product is disposed of to another in exercise of a right conferred by subsection (4) or (5) above, that other and any person claiming through him may deal with the product in the same way as if it had been disposed of by the applicant.

   (6A) The above provisions apply in relation to the use of a patented invention for the services of the Crown as they apply in relation to infringement of the rights conferred by publication of the application for a patent (or, as the case may be, infringement of the patent). "Patented invention" has the same meaning as in section 55 below.

   (7) In this section "termination", in relation to an application, means—

   (a) the refusal of the application, or

   (b) the application being treated as having been refused or withdrawn.

COMMENTRAY ON SECTION 20B

20B.02 | *Scope of the section*

New section 20(B) specifies the provisions which apply when reinstatement is allowed under section 20A (as discussed in § 20A.03 *supra*) of an application which has been terminated as the result of refusal of the application or where an application has been refused or withdrawn (subs. (7)), the word "termination" (as used in the Rules) being defined by an addition to rule 2 (definitions), for which see § 123.02 *supra*). These provisions (which are often called "third party rights" generally follow those which apply when a lapsed patent is restored under section 28 and, therefore, are generally analogous to the provisions set out in section 28A, for which see §§ 28A.02–28A.06 of the Main Work. There are also analogies with the third party rights which arise under new section 117A when an application is resuscitated for having been withdrawn in error or by mistake (see § 117A.02 *infra*) and also those which arise under section 64 in a situation of prior secret use, for which see §§ 64.02–64.07 in the Main Work and *infra*.

Under section 20B, anything done during the period between termination and reinstatement (conveniently termed the "interim period") is treated as valid (subs. (2)); and, where the application had been published under section 16 before the termination occurred, acts which would have constituted an infringement of the rights arising from the existence of the application (under s. 69) are to be treated as an infringement of those rights, but only if these acts were done at a time when it was possible for the period specified in section 20(A)(1) to be extended or the act was a "continuation" or "repetition" of an earlier act infringing those rights (subs. (3)).

However, where the application was published under section 16 before its termination and after the termination and before publication of the request for reinstatement, then third party rights will exist to allow a person who had during such period "begun in good faith" to do what would otherwise have been an infringing act or had made "in good faith effective and serious preparations to do"such an act, that person will have the right to continue to do the act notwithstanding the subsequent reinstatement of the application and the grant of a patent thereon, but without a right to grant a licence to another to do the same act (subs. (4). Where such a third party right has been acquired as part of a business, the rights can be exercised by others in the same business and it can be assigned (or transmitted on death or dissolution of a company) to a person acquiring the relevant part of that business (subs. (5)). Where a product is disposed of in exercise of a right acquired under either of subsections (4) or (5), any person receiving that product may deal with it in the same way as if it had been disposed by the applicant (subs. (6)).

SECTION 21—Observations by third party on patentability

PRACTICE UNDER SECTION 21   **21.06**

Central Research Laboratories' Application (BL O/419/00) is an example of a confidentiality order being made on observations (sent by email) containing commercially sensitive information.

Security and safety [National Security] [Sections 22 and 23]

SECTION 22—Information prejudicial to national security [*defence of realm*] or safety of public

22.01

All with effect from January 1, 2005 (S.I. 2004 No. 3205, a. 2(f)(k)), the Patents Act 2004 (c. 16, Sched. 2(8)) amended the introductory heading and the section title, each as shown *supra*, and amended subsections (1) and (5)(a), (c) and (d) by replacing, in each instance, the words "the defence of the realm" by "national security".

Also, subsection (6)(a) was amended as follows:

(6) The Secretary of State may do the following for the purpose of enabling him to decide the question referred to in subsection (5)(c) above;

    (a) where the application contains information relating to the production or use of atomic energy or research into matters connected with such production or use, he may at any time do one or both of the following, that is to say,

        (i) inspect [*and authorise the United Kingdom Atomic Energy Authority to inspect*] the application and any documents sent to the comptroller in connection with it;

(ii) **authorise a government body with responsibility for the production of atomic energy or for research into matters connected with its production or use, or any person appointed by such a government body, to inspect the application and any documents sent to the comptroller in connection with it;** and

(b) in any other case, he may at any time after (or, with the applicantís consent, before) the end of the period prescribed for the purposes of section 16 above inspect the application and any such documents;

and where a **government body or a person appointed by a government body carries out an inspection which the body or person is authorised to carry out under paragraph (a) above, the body or (as the case may be) the person shall report on the inspection to the Secretary of State as soon as practicable** [*that authority are authorised under paragraph (a) above they shall as soon as practicable report on their inspection to the Secretary of State*].

Note. The amendment noted for subsection (9)(b) is now a consequence of S.I. 2003 No. 1249.

COMMENTARY ON SECTION 22

22.02 | *Scope of the section*

The amendments made to section 22 do not change its scope as such, but its terminology is updated by changing the references to "defence of the realm" to "national security". The new wording also addresses an anomaly caused by removal of duties from the UKAEA, see § 22.05 *infra*. While it could be argued that the phrase "prejudicial to the defence of the realm" to "prejudicial to national security" represents a broadening of the scope of the section, it is understood that this is not intended. Certainly, the phrase "national security" is vague and can be given such meaning as one wants. However, it is understood that the Comptroller's view as to the meaning of the words is likely to be guided by the rules which regulate the export of goods and information as to be found in the Export of Goods, Transfer of Technology and Provision of Technical Assistance (Control) Order 2003 (S.I. 2003 No. 2764), particularly the goods falling within the definitions of Schedules 1 and 2 thereof, and that there is likely to be little or no change in the practice under the section. Guidance as to whether particular subject matter is likely to be found to fall within the terms of section 22(1) can be obtained by enquiry to the Security Section of the Patent Office, see also § 22.14 *infra*.

22.05 | *Notice of directions to Secretary of State (subss. (5) and (6))*

The amendments made to subsection (6) replace the references to inspection of an application by the UKAEA with references to inspection by a government body (or a person appointed by such) with responsibility for the production of atomic energy or for research into matters connected with its production or use; this responsibility is no longer that of the UKAEA.

PRACTICE UNDER SECTION 22

Effect of other statutes

22.13 | *—Official Secrets Act*

The Official Secrets Act 1989 c. 6 has updated the 1911 and 1920 Acts.

—Export of Goods (Control) Order **22.14**

The Export of Goods Control Act 2002 (c. 28) has replaced the provisions of the Import, Export and Customs Powers (Defence) Act 1939 (c. 69). The implementing rules are now to be found in the Export of Goods, Transfer of Technology and Provision of Technical Assistance (Control) Order 2003 (S.I. 2003 No. 2764), see particularly the list of goods set out in Schedules 1 and 2 thereto. Enquiries as to the extent of the export restrictions of such goods can be made to the Department of Trade and Industry (tel. 020 7215 8070 fax. 020 7215 0558).

SECTION 23—Restrictions on applications abroad by United Kingdom residents

23.01

Subsection 23(1) was amended and new subsections (1A) and (3A) inserted by the Patents Act 2004 (c. 16, s. 7), each with effect from January 1, 2005 (S.I. 2004 No. 3205, a. 2(c)) as follows:

In subsection (1), after the word "invention" (in line 4 of the reprint on page 302 of the Main Work), the words "if subsection (1A) below applies to that application", were added.

(1A) This subsection applies to an application if—
  (a) the application contains information which relates to military technology or for any other reason publication of the information might be prejudicial to national security; or
  (b) the application contains information the publication of which might be prejudicial to the safety of the public.
(3A) A person is liable under subsection (3) above only if—
  (a) he knows that filing the application, or causing it to be filed, would contravene this section; or
  (b) he is reckless as to whether filing the application, or causing it to be filed, would contravene this section.

Note. As these amendments were made without any transitional provision, it would appear that they only have effect in relation to applications filed on or after the above mentioned commencement date.

The amendment noted for subsection (3)(b) (wrongly recorded as for subsection (4)(b)) is now a consequence of S.I. 2003 No. 1249.

COMMENTARY ON SECTION 23

Scope and general purpose of the section **23.02**

The O.J. now carries a notice that a request under section 23 for permission to make an application abroad should be made even if for example such an application is required by contract with a foreign firm.

New subsections (1A) and (3A), greatly ease the burden imposed by the original section 23, although with some uncertainty for an applicant and his agents. First (by new subsection (1A)) the prohibition imposed by subsection (1) against filing a patent application outside the United Kingdom, either initially or without first waiting six weeks from the date of filing in the United Kingdom to see if a secrecy order is imposed, without first seeking permission from the Patent Office, now only applies if the application "contains information which relates to military technology" **or**, if publication of such information "might be prejudicial to national security", **or** if the application contains information contains information the publication of which "might be prejudicial to the safety of the public". Secondly, breach of this provision makes a person criminally liable only if "he knows that filing the application, or causing it to be filed, would contravene the section" **or** if that person is "reckless" as to whether such an action would do so.

Thus, (while subsection (2) does not absolve a person from liability, for which see § 23.05 in the Main Work), section 23 (as so amended) is only likely to lead to a criminal penalty if an applicant (or his agent), either of whom is "resident" in the United Kingdom, files an application abroad either initially or without waiting until the six week period has expired without seeking consent from the Patent Office for foreign filing of an application **when he knows, or ought to have known**, that the application contains information relating to military technology which "might" be prejudicial to national security or the safety of the public. Thus, an honestly held and considered view that filing abroad would not contravene subsection (1), as modified by subsections (1A) and (2), absolves a person from criminal penalty even if that view turns out to have been erroneous. However, obviously, there can be no absolution in the case of an application arising from research and development work carried out under a defence contract, or one obviously relating to technology of military significance. This is especially so where (as often will be the case) the contract contains a provision requiring any patent application to be made under a secure filing procedure on the assumption that a secrecy order under section 22 will be made upon filing.

The references to "military technology" and to "information which **might** be prejudicial to national security or the safety of the public" are potentially far reaching in their effect, if only because of the vagueness of these terms and their subjective nature. This is particularly so in the case of public safety. However, it is understood that the term "public safety" is not intended to cover inventions which merely could be dangerous if misused and, while no specific examples are appropriate, it is understood that the term is likely only to be applied to an invention, or information presented in a patent application, which the general public would understand as constituting a threat to their safety and security. Where an applicant or agent is in any doubt as to whether permission under section 23 is needed, he is advised not to file abroad without first seeking advice from the security section of the Patent Office.

24.01

SECTION 24—Publication and certificate of grant

The Patents Act 2004 (c. 16, Sched. 2(9)) prospectively amended subsection 24(4) by inserting new subsection (4) reading:

(4) Subsection (3) above shall not require the comptroller to identify as inventor a person who has waived his right to be mentioned as inventor in any patent granted for the invention.

Note. This amendment remains to be brought into effect.

[FORM OF CERTIFICATE OF GRANT OF PATENT]

The current form of the Certificate of Grant is reproduced below:

The Patent Office

Certificate of Grant of Patent

Patent Number: *(Patent Number appears here)*

Proprietor(s): *(Proprietor(s) name(s) appears here)*

Inventor(s): *(Inventor(s) name(s) appears here)*

This is to Certify that, in accordance with the Patents Act 1977,

a Patent has been granted to the proprietor(s) for an invention entitled " *(Title of invention appears here)* " disclosed in an application filed *(Filing date appears here)*

Dated *(Date of Certificate appears here)*

(Comptroller General's signature and name appear here)

Comptroller General of Patents, Designs and Trade Marks
UNITED KINGDOM PATENT OFFICE

The attention of the proprietor(s) is drawn to the important notes overleaf.

IMPORTANT NOTES FOR PROPRIETORS OF UNITED KINGDOM PATENTS

1. DURATION OF PATENT AND PAYMENT OF RENEWAL FEES

(i)   Your patent took full effect on the date of the certificate, as shown overleaf.

(ii)   By paying annual renewal fees, you can keep your patent in force for 20 years from the date of filing of the patent application, which is also shown overleaf.

(iii)   The annual renewal fee is due on the fourth and each subsequent anniversary of the date of filing of the patent application. The fee can be paid up to three months before each such anniversary of the filing date. Each renewal fee payment should be accompanied by Patents Form 12/77. If the Form with the fee is not lodged in the Patent Office by the anniversary of the filing date, the fee can still be paid at any time during the following six months. However, you may have to pay a late payment fee. The patent will cease if the renewal fee (and any late payment fee) is not paid before the end of the six month period. When renewing the patent it is advisable to check the current fee rates.

(iv)   **It is important that you should set up and maintain effective renewal arrangements to ensure that renewal fees are paid on time.** You should not wait for any reminder from the Patent Office before paying the fee. The Patent Office will send a reminder to the last recorded address for service within six weeks after the anniversary of the date of filing, but this reminder is only intended to alert you to the possible failure of your renewal arrangements.

2. PROCEDURE FOR PAYMENT OF RENEWAL FEES

Patents Form 12/77, together with the fee(s) and fee sheet (FS2) should be addressed to "The Cashier, The Patent Office, Concept House, Cardiff Road, Newport, South Wales NP10 8QQ" and may be posted or delivered by hand to this address. Alternatively, they may be **delivered by hand** to The Patent Office at Harmsworth House, 13–15 Bouverie Street, London, EC4.

Blank Patents Forms 12/77 and fee sheets (FS2) can be requested by post from The Central Enquiry Unit, The Patent Office, Concept House, Cardiff Road, Newport, South Wales NP10 8QQ, by telephone on 08459-500505 (Minicom 08459-222250), by fax on 01633-813600 or by e-mail (enquiries@patent.gov.uk). The Forms and fee sheets can also be downloaded from the Patent Office website (www.patent.gov.uk).

3. REGISTRATION OF OWNERSHIP AS EVIDENCE OF ENTITLEMENT

Any person who becomes legally entitled to a patent or to a share or interest in a patent should apply to the Patent Office to register their entitlement, share or interest.

(*Address For Service appears here*)

For further information or assistance you can contact the Central Enquiry Unit of the Patent Office as indicated above.

COMMENTARY ON SECTION 24

24.06 | *Date of grant*

To prevent publication of a granted patent, notice of withdrawal must be received before issue of the letter notifying the date of grant. See § 16.06 *supra* as to the manner in which withdrawal should now be effected.

Publication of patent specification(subss. (4))　　　　　　　　　**24.08**

New subsection (4), when given effect, will remove the requirement of the Comptroller to identify an inventor, provided that he has waived his right to be mentioned as such in the granted patent. This is for reason given in § 16.03 *supra*. The way in which that waiver can be made will need to be specified in a future rule.

SECTION 25—Term of patent　　　　　　　　　**25.01**

The Patents Act 2004 (c. 16, s. 8) has prospectively replaced subsection 25(3), and amended subsection (4), as follows:

The new wording of subsection (3) is:

(3) Where any renewal fee in respect of a patent is not paid by the end of the period prescribed for payment (the "prescribed period") the patent shall cease to have effect at the end of such day, in the final month of that period, as may be prescribed.

In subsection (4), the words "the period of six months immediately following the end of the prescribed period" are replaced by "the period ending with the sixth month after the month in which the prescribed period ends".

COMMENTARY ON SECTION 25

Renewal fees (subs. (3))　　　　　　　　　**25.07**

The revised form of subsection (3) (set out in § 25.01 *supra*) will, when brought into force, provide a prescribed degree of flexibility as to the final date when a renewal fee is payable (without formal extension) but, where such fee is not paid by this date, rules may provide for the patent to cease to have effect from an earlier date. It is expected that, in conformity to the position in many other European countries, the prescribed period for paying a renewal fee (without formal extension) will be the last day of the calendar month in which the anniversary of the filing, or deemed filing, date falls, but that (under the Act) when such fee is not paid, then the patent will cease to have effect on that anniversary date. These dates will need to be prescribed by the Patents Rules.

Late payment of renewal fees (subs. (4))　　　　　　　　　**25.08**

The change to subsection (4) (noted in § 25.01 *supra*) is consequential to the amendment of subsection (3) (for which see § 25.07 *supra*) and provides that the period of six months' grace for the late payment of a renewal fee (with extension fee) ends at the end of the sixth month after the extended date prescribed for the payment of the renewal fee as prescribed under subsection (3). Corresponding changes are prospectively made to sections 28(3), 46(3) and (3A).

SECTION 27—General power to amend specification after grant　　**27.01**

New subsection 27(6) was prospectively added by the Patents Act 2004 (c. 16, s. 2). It will be brought into effect when the EPC revisions agreed in 2000 come into force. It reads:

(6) In considering whether or not to allow an application under this section, the comptroller shall have regard to any relevant principles applicable under the European Patent Convention.

RELEVANT RULE—RULE 40

27.02 Rule 40—Amendment of specification after grant

With effect from April 1, 2003, Rule 40 was amended by the Patents (Electronic Communications) (Amendment) Rules 2003 (S.I. 2003 No. 513) to replace paragraph (1) and add new paragraphs (1A) and (1B) reading:

(1) An application to the comptroller for leave to amend the specification of a patent shall—

    (a) be made on Patents Form 11/77, and

    (b) clearly identify the proposed amendment and state the reasons for it.

(1A) If it is reasonably possible, the proposed amendment and the reasons for it shall also be set out and delivered to the comptroller in electronic form or using electronic communications.

(1B) The comptroller shall advertise in the Journal notice that an application has been made to amend the specification of a patent, and the advertisement shall state that any person may apply to the comptroller for a copy of the proposed amendment and the reasons given for it.

Paragraph (6) was amended by S.I. 2004 No. 2358 (Sched. 2(5)), with effect from January 1, 2005, by deleting (i) from sub-paragraph (a) the words "verified to the satisfaction of the comptroller as corresponding to the original text" where these words first appear; and (ii) the final words "verified to his satisfaction as corresponding to the original text".

COMMENTARY ON SECTION 27

27.03 *Scope of the section*

The term "amendment", as used throughout the Act will (from the coming into force of new subsection 130(5A), for which see § 130.01 *infra*) include any amendment made in the EPO (under new EPCa. 105A) by way of limitation of the claims of a granted European patent, see § 130.07 *infra*.

27.05 *Discretion*

Amendment was allowed in *Baker Hughes' Patents* (BL O/332/02) as a matter of discretion under s. 27 but not as a correction under s. 117 see §§ 27.06, 27.07, 27.08, 76.08 and 117.06 *infra*.

The first instance decision in *Sara Lee v. Johnson Wax*, cited in the Main Work, was reported at [2001] FSR 261.

Although there does not appear to be a definitive decision from the EPO on the point, it has not been the practice of the EPO to permit issues of discretion to be raised in proceedings before it. Rather, amendment (within the terms of EPCa. 123) is considered to be available as of right. When brought into force, the new form of EPCa. 123 (created by EPC(2000)), permits amendment of a European patent application or European patent (UK) patent at any time after its grant (although only by way of limitation of its claims). A request for such amendment may be made by application to the EPO (under EPCa. 105A) at any time after grant, but subject to the continuing provisions of EPCa. 123(2) and (3) which prohibit any addition of subject matter or the broadening of the extent of protection provided by the patent. Such a procedure is to arise outside of invalidity opposition and, is to be strictly *ex parte* so that third party opposition thereto will not be possible. Consequently, there will be no opportunity in EPO limitation proceedings under

EPCa. 105A for issues of *mala fides* to be considered, whereas under existing UK law discretion to permit amendment can be refused in such circumstances, as discussed in the Main Work.

With the aim of bringing the national law on patent amendment into conformity with the provision of the EPC and its Implementing Regulations, and for consistency of approach to the allowability of post grant amendments, new subsections 27(6) and 75(5) have been inserted. These require a tribunal or court, when considering a request for amendment, to "have regard to any relevant principles applicable under the EPC". Unless the attitude of the EPO should change, this provision is likely to have the effect of removing consideration of discretion when considering an issue of amendment.

However, an issue of discretion can still arise as a possible sanction against the assessment of damages for infringement of the amended patent, as amended, see the amendments to sections 58(6) and (8), 62(3) and 63(2). These provide for the curtailment of monetary relief for infringement (or Crown user) unless "the relief is sought in good faith". This provision ought to be effective when a patentee has delayed seeking amendment while issuing or threatening proceedings under a form of the patent which the patentee ought to have known to be partially invalid, as discussed in §§ 58.05, 62.05 and 63.03 *infra*.

—Duty of full disclosure   27.06

The principles set out in *Smith Kline & French v. Evans Medical* (cited in the Main Work) were rigidly applied by the Comptroller in *Kaiser's Patent* (BL O/279/00) where it was held that a failure to inform the Comptroller that a warning letter had in the past been issued to a third party required refusal of a validating amendment, even though it was held that, when that letter was sent, the proprietor had no reason to believe the patent to be invalid, the prior art necessitating amendment only having come to his attention at a later date, it being insufficient that the opponents to the amendment had been aware of that letter.

Oxford Gene Technologies v. Affymetrix (No. 2) ([2001] RPC 310) made it clear that a patentee need disclose documents on the issue of discretion only to the extent that an opponent has made out a case that these should be produced; and, even then, such disclosure can be made with restricted access to the documents and without any waiver of privilege in the documents.

On balance it was found there had been sufficient disclosure in *Baker Hughes' Patents* (BL O/332/02) see § 76.08. In considering the matter on appeal (BL C/49/02, *noted* IPD 26003), the court observed that the law had "moved on" since *Hsiung's Patent* (cited in the Main Work) and there was now no obligation on the patentee to make full disclosure when seeking amendment, particularly not as regards privileged documents. The patentee had made a *prima facie* case for discretion to be exercised and the onus had therefore shifted to the opponent who had not made out a convincing case against the amendments.

—Undue delay   27.07

There is no undue delay where a proprietor seeks (after receiving professional advice) unsuccessfully to contest an allegation of invalidity due to prior art and, only thereafter, seeks to make an invalidating amendment, nor if a warning letter is sent to a third party before he was made aware of that invalidating prior art (*Kaiser's Patent* BL O/279/00), but here amendment was not allowed because the Comptroller held that there had been a failure to make a full disclosure, see § 27.06.

In *Instance v. CCL* ([2002] FSR 430; [2002] IP&T 721) permission to amend was refused where the patentee had been aware since August 1999 of the anticipation (by one of its own earlier patents) of one of the claims but an application to amend was not made until December 2000, the patent in the meantime having been deployed in litigation without informing the defendants of the need for amendment. Further, amendment had been sought earlier in Germany. See the case comment by P. Cliffe at [2002] EIPR 277.

No undue delay was found in *Baker Hughes' Patents* (BL O/332/02) see § 76.08, nor in *Calix Technology's Patent* (BL O/62/03), in which the agents for the applicant had been of the opinion that no amendment was required until advised otherwise by their QC. It was held that the applicant had acted throughout on the advice of their agents and there was no evidence of bad faith on their part.

27.08   *—Lack of good faith and covetous claiming*

Kimberly-Clark v. Procter & Gamble (No. 2) (BL C/25/00, *noted* IPD 23087) has been reported in [2001] FSR 339; and the *Nutrinova* decision, cited in the Main Work, has been published as *Nutrinova v. Scanchem (No. 2)* ([2001] FSR 831). No "bad faith" was found in *Baker Hughes' Patents* (BL O/332/02) —see § 76.08.

27.10   *Inapplicability of section 27 (subs. (2))*

In *Luk Lamellan's Patent* (BL O/379/02) it was made clear that where amendments had been advertised under section 27 and an application for revocation under section 72 was subsequently filed, the amendment application under section 27 would still be stayed since the amendments had not at that point been "allowed". See also § 72.30.

PRACTICE UNDER SECTION 27

27.15   *Procedure for amending a patent*

Under revised rule 40 (for which see § 27.02 *supra*), made under new section 124A (reprinted in § 124A.01 *infra*), an applicant seeking amendment is required to deliver the amendment (and where possible the reasons for making the amendment) to the Comptroller electronically. While PF 11/77 must be filed in the normal way, because of the need to pay the fee therefor, the amendment details should be sent either: (a) using e-mail addressed to litigationamend@patent.gov.uk and presented as a "plain text" message [MS-TNEF/RTF and HTML formats, and encrypted or digitally signed documents are not acceptable], optionally with the details presented in an attachment; or (b) on a data carrier (*e.g.* on a disk or CD-ROM) delivered to the Patent Office accompanied by a letter. The attached text, or that so recorded, may be presented in any of theMicrosoft Word, WordPerfect or PDF formats. A notice on the Patent Office website states that applicants are encouraged to use conventional word processing features such as markup, coloured text and strikeout/strikethrough to set out the amendments on the original version of the text in a way that makes it easy for the reader to appreciate the changes.

The fact that amendment is being sought will be advertised in the O.J. but details of the amendments are no longer being published therein. Instead, copies of the amendments and of the reasons therefor are available for supply by the Patent Office upon request. If possible, these documents are transmitted electronically to those making such a request.

27.16   *Amendment of European patent (UK)*

The amendment to rule 40 (noted in § 27.02 *supra*) removes the previous obligation for any required translation to be "verified to the satisfaction of the comptroller", but (under new rule 113A, reprinted in § 123.11A *infra*) the Comptroller can take action where he has reasonable doubts about the accuracy of any translation filed at the Patent Office by any person in accordance with the Act or rules, for which see § 123.43 *infra*.

Procedure on opposition **27.19**

In *Intel's Patent* (BL O/87/03) the opponent was unsuccessful in opposing the amendment, which was therefore allowed. Nevertheless the opponent argued that it should have its costs because the applicant for an amendment had been seeking an indulgence in applying to amend its patent. The Comptroller rejected this position as suggesting that anyone might raise spurious objections to amendment with impunity. The opponent was ordered to pay costs on the normal scale.

SECTION 28—Restoration of lapsed patents | **28.01**

The RRO (a. 9) replaced subsection 28(3), but this wording was, prospectively, amended by the Patents Act 2004 (c. 16, s. 8). This further change is shown by bold type (for the further new wording) and italic type (for the wording which has been deleted (either as noted in the Main Work or by this provision in the Patents Act 2004).

(3) If the comptroller is satisfied that [*—(a) the proprietor of the patent took reasonable care to see that any renewal fee was paid within the prescribed period or that that fee and any prescribed additional fee were paid within the six months immediately following the end of that period, and (b) those fees were not so paid because of circumstances beyond his control*], **the failure of the proprietor of the patent —**
  (a) to pay the renewal fee within the prescribed period; or
  (b) to pay that fee and any prescribed additional fee within the period ending with the sixth month after the month in which the prescribed period ended [*within the period of six months immediately following the end of that period*],
was unintentional, the comptroller shall by order restore the patent on payment of any unpaid renewal fee and any prescribed additional fee.

Note. The original replacement of subsection (3) took effect on January 1, 2005, the Commencement Date of S.I. 2004 No. 2358 (but without effect on any patent which before that date had ceased to have effect, RRO, a. 23). At the time of writing, the further amendment of subsection (3) is prospective.

COMMENTARY ON SECTION 28

Application for restoration **28.05**

The words in subsection (2) "any other person who would have been entitled to the patent if it had not ceased to have effect" apply to the position as at the date of that cessation and such a person must be able to prove entitlement in a legal sense, an allegation that there is an entitlement to an assignment being insufficient (*Classlife's Patent*, BL O/278/00).

Reasonable care (subs. (3)) **28.06**

The main change made to subsection (3) by the RRO, and already effective for patents which lapsed after January 1, 2005 (see § 28.01 *supra*) replaced the requirement for the proprietor (in order to obtain an order for restoration) to have shown that he took "reasonable case" to pay the renewal fee within the prescribed time has been replaced by a requirement that the proprietor show that his failure to pay that fee was "unintentional". This is a far less stringent test, but it involves a negative proposition which can never be proved with logical certainty. Thus, circumstantial evidence will usually need to be produced to show that, on the balance of probabilities, the proprietor did have an intention to make a timely payment of the due renewal fee. However, where (under the former test of "reasonable care") restoration of a patent has been allowed, the circumstances were probably such that they also showed that the failure was "unintentional". However, the converse is not true so that refusals to allow restoration in circumstances arising in former decisions are probably of little value in applying the revised wording. Accordingly, the continuing validity of the decisions cited in §§ 28.06–28.13 (in the Main Work and herein) must be problematical. Certainly, what will be fatal to obtaining restoration under the new provision will be evidence indicating a positive lack of any initial intention to pay or of a change of mind, *e.g.* evidence of any intention to allow the patent to lapse.

The further amendment prospectively made to paragraph (b) is one consequential to the variation in the period for paying the renewal fee (with further fee for late payment) following the change of the prescribed normal period for paying a due renewal fee without additional fee, for which see § 25.08 *supra*.

Whereas it might be reasonable for a patentee to rely on his patent agent to send him reminders, it remains his responsibility to interpret them correctly and act on them (*Harris's Patent*, BL O/100/01). In *Harris*, the patent agents wrote requiring payment of outstanding fees before attending to renewal. Their letter was clear. The patentee could have paid the fees to the Patent Office himself if he had wanted so the stipulation in the agents' letter about outstanding fees had no bearing on the matter.

In *Richard Pearson's Patent* (BL C/78/01) computer errors had defeated the patentee's own system of reminders and his renewals agency had taken ten days to furnish a list of patents requiring renewal, after the errors had been noted. In the meantime the patent in issue lapsed. The Comptroller accepted that more could have been done, but held that prompt and reasonable action had been taken in unfortunate circumstances so that restoration should be permitted.

Hardman's Patent (BL O/423/02) provides an example where reasonable care on the part of an individual proprietor was lacking and therefore restoration was refused.

In *Omnicell's Patents* (BL O/329/02) the lapsed patents had been transferred to a new owner but had not been added to its renewal reminder system. It was held that the obligation to "take reasonable care that the renewal fee is paid" is not satisfied if care is not taken to add newly acquired patents to an existing renewal system.

Restoration was refused in *Comet Technology's Patent* (BL O/337/03), where the proprietor had received a notice to pay an additional fee (because the renewal fee had been paid late), but had ignored this because he thought he had sent the additional payment. It was held that he had not taken the "necessary care" to see that the required fees had been paid.

28.07   *—Employee error*

In *Sumitomo Rubber's Patent* (BL O/351/03), an error in information about the patent made by an employee of 13 years standing, who was regarded as reliable and well-trained, had contributed to a decision to allow the patent to lapse, which was later seen to be a mistake. Restoration was allowed as the error was seen to be an isolated and unpredictable event. [*Note*: the proposed Patents Act 2004 prescribes that the failure to pay the fee should be "unintentional". It is not clear that the circumstances of this case would fulfil that requirement as the decision not to pay the fee was deliberate, albeit based on information which was later found to be incorrect.]

28.08   *—Patent agent error*

Harris's Patent (BL O/100/01) is to be contrasted with *Lister's Patent*, cited in the Main Work. In *Harris*, the agents' letter was clear and there was no error. The patentee had the responsibility for renewal and had not acted reasonably.

—Change of Address   **28.09**

Where there has been a change of agents, reasonable care is not taken when the proprietor ignores an invitation to make a change of address for service, thereby causing the official reminder letters not to be received (*Matelect's Patent*, BL O/458/00).

Hidalgo's Patent (BL O/243/02) provides an example where non-receipt of a change of address sent by e-mail contributed to the renewal date being missed. Even though no check was made whether or not the e-mail had been received, reasonable care was found to have been exercised in the circumstances of the particular case so the patent was restored.

[*Editor's note*: it would be unwise to rely on this case as indicating that non-receipt of e-mails could always be used as an excuse in such cases. It is preferable to obtain at least an automated "read receipt" or delivery receipt for e-mails or, better still, a positive acknowledgement from the recipient, since the sending of an e-mail provides no proof of receipt.]

—Illness   **28.10**

In *Hoerrman's Patent*, BL O/7/02 the patentee, despite a request from the Patent Office, did not provide independent evidence of his illness, and other matters remained unexplained, such that the Hearing Officer was not satisfied that reasonable care had been exercised.

—Financial problems and late payments   **28.12**

"Exceptional and extenuating" circumstances were found in *Collins' Patent* (BL O/322/01) in which the patentee had died and his executor had omitted payment of a renewal fee despite having obtained probate and dealing with other formalities including recording himself as the new proprietor. It was held that reasonable efforts had been taken and the patent should be restored. But reasonable care was not found to have been exercised in *Interroof Products' Patent* (BL O/23/02) in which the patentee's "preoccupation with his other business and personal activities" was held not to absolve him from the need to take reasonable care to see that renewal fees were paid.

PRACTICE UNDER SECTION 28   **28.15**

The automatic extension of the time period specified by rule 41(4) for the filing of PF 12/77 and 53/77 which is available under revised rule 110(3) is now two months, with a further extension available with discretion under rule 110(4), as discussed in §§ 123.33 and 123.34 *infra*, although there any discretionary extension under rule 110(4) is not limited by Rules, Schedule 4A, Part 4, see § 123.09D *infra*.

SECTION 29—Surrender of patents

COMMENTARY ON SECTION 29

Acceptance of offer to surrender (subs. (3))   **29.06**

In *Dyson's Patent* ([2003] RPC 473) an action for revocation of the relevant UK patent was proceeding before the court. The patentee had applied to the court to stay the revocation proceedings until the patent was revoked by the Comptroller under section 73(2), there being a corresponding European application still undergoing prosecution. However, the court had declined to order the stay. The patentee then offered to surrender the UK patent. The Patent Office initially declined to accept the offer of surrender on the basis that it was not one appropriate to accept without the view of the court as to how this would affect the revocation proceedings. Upon the matter being further argued ([2003] RPC 878), the offer of surrender was accepted, the patentee's reasons being accepted as "satisfactory", no-one, including the applicants for revocation, having opposed the surrender, and the court having expressed no view in the matter, although having been made aware of the surrender application. The Hearing Officer commented that the surrender would not adversely affect the continuance of the revocation action (should the applicant for revocation wish to proceed with it), but it was not the practice of the Patent Office to initiate proceedings under section 73(2) if, at the relevant date, the UK patent is no longer in force or if an offer to surrender it has been made (reference being made to paragraph 73.09 of the *Manual*). The Office would therefore take no further action under section 73(2).

PRACTICE UNDER SECTION 29

29.07 *Making an offer of surrender*

In view of the amendment made to rule 43(1) (noted in the Main Work) the wording of this paragraph should be amended to reflect the fact that an offer to surrender may be made in writing and does not have to be on PF 2/77, although it may still conveniently be made using that form. A statement of reasons is no longer required.

30.01 **SECTION 30—Nature of, and transactions in, patents and applications for patents**

The RRO (a. 10) amended subsection (6) and introduced new subsection (6A), as follows:

In subsection (6): (i) the words "the parties to the transaction" (reprinted in lines 5–6 in the Main Work) were replaced by "the assignor or mortgagor"; and (ii) the words "or in the case of a body corporate" to the end of the subsection were deleted.

New subsection (6A) reads:

(6A) If a transaction mentioned in subsection (6) above is by a body corporate, references in that subsection to such a transaction being signed by or on behalf of the assignor or mortgagor shall be taken to include references to its being under the seal of the body corporate.

Note. These amendments took effect on January 1, 2005, the Commencement Date of the RRO.

COMMENTARY ON SECTION 30

30.06 *Execution of documents (subs. (6))*

The amendment made to subsection 6, and the introduction of new subsection (6A), removes the former requirement for dual signature of an assignment or mortgage of a patent or application therefore by both the assignor/mortgagor and assignee/mortgagee. It is now sufficient for such a document to be executed solely by the assignor or mortgagor (subs. 6)).

Moreover, where such a person is a body corporate, then application of the seal of that body to an assignment or mortgage of a patent or application satisfies the requirement for "signature by or on behalf of" that body corporate (subs. (6A)).

PRACTICE UNDER SECTION 30

Stamp Duty   **30.10**

The Finance Act 2002 (c.23), section 116, abolished stamp duty on the "sale, transfer or other disposition of goodwill" as regards instruments executed after April 23, 2002, so there is now no need for an apportionment of value as suggested in the Main Work in assignments executed after that date.

For a summary of the position since the abolition of Stamp Duty in relation to the transfer of Intellectual Property Rights, see the article on that subject by R. Williams ([2002] *CIPA* 16).

Income and corporation tax   **30.12**

A new regime of taxation of intangibles, including intellectual property rights, in the United Kingdom came into force on April 1, 2002, providing for certain important new tax reliefs for companies.

SECTION 31—Nature of, and transactions in, patents and applications for patents in Scotland

COMMENTARY ON SECTION 31

Grant of security under Scots law   **31.05**

The decision in *Buchanan v. Alba Diagnostics [Scotland]*, cited in the Main Work, was upheld on appeal ([2001] RPC 851). The appeal decision contains a useful synopsis of precedent decisions on the meaning of "improvement inventions" although each case must be decided on its own particular facts. The decision was upheld on further appeal to the House of Lords ([2004] RPC 681), the House finding that the right to improvements had been an important element of the security provided, and an agreement to assign improvements was not *per se* contrary to public policy as an unreasonable restraint of trade.

SECTION 32—Register of patents, etc.   **32.01**

Subsection 32(2) was prospectively amended by Patents Act 2004 (c. 16, s. 13(3)) by adding (after paragraph (b)) a new paragraph (ba) reading:

(ba) the entering on the register of notices concerning opinions issued, or to be issued, under section 74A below.

Subsection 12 was repealed by the Youth Justice and Criminal Evidence Act 1999 (c. 21, Sched. 6) and, as a consequence, in subsection (9) the words "Subject to subsection 12 below" and in subsection (11) the words, "subject to subsection (12) below", were each subsequently deleted by the Criminal Justice Act 2003 (c. 44, Sched. 37(6)).

RELEVANT RULES—RULES 30, 44–47, 50–53, 79 AND
PATENTS (COMPANIES RE-REGISTRATION RULES) 1982

Rule 30—Address for service   **32.02**

In the reprinting of rule 30(2) in the Main Work, the opening words should be "(2) Upon grant of an application …".

Rule 45—Alteration of name or address   **32.04**

By S.I. 2004 No. 2358, with effect from January 1, 2005, paragraph (2) was replaced by:

(2) Where the comptroller has doubts about whether he should make the alteration to a name—

    (a) he shall inform the person making the request of the reason for his doubts; and

    (b) he may require that person to furnish proof in support of the request.

32.05 **Rule 46—Registration under section 33**

Paragraphs (2) and (3) were amended by S.I. 2004 No. 2358, with effect from January 1, 2005. In the reprinting of these paragraphs in the Main Work some errors occurred. The reproduction below of these paragraphs show the changes in wording which have been made to the original form thereof, as subsequently amended as indicated in the Main Work.

(2) An application under paragraph (1) above shall—

    (a) where it relates to an assignment or assignation referred to in section 33(3)(a) or (c), be signed by or on behalf of the parties thereto or the assignor only;

    (b) where it relates to a mortgage or the granting of a licence or sub-licence or security referred to in section 33(b) or (c), be signed by or on behalf of the mortgagor or the grantor of the licence or security, as the case may be; or

be accompanied by [*such documentary evidence as suffices to establish*] **documentation establishing** the transaction, instrument or event.

(3) The comptroller may direct that such [*evidence*] **documentation** as he may require in connection with the application shall be sent to him within such period as he may specify.

32.06 **Rule 47—Request for correction of error**

Paragraph (2) has been replaced and new paragraph (3) added by S.I. 2004 No. 2358, with effect from January 1, 2005, to read:

(2) Where the comptroller has doubts about whether there is an error—

    (a) he shall inform the person making the request of the reason for his doubts; and

    (b) he may require that person to furnish a written explanation of the nature of the error or evidence in support of the request.

(3) Where the comptroller is satisfied that an error has been made he shall make such correction as he may agree with the proprietor of the patent (or, as the case may be, the applicant).

COMMENTARY ON SECTION 32

32.15 *Address for service (r. 30)*

CPR 49EPD 1.3 and CPR 49EPD 3.2 have been respectively replaced by CPR 63.1(2)(e) and CPR 63.16 (reprinted in §§ E63.1 and E63.16 *infra*).

32.18 *Transactions, instruments and events (rr. 45 and 46)*

Rules 45 and 46 have been amended (for which see §§ 32.04 and 32.05 *supra*) to limit the obligation on applicants to provide evidence to those situations where the Comptroller has doubts about the relevant issue.

Correction of errors **32.20**

Rule 47 has been amended (for which see § 32.06 *supra*) to limit the obligation on applicants to provide evidence to those situations where the Comptroller has doubts about the relevant issue.

Register entries as prima facie evidence (subss. (9)–(13)) **32.21**

Eveready Battery's Patent, cited in the Main Work, has been reported ([2000] RPC 852).

Registration of transactions, instruments and events

—General **32.25**

It is understood that an application to register an assignment of a lapsed patent, which is subject to a restoration application under section 28, can now proceed without a stay and likewise for assignment of a patent which is the subject of proceedings before the Comptroller, whether *inter partes* or *ex parte*, although for *inter parte* s proceedings a subsequent application will be required for substitution or addition of a party. However, where an application or patent is the subject of entitlement proceedings, an assignment will only be registered before the completion of these proceedings if consent thereto is given by all parties to the dispute, or where there are special circumstances. Where entitlement proceedings are known to be pending before the court, there will normally be a stay unless all parties to the dispute consent to the registration or if evidence is provided that the court is content for the substitution of the parties (under CPR 19.4, not reprinted in the Main Work or herein). In all cases, a notice will be published in the O.J. of the application to register the assignment.

Certification of priority documents **32.37**

According to a notice in the O.J. of December 17, 2003, priority documents required to be filed with the International Bureau for PCT applications must be "signed and sealed". This form of certification should be specifically requested on PF 23/77.

SECTION 34—Rectification of register

PRACTICE UNDER SECTION 34

Procedure for rectification before the Patents Court **34.06**

This procedure is now governed by CPR 63PD15 (reprinted *infra* at § F63PD.15). Former CPR 49EPD 3 has been replaced by CPR 63PD 16(2) (reprinted *infra* in § F63PD.16). For the references to §§ G02 and G15 in the Main Work, substitute respective references to §§ G03 and G16, each as reprinted in Appendix G *infra*.

36.01   **SECTION 36—Co-ownership of patents and applications**

The Patents Act 2004 (c. 16, s. 9) prospectively amended subsection 36(3) by adding, after the word "others" (reprinted in line 2 on page 389 of the Main Work), the words:

(a) **amend the specification of the patent or apply for such an amendment to be allowed or for the patent to be revoked, or**

(b)

COMMENTARY ON SECTION 36

36.03   *Prima facie entitlement of co-owners to equal undivided shares in patent*

In *Magill's Application* (BL O/256/00), a payment default provision in an agreement providing a condition for assignment of "30% of the patent application" was held to be void for uncertainty, such phrase having no clear meaning, particularly in view of the wording of section 36.

36.04   *Rights and freedoms of each co-owner (subss. (2), (4) and (5))*

Minnesota Mining's International Application ([2003] RPC 541) considered the rights of co-owners and whether there should be an order for cross-royalties to be paid between two co-owners. Although it was held that such an order would be possible under section 36, it was considered inappropriate in this case. The decision also considered the division of patenting costs, and marking requirements.

36.05   *Rights not exercisable by co-owners individually without consent (subs. (3))*

The prospective amendment of section 36(3) places an additional restraint on a co-owner in that, without consent of all other co-owners, or by virtue of a prior agreement, no application may be made to amend, or revoke the patent, nor may the patent be amended. For example, if A and B are the original proprietors, but in entitlement proceedings C, rather than B, is found to be a rightful co owner, C is not entitled to have the patent revoked. Instead, C (under s. 37) should apply to be added as a co-owner and for B to be removed. If A and B were found both to be wrongly entitled, with C and D found to be the rightful co owners, the patent could be revoked and leave granted to the filing of a replacement application by C and D, provided that both agree to do this.

SECTION 37—Determination of right to patent after grant

COMMENTARY ON SECTION 37

37.06   *Types of entitlement questions which can arise under sections 8, 12 or 37*

In *Magill's Application* (BL O/256/00), entitlement was claimed (under s. 12) under a payment default provision in an agreement between two companies (CRL and IC, a company apparently owned by the applicant, M) specifying that, if IC defaulted on the agreed payments (as was held to have happened) "CRL will be assigned 30% of the patent application". This phrase was found to have no clear meaning (s. 36 requiring a 50% ownership for co-proprietors) and so was held void for uncertainty, leaving the patent rights seemingly with M. However, the agreement was seen as evidence that IC was the true owner of the rights. The Comptroller was therefore minded to make an order for assignment of the rights to IC forthwith, subject to any further representations from M or IC, but there were none and this order was made (BL O/362/00). However, no order could be made under section 12 in respect of the United States application which had already proceeded to grant.

In *Minnesota Mining's International Application* ([2003] RPC 541), a third party had made a non-confidential disclosure which was communicated to an inventor employed by the applicant and which then found its way into the application in suit. The applicant contended that since the disclosure had not been subject to confidentiality restrictions they were entitled to treat it as though it were in the public domain. It was however held that the disclosure had contributed to the inventive concept of some of the claims, and the third party was thus entitled to be a joint applicant in respect of them. However some of the claims derived only from the work of the applicant's employee and some only from the work of the third party so that further time was allowed for the parties to make submissions as to the appropriate order in the circumstances (see § 36.04 *supra*).

Raising questions of entitlement

—Types of relief available under sections 8 and 37   37.08

Following the initial decision of joint entitlement in *Minnesota Mining's Patent* (BL O/237/00), the parties failed to reach agreement and the Comptroller could then do no more than order (BL O/452/00) joint ownership under the terms of section 36 despite the fact that the customers of the new co-owner (E) would require to obtain a licence from the original owner (M), but it was pointed out to M "that it is incumbent on them to recognise how E carry out their business as suppliers of adhesives in order that E might gain some advantage from the patents".

In *Quantum Glass v. Spowart [Scotland]* (*noted* [2001] *CIPA* 99), the Court of Session thought it appropriate to impose interim interdicts upon a patent applicant and inventor from further prosecuting an international application pending full trial of the issues of entitlement to this application and of alleged breach of confidence in its disclosure, even though the outcome of these interdicts seemed likely to be that the application could not proceed within the required time limits.

Powers of the Comptroller and court to determine entitlement disputes   37.09

In *Pico's Patent* (BL O/303/00), the Comptroller declined jurisdiction solely because this was the unopposed wish of the proprietor, although otherwise no sufficient ground had been put forward as to why jurisdiction should be declined under subsection (8).

In *West Pharmaceuticals International Application* (BL O/58/2) the matter was referred to the court not because the case was a complex one (which was seen as no reason to decline jurisdiction) but since court proceedings involving essentially the same issue were in being, and it was not desirable that there be parallel proceedings.

Relief granted under sections 8 and 31   37.11

In a sequel (BL O/410/00) to *McGriskin's Patent*, cited in the Main Work requiring the referrer (W) to become a joint proprietor, the original proprietor (M) failed to pay her half share of a renewal fee "in a timely manner" as required by an earlier decision. An order was therefore made for W to become the sole proprietor, but with M having an irrevocable, royalty-free, non-exclusive licence with power to grant sub-licences, but any party granted a sub-licence must be required to provide to W a bi-annual report of the amount of product produced and sold by it. W was also required to pay the other half-renewal fee which was accepted out of time.

In *Solenzaro's Patents* (BL O/156/01) it was held not fatal to an argument that rights in the relevant patent had been transferred that no written documents had been signed because the Comptroller was entitled to take account of the position in equity, and the actions of the parties were consistent with transfer having taken place.

PRACTICE UNDER SECTION 37

37.13 *Proceedings under section 37 before the Comptroller*

In *Thibierge & Connor's Application* (BL O/345/01), an application for a stay of entitlement proceedings before the Comptroller when parallel proceedings had been commenced in France was refused. It was held that the applicant for the stay had the onus of showing that it was appropriate. A relevant consideration was the relative speed of proceedings before the English and French courts (the English proceedings being likely to be quicker) but not the availablity of cross-examination and disclosure of documents because it would be improper to decide that one national proceedure would be superior to another. The Comptroller's decision was upheld when this case came before the Patents Court in *Thibierge & Comar v. Rexam* ([2002] RPC 379); see also § .

37.15 *Procedure before the court in entitlement proceedings*

CPR 49EPD 13 and 18 and CPR 49EPD 5 have been respectively replaced by CPR 63.11, CPR 63PD 16 and CPR 63.5 (reprinted respectively in §§ F63.11, F63PD.16 and F63.5 *infra*, but note that the time for referring a matter to the court has been reduced (under CPR 63.11) from 28 to 14 days.)

38.01 ## SECTION 38—Effect of transfer of patent under section 37

The Patents Act 2004 (c. 16, Sched. 2(10)) amended (with effect from January 1, 2005, S.I. 2004 No. 3205. a. 2(f)(k)) subsections 38(3) and (5), as follows:

(1) in subsection (3), after the words "new proprietor or proprietors" (in line 8 of the reprint in the Main Work), inserting the words "or, as the case may be, the new applicant"; and

(2) in subsection (5), after the words "proprietors of the patent" (in line 1 of the reprint in the Main Work), inserting the words "or, as the case may be, the new applicant".

RELEVANT RULES—RULES 57 AND 58

38.02 ### Rule 57—Orders under section 37

57.—(1) Where an order is made under section 37—

(a) that a patent shall be transferred to one or more persons none of whom was an old proprietor; or

(b) that a person other than an old proprietor may make a new application for a patent,

the comptroller shall give notice of the making of the order to the old proprietor or proprietors, and to any of their licensees of whom he is aware; and a person who makes a request under section 38(3) must do so before the end of the relevant period.

(2) The relevant period is—

(a) where the request is made by an old proprietor, the period of two months starting on the date the notice is sent to him;

(b) where the request is made by a licensee, the period of four months starting. on the date the notice is sent to him.

Note. This rule replaced its former form with effect from January 1, 2005 (S.I. 2004 No. 3205, a. 6).

Rule 58—Reference to the comptroller under section 38(5)   **38.03**

58.—(1) A reference under section 38(5) shall be made on Patents Form 2/77 and shall be accompanied by a copy and by a statement in duplicate setting out fully—

(a) the question referred;

(b) the facts upon which the person making the reference relies; and the period or terms of the licence which he is prepared to accept or grant.

(2) The comptroller shall send, except to the person who made the reference, a copy of the reference and statement to—

(a) the new proprietor or proprietors or, as the case may be, the new applicant; and

(b) every person claiming to be entitled to be granted a licence,

and any such person who receives a copy of the reference and statement may, before the end of the period of six weeks starting on the date the copies were sent to him, file a counter-statement (which must be in duplicate) setting out fully his grounds of objection.

(3) The comptroller shall send a copy of the counter-statement to the person who made the reference.

(4) The comptroller may give such directions as he thinks fit with regard to the subsequent procedure.

Note. This rule replaced its former form with effect from January 1, 2005 (S.I. 2004 No. 3205, a. 7).

COMMENTARY ON SECTION 38   **38.04**

The amendments prospectively made to subsections (3) and (5) clarify that these provisions apply both when the successful party has opted to continue with the existing patent and when a choice has been made to file a replacement application. Rules 57 and 58 have been re written accordingly (see §§ 38.02 and 38.03 *supra*).

SECTION 39—Right to employees' inventions

COMMENTARY ON SECTION 39

Ownership of employee inventions by an employer

—The employee's normal duties   **39.08**

Following *Greater Glasgow Health Board's Application*, cited in the Main Work, it was held that the job description for a hospital surgeon had merely provided a hope, rather than an obligation, that research would be done under the employment contract. Hence, the surgeon should have entitlement to an invention made by him in his own time and not during either his normal, or specially assigned, duties (*Bradford Hospital's Application* (BL O/37/01)).

—Performance of normal or specifically assigned duties   **39.10**

In *West Glamorgan's Application* (BL O/235/01), it was held that, in contrast to the situation in *Harris's Patent* ([1985] RPC 19) the inventor had not been asked to apply himself to any technical problem so that although the invention had been made in the course of his normal duties, these were not such that the invention might reasonably have been expected to result, so the inventor was entitled to the invention. The Comptroller also held in this case that "specially assigned duties" under section 39(1)(a) must be outside "normal duties".

39.11   *—Employees with special obligations*

In *West Glamorgan's Application* (BL O/235/01), the Comptroller also held that the "special obligation" referred to in section 39(1)(b) must be something special over and above the obligations which any employee has to his employer.

40.01   **SECTION 40—Compensation of employees for certain inventions**

The Patents Act 2004 (c. 16, s. 10) amended section 40 by replacing subsection (1) and amending subsection (2), as set out below. These amendments took effect from January 1, 2005 (S.I. 2004 No. 3205, a. 2(d)), but only as regards inventions the patent for which is applied for on or after that date (2004 Act, s. 10(8)).

The new form of subsection (1) is:

(1) Where it appears to the court or the comptroller on an application made by an employee within the prescribed period that—

> **(a) the employee has made an invention belonging to the employer for which a patent has been granted,**
>
> **(b) having regard among other things to the size and nature of the employer's undertaking, the invention or the patent for it (or the combination of both) is of outstanding benefit to the employer, and**
>
> **(c) by reason of those facts it is just that the employee should be awarded compensation to be paid by the employer,**

the court or the comptroller may award him such compensation of an amount determined under section 41 below.

In subsection (2)(c), the word "patent" (last line on page 423 of the Main Work has been replaced by:

"the invention or the patent for it (or both)."

Commentary on Section 40

40.06   *Time for making application for compensation*

CPR 49EPD 14 has been replaced by CPR 63.12 and CPR 63PD.13 (reprinted *infra* respectively in §§ F63.12 and F63PD.13).

Invention belonging to the employer (subs. (1))

40.09   *—Meaning of "outstanding benefit"*

First, it is important to note that the amendments (made to sections 40, 41 and 43) only have application to an invention, the patent for which is applied for on or after the amendments have been brought into effect, *i.e.* from January 1, 2005, see the note to § 43.01 *infra*. However, when effective, the changes to subsections (1) and (2) (noted in

§ 40.01 *supra*) are significant. Under the new terms, compensation may be awarded to an employee, not only where the patent has been of outstanding benefit to the employer, but also where the invention (or a combination of the patent and the invention) has provided such benefit. The decision in *Memco Med's Patent* ([1992] RPC 403) has therefore been overruled to the extent that only benefit arising directly from "the patent" can be taken into account when assessing compensation under section 40. Benefits arising from the invention as such can also now be taken into account.

In *Entertainment UK's Patent* ([2002] RPC 291), the Comptroller held that although section 40 used the words "is of outstanding benefit", section 41(1) seemed to suggest that future benefit could not be ruled out.

Procedure, hearing, costs and appeals   40.14

CPR 49EPD 1 and 2 have been replaced by CPR 63.1–63.5 (reprinted at §§ F63.1–63.5 *infra*); and CPR 49EPD 13 and 14 have been replaced by CPR 63.11, CPR 63.12 and CPR 63PD.13 (for which see §§ F63.11, F63.12 and F63PD.13, each reprinted *infra*).

PRACTICE UNDER SECTION 40

Application to the Comptroller   40.16

The Comptroller refused to order summary judgment for the patentee in *Entertainment UK's Patent* ([2002] RPC 291), holding that the power to do so did exist, but should only be exercised in a clear case in accordance with what is now CPR 63.12. Although unlikely to be able to show "outstanding benefit" on the facts, the applicant's case was not hopeless.

Application to the court   40.17

CPR 49EPD 14 has been replaced by CPR 63.12 and CPR 63PD.13 (reprinted *infra* respectively in §§ F63.12 and F63PD.13); and CPR 49EPD.16 has been replaced by CPR 63.17 (reprinted *infra* at § F63.17).

SECTION 41—Amount of Compensation   41.01

The Patents Act 2004 (c. 16, s. 10(3) and Scheds. 2(11) and (3)) amended section 41 (with effect from January 1, 2005, S.I. 2004 No. 3205, a. 2(d)(f)(k)) by replacing subsection (1) and amended subsections (4), (5) and (10), as follows:
The new form of subsection (1) is:

(1) An award of compensation to an employee under section 40(1) or (2) above shall be such as will secure for the employee a fair share (having regard to all the circumstances) of the benefit which the employer has derived, or may reasonably be expected to derive, from any of the following—
    (a) the invention in question;
    (b) the patent for the invention;
    (c) the assignment, assignation or grant of—
        (i) the property or any right in the invention, or
        (ii) the property or any right in the invention, or

In subsections (4) and (5), the words "a patent for" (reprinted in line 2 of each subsection in the Main Work) have been omitted; and in subsection (5)(a) the words "for it" have been added at the end of that paragraph. In subsection (10), the words "a recorded decree arbitral" have been replaced by:

"an extract recorded decree arbitral bearing a warrant for execution issued by the sheriff court of any sheriffdom in Scotland."

Note. The amendment noted for subsection (12) is now a consequence of S.I. 2003 No. 1249.

COMMENTARY ON SECTION 41

41.03   *Scope of the section*

The amendments made to the subsections (1), (4) and (5) (as noted in § 41.01 *supra*) are consequential upon the amendments made to section 40(1) and (2), as discussed in § 40.09 *supra*. The amendment of subsection (10) brings its wording into conformity with the wording already existing in sections 93(b) and 107(3) and also as now added by new section 61(7). However, these amendments only have application to an invention, the patent for which is applied for on or after January 1, 2005, see the note to § 43.01 *infra*.

41.09   *Procedure*

CPR 49EPD 14 has been replaced by CPR 63.12 and CPR 63PD.13 (reprinted *infra* respectively in §§ F63.12 and F63PD.13).

41.10   PRACTICE UNDER SECTION 41

For the procedure in any application to the Patents Court or Patents County Court, see now CPR 63 (reprinted *infra* in Appendix F) and, more particularly, CPR 63.12 and CPR 63PD 13 (reprinted *infra* in §§ F63.12 and F63PD.13). Any appeal from a decision of the Comptroller is now governed by CPR 63.17 (reprinted *infra* at § F63.17), for which see § 97.16 in the Main Work and *infra*.

43.01   **SECTION 43—Supplementary**

The Patents Act 2004 (c. 16, s. 10) amended section 43(5) and inserted new subsection 43(5A), each with effect from January 1, 2005 (S.I. 2004 No. 3205, a. 2(d)), to read:

(5) For the purposes of sections 40 and 41 above the benefit derived or expected to be derived by an employer from an invention or patent shall, where he dies before any award is made under section 40 above in respect of it, include any benefit derived or expected to be derived from it by his personal representatives or by any person in whom it was vested by their assent.

(5A) For the purposes of sections 40 and 41 above the benefit derived or expected to be derived by an employer from an invention shall not include any benefit derived or expected to be derived from the invention after the patent for it has expired or has been surrendered or revoked.

Note. The amended form of Section 43 (and therefore also of sections 40–42) came into effect on January 1, 2005 (S.I. 2004 No. 3205), but applies only "in relation to an invention, the patent for which is applied for on or after this date. For this, the word "patent" has the meaning given to it by section 43(4) [1977] (Patents Act 2004, s.10).

COMMENTARY ON SECTION 43

Scope of the section **43.02**

The amendments made to the section (as noted in § 43.01 *supra*) are consequential upon the amendments made to section 40(1) and (2), as discussed in § 40.09 *supra*.

SECTION 44 [REPEALED]—Avoidance of certain restrictive conditions | **44.01**

Note. The repeal of this section has been applied to the Isle of Man (S.I. 2003 No. 1248).

COMMENTARY ON SECTION 44

The Competition Act 1998

—General **44.04**

The Office of Fair Trading (OFT) has issued a draft Guideline (OFT 418) on the application of the Competition Act 1998 to agreements concerning intellectual property rights. This was made available on the OFT website (www.oft.gov.uk).
The Enterprise Act 2002 (c. 40) has greatly increased the powers of the Competition Commission, and the Secretary of State, in relation to features in merger and marketing situations which are seen as anti-competitive or contrary to the public interest. These are outside the scope of this Work, but it is to be noted that they have included the introduction of section 50A and revision of sections 51(2) and 53(2), as indicated and discussed in §§ 50A.01, 50A.02, 51.01 and 53.01 *infra*.
The Enterprise Act also repealed (by Sched. 26) the exception for patent agents and European patent attorneys from allegations of unfair trading for activities "in their capacity as such", as mentioned in the Main Work.

SECTION 45—Determination of parts of certain contracts | **45.01**

Note. The repeal of this section has been applied to the Isle of Man (S.I. 2003 No. 1248).

SECTION 46—Patentee's application for entry in register that licences are available as of right | **46.01**

The Patents Act 2004 (c. 16, s.8) prospectively amended section 46 by replacing subsection (3)(d) and inserting a new subsection (3B), each to read as follows:

(d) if the expiry date in relation to a renewal fee falls after the date of the entry, that fee shall be half the fee which would be payable had the entry not been made.

(3B) For the purposes of subsection (3)(d) above the expiry date in relation to a renewal fee is the day at the end of which, by virtue of section 25(3) above, the patent in question ceases to have effect if that fee is not paid.

PRACTICE UNDER SECTION 46

Making of entry in register **46.18**

Although the prospective changes to section 25 (noted in § 25.01 *supra*) provide an extended period for the payment of a renewal fee (for which see § 25.07 *supra*), the changes made to section 46 (as noted in § 46.01 *supra*) will (when given effect) ensure that, in order to obtain the advantage of a half fee renewal payment, the application under section 46 must be filed BEFORE the anniversary date, *i.e.* before the commencement of the next renewal period.

48.01   **SECTION 48 [SUBSTITUTED]—Compulsory licences**

Note. This substituted section has been applied to the Isle of Man by S.I. 2003 No. 1249.

RELEVANT RULES—RULES 68 AND 70

48.03   *Rule 70—Procedure on receipt of application under sections 48, 51 or 52*

The reprinting of this rule in the Main Work should be corrected so that: in paragraph (1)(a), "an" should appear before "entry"; in paragraph (1)(b) "the" should appear before "revocation" and "making" before "such notification"; in paragraph (2), line 2, "an opportunity" should read "the opportunity"; paragraph (3)(a) should read: "the making of an order or an entry"; and paragraph (3)(b) should commence "**the revocation** ".

COMMENTARY ON SECTION 48

48.04   *The provisions for the grant of compulsory licences*

See § 1.21 for mention of the regime for cross-licences between patents and plant breeders' rights under The Patents and Plant Variety Rights (Compulsory Licensing) Regulations (S.I. 2002 No. 247). Note that the procedure under section 48(1) is taken to apply to proceedings under the Regulations, but the provisions of sections 48, 48A, 48B, 49, 50 and 52 do not otherwise apply to compulsory patent licences and cross-licences obtained under these Regulations.

48A.01   **SECTION 48A [ADDED]—Compulsory licences: WTO Proprietors**

Note. This added section has been applied to the Isle of Man by S.I. 2003 No. 1249.

COMMENTARY ON SECTION 48A

48A.04   *Scope of the section*

Meijer's Plant Variety Right (*noted* [2002] EIPR N–38) was the first application to the Controller of Plant Varieties for a compulsory licence under the Plant Varieties Act 1997 (c.66), and was unsuccessful. It was held that nothing in the Act required the rights holder to grant a licence so the Controller had a wide discretion. A compulsory licence should only be granted when to do so was clearly in the public interest, and then only if at least one of the prescribed grounds was seen to be met. The same principles could be held to apply to an application for a patent compulsory licence, when made by a WTO proprietor under this section.

48A.07   *Failure to meet demand for patented product (subs. (1)(a))*

An example of a compulsory licence case in which the question of a failure to supply was considered (application failed on the facts) is *Swansea Imports v. Carver Technology* (BL O/170/04).

48B.01   **SECTION 48B—Compulsory licences: other cases**

Note. This added section has been applied to the Isle of Man by S.I. 2003 No. 1249.

SECTION 50—Exercise of powers on applications under section 48	**50.01**

Note. The amendments noted for subsections (1) and (2) were each applied to the Isle of Man by S.I. 2003 No. 1249.

SECTION 50A [ADDED]—Powers exercisable following merger and market investigations	**50A.01**

Section 50A was added by the Enterprise Act 2002 (c. 40, Sched. 25(8)). It reads:

50A.—(1) Subsection (2) below applies where—

(a) section 41(2), 55(2), 66(6), 75(2), 83(2), 138(2), 147(2) or 160(2) of, or paragraph 5(2) or 10(2) of Schedule 7 to, the Enterprise Act 2002 (powers to take remedial action following merger or market investigations) applies;

(b) the Competition Commission or (as the case may be) the Secretary of State considers that it would be appropriate to make an application under this section for the purpose of remedying, mitigating or preventing a matter which cannot be dealt with under the enactment concerned; and

(c) the matter concerned involves

   (i) conditions in licences granted under a patent by its proprietor restricting the use of the invention by the licences; or

   (ii) a refusal by the proprietor of a patent to grant licences on reasonable terms.

(2) The Competition Commission or (as the case may be) the Secretary of State may apply to the comptroller to take action under this section.

(3) Before making an application the Competition Commission or (as the case may be) the Secretary of State shall publish, in such manner as it or he thinks appropriate, a notice describing the nature of the proposed application and shall consider any representations which may be made within 30 days of such publication by persons whose interests appear to it or him to be affected.

(4) The comptroller may, if it appears to him on an application under this section that the application is made in accordance with this section, by order cancel or modify any condition concerned of the kind mentioned in subsection (l)(c)(i) above or may, instead or in addition, make an entry in the register to the effect that licences under the patent are to be available as of right.

(5) References in this section to the Competition Commission shall, in cases where section 75(2) of the Enterprise Act 2002 applies, be read as references to the Office of Fair Trading.

(6) References in section 35, 36,47, 63, 134 or 141 of the Enterprise Act 2002 (questions to be decided by the Competition Commission in its reports) to taking action under section 41(2), 55, 66, 138 or 147 shall include references to taking action under subsection (2) above.

(7) Action taken by virtue of subsection (4) above in consequence of an application under subsection (2) above where an enactment mentioned in subsection (1)(a) above applies shall be treated, for the purposes of sections 91(3), 92(1)(a), 162(1) and 166(3) of the Enterprise Act 2002 (duties to register and keep under review enforcement orders etc.), as if it were the

making of an enforcement order (within the meaning of the Part concerned) under the relevant power in Part 3 or (as the case may be) 4 of that Act.

COMMENTARY ON SECTION 50A

50A.02 | *Scope of the section*

In effect, new section 50A expands the scope of section 51 (and also re-locates some of the provisions of section 51) by providing that, in certain circumstances, the Competition Commission, or the Secretary of State (as the case may be), can apply to the Comptroller for him to vary the terms of a licence under a patent or to make an entry in the register of patents that licences under the patent are to available as of right. The circumstances under which section 50A applies is where a decision has been made, or a report issued by the Competition Committee of the Secretary of State (as the case may be) each acting under the terms of the Enterprise Act 2002 (c. 40) that a merger situation, or marketing activities, may have an adverse effect on the public and, accordingly, that some remedial action is desirable in relation to the exercise of patent rights or for the variation of conditions in an existing patent licence. These powers are wider in effect than those under the form of section 51 which existed prior to its amendment as a consequence of the addition of section 50A (for which see § 51.01 *infra*). This is because the terms of the Enterprise Act 2002 (c. 40) are considerably more extensive, particularly as regards mergers and marketing activities, than those which were previously applied under the terms of the Competition Act 1980 (c. 21). Section 53(2) has been consequentially amended to provide that reports made under Parts 3 or 4 of the Enterprise Act 2002 shall also be prima facie (or sufficient) evidence of the report matters.

When section 50A is sought to be applied, the provisions of section 52 will govern the procedure providing for possible opposition, appeal and arbitration.

51.01 | **SECTION 51 [SUBSTITUTED]—Powers exercisable in consequence of report of Competition Commission**

Section 51(1)(a) and (b) have now ceased to have effect (Enterprise Act 2002, c. 40, Sched. 15(8)(3)), but the powers provided by these provisions are now to be found, in expanded form, in the added section 50A (reprinted in § 50A.01 *supra*) as briefly discussed in § 50A.02 *supra*.

Note. The amendments noted for the title and subsection (1) were each applied to the Isle of Man by S.I. 2003 No. 1249.

52.01 | **SECTION 52 [SUBSTITUTED]—Opposition, appeal and arbitration**

Note. This substituted section was applied to the Isle of Man by S.I. 2003 No. 1249 with changes to subsection (4) deleting "or" after "1857 [c. 44]" and adding after "Northern Ireland" the words "or the Attorney General for the Isle of Man".

53.01 | **SECTION 53—Compulsory licences: supplementary provisions**

Subsection (1) (which had never been brought into force) was deleted by the Patents Act 2004 (c. 16, Scheds. 2(12) and 3) on January 1, 2005 (S.I. 2004 No. 3205, a. 2(f)(g)(k)) as part of the removal from the Act of all references to the CPC which never came into force.

Subsection (2) was amended by the Enterprise Act 2002 (Sched. 25(8)(4)) by adding after the words "Competition Act 1980 [c. 21] (reprinted in the final line of page 510 in the Main Work) the words: or published under Part 3 or 4 of the Enterprise Act 2002 [c. 40]".

Note. The amendment noted for subsection (2) (as regards the Competition Commission) was applied to the Isle of Man by S.I. 2003 No. 1249.

SECTION 54—Special provisions where patented invention is being worked abroad — 54.01

Note. The amendment noted for subsection (2) was applied to the Isle of Man by S.I. 2003 No. 1249.

SECTION 55—Use of patented inventions for services of the Crown — 55.01

Note. By the Visiting Forces and International Headquarters (Application of Law) Order 1999 (S.I. 1999 No. 1736, art. 6 and Sched. 4(2)), the powers conferred by section 55 have been extended as follows:—

Schedule 4(2)—Use of patented inventions

2.—(1) Subject to sub-paragraph (2), the power conferred by section 55(1) of the Patents Act 1977 (c. 37) on a government department, or person authorised in writing by a government department, in relation to the use of patented inventions for the services of the Crown shall be exercisable for the purposes of a visiting force or headquarters to the extent that it would be exercisable if the visiting force or headquarters were part of any of the home forces.

(2) Sub-paragraph (1) shall not have effect to authorise—

  (a) the doing of any act falling within section 55(1)(a)(ii) or (c) of the Patents Act 1977, or

  (b) the doing of anything which is for a purpose relating to the production or use of atomic energy or research into matters connected therewith.

(3) In relation to the exercise of the powers conferred by sub-paragraph (1), sections 55 to 58 of the Patents Act 1977 (apart from section 56(2) to (4)) shall have effect with any reference in those provisions to the use of a patented invention for the services of the Crown being construed as a reference to the use of such an invention for the purposes of a visiting force or headquarters.

Paragraphs 4(1) and 4(3) of Schedule 4 of S.I. 1999 No. 1736 provide respectively corresponding provisions for the use of registered designs and design rights.

COMMENTARY ON SECTION 55

The Defence Contracts Act 1958 — 55.11

CPR 49EPD 1.3 has been replaced by CPR 63.3(2)(c) (reprinted in § F63.3 *infra*). For the former procedure under CPR 49EPD 15.1, see § *supra*.

SECTION 56—Interpretation, etc., of provisions about Crown use — 56.01

Notes.

  1. Subsection (4) has been amended, first by the Health and Social Care Act 2001 (c. 15, Sched. 5(4)) and then further by the Health and Social Care (Community Health and Standards) Act 2003 (c. 43, Scheds. 11(6) and 14(4)) so that this now reads:

(4) For the purposes of section 55(1)(a) and (c) above and subsection (2)(b) above, specified drugs and medicines are drugs and medicines which are both—

    (a) required for the provision of—

        (i) primary medical services or primary dental services under Part I of the National Health Service Act 1977 or any corresponding provisions of the law in force in Northern Ireland or the Isle of Man, or

        (ii) pharmaceutical services, general medical services or general dental services under Part II of the National Health Service Act 1977 [c. 49] (in the case of pharmaceutical services), Part II of the National Health Service (Scotland) Act 1978 [c. 29], or the corresponding provisions of the law in force in Northern Ireland or the Isle of Man, or

        (iii) personal medical services or personal dental services provided in accordance with arrangements made under Section 17C of the 1978 Act, or the corresponding provisions of the law in force in Northern Ireland or the Isle of Man, and

        (iv) local pharmaceutical services provided under a pilot scheme established under section 28 of the Health and Social Care Act 2001 or an LPS scheme established under Schedule 8A to the National Health Service Act 1977, or under any corresponding provision of the law in force in the Isle of Man, or

        (v) personal dental services provided in accordance with arrangements made under section 28 C of the 1977 Act, and

    (b) specified for the purposes of this subsection in regulations made by the Secretary of State.

    2. The operation of section 56(1) has become subject to the provisions of S.I. 1999 No. 1736, for which see § 55.01 *supra*.

Note. Sub-paragraph (v) was inserted by S.I. 2004 No. 288 (for England) and by S.I. 2004 No. 480 (for Wales) and is a transitional and temporary provision until section 172(1) of the aforesaid 2003 Act is brought into force when a reference to general dental services will be added to paragraph (4)(ai) and this sub-paragraph (v) deleted. There appears to be no sub paragraph (iv) or, alternatively, sub-paragraph (v) should have been designated in these two S.I.'s as sub-paragraph (iv).

COMMENTARY ON SECTION 56

56.02   *Scope of the section*

    CPR 49EPD 1.3 has been replaced by CPR 63.3(2)(c) (reprinted in § F63.3 *infra*).

57A.01   **SECTION 57A—Compensation for loss of profit**

Note. The operation of section 57A has become subject to the provisions of S.I. 1999 No. 1736, for which see § 55.01 *supra*.

SECTION 58—Reference to disputes as to Crown use | **58.01**

Subsections 58(6) and (8) were prospectively amended, and new subsection 58(9A) added, by the Patents Act 2004 (c. 16, ss. 2 and 3), each to brought into effect when the EPC revisions agreed in 2000 come into force, so that:

in subsection (6), lines 4–6 (as reprinted in the Main Work) will then read:

"allow the amendment unless the court is satisfied that—
> **(a) the specification of the patent as published was framed in good faith and with reasonable skill and knowledge, and**
> **(b) the relief is sought in good faith";**

and, subsection (8), lines 3 and 4 (as reprinted in the Main Work) will then read:

"except where the proprietor of the patent proves that—
> **(a) the specification of the patent was framed in good faith and with reasonable skill and knowledge, and**
> **(b) the relief is sought in good faith."**

New subsection (9A) reads:

(9A) The court may also grant such relief in the case of a European patent (UK) on condition that the claims of the patent are limited to its satisfaction by the European Patent Office at the request of the proprietor.

Notes
1. The operation of section 58 has become subject to the provisions of S.I. 1999 No. 1736, for which see § 55.01 *supra*.
2. The amendment noted for subsection (12) is now a consequence of S.I. 2003 No. 1249.

COMMENTARY ON SECTION 58

Scope of the section   **58.02**

CPR 49EPD 1.3 has been replaced by CPR 63.3(2)(c) (reprinted in § F63.3 *infra*).

Determination of relief (subss. (3)–(11)) | **58.05**

The amendments made to subsections (6) and (8) parallel those made to sections 62(3) and 63(2) and have effect to provide that, in the case of a patent found to be only partially valid or which has been amended, relief for Crown use is predicated on the patentee satisfying the court that, not only was the patent framed in good faith and with reasonable skill and knowledge, but also that the proceedings for relief were "brought in good faith". Thus, when these statutory amendments are brought into force, Crown use compensation may be denied where the patentee knew, or ought to have known, that during a period in respect of which a claim for compensation is made, or was threatened, the patent was not wholly valid. In relation to a claim for compensation for Crown use of a European patent (UK), new subsection (9A) has similar effect to that of new subsection 63(4), as discussed in § 63.04 *infra*.

PRACTICE UNDER SECTION 58   **58.08**

The provisions of former CPR 49EPD 15.1 have been subsumed into the general CPR with particular effect under CPR Part 63 and the Practice Directions thereunder (reprinted under Appendix F *infra*).

59.01   **SECTION 59—Special provisions as to Crown use during emergency**

In the reprinting of section 59(2) "the addition" in the first line should read "in addition".

60.01   **SECTION 60—Meaning of infringement**

Subsection (4) (which had never been brought into force) was prospectively deleted by the Patents Act 2004 (c. 16, Scheds. 2(13) and 3) on January 1, 2005 (S.I. 2004 No. 3205. a. 2(f)(g)(k)) as part of the removal from the Act of all references to the CPC which never came into force.

Subsection (6)(b) was further amended by the RRO (a. 11), with effect from January 1, 2005, to read:

(6) . . .

   (b) a person who by virtue of section **20B(4) or (5) above or section 28A(4) or (5)** [*28(6)*] above or section 64 below **or section 117A(4) or (5) below** is entitled to do an act in relation to an invention without it constituting such an infringement shall, so far as concerns that act, be treated as a person entitled to work the invention.

The amendments noted for subsections (5), (6A), (6B), (6C) and (7) [re. "relevant ship", etc.] were each applied to the Isle of Man by S.I. 2003 No. 1249.

Note: Subsection (5) may need to be amended to conform with EU Directives 2004/27/EC and 2004/28/EC (OJEC L 136/34 abd 58) see § 60.14 *infra*.

COMMENTARY ON SECTION 60

60.02   *Origin and scope of the section*

The decision in *Buchanan v. Alba Diagnostics [Scotland]*, cited in the Main Work, was upheld on appeal ([2001] RPC 851) and again on appeal to the House of Lords ([2004] RPC 681), see § 31.05 *supra*.

The intention of an alleged infringer as to whether an act in fact infringes is normally irrelevant, but in *Monsanto v. Schmeiser* (12 CPR (4th) 204), a decision of the federal Court of Canada, it was held to be an open question whether a remedy for infringement could be obtained where a plant containing a patented gene came onto the property of a person who may tolerate the continued presence of the plant without doing anything to cause or promote its propagation or that of its progeny (except for example by saving and planting its seeds, as in this case). The court did not decide the question since it had been found as a fact that the defendant knew or ought to have known of the relevant property of the plant (glycophosphate resistance). On appeal, the Supreme Court of Canada confirmed the general rule that the defendant's intention is irrelevant to a finding of infringement, citing *Stead v. Anderson* (1847) 4 CB 806; 136 E.R. 724), but may be relevant if the infringement is alleged to consist of possession with an intention to use (*Adair v. Young* (1879) 12 Ch. D 13 (CA)).

Direct (or substantive) infringement (subs. (1))

60.03   *—Scope of subsection (1)*

Monsanto v. Merck, cited in the Main Work, was published [2002] RPC 709. The decision on infringement was reversed by the Court of Appeal (cited as *Pharmacia v. Merck* ([2002] RPC 775)), see § 125.16 *supra*.

—Infringement of product invention (subs. (1)(a))   **60.04**

In *SABAF v. MFI and Meneghetti* (BL C/37/01, *noted* IPD 24059) the arrangements for importation into the United Kingdom were made by the Italian manufacturer. On appeal ([2003] RPC 264) the finding of infringement at first instance was reversed on the basis that a seller who had no title to goods but made the contract of carriage did not import the goods for the purposes of section 60(1)(a). The House of Lords ([2005] RPC 209) agreed with the finding of non-infringement—see also §§ 60.18 and 60.25 *infra*, and the case comment by E. Cheyrey in *Patent World*, February 2003 (No. 149), page 18.

—Infringement by direct product of patented process (subs. (1)(c))   **60.06**

The underlying facts and evidence involved in *Nutrinova v. Scanchem* now published ([2001] FSR 797), cited in the Main Work, were described by S. Chen and N. Stoate ([2000] BSLR 246).

Indirect (or contributory) infringement under subsection (2)

—Scope of subsection (2)   **60.08**

A German court has held that a supplier of a part of a patented combination infringes under the equivalent provision when he knows, or ought to have known, that the customer would use the part supplied in that combination, actual knowledge not being required, and this even when the part supplied has other uses (*D.I. BV v. H.S. [Germany]* [2000] ENPR 194).

In *Menashe v. William Hill* ([2002] RPC 950 and [2003] RPC 575; [2003] IP&T 32; [2003] All ER 279 (CA)) the patent related to a gaming system. The claims called for a host computer, terminal computer(s), a communication means between them and a program means for operating the terminals. The host computer in the defendants' system was placed abroad, in the Netherlands Antilles. The Court was asked to determine as a preliminary point of law the question "Is it a defence to the claim under section 60(2) of the Patents Act 1977, if otherwise good, that the host computer claimed in the patent in suit is not present in the UK, but is connected to the rest of the apparatus claimed in the patent". In answering "no" to the question, the judge said that the patentee's invention was in substance *the combination* of elements. The invention was the system and the words of the subsection therefore looked to where the effect of the system was felt. The Court of Appeal agreed. The location of the host computer was irrelevant to a user supplied with software by the defendant. That person used the invention on his own terminal and it was "not a misuse of language to say that that he used the host computer in the United Kingdom". Thus the supply of software on CD by the defendant was intended to put the invention into effect in the UK. See the case comment by D. Knight in *Patent World*, February 2003 (No. 149), page 20.

Exhaustion of rights (subs. (4))   **60.11**

Subsection (4) has been formally repealed (see § 60.01 *supra*). It had always been redundant, not only because the CPC never came into effect, but also because of the primacy of the doctrine of exhaustion of rights (as developed under CTaa. 81 and 82), as discussed in §§ D16 and D36–D39 of the Main Work and *infra*.

Acts exempted from infringement (subs. (5))   **60.12**

The development during the life of a patent of an infringing product, including the making of a prototype, has been seen as involving infringement for which post-expiry relief may be appropriate, see *Dyson v. Hoover (No. 2)* ([2001] RPC 544) discussed in § 61.22 *infra*.

60.14   —*Acts done for experimental purposes (subs. (5)(b))*

For former CPR 49EPD 10, see now CPR 63PD.9 (reprinted at § F63PD.9).

In *Inhale Therapeutics v. Quadrant* ([2002] RPC 419) the defendant raised a defence of experimental use, but this failed on the facts because the defendant was trying to exploit and sell its technology to third parties, which is not experimental use.

The Editor's attention has been drawn to the fact that the passage from *Monsanto v. Stauffer* recited in the second paragraph of the corresponding section of the Main Work is not a strict quotation from the judgment and therefore the quotation marks surrounding it should be removed. In particular the reference to "or even perhaps to see if the experimenter could manufacture commercially in accordance with the patent" does not form part of the decision and is to be regarded only as an editorial comment. For the reader's convenience the relevant quotation from the case as reported in [1995] RPC 515 is set out in full below:

Trials carried out in order to discover something unknown or to test a hypothesis or even in order to find out whether something which is known to work in specific conditions, *e.g.* of soil or weather, will work in different conditions can fairly, in my judgment, be regarded as experiments. But trials carried out in order to demonstrate to a third party that a product works or, in order to amass information to satisfy a third party, whether a customer or a body such as the PSPS or ACAS, that the product works as its maker claims are not, in my judgment, to be regarded as acts done "for experimental purposes".

EC Directives Nos. 2004/27/EC (Art. 10(6)) and 2004/28/EC (Art. 13(6)) ([2004] OJEC L136/34 and 58) relate respectively to medicinal products for human use and veterinary medicinal products. Each requires that EU Member States make (no later than October 30, 2005) provision that conducting the necessary studies, tests and trials for the further marketing of pharmaceutical and veterinary products for which marketing authorisations have previously been given to another "shall not be regarded as contrary to patent-related rights or to supplementary-protection certificates". Some statutory change may be necessary as the Directives require the law to provide greater exemption for tests of an experimental nature than was provided by the *Monsanto v. Stauffer* decision and this seems to accord with the *Bolar* provision under US patent law.

60.16   —*Acts done on transiently visiting ships, aircraft, etc. (subs. (5)(d)–(f))*

In *Stena v. Irish Ferries* ([2002] RPC 990 and [2003] RPC 668) the defendants' vessel was held to fall within valid claims of the patent. However, infringement was avoided because the vessel (a ferry operating between its home port of Dublin and Holyhead) was deemed only ever to be "temporarily" in UK waters and therefore to be exempted under section 60(1)(d). The judge agreed with a decision of the German District Court of Hamburg (*Rolltraller* GRUR Int. (1973), 703) that the underlying purpose of the subsection and that of subsection (e) was to promote international trade. An argument that the exemption only applied to products and processes used on ships and not to the ship itself was rejected on a purposive construction of the subsection. The *Stena* decision was upheld on appeal ([2003] RPC 668; [2004] IP&T 301).

A case comment on the *Stena* Case by R. Sharma and H. Forrest has been published at [2003] EIPR 430.

60.17   *Entitlement of persons to work the invention (subs. (6))*

The amendments made to subsection 6(b) (as noted in § 60.01 *supra*) expand the immunity from infringement proceedings also to situations where a patent has been restored (under s. 28, with effect under s. 28A) and to the new situations where a lapsed application has been reinstated (under new s. 20A, with effect under new s. 20B) or resuscitated (under new s. 117A).

Territorial scope of infringement   **60.18**

In *SABAF v. MFI and Meneghetti* ([2003] RPC 264 and [2005] RPC 209 HL), in which the Italian manufacturer entrusted its products to an independent haulier for transport to the English retailer for sale in England, the Court of Appeal (reversing a finding of infringement at first instance) held that it is artificial to regard someone as importer who has no legal or beneficial interest in the goods, so the Italian company was held not liable for importation for the purposes of section 60(1)(a). The House of Lords ([2005] RPC 209) agreed with the finding of non-infringement. (See also § 60.25 *infra* in which the facts were not found sufficient to establish a common design between the manufacturer and the customer.)

Authorised use of invention   **60.19**

The decision in *Oxford Gene Technology v. Affymetrix and Beckman* (noted in the Main Work) was partially overturned on appeal ([2001] FSR 136 (CA)), it being held that there had been a purchase of a "business", giving that word a broad meaning.

Implied licence to repair   **60.20**

The House of Lords judgment in *United Wire v. Screen Repair Services*, cited in the Main Work, has been fully reported and both the Court of Appeal and House of Lords decisions are to be found at [2001] RPC 439.

Laches, acquiescence and estoppel   **60.21**

In *Building Products v. Sandtoft Roof Tiles* ([2004] FSR 834), the court had excluded from the damages inquiry in an earlier action certain products which had not been specifically pleaded in that case, because these had to be considered different types of infringement. Upon the claimants launching a new action in respect of these products, the action was struck out on the basis of issue estoppel because infringement by these products could have been included in the earlier case. In accordance with CPR 63 PD11.1(1)(b), it is important that each type of infringement be specifically pleaded.

—Joint tortfeasance by acting in a "common design"   **60.25**

In *SABAF v. MFI and Meneghetti* ([2003] RPC 264) the Italian manufacturer supplied its products to the English retailer for sale in England and supplied instruction manuals in the English language to facilitate their sale here, but this was not held sufficient to establish that it had a common design to market the products in England. The goods were its standard products and the retailer "could have decided to store or destroy the stock or send them to a market where there were no SABAF patents". This aspect of the case was upheld on appeal. The Italian company was merely acting as a supplier of goods to its English customer (MFI) and did not thereby "make MFI's infringing acts its own". The House of Lords ([2005] RPC 209) agreed with the finding of non-infringement. The question of common design was not argued before the House.

In *Warheit v. Olympia Tools* (Pumfrey J. February 2, 2001) an exception to the normal position that a parent subsidiary relationship is not sufficient to make the foreign parent a joint tortfeasor was made on the basis that the foreign company had given the subsidiary's customers a lifetime warranty and had provided financial support to the subsidiary.

61.01 **SECTION 61—Proceedings for infringement of patent**

The Patents Act 2004 (c. 16, Sched. 2(14)) changed the word "plaintiff" in subsection (4)(b) to "claimant" in conformity with the current practice under the CPR; and (by s. 11) also inserted new subsection 61(7), both changes being effective from January 1, 2005 (S.I. 2004 No. 3205, a. 2(d)(f)(k)). This new subsection reads:

(7) If the comptroller awards any sum by way of damages on a reference under subsection (3) above, then—

(a) in England and Wales, the sum shall be recoverable, if a county court so orders, by execution issued from the county court or otherwise as if it were payable under an order of that court;

(b) in Scotland, payment of the sum may be enforced in like manner as an extract recorded decree arbitral bearing a warrant for execution issued by the sheriff court of any sheriffdom in Scotland;

(c) in Northern Ireland, payment of the sum may be enforced as if it were a money judgment.

RELEVANT RULES—RULES 72–73

61.02 **Rule 72—Procedure on reference to comptroller under section 61(3)**

In the reprinting of the rule in the Main Work, "to" at the end of line 1 should be "by".

In rule 72, the words "plaintiff" and "plaintiff's", wherever they occur have been respectively replaced by "claimant" or "claimant's" with effect from January 1, 2005 (S.I. 2004 No. 3205, a. 8).

61.03 **Rule 73—Procedure where validity of patent in dispute**

In rule 73, the words "plaintiff" and "plaintiff's", wherever they occur have been respectively replaced by "claimant" or "claimant's" with effect from January 1, 2005 (S.I. 2004 No. 3205, a. 8).

COMMENTARY ON SECTION 61

61.04 *Scope of the section*

In *Hartington Conway's Applications* ([2004] RPC 161), it was held that the right to bring proceedings was conferred by s. 61 on the "proprietor of the patent". The word "proprietor" did not mean "registered proprietor" and the statutory right of action was conferred on the person who could trace his title as set out in s. 7 of the Act. Section 30(6) requires the specified transactions to be written, but an estoppel at common law could operate to bind the true owner notwithstanding the lack of writing.

61.05 *The forum for infringement proceedings*

CPR 49EPD 1 and 2 have been replaced by CPR 63.1–63.5 and CPR 63PD.2–63PD.3 (reprinted in §§ F63.1–F63.5 and F63PD.2–F63PD.3 *infra*).

In *GAT v. LuK* (ECJ Case C–4/03, Opinion of A G Geelhoed, September 16, 2004, (available, in French, via www.europa.eu.int/jurisp/)) a German court had asked the ECJ to decide the meaning of Article 16(4) of the Brussels Convention which states that in proceedings concerned with the registration or validity of IP rights required to be deposited or registered in a particular Contracting State the courts of that State "shall have exclusive jurisdiction, regardless of domicile of the defendant". Action had been brought by GAT in a German court for infringement of a French patent. GAT (and the German government) argued that this Article had to be construed strictly and therefore did not apply at all to actions of infringement, or non-infringement, commenced as such. LuK, together with the French and UK governments, argued that, because actions for patent infringement cannot in practice be disassociated from issues of validity, that issue had also to be decided solely by the courts of the country where the patent was granted. The Commission proposed the interpretation that, while only the tribunal in the country of registration is competent to decide validity questions, all other matters (*e.g.* infringement, or non-infringement) fall outside the scope of Article 16(4) and can therefore be determined by a court other than the court where the patent is granted. It was the opinion of the Advocate General that this third interpretation should be the one which the ECJ should adopt. This must await the court's decision following the hearing which was held on July 14, 2004.

[*Editor's Note*: This would leave it unclear as to how a court should proceed when faced with an allegation of infringement of a foreign patent where the defendant seeks to deny liability on grounds of invalidity; should the court stay the proceedings until the foreign court has decided on validity, or can it decide on infringement if it considers that the invalidity defence has no merit? But how can the court decide this without going into the validity contentions in some detail? The issues discussed here would appear to remain the same under the Brussels Regulation which replaces the Convention—see § 96.09 *infra*.]

Interim injunctions

—The principles upon which pre-trial relief is granted   **61.09**

The reference to paragraph 21 of the *Patent Court Guide* remains unchanged in the new version of the Guide, see § G21 *infra*.

—The balance of injustice   **61.13**

In *SmithKline Beecham v. Generics UK* (BL C/50/01, *noted* [2001] *CIPA* 628 and IPD 25005) the court said that it was impossible to judge the merit of the defendant's proposed defences based on non-infringement and invalidity of the patent at the stage of an interim injunction request and so proceeded to an analysis of the *American Cyanamid* questions. The claimants had entered into an agreement with another generics manufacturer to assist in marketing the relevant product after patent expiry and the court held that although both parties were likely to suffer unquantifiable and irreparable damage, those likely to be suffered by the claimant would be the greater. The judge also noted that, if the indicated defences had been strong, the defendant could have brought revocation proceedings or sought a declaration of non-infringement, but had not done so. Therefore an injunction was imposed, limited to acts of sale or offers for sale but not so as to prohibit importation or any experiments for the purposes of possible challenges to validity.

Another such case (and under the same patent) is *SmithKline Beecham v. Apotex* ([2003] FSR 524) in which the entry of the defendant into the market would have given rise to substantial but not adequately quantifiable damage and the judge again commented that the defendant could have cleared its way by proceedings for revocation or a declaration of non-infringement, but had chosen not to do so. This view was upheld by the Court of Appeal ([2003] FSR 544), which found that the judge had been entitled to take into account that, by failing to seek revocation, the defendant had "walked into the situation they find themselves in with their eyes open to the risk they were taking" but if they turned out to be right "the court would have to do the best it can to compensate them under the cross-undertaking". See the case comment by E. Nettleton and B. Cordery (*Patent World*, March 2003 (No. 150), page 14.)

[*Editor's comment*: It would therefore seem that a party which may be at risk of a challenge for infringement of a patent must think seriously about the option of applying for a declaration of infringement or revocation of the patent rather than waiting to be sued, because the court may construe the fact that these steps were not taken as counting against it as a defendant in interim injunction proceedings.]

In *Approved Prescription Services v. Merck* (BL C/3/03 —see § 71.04) the Patents Court ordered an early trial of the issue of non-infringement where the claimant had brought proceedings for a declaration.

61.18   —*Interim injunctions without notice*

For the reference to § G06 in the Main Work, substitute § G08, as reprinted in Appendix G *infra*.

61.22   *Relief by post-trial injunction (subs. (1)(a))*

The final decision on the scope of the injunction in *Coflexip v. Stolt Comex* (cited in the Main Work as BL C/32/00 (CA)) has been reported ([2001] RPC 182) but see § 125.15 *infra* for comment on further proceedings in this case. Also the *Nutrinova* decision, cited in the Main Work, has been published as *Nutrinova v. Scanchem (No. 2)* ([2001] FSR 831).

Following on from the discussion in the Main Work as to the possibility of a post-expiry injunction, such was granted in *Dyson v. Hoover (No. 2)* ([2001] RPC 544]). Here, it was noted that section 61(1) does not preclude other relief for infringement and that (under the Supreme Court Act 1981, c. 54, s. 37) an injunction can be granted where it appears "just and convenient" to do so. Springboard damages for post-expiry acts had been found allowable in *Gerber Garment v. Lectra Systems* ([1995] RPC 383 and [1997] RPC 443 (CA)), but such damages were seen as notoriously difficult to assess and a post-expiry injunction could be granted to ameliorate that difficulty. However (as held in *Gerber Garment*), an award of damages has to be limited to damages which were "foreseeable, caused by the wrong and not excluded by public policy". As Hoover had taken about 12 months to develop the infringing device (such development itself being an infringing act), an injunction was ordered to run for the same period from the patent expiry date, but this would be limited in scope to the device upon which the trial had taken place. A request for an injunction against use of the trade mark used to promote marketing of the infringing device was rejected as not being a foreseeable consequence of the patent infringement; any goodwill generated by that use having conveyed the message of a new Hoover product regardless of how it had been made.

For discussion of other cases in which post-trial injunctions have been granted in limited form, see Heidi Hurdle (*Patent World* No. 127 (November 2000), 14).

In *Kirin-Amgen v. Transkaryotic Therapies (No. 2)* ([2002] RPC 203) the claimant sought an injunction extending to activities outside the United Kingdom. The court refused the relief holding that it was highly questionable as going beyond the ambit of the patent which relates only to activities in the United Kingdom in the absence of any special facts. The claimant was permitted to amend its pleadings to claim "springboard" relief (as approved in *Dyson v. Hoover (No. 2)*, *supra*) in respect of any losses arising after expiry as a result of pre-expiry infringing activities. In a further hearing relating to the same patent (*Kirin-Amgen v. Transkaryotic Therapies (No. 3)*, [2002] RPC 851; [2002] IP&T 331) an injunction pending the hearing of the appeal was imposed with certain caveats. The substantive appeal subsequently succeeded (*Kirin-Amgen v. Transkaryotic Therapies* [2003] RPC 31), and the patentee eventually lost in the House of Lords ([2005] RPC 169).

Relief by delivery up or damages (subs. (1)(b))　　　　　　　　　　**61.23**

The "necessary fee" referred to in line 7 of the final paragraph of § 61.23 has been abolished, see S.I. 2003 No. 2316.

Relief by damages (subs. (1)(c))

—Time when damages are assessed　　　　　　　　　　**61.24**

In *Kirin-Amgen v. Transkaryotic Therapies, (No. 2)* ([2002] RPC 203) the claimant was permitted to amend its pleadings to claim "springboard" relief (as approved in *Dyson v. Hoover (No. 2)*, see § 61.22) in respect of any losses arising after expiry as a result of preexpiry infringing activities.

—Basis for assessment　　　　　　　　　　**61.25**

In *Coflexip v. Stolt Comex* (BL C/34/02) the claimant was ordered to amend its pleadings to specify how and why the use of the invention was causative of the loss of prospect of "infringing contracts" (being contracts entered into between the defendant and its customers), which contracts it was alleged might have been awarded to the claimant. On referral to the Court of Appeal ([2003] FSR 728) that court declined to express a view until the facts relating to the contracts had been established, but agreed that detailed re-pleading was required before legal argument could proceed. The claimant would however be permitted to plead its view of causation even though that appeared to differ from that of the judge.

Relief by account of profits (subs. (1)(d))　　　　　　　　　　**61.29**

In *Spring Form v. Toy Brokers* ([2002] FSR 276) the Patents Court determined that while a co-claimant exclusive licensee can claim this relief, there is only one "profits pot" to be shared between him and the patentee. All co-claimants must make the same election between damages and an account. Accounts against multiple defendants needed to be taken together and no payment should be made in respect of any infringing article until the claimant undertakes not to make a claim in respect of the same article against any other defendant, otherwise the taking of an account would become hopelessly complicated.

Euro-defences　　　　　　　　　　**61.34**

In *Intel v. Via Technologies* ([2003] FSR 175), summary judgment for the claimant was ordered in relation to a series of defences based on Arts. 81(1) and 82 of the EC Treaty. However, on appeal ([2003] FSR 574), it was held that, following *Magill v. European Commission* ([1995] ECR I, 743) which said that "the exercise of an exclusive right by the proprietor may, in exceptional circumstances, involve abusive conduct" the judge had been wrong to deny a full trial of the issue whether Intel's conduct should be regarded as "exceptional circumstances". The appeal was therefore allowed with an order that the parties should return to the High Court for directions for trial of the "Euro-defences", but the action was subsequently settled. See the case comment on this decision in *Patent World*, October 2002 (No. 146), page 12.

Costs

—The principles for award and assessment of costs　　　　　　　　　　**61.35**

The amendments made to section 106 (for which see § 106.01 *infra*) may affect awards |

of costs in patent litigation. As discussed in § 106.02 *infra*, the new provisions extend the powers under section 106 to proceedings before the court, not only to those under section 40, but also in respect of acts of infringement and/or actions under sections 70 and/or 71, and so require the court in assessing awards of costs in such proceedings to "consider all the relevant circumstances, including the financial position of the parties", as to which see § 106.02 *infra*. These provisions are additional to (or perhaps merely explanatory of) CPR 44.3 (reprinted in § E44.3 of the Main Work) which requires the court, when making a costs order, "to have regard to all the circumstances".

The *Nutrinova* decision, cited on page 594 in the Main Work, has been published as *Nutrinova v. Scanchem (No. 2)* ([2001] FSR 831).

In *McGhan Medical v. Nagor* ([2002] FSR 162) the defendant had succeeded in its arguments that the patent was not infringed but failed in its attack on the validity of the patent. The court considered the appropriate award of costs under CPR 44.3 and concluded that in normal circumstances the overall winner of a patent infringement suit containing a counterclaim should get its entire costs, subject only to the possibility of a discretionary discount for any unreasonable conduct on the defendant's part (whether by commission, omission, exaggeration or "over-zealous application"). However, the judge was urged to take into account the observations of Lord Woolf in *AEI Rediffusion Music Ltd v. Phonographic Performance Ltd* ([1999] 1 WLR 1507) in which he said that "too robust an application of the 'follow the event principle' ... discourages litigants from being selective as to the points they take ..." and may encourage them to "leave no stone unturned" in their efforts to do so. In the light of that the judge applied a "modest" discount in relation to one aspect of the case (an allegation of prior use) which he held had initially been pleaded as a "makeweight".

In the decision on costs in the Court of Appeal in *Pharmacia v. Merck* ([2002] RPC 775 but unreported on this aspect) the defendants had succeeded overall but were unsuccessful on one aspect (infringement), where the appeal was successful in overturning the decision below. The court was not inclined to order assessment of both parties' costs on this aspect but instead applied a discount to the total costs of the overall winner, which in this case was quantified at 10%; see the commentary on this case by Sara Ashby "Costs in United Kingdom Patent Actions: Patent Valid but Not Infringed" ([2001] EIPR 380).

The matter was further considered in *Apotex v. SmithKline Beecham* ([2004] EWHC 964 (Ch), May 5, 2004, BL C/48/94 and [2004] EWHC 2051 (Ch), C/99/04) in which the court stated the general principal as follows: "A party successful on the issue of invalidity will not generally recover its costs of the objections to validity that failed unless they are so tied in with successful objections that it would not be fair to treat them differently. It may, but must not, have to pay the unsuccessful patentee's costs of the issues upon which it fails if those issues were unreasonably raised or persisted in. Where a defendant is successful on the issue of infringement, an order for it to recover its assessed costs of that issue will normally be made unless it is possible at the stage when the order for costs is made to identify discrete 'infringement issues' which failed unreasonably in respect of which it is possible without detailed assessment fairly to make an estimate and so reduce the recovery to that extent. Equally, if in an otherwise successful defence to the allegation of infringement it is clear that the Defendant is responsible for raising issues that failed and in respect of which it is fair that the unsuccessful patent should receive its costs then a further adjustment can be made".

Warheit v. Olympia Tools (referred to in § 60.25 *supra* in relation to a preliminary point) was eventually heard in the Patents County Court. The Court of Appeal reversed the finding of the deputy judge on infringement by one of the defendants' products, but declined to interfere with the finding on validity. The Court of Appeal (reported on the issue of costs only at [2003] FSR 95) ordered the defendants to pay the claimants' costs in both courts but expressed concern that the amounts claimed were £250,000 for the two day trial and a further £112,000 for the appeal. It expressed the view that such costs could not have been envisaged by the Lord Chancellor when setting up the Patents County Court as a forum to encourage cheaper litigation. Also, the sums were not such as would normally be recovered in other complex cases in a County Court. The Court of Appeal therefore hoped that the costs judge would present his views in writing so that these could be reported and brought to the attention of practitioners.

[*Editor's Note*: the remarks of the Court of Appeal seem to disregard the lack of any threshhold either of financial value or of complexity determining whether cases should be brought in the Patents County Court or in the High Court. Although the technology involved in the case in point was relatively simple, the costs would be broadly in line with what would be expected in a Patents Court hearing, and there is no reason why the costs before the Patents County Court should be significantly different, other things (*e.g.* the representatives chosen) being equal. The Court of Appeal may be suggesting that a different approach to cases in the Patents County Court is appropriate, and it will be interesting to see if and in what way this suggestion is taken up.]

As mentioned in § 61.59 *infra* the judge in *Merck v. Generics [Alendronate product]* ([2004] RPC 607) was critical of costs incured, particularly as a result of experiments. He commented that "while the parties must continue to have a major say in the way the litigation is run, this is subject to the court's management responsibilities under the CPR".

Admiral Management Services v. Para Protect Europe (*noted The Times*, March 26, 2002) applied the principles of *Nossen's Patent* [1969] 1 All ER 775 to the costs of an employee of a party acting as an expert witness.

In *Inline Logistics v. UCI Logistics* (BL C/14/02; [2002] IP&T 444) a party was allowed to claim as part of its costs an insurance premium which it had paid shortly before trial to guard against its costs in case it had been unsuccessful in its defence.

A party who threatens proceedings but withdraws before they are issued may be liable for the costs of the other party in preparing itself to defend the proceedings: *c.f. Associated Newspaper v. Impac* ([2002] FSR 293).

In *Stena v. Irish Ferries (No. 2)* ([2003] RPC 681) the Court of Appeal upheld the decision at first instance to award costs on an "issue" basis, where the defendant had been successful on a narrow ground (see § 60.16 *supra*) but its substantial attack on validity had failed. Accordingly the claimant was ordered to pay 20% of the defendant's costs, and the defendant 80% of the claimant's.

Costs of the attendance of the claimant's experts at an inspection of its process in India were awarded even though the patentee conceded, as a result of the inspection, that the requested declaration of non-infringement should be granted. The court held that the claimants were justified in protecting their interests when the outcome of the inspection was in doubt (*Niche Generics v. Lundbeck,* [2004] FSR 392).

—*The "Earth Closet" or "See v. Scott-Paine" order*   **61.36**

Another case in which a *See v. Scott-Paine* order has been refused in accordance with the principles stated in the Main Work is *CIL International v. Vitrashop* ([2002] FSR 67). The court held that the amendment to the pleadings would have come as no surprise to the claimant, and an allegation that the defendant had not been diligent in making the amendment was dismissed, the application having been made within a month of the facts coming to the defendant's attention. An order was also refused in *Monitoring Technologies v. Bell Group* ([2003] EWHC 3136 (Pat), Laddie, J., July 23, 2003, IPD 27015) in circumstances where the court concluded that it would not be just to do so in relation to late pleaded prior uses.

The Standard Form of the Order for Directions in patent litigation now contains specific provisions for use when the defendant amends the Grounds of Invalidity and the patentee then seeks to discontinue the litigation, see § G22A.4 *infra*.

—*Effect on costs of offers of settlement*   **61.38**

Complex issues as to payment of costs following Part 36 offers and payments in were addressed in further proceedings in *Dyson v. Hoover* ([2003] FSR 394). The court held that CPR 36.13(4) precluded the assessment of costs other than on the standard basis once a payment in had been accepted.

61.39 *Proceedings before the Comptroller (subs. (3))*

CPR 49EPD 13 has been replaced by CPR 63.11 (reprinted *infra* at § F63.11), but with reduction of the time for referring the matter to court reduced from 28 to 14 days.

New subsection (7), for which see § 61.01 *supra*, provides a mechanism for enforcement of an award of damages made by the Comptroller under subsection (3). This mechanism is the same as that for enforcement of an award of damages by a county court in England and the corresponding mechanisms in Scotland and Northern Ireland, the wording for Scotland being brought into conformity with that already present in sections 93(b) and 107(3). There is therefore now a uniform mechanism for the recovery of compensation or costs arising from a decision of the Comptroller under any of sections 41, 61, 93 and 107.

PRACTICE UNDER SECTION 61

61.41 *Basic essentials of procedure before the Patents Court*

The former specialist Practice Direction for proceedings in the Patents Court, CPR 49EPD, has been replaced by CPR Part 63 and the Practice Directions thereunder. These are reprinted in Appendix F *infra*. More specifically, CPR 49EPD 2.4 and 2.5 have been replaced by CPR 63.7(1) and CPR 63PD.4(4) (reprinted in § F63PD.7 and § F63PD.4 *infra*), The Patents Court Guide has also been amended and is reprinted in its new form in Appendix G *infra*. For the new form of the Standard Form of Order for Directions, see § G21A therein. The cross-references to §§ G02, G03, G04, G10, G14, G15 and G16 in the Main Work should now be respectively replaced by §§ G03, G05, G06, G12, G15, G16 and G17 *infra*. The Patents Court no longer routinely sits in September, see new § G06 *infra*.

Attention is specifically drawn to the new provisions for a "Streamlined Procedure" set out in § G10 *infra*. These replace the former provisions for a "Simplified Trial" reproduced in § G08 of the Main Work. Paragraph G10(e) requires that the parties' legal advisers *must* draw their clients' attention to the availability of this procedure in the Patents Court and the Patents County Court. The judge in *Merck v. Generics [Alendronate process]* [the latter being part of the general correction noted in item 1 *supra*] ([2004] RPC 607) drew attention to this requirement and said that it was to be expected that the court will take it seriously and will montitor compliance with it. He also remarked that the court has power to impose this procedure of its own motion, and this may mean that the court will, at an early stage, require the parties to give it a fuller understanding than normal of the issues, so that it is better placed to decide whether to do so.

61.42 *Statements of Case*

CPR 49EPD.5–7 have been respectively replaced by CPR 63.5, CPR 63.9 and CPR 63PD.11 (reprinted in §§ F63.5, F63.9 and F63PD11 *infra*); and references to §§ G10, G11 and G12 in the Main Work now refer respectively to §§ G12, G13 and G9(b) of the new Patents Court Guide (reprinted in replaced Appendix G *infra*).

Where there is challenge to validity (including a claim for revocation of the patent), there must now be served a separate document entitled 'Grounds of Invalidity' specifying the grounds upon which validity of the patent is challenged (CPR 63PD 11.2(2)). A copy of each document referred to therein (and, if necessary, a translation thereof) must be served with the 'Grounds of Invalidity' document (CPR 63PD 11.2(3)). Moreover, a new provision requires that a copy of the 'Grounds of Validity' document must be sent to the

Comptroller and, likewise, when any amendment to this document is effected, a copy thereof must also be sent to the Comptroller (CPR 63PD 11.2(4)): such document should then appear on the patent file available for inspection in the Patent Office (for which see § 118.14 in the Main Work). Service upon the patentee can be effected at the address for service recorded in the Patent Office Register, see CPR 63.16(2) (reprinted in § F63.16). Case management is now governed by CPR 63.7 and CPR 63PD.4 (reprinted respectively in §§ F63.7 and 63PD.4).

CPR 63 PD11.1(1)(b) requires that each type of infringement be specifically pleaded. If not, the action may not run against those products not included in the pleadings and it may not be possible to include such products in a later action because of issue estoppel, as in *Building Products v. Sandtoft Roof Tiles* ([2004] FSR 834), see § 60.21 *supra*.

Striking-out of pleadings

—For lack of an arguable case   **61.43**

The decision at full trial in *Monsanto v. Merck*, cited in the Main Work, was published at [2002] RPC 709.

In *Storage Computer v. Hitachi* (BL C/34/01, *noted* IPD 24065) the court refused to strike out the proceedings even though the case for non-infringement was seen to be "very strong indeed" because it was "not inconceivable" that infringement could be found under the Protocol to EPCa. 69.

In *Schering v. CIPLA* (BL C/134/04 *noted The Times*, December 1, 2004), an action for infringement was struck out, because without being able to rely on a "without prejudice" letter there was no evidence of infringement see § 61.60 *supra*.

Hearing of a preliminary point   **61.45**

The Court of Appeal decision in *American Home Products v. Novartis*, cited in the Main Work as BL C/31/00, has been published ([2001] RPC 159).

Application to stay proceedings   **61.46**

In *Storage Computer v. Hitachi* (BL C/35/01, *noted* IPD 24065) the court took into account that the patentee was of limited means such that a stay would be "immensely harmful" to it whilst less so to the defendant, a substantial company. Accordingly a stay was refused, even though probable amendment of the patent during pending EPO proceedings might strengthen the case for non-infringement.

For a review of the circumstances in which English patent infringement proceedings may be stayed pending the outcome of EPO Opposition proceedings see the articles "*Staying Alive!* " by W. Cook ([2001] EIPR 304) and " *Stay Applications: From Kimberly Clark v. Procter & Gamble to Rambus v. Micron* " by I. Kirby and Louise Pearson ([2001] EIPR 367), also the paper by J. Radcliffe (*Patent World* 138 (December 2001/January 2002), 16).

In *General Electric v. Enercon* (Laddie J., February 17, 2003; [2003] EWHC 1248 (Pat)), the patent (concerning wind generators) was the subject of ten EPO oppositions with a final decision, after appeal, likely only in 2006. The defendant sought a stay of infringement proceedings until after the final determination of the oppositions. If this stay were granted, the Court could foresee that the UK proceedings might not be concluded before 2008/2009 with patent expiry in 2102. It was argued that the wind power market is set for significant growth and the Court saw that, if infringement were eventually proved, it might have a reluctance to stop projects already in construction. Although it was not an easy decision to make, it was held that the infringement proceedings should continue and so a stay was refused. In subsequent proceedings ([2003] EWHC 3089 (Pat), BL C/71/03), after the EPO Opposition proceedings had been successful (the patent having been revoked), but were subject to appeal, the patentee itself requested a stay. It was held that the balance had shifted in favour of granting the request, the patentee having offered various safeguards for the position of the defendant and other parties during the period of the stay, "in effect cutting out their monopoly for two or three years".

A stay of proceedings pending resolution of an EPO opposition was ordered in the Irish *Monsanto v. Merck* case reported as *Searle and Monsanto's Patent* ([2002] FSR 381).

In *Affymetrix v. Multilyte* (BL C/9/04), the defendant sought a stay of UK declaration of non-infringement proceedings pending determination of infringement proceedings which it had brought in Germany. The Claimant had also brought similar proceedings in the USA, so that the defendant argued that it could not afford to pursue proceedings in more than one jurisdiction. The stay was refused since each party was entitled as of right to bring proceedings in each jurisdiction.

In *Ivax Pharmaceuticals v. AstraZeneca* (May 28, 2004), the patentee sought to stay proceedings for revocation pending determination of EPO opposition proceedings which would probably take a further four and a half years. Here the applicant, having delayed bringing the revocation proceedings and having filed its opposition on the last permitted day, failed to satisfy the court that it could not afford to wait for the EPO decision. The *prima facie* desirability of a stay had not been rebutted and it was therefore granted.

Disclosure

61.49   *—Breadth of disclosure in patent litigation*

The provisions of former CPR 49EPD 9 are now to be found in CPR 63PD 5, see also CPR 63.8 (reprinted respectively *infra* in §§ F63PD.5 and F63.8)

Where disclosure is sought from a third party under CPR 31.17, it is necessary to identify the documents sought and show (in respect of each) that disclosure would be material to the decision sought. This is not so if the anticipated disclosure amounts only to a personal expression of obviousness (*American Home Products v. Novartis* BL C/53/00, *noted* IPD 24010). However, this decision was reversed on appeal ([2001] FSR 784) because the issue was seen as one of possible lack of novelty depending on whether the inventor had made a prior, non-confidential, disclosure to that third party. In assessing whether any relevant disclosures had been made in confidential circumstances, all the requested documents dated less than two years after the priority date were seen to be relevant to the issue of implied confidentiality by conduct.

For the possibility of obtaining disclosure in the United States for use in foreign proceedings under 28 USC 1782, see the paper by J. Fellas ([2000] EIPR 546).

61.50   *—Disclosure in patent litigation*

The provisions of former CPR 49EPD 9 are now to be found in CPR 63PD 5. See also CPR 63.8 (reprinted respectively *infra* in §§ F63PD.5 and F63.8)

In *Oxford Gene Technology v. Affymetrix (No. 2)* ([2001] RPC 310 (CA)), the decision in *Bonzel v. Intervention (No. 2)*, cited in the Main Work, was re-interpreted as not necessarily requiring full disclosure of background documents relating to the issue of discretion, the extent of such disclosure being within the discretion of the court; and, where disclosure is given, this can be done by restrictions on inspection of the documents and without waiver of privilege.

61.53   *—Application for further disclosure*

In *Rockwater v. Coflexip* (BL C/46/02, *noted* IPD 25085) the defendant had served a process description under CPR PD49E, para. 9.2(1) (now CPR 63PD 5.1). The claimant contended that the description was not adequate and sought full disclosure. The court declined holding that disclosure should only be required if found to be essential, but ordered that the alleged deficiencies be identified in correspondence and the description then clarified. In further proceedings in relation to the same patent (*Technip's Patent* ([2004] RPC 919)) see § 125.15 *infra*, and the case comment by Katharine Stephens in [2004] *CIPA* 224), the Court of Appeal commented that it would be desirable in future cases if the claimant required that the process description be formally proved by a witness at trial.

—Limitation on use of documents produced on disclosure   **61.54**

Instance v. Denny Bros, cited in the Main Work, has been reported ([2000] FSR 869 and on appeal at [2002] RPC 321). In *Bourns v. Raychem*, cited in the Main Work, subsequent proceedings took place in which leave was sought to use in contempt proceedings a document disclosed on compulsion during taxation of costs: such leave was refused because previously the claimant had been awarded indemnity costs with damages to be assessed so that it was considered now too late to bring contempt proceedings on the same facts ([2000] FSR 841).

Permission to use, in foreign litigation, test results produced in the course of English litigation but not yet presented in open court was refused in *SmithKline Beecham v. Apotex* (BL C/7/03, *noted* IPD 26071), but was allowed on appeal ([2004] FSR 133; [2004] IP&T 62).

The provisions of former CPR 49EPD 9 are now to be found in CPR 63PD 5. See also CPR 63.8 (reprinted respectively *infra* in §§ F63PD.5 and F63.8).

—Further confidentiality restrictions on disclosure documents   **61.55**

In a further judgment in relation to *Pfizer's Patent* (cited as *Lilly Icos v. Pfizer* ([2002] FSR 809)) it was held that advertising figures disclosed by Pfizer in support of an argument of commercial success should be kept confidential as an exception to the general rule that justice should take place in open court and that confidentiality restrictions should normally cease on the document being referred to in evidence. In this case the expenditure had not been in issue in the trial. It was emphasised that this was not to be taken as deciding that figures for advertising expenditure can be kept confidential in every case, without, as here, a particularly good reason.

In *Dyson v. Hoover (No. 3)* ([2002] RPC 841) (the inquiry into damages) it was confirmed that all parties should have access to the same material that the judge himself had access to in coming to his conclusion. It was only in exceptional cases that a party could be prevented from having access to information which would play a substantial part in the case. The burden of showing why disclosure should not be given was on the party seeking to restrict disclosure. There was a necessity for disclosure which could only be displaced for good cause. The relevant documents were ordered disclosed subject to confidentiality arrangements already in place.

Cross-applications for further disclosure subject to confidentiality restrictions were allowed in *Intel v. Via Technologies* (BL C/36/02).

An application for early limited disclosure of sales figures was made in *Unilin Beheer v. Berry Floor* (PCC January 17, 2003, *noted* IPD 26012) to allow the claimant to consider the viability of a possible claim for relief under section 69, subject to restrictions on disclosure to solicitors and counsel only.

Inspection of property   **61.57**

Former CPR 49EPD 7.4 has been subsumed into the general CPR which require a case to be fully pleaded. CPR 49EPD 12.3 has been replaced by CPR 63PD 11.5(2) (reprinted *infra* in § F63PD.11).

Leave for employees of the patentee to attend an inspection of the processes of the defendant in India were refused as excessive in *Niche Generics v. Lundbeck* (BL C/17/03). Inspection of confidential procedures by a competitor should be strictly controlled.

61.58 *Admissions*

Former CPR 49EPD 8 has been subsumed into the general CPR, see particularly § E32.18 in the Main Work. Paragraph 11 of the Patents Court Guide has become paragraph 13 in its new version, see § G13 *infra*.

61.59 *Experiments*

Former CPR 49EPD 10 has been replaced by CPR 63PD 9 (reprinted *infra* at § F63PD.9). For the reference to § G22A.10, see the new version thereof reprinted *infra*.

In *SmithKline Beecham's* [PMS] *Patent (No. 2)* ([2003] RPC 607) experiments had been conducted on the question of anticipation by an earlier application forming part of the state of the art under s. 2(3) (see § 2.24). The experimenters chosen were a highly distinguished team consisting of Professor Sir Jack Baldwin FRS of Oxford University and Dr Robert Adlington, described by the professor as "the best practical organic chemist he had ever had working for him". The judge commented that "one might have thought that a team of ordinary ability might have been engaged, ... not world champions". Surprise was also expressed that in attempting to determine what the effect of carrying out the experiments described in the prior application was, the experimental team had not simply been given the relevant application and asked to carry out its teaching. In fact they had been given a somewhat different protocol and this had not been explained. Nevertheless the results obtained by the Oxford team were accepted and formed an important part in the subsequent decisions on anticipation. At first instance the claim was held to lack novelty but on appeal ([2003] RPC 769), the decision was reversed because it was not possible to repeat the example of the prior art without modification and so there were no clear and unmistakeable directions to make the claimed compound (see §§ 2.09, 2.12 and 2.24 *supra*). A further appeal to the House of Lords is scheduled for April 2005.

The judge in *Merck v. Generics [Alendronate process]* ([2004] RPC 607) was critical of the experiments conducted and the expense incurred. He indicated that, in the future, "no experiments should be conducted going to *Catnic* -type questions of construction unless the court has given informed permission for them in advance".

In *Unilin Beheer v. Berry Floor* ([2004] FSR 238), the court indicated that the experiments performed by both parties on the issue of infringement had been of no real assistance to the court, and that it would not be normal for experiments to be approved in proceedings before the Patents County Court.

61.60 *Evidence*

Former CPR 49EPD 12 has been subsumed into the general CPR requiring a case to be distinctly pleaded. The provisions concerning a pleading of commercial success are now to be found in CPR 63PD 5.1(3) and 5.2 (reprinted *infra* in § F63PD.5). The reference to paragraph 12 of the *Patents Court Guide* has become paragraph 13 in its new version, see § G22A.13 *infra*. The use of models or apparatus now requires an application to the court for directions, see CPR 63PD 10 (reprinted *infra* at § F63PD.10) and paragraph 12 of the new *Patents Court Guide* (reprinted at § G22A.12 *infra*).

It is inadmissible for a witness to opine on questions which the court itself has to decide, such as claim construction, infringement, obviousness and added matter, see *Amersham v. Amicon* (BL C/49/00, *noted* IPD 24011) where the court deprecated the expense incurred in this inappropriate exercise.

There is no property in a witness and, hence, any attempt to limit by contract a person's freedom to give evidence on behalf of another party, especially as an expert witness, would be contrary to public policy, see *Pfizer's Patent* (BL C/36/00, *noted* IPD 23089).

In *Cadcam Technology v. Proel* (BL CC/61/00) the Patents County Court Deputy Judge criticised certain expert witnesses for lack of impartiality. One expert was found not to have complied with the rule which requires the first duty of an expert witness to be to the court, rather than to the party who calls him.

Another case in which the evidence of an expert was criticised is *Tickner v. Honda* (BL C/68/01, *noted* IPD 25020) in which one witness was held to have given "astonishing answers" to questions. The cross-examiner elected to terminate the examination, which the court held he was entitled to do: "once it has been shown that an expert's evidence ... is clearly and obviously untenable it is legitimate for the tribunal to ... disregard his evidence".

In *AB Hässle's Patents* ([2002] FSR 564) the judge summarised the function of experts thus: "In considering the issue of obviousness, it is necessary to determine what the notional skilled addressee would have thought and done at the priority date.... In the end, this is a question which must be answered by the court. In doing so it is normally assisted by the evidence of experts on either side". The judge referred to the reference made in *Pfizer's Patent* ([2001] FSR 16) that the witnesses will frequently be at the top of their fields, may well be inventive and will come to the case with personal idiosyncrasies, and thus will not be typical of the notional uninventive worker. "Subject to that caveat, the evidence of experts is valuable and frequently essential in helping the court to understand a field of technology and the approaches which are likely to have occurred to relevant workers. In the *AB Hässle* case the evidence of one of the witnesses was criticised for being "more akin to that of an advocate than an expert" possibly because of "over exposure to the patentee's case", the same witness having been involved as an expert in the same case in several other countries. The patentee's application to the Court of Appeal for a new trial on the grounds of apparent bias on the part of the judge was refused (see [2003] FSR 413; [2003] IP&T 266 and § 97.19 *infra*).

In *Glaxo Group's Patent* ([2004] RPC 843), an expert for one of the claimants revealed that he had been telephoned by a representative of the defendant in which he was said to have expressed surprise that the expert was acting for the claimants and indicating that this was viewed unfavourably by the defendant and might have consequences for the receipt by the expert of research funding from the defendant in the future. The judge required the representative of the defendant to appear before him and, although he decided not to take the matter further in that instance, made the comment that " ... expert witnesses are relied on by the court to express a disinterested view. Any pressure, and any act which may have the effect of placing pressure, on a witness may be a contempt of court and dealt with accordingly".

In *Smithkline Beecham v. Apotex* ([2004] FSR 523), evidence was given for the patentee by one of the inventors who had been involved with the patented product for many years such that the judge commented that he "came to the case with much special knowledge and belief that would not be part of the skilled person's qualities".

In *Marshalltown Trowel v. Ceka Works* ([2001] FSR 633), an action for infringement in relation to one patent originally included in the claim had been dropped when experts' reports were exchanged. The court felt that the claimant should have realised that it could not maintain its case of infringement on the evidence by the date when the parties had agreed to exchange the names of their experts and should not have left the decision until after the experts' reports had been completed and exchanged. Accordingly the defendants would obtain their costs on an indemnity basis in relation to that part of the action from the date agreed for the exchange of experts' names. The claimants were also held to have been unreasonable in requiring proof by witnesses of the dates of certain publications when there was no apparent reason to doubt their dates. Indemnity costs were awarded on that issue also, and an interim award of costs was made.

In *Micromatic v. Dispense Systems* (BL C/20/01), the judge found it very helpful to have samples of the products (valves) in court and commented that "a model is worth a thousand words".

In *Arrow Generics v. Generics UK* (BL C/52/02), the parties were each applicants for revocation of a patent of Merck, and one was ordered to supply details of its experiments to the other since the applications had been ordered to be tried together.

In *Schering v. CIPLA* (BL C/134/04 *noted*, IP D 28009, *The Times*, December 1, 2004), the defendant wrote to the patentee stating that it intended to market a patented product with a view to reaching a commercial settlement. The letter was marked "without prejudice". Infringement proceedings brought by the patentee were struck out on the basis that the court should assess what the reasonable recipient would perceive as the message which the author had intended to convey; on that basis the letter indicated a willingness to negotiate and the action was therefore struck out, because without the letter there was no evidence of infringement.

61.62 *Procedure at trial*

Case management of a case in the Patents Court or Patents County Court is now governed by CPR 63.7 (reprinted *infra* at § F63.7) and see also §§ F63PD.4–63PD.9 (reprinted *infra*). The *Patents Court Guide* has been reissued as reprinted in Appendix G *infra*. It contains a revised form of the Standard Form of Order for Directions, for which see §§ G22A.1–G22A.19 *infra*. The procedure is now more generally aligned to that of other litigation in the Chancery Division, but particular attention should be paid to paragraphs 2, 3, 9, 11, 14 and 20 of the revised *Patents Court Guide* (reprinted in §§ G02, G03, G11, G14 and G20 *infra*). Paragraph 9(a) states that:

"Bundling is of considerable importance and should be done intelligently. The general guidance given in Appendix 2 of the *Chancery Guide* should be followed. Solicitors and patent agents who fail to do so may be required to explain why and may be penalised personally in costs."

This Appendix is available on the website at www.courtservice/using__courts/guides__notices/notices/chanc/index.htm.

Paragraph 10 of the *Patents Court Guide* introduces a "Streamlined procedure" (replacing the former "Simplified procedure", for which see § G08 in the Main Work), this generally avoiding disclosure and cross-examination if there is agreement between the parties. Paragraph 10(e) states that "The parties' legal advisers must draw their clients' attention to the availability of a streamlined procedure in the Patents Court and the Patents County Court".

62.01 **SECTION 62—Restrictions on recovery of damages for infringement**

Subsections 62 (2) and (3) were each prospectively amended by the Patents Act 2004 (c. 16, s. 2 and Sched. 2(15)), as follows, each to be brought into effect when the EPC revisions agreed in 2000 come into force.

In subsection (2), the words "any further period specified under" (appearing in lines 3 and 4 of the reprint in the Main Work) were replaced by the words "the further period specified in"; and, In subsection (3), lines 4–6 (as reprinted in the Main Work) were amended to read:

"allow the amendment unless the court or comptroller is satisfied that—

(a) the specification of the patent as published was framed in good faith and with reasonable skill and knowledge, and

(b) the proceedings are brought in good faith."

62.04 *Lost rights after restoration or late renewal (subs. (2))*

The amendment to subsection (2), noted in § 62.01 *supra*, conforms to the reference to the period which is specified in section 25(4), as amended (for which see § 25.01 *supra*).

Damages after infringement (subs. (3))   **62.05**

The amendment of subsection (3) (as noted in § 62.01 *supra*), has the effect of providing that, where damages are claimed for a period before (validating) amendments are made to the patent, the court is entitled to refuse to award such damages unless it is satisfied, not only that the patent as published was framed in good faith and with reasonable skill and knowledge, but also that the infringement claim was "brought in good faith". Thus, when this statutory amendment is brought into force, infringement damages may be denied where the patentee knew, or ought to have known, that during a period in respect of which a claim for damages is made the patent was not wholly valid. However, this further provision does not apply in respect of acts of infringement occurring after the date of the amendment.

SECTION 63—Relief for infringement of partially valid patent   **63.01**

Subsection (2) was prospectively amended, and new subsection (4) added, by the Patents Act 2004 (c. 16, ss. 2 and 3) and Sched. 2(16)), each to be brought into effect when the EPC revisions agreed in 2000 come into force. However, that Act (by Sched. 2(16)) also replaced the word "plaintiff" in subsection (2) by "claimant", this change being effective from January 1, 2005 (S.I. 2004 No. 3205, a. 2(f)(k)). When the prospective amendments are brought into effect, subsection (2), (as reprinted in lines 1–3 of page 633 of the Main Work) will then read:

"... or expenses, except where the claimant or pursuer proves that—
>   **(a) the specification of the patent was framed in good faith and with reasonable skill and knowledge, and**
>   **(b) the proceedings are brought in good faith, and in that event the court or comptroller may grant relief in...; "**

and new subsection (4) will read:

(4) The court or the comptroller may also grant relief under this section in the case of a European patent (UK) on condition that the claims of the patent are limited to its or his satisfaction by the European Patent Office at the request of the proprietor.

COMMENTARY ON SECTION 63

Scope of the section   **63.02**

In *SmithKline Beecham v. Apotex* ([2003] FSR 524 and 544), no reason was seen why an interim injunction could not be based on a partially valid patent.

Requirement for good faith, skill and knowledge in patent draftmanship   **63.03**
(subs. (2))

The *Nutrinova* case, cited on page 635 of the Main Work, has been published as *Nutrinova v. Scanchem (No. 2)* ([2001] FSR 831).

Relief was granted in *Kirin-Amgen's Patent* ([2002] RPC 851), the court holding that the fact that "a patent may have been drafted so as to include invalid claims should not, in the absence of special factors, prevent the patentee being entitled to the full range of relief against an infringer of one or more of the valid claims, provided it is a case where section 63(2) does not apply". The court found that errors in a minor proportion of the description had not influenced the decision on the invalidity of the claims sought to be deleted and had not led to the EPO or readers of the specification being particularly adversely affected. The claims were held valid in the Court of Appeal (*Kirin-Amgen v. Transkaryotic Therapies* [2003] RPC 31), but then found invalid by the House of Lords ([2005] RPC 169).

The amendments made to subsection (2) (as noted in § 63.01 *supra*): (1) have the effect of: changing the word "plaintiff" to "claimant" in conformity with the current practice under the CPR; and (2) providing that, where damages are claimed for infringement of a patent which is held to be only partially valid, the court or Comptroller is entitled to refuse to award such damages unless it/he is satisfied, not only that the patent as published was framed in good faith and with reasonable skill and knowledge, but also that the infringement claim was "brought in good faith".

Thus, when these statutory amendments are brought into force, infringement damages may be denied where the patentee knew, or ought to have known, when the claim was made, that the patent was not wholly valid. Where the patent is satisfactorily amended to remove the partial invalidity, section 62(3) will then apply instead and damages are then available for acts of infringement committed after the date of the amendment, see § 62.05 *supra*.

63.04 *Amendment required as a condition of relief on partially valid patent (subss. (3) and (4))*

New subsection (4) applies to European patents (UK) and is parallel to subsection (3). However, when the amendments to the section are brought into effect, and such a patent is found partially valid in UK proceedings, the patentee, instead of being required to amend that UK patent, may be required to limit the claims of the European patent as a whole in limitation proceedings brought before the EPO under EPCa. 105A in a way which satisfies the court or the Comptroller as the case may be. Damages may then perhaps only become available from the date when the necessary approval of the amendments has been given by the court or Comptroller, assuming that damages are anyway not precluded because of a finding of non compliance with (amended) subsection (2).

SECTION 64 [SUBSTITUTED]—Right to continue use begun before priority date

COMMENTARY ON SECTION 64

64.03 *The requirement for the rights to arise from an "infringing act"*

The Court of Appeal decision in *Bristol-Myers Squibb v. Baker Norton*, cited in the Main Work, has now been reported at [2001] RPC 1.

64.06 *The nature and extent of the right provided by section 64*

In "*Biegevorrichtung* ", [2002] GRUR 231, the German Supreme Court held that the prior user right in German law equivalent to that provided by section 64 does not go beyond what is actually used so that a prior user cannot use further developments going beyond the prior use. This case is noted in *Patent World*, August 2002 (No. 144), page 5.

SECTION 65—Certificate of contested validity of patent

COMMENTARY ON SECTION 65

65.03 *Grant of certificate of contested validity (subs. (1))*

In the Australian case of *Datadot v. Alpha Microtech* ((2004) 59 IPR 402), the court declined to issue a certificate of contested validity because no evidence had been led on the claim for revocation and therefore there had been no contest to validity.

SECTION 67—Proceedings for infringement by exclusive licensee

COMMENTARY ON SECTION 67

Definition of "exclusive licence"   **67.03**

An exclusive sub-licence granted by the licensee with the patentee's consent which conferred the exclusive licence on the sub-licensee to the exclusion of the licensee was accepted as an exclusive licence giving the sub-licensee the entitlement to sue instead of the licensee in *Dendron v. Regents of the University of California* ([2004] FSR 861).

Right of exclusive licensee to sue for infringement   **67.04**

That the exclusive licensee's entitlement to sue does not depend on registration of the licence was accepted in *Dendron v. Regents of the University of California* ([2004] FSR 861), the only limitation being on the recovery of damages (s.68).

SECTION 68—Effect of non-registration on infringement proceedings

COMMENTARY ON SECTION 68

Effect of non-registration of an assignment or exclusive licence   **68.04**

In *LG Electronics v. NCR Financial Solutions* ([2002] FSR 428) there had been a series of assignments, each of which was stated to include the right to claim damages for past infringements. However, until registration of the assignments there was no valid claim to damages or an account of profits in the name of the subsequent assignees, and relief for the current owner was therefore limited to damages accrued during the period of ownership of the original owner, and the period after registration of the assignments, but not the intervening periods.

SECTION 69—Infringement of rights conferred by publication of application

COMMENTARY ON SECTION 69

Rights conferred by the section (subs. (1))   **69.04**

In *Spring Form v. Toy Brokers* ([2002] FSR 276) it was held that an account of profits could be claimed in respect of infringing activities before the grant of the patent. Subsection 69(1) refers only to damages in this context and the Main Work accordingly refers to the subsection conferring "… the right to bring proceedings for damages (but not for an account of profits) …". Unless this point should be reconsidered by the Court of Appeal, the statement in the Main Work (although reflecting the plain words of the statute) must be taken to be wrong, and claims to accounts of profits for infringements between publication and grant will apparently (as in this case) be entertained by the Courts.

70.01 **SECTION 70—Remedy for groundless threats of infringement proceedings**

The Patents Act 2004 (c. 16, s. 12 and Sched. 2(17)) amended section 70, with effect from January 1, 2005, although the unamended section continues to apply to any alleged threat communicated before that date (S.I. 2004 No. 3205. aa. 2(d)(f)(k) and 9(3)). These amendments substituted new forms of subsections (2), (4) and (5) and inserted new subsections (2A) and (6), respectively reading:

(2) In any such proceedings the **claimant** [*plaintiff*] or pursuer shall, **subject to subsection (2A) below, be entitled to the relief claimed** if he proves that the threats were so made and satisfies the court that he is a person aggrieved by them [*be entitled to the relief claimed unless —*

(a) the defendant or defender proves that the acts in respect of which proceedings were threatened constitute or, if done, would constitute an infringement of a patent; and

(b) the patent alleged to be infringed is not shown by the plaintiff or pursuer to be invalid in a relevant respect].

(2A) If the defendant or defender proves that the acts in respect of which proceedings were threatened constitute or, if done, would constitute an infringement of a patent—

    (a) the claimant or pursuer shall be entitled to the relief claimed only if he shows that the patent alleged to be infringed is invalid in a relevant respect;

    (b) even if the claimant or pursuer does show that the patent is invalid in a relevant respect, he shall not be entitled to the relief claimed if the defendant or defender proves that at the time of making the threats he did not know, and had no reason to suspect, that the patent was invalid in that respect.

(4) Proceedings may not be brought under this section for—

    (a) a threat to bring proceedings for an infringement alleged to consist of making or importing a product for disposal or of using a process, or

    (b) a threat, made to a person who has made or imported a product for disposal or used a process, to bring proceedings for an infringement alleged to consist of doing anything else in relation to that product or process.

(5) For the purposes of this section a person does not threaten another person with proceedings for infringement of a patent if he merely—

    (a) provides factual information about the patent,

    (b) makes enquiries of the other person for the sole purpose of discovering whether, or by whom, the patent has been infringed as mention in subsection (4)(a) above, or

    (c) makes an assertion about the patent for the purpose of any enquiries so made.

[*It is hereby declared that a mere notification of the existence of a patent does not constitute a threat of proceedings within the meaning of this section].*

(6) In proceedings under this section for threats by one person (A) to another (B) in respect of an alleged infringement of a patent for an invention, it shall be a defence for A to prove that he used his best endeavours, without success, to discover—

    (a) where the invention is a product, the identity of the person (if any) who made or (in the case of an imported product) imported it for disposal;

   (b) **where the invention is a process and the alleged infringement consists of offering it for use, the identity of a person who used the process;**

   (c) **where the invention is a process and the alleged infringement is an act falling within section 60(1)(c) above, the identity of the person who used the process to produce the product in question;**

and that he notified B accordingly, before or at the time of making the threats, identifying the endeavours used.

COMMENTARY ON SECTION 70

Scope of the section   **70.02**

The amendments made to section 70 first replace the word "plaintiff" by "claimant" in conformity with the current practice under the CPR. Of more importance is that the grounds for bringing a successful action under the section against a person who has made threats of infringement have been considerably restricted, as indicated in §§ 70.05, 70.07 and 70.08 *infra*, and see also an article by W. Cook ([2004] *CIPA* 698). Obviously, it will take time for decisions of the courts to determine the actual effect of these changes, which applies only to threats made after January 1, 2005. The effect of decisions given under the original form of the section is therefore problematical, and these decisions should thus be treated with caution.

Icon Health v. Precise Exercise Equipment (BL C/29/01, *noted* IPD 24050) was an example of a case where relief for unjustified threats was ordered, the patent being held not to be infringed and it therefore not being necessary to consider the validity of the patent.

In *Kenburn Waste Management v. Bergmann* ([2002] FSR 696) the parties had previously settled a threats action by means of undertakings by the German defendant that it would not utter further threats. Upon the defendant being alleged to have breached the undertakings, questions arose as to the proper forum for adjudication of this further dispute. The defendant argued that because he was domiciled in Germany and operated his business from there, the proper forum for the dispute was Germany. The court considered the relevant provisions of the Brussels Convention and held that because the object of the contract was to achieve results in the UK (fulfilment of the negative obligation not to make threats), and because the contract was concerned with the purely English right of action under section 70, the contract was strongly connected with the UK and therefore the matter was actionable there. The judgment was upheld on appeal ([2002] FSR 711).

What constitutes a threat (subs. (1))   **70.03**

Kooltrade v. XTS, cited in the Main Work, has been published ([2001] FSR 158).

Malicious falsehood and contempt of court   **70.04**

In a dispute in which records were produced of processes used by the defendant which the claimant alleged to have been forged, the claimant issued statements implying that the court had ordered investigations into the alleged forgery. An order for disclosure as to the origin of these statements was made, the court making it clear that there had as yet been not even a preliminary finding with regard to the allegations (*Lundbeck v. Lagap* (BL C/5/03)).

Justification (subss. (2) and (2A))   **70.05**

New subsection (2A) provides that, in addition to a defence that the threat was justified because there had been infringement, the defendant can counter a plea that the patent was invalid (and hence not infringed) and hence avoid sanction under the section by a showing that he did not know, and had no reason to suspect, that the patent was invalid. Of course, the onus for establishing that invalidity remains with the claimant, but that of itself will not provide grounds for relief under the section where the ground of invalidity is one not envisaged by the person when issuing the threat.

70.06 *Relief (subs. (3))*

In further proceedings in *Kooltrade v. XTS* ([2002] FSR 764), the claimant sought to enforce the court's judgment by joinder of other parties (including a director of the defendant and the solicitors who had issued the threats), the defendant itself having gone into liquidation. The court held that a new trial would be required to assess the liability of the proposed further defendants and fresh proceedings would need to be commenced to deal with any claim against them.

70.07 *Exclusion of threats made to primary infringers (subs. (4))*

The amendments to section 70 set out in § 70.01 *supra*, amend subsection (4) to provide that the protection previously provided thereby that the threat was only made in respect of an act alleged to consist of making or importing the patented product for disposal, or of using the patented process (*i.e.* acts of "primary" infringement), is now extended (by subsection (4)(b)) to threats to bring proceedings in respect of "secondary" acts of infringement, *i.e.* of selling or stocking the patented product or offering the patented product for use, but provided that the person threatened has made or imported that product for disposal (or used that process).

70.08 *Mere notification of patent existence is not a threat (subss. (5) and (6))*

Under the amendments set out in § 70.01 *supra*, subsection (5) has been re written to enlarge the definition of acts which cannot be construed as a threat to bring proceedings. These are now:
(a) providing any purely factual information about the patent (not merely, as formerly, the mere notification of its existence);
(b) making enquiries to find out if there has been a primary infringement and, if so, by whom; and
(c) making assertions about the patent for the purposes of making such enquiries.

It is apparently envisaged that, as a result of these changes, an enquirer will be able to make assertions regarding an alleged primary infringement, as part of his attempt to trace the primary infringer, but that assertions regarding an alleged secondary infringement will not necessarily be excluded from the definition of a "threat". Of course, whether an assertion does in fact amount to a threat will have to be decided taking into account all the relevant circumstances.

Moreover, new subsection (6) provides a further defence to a claim under the section, even when the threat is made against a secondary infringer, although only in limited circumstances. Under this subsection, it is a defence to the threatener to prove that he had used his best endeavours, without success, to discover the identity of a person who has made, or imported for disposal, the patented product, or has used the patented process, or has used that process to produce the product in question, although only where the threatener had notified the person threatened before, or at the time of making the threat, and has identified the endeavours used. This provision is intended to enable a proprietor to approach, for example, a retailer or stockist, in order to get the infringement dispute resolved (and in doing so threaten the latter with infringement proceedings). However, the defence is only available when "best" endeavours have been used to obtain the information identifying the primary infringer and, when the person threatened is supplied (no later than the time of making the threat) with information setting out the scope of these (unsuccessful) endeavours.

PRACTICE UNDER SECTION 70

70.09

CPR 49EPD has been replaced by CPR 63 and the Practice Directions thereunder. These are reprinted in Appendix F *infra*. CPR EPD 3.2 has become CPR 63.16 (reprinted at § F63.16 *infra*). CPR 63PD 2.2(c) (reprinted in § E63PD.2 *infra*) specifically requires actions under section 70 to be brought in either the Patents Court or a Patents County Court. *The Patents Court Guide* has also been re-issued, for which see Appendix G *infra*.

SECTION 71—Declaration or declarator as to non-infringement

COMMENTARY ON SECTION 71

The advantages and disadvantages of using the section   **71.04**

In *Approved Prescription Services v. Merck* (BL C/3/03, *noted* IPD 26026) the Patents Court ordered an early trial of an issue of non-infringement limited to one day where this had the possibility to determine whether or not the claimant could market its product, even though the patent was also the subject of an invalidity challenge by other parties.

Requirements for seeking a declaration (subs.(1))   **71.05**

In *Denman's Patent* (BL O/369/01), the practice reflected in the Main Work of commencing proceedings for a declaration without waiting for the proprietor to give an acknowledgement of non-infringement was disapproved. The applicant in this case had written to the proprietor for an acknowledgement as required, but then applied for the declaration on the next working day. This was held to be at odds with the Civil Procedure Rules in accordance with which "parties are expected to try and settle their disputes first before resorting to litigation." Because the decision in *MMD Design's Patent* (and the passage referring to it in the Main Work) had encouraged practitioners to believe that it was acceptable to proceed in this way (or even to defer seeking an acknowledgement until after the application under section 71(1) had been filed), the Hearing Officer declined to dismiss the application in the *Denman* case. However it has been made clear that the Comptroller is likely to take a different line in future cases. (See [2001] *CIPA* 504).

The Main Work records the decision in *Impro's Patent* ([1998] FSR 299) in which a declaration of non-infringement was refused. In a decision in the same court concerning the same patent but by a different judge, *Arjo and Impro v. Liko* (BL C/52/01, *noted* [2001] *CIPA* 575, 628 and IPD 25006), the court held that it could not agree with the construction placed on the patent in the previous case and granted a declaration, holding that certain features previously determined as inessential were in fact essential features (see also § 125.19 *infra*).

Effect of declaration   **71.07**

The effect of the onus of proof being on a claimant is well-illustrated by *Rohm & Haas v. Collag* ([2001] FSR 426) where a declaration was refused under the section, but where a finding of infringement might well have failed had the patentee been the claimant. This view was upheld on appeal ([2002] FSR 445).

PRACTICE UNDER SECTION 71

71.08 *Procedure before the Comptroller*

In *Ash & Lacy's Patent No. 2240558* ([2002] RPC 939), section 71 proceedings were stayed in favour of section 72 proceedings in order that the declarant applicant would not have to make inconsistent statements as to the extent of protection proved by the claims in relation to an insufficiency allegation. It was here noted that section 107(4) provides no power for the Comptroller to order security for costs in proceedings under section 71.

71.09 *Proceedings before the court*

CPR 49EPD has been replaced by CPR 63 and the Practice Directions thereunder. These are reprinted in Appendix F *infra*. CPR 49EPD 3.2 has become CPR 63.16 (reprinted at § F63.16 *infra*). *The Patents Court Guide* has also been re-issued, for which see Appendix G *infra*.

72.01 **SECTION 72—Power to revoke patents on application**

The RRO (a. 12) amended subsection 72(1)(d) by replacing the words "section 15(4)" by "section 15(9)". This amendment took effect from January 1, 2005, but the previous version of the section continues to apply to patents granted on applications then "pending", a term defined in Note 3 to § 15.01 *supra*.

Also, the Patents Act 2004 (c. 16, Scheds. 2(18) and 3) prospectively amended the preamble to subsection (1) to read:

"Subject to the following provisions of this Act, the court or comptroller may [*on the application of any person*] by order revoke a patent for an invention **on the application of any person (including the proprietor of the patent)** on (but only on) any of the following grounds, that is to say—;"

and this Act (by s. 4 and Sched. 3) also prospectively amended subsection 72(4) by omission of the words "under section 75 below" (appearing in lines 5 and 6 of the reprint in the Main Work); and adding new subsection 72(4A) reading:

(4A) The reference in subsection (4) above to the specification being amended is to its being amended under section 75 below and also, in the case of a European patent (UK), to its being amended under any provision of the European Patent Convention under which the claims of the patent may be limited by amendment at the request of the proprietor.

These prospective amendments will be brought into effect when the EPC revisions agreed in 2000 come into force.

RELEVANT RULES—RULES 21, 75, 76, 103, 107, 109 AND 112

72.06 **Rule 104—Statutory declarations and affidavits**

and

Rule 104A—Witness statements

In the reprinting of rule 104A(1)(a) in the Main Work, the words "and dated" should follow "signed".

72.08 **Rule 106—Directions to the furnishing of documents**

The rule title reprinted in the Main Work should be as given above.

Rule 107—Supporting statements or evidence

In rule 107(2), "36A," has been inserted before "40(3)" (S.I. 2004 No. 2358).

COMMENTARY ON SECTION 72

Forum for revocation

72.13

CPR 49EPD has been replaced by CPR 63 and the Practice Directions thereunder. These are reprinted in Appendix F *infra*. *The Patents Court Guide* has also been re-issued, for which see Appendix G *infra*. When proceedings are brought in the Patents Court or the Patents County Court, CPR 63PD 11.2(4) (reprinted in § F63PD.11 *infra*) requires (as from April 1, 2003) that a copy of the required 'Grounds of Invalidity' document (and any amendment thereof) must be sent to the Comptroller where it should become available to public inspection on the patent file, on which see § 61.42 *supra*.

Who may apply to revoke, and when

72.15

The amendment to subsection (1), noted in § 72.01 *supra*, will (when made effective) make it clear that even a proprietor may seek to revoke his own patent; however, presumably only in part. The amendment being made to section 36(3) (for which see § 36.05 *supra*) makes clear that, unless co owners agree that it should be possible, one co owner may not seek revocation against the wishes of the others.

In *Cairnstores v. AB Hässle* ([2002] FSR 564) the defendant tried to have the action struck out as an abuse of process because the defendant company had only recently been incorporated and appeared to lack assets or trading activities. However the action was allowed to proceed subject to security for costs being given. The court held that the words "any person" in section 72 of the Act did not require a person applying to revoke a patent to have any interest, commercial or otherwise, in the outcome of the proceedings. There were circumstances in which it could be envisaged that the commencement of revocation proceedings might amount to an abuse of process, which the court defined as the use of the court's procedure for an improper or collateral purpose, but there was no suggestion of that in the case in hand.

In *Oystertec's Patent* (BL O/298/02) a revocation action was allowed to proceed in the name of a firm of patent agents, the decision in *Cairnstores* (*supra*) being seen as a precedent binding on the Patent Office, despite a further argument that to permit an application for revocation in the name of a "man of straw" was contrary to the Human Rights Act 1998. Potential difficulties as to disclosure, cross-examination and estoppel were not seen as sufficient to change that view although they might have to be considered at a later stage in the proceedings. The Patent Office decision was upheld on appeal to the court ([2003] RPC 559).

Insufficient description (subs. (1)(c))

—General

72.18

Where insufficiency is pleaded as a ground of invalidity before the Patents Court or the Patents County Court, CPR 63PD 11.3(2) (reprinted *infra* in § F63PD.11) requires that the 'Grounds of Invalidity' document must state "which examples of the invention cannot be made to work and in which respects they do not work or do not work as described in the specification".

Impermissible amendments (subs. (1)(d) and (e))

72.25 | *—General*

Divisional applications are now made under replaced section 15(9), rather than as under section 15(4) as stated in the Main Work. Subsection (1)(d) has been amended accordingly (see § 72.01 *supra*).

72.26 *—Effect of subsection (1)(d) and (e) in practice*

Monsanto v. Merck and the Court of Appeal decision in *Cartonneries de Thulin v. CTP White Knight,* each cited in the Main Work, have been respectively published [2002] RPC 709; [2002] IP&T 828 and [2001] RPC 107. *Stoves v. Baumatic* (BL C/27/00), likewise cited, has been noted (IPD 23086).

Monsanto v. Merck was upheld on this point on appeal (cited as *Pharmacia v. Merck* ([2002] RPC 775)), the court finding that the amendment to make the methylsulphonyl group obligatory amounted to making a new selection of compounds, but that that an amendment to further restrict the claim to a substituent already described as optional would not add matter but be a disclaimer which the patentee is entitled to make. The Main Work refers to the EPO Opposition Division coming to the opposite conclusion on added subject matter. However, the EPO Board of Appeal subsequently overruled that decision and revoked the patent for added matter.

In the quotation from *Bonzel v. Intervention (No.3)* ([1991] RPC 553) on page 682 the last two lines of sub-paragraph (3) should read:

"... subject-matter will be added *unless* such matter is clearly and unambiguously disclosed in the application either explicitly or implicitly."

72.27 | *Partial revocation (subss. (4) and (4A))*

In the case of a European patent (UK) which the court finds to be partially invalid, it may (under new subsection (4A), reprinted in § 72.01 *supra,* and when this is brought into force), instead of ordering this patent to be validated by amendment under section 75, allow the claims of the European patent as a whole to be limited by proceedings in the EPO under EPCa. 105A. Subsection (4) has been prospectively amended accordingly.

72.28 | *Estoppel (subss. (5) and (6))*

In *Coflexip v. Stolt Comex* ([2004] FSR 118 and 708) the plaintiffs sought a stay of proceedings in the damages enquiry on the basis that the patent in suit had been found invalid in subsequent proceedings (*Rockwater v. Coflexip* (BL C/15/03 , *noted* IPD 26039), subject to appeal (see § 125.13 *infra*). However, the patentee relied on the decision in *Poulton v. Adjustable Cover* (1908) 25 RPC 529 and 661, where it was held that the decision of patent validity and liability for damages created a cause of action estoppel preventing the defendant from relying on the decision in later proceedings. On that basis the inquiry into damages was ordered to continue. In appeal proceedings (*Technip's Patent,* [2004] RPC 919—see § 125.15 *infra*) the decision in the Rockwater case was then overturned and the patent again found to be valid.

72.30 *Concurrent proceedings*

In *Luk Lamellan's Patent* (BL O/379/02) it was pointed out that *Gibbons' Patent* referred to in the Main Work is in fact a case under the 1949 Act and is no longer applicable in view of the express terms of section 27(2) which provide that the amendment cannot be allowed where there are concurrent proceedings as to validity.

PRACTICE UNDER SECTION 72

Scope of this commentary on practice in revocation and other proceedings   **72.31**

CPR 49EPD has been replaced by CPR 63 and the Practice Directions thereunder. These are reprinted in Appendix F *infra*. *The Patents Court Guide* has also been re-issued, for which see Appendix G *infra*.

General procedure in inter partes applications made to the Comptroller   **72.33**

The revision of rule 107(2) (noted in § 72.09 *supra*) adds to it the procedure under rule 36A for reinstatement of an unintentional withdrawal of an application under new section 20A. for which see §§ 20A.02 and 20A.03 *supra*.

In *Ash & Lacy's Patent No. 2240558* ([2002] RPC 939), a Case Management Conference was held to decide various procedural disputes and an immediate award of costs was made to the party wholly successful at that Conference. In a subsequent decision (BL O/175/01), although the application for revocation had been withdrawn, the Comptroller in accordance with "long-standing practice" (as referred to in the Main Work) went on to consider whether to accept the notice of withdrawal or whether there were questions which should be considered further in the public interest. Having done so, it was held that the grounds for revocation of the patent had not been made out. The power of the Comptroller to continue the proceedings in this way was upheld in an application for judicial review of that decision before Mr Justice Laddie sitting as a judge of the Queen's Bench Division (Administrative Court) (*R v. Comptroller-General ex parte Ash & Lacy Building Products* [2002] RPC 939; [2002] IP&T 709). The same patent was then the subject of proceedings in the Patents County Court (*Ash & Lacy v. Fixing Point* (PCC July 24, 2002)). The patentee argued for a broader construction of claim than that given by the Patent Office but validity was upheld on the basis of a relatively narrow construction, which then led to a finding that it was not infringed by the defendant's product. So, in effect, the Patent Office's decision was vindicated.

Evidence was given by video link in *Interfilta (UK)'s Patent* ([2003] RPC 411) and an application to reopen the hearing on the ground that the witness had been accompanied and assisted by his own attorney such that his evidence was tainted was refused. It was indicated however that the Hearing Officer's Manual had been amended to make it clear that in future such cases the Patent Office would insist on the witness being supervised by an attorney who is independent of the parties.

The Patent Office has published a Litigation Section Manual which deals with the various procedures applicable to litigation before the comptroller. This is available on the Patent Office web site www.patent.gov.uk.

Time limits and extensions of time   **72.34**

Where, in proceedings before the Comptroller, the time of filing evidence by one party is set to begin when the other party has filed its evidence and that other party notifies the Comptroller that he does not wish to file any evidence, the Comptroller may now set a limit for the first party to file its evidence within such period as he may specify (see r. 110(11), reprinted in § 123.09 *infra*).

Statement of case   **72.37**

In *Ash & Lacy's Patent No. 2240559* (BL O/60/02) the claimant's statement of case as originally filed was described as "lamentable" having failed to plead the stated grounds properly, in particular having given no details of alleged "common general knowledge".

The claimant was allowed to amend the statement subject to a costs penalty (see § 72.53 *infra*), because it "is not in the public interest for bad patents to remain on the Register". The Hearing Officer also took note that the claimant could have refiled the application for revocation and observed that the "interests of speedy justice and minimising the period of uncertainty for the public at large would be better served by admitting the amendments than by requiring everything to start all over again".

On the sufficiency of a statement of case, the former CPR 49EPD 7.5 has been replaced by CPR 63PD 11.3(2) (reprinted in § F63PD.11).

72.39   *Counter-statement*

Where claim construction was the basis for an allegation of insufficiency, the patentee was ordered to expand his counter-statement which had made a mere denial of this allegation (*Ash & Lacy's Patent No. 2240558*, [2002] RPC 939).

An application for leave to amend a counter-statement was allowed as a matter of discretion in *Robinson Wiley's Patent* (BL O/228/02), the amendments being largely by way of clarification and not substantive.

Evidence

72.42   *—Powers of the Comptroller concerning evidence*

After the rounds of evidence provided by the rules, further evidence may be admitted in the discretion of the Comptroller. This discretion will not be exercised for evidence which could have been filed earlier, especially where it would result in delay because of the need to provide an opportunity for response thereto, see *Baker Hughes' Patents* (BL O/1/01).

Requests for admission of further evidence and for cross-examination were allowed in *Hartington Conway's Application* (BL O/438/02).

In *Intel's Patent* ([2002] RPC 957) it was commented that it was normal practice in amendment proceedings before the Patent Office for the opponent to put in its evidence first, but the practice in the High Court was for the patentee to go first. There was seen to be no good grounds for this difference in practice so the practice in the Patent Office should be changed to align it with the court and therefore the patentee was ordered to file its evidence first.

72.44   *—Disclosure and power to require production of documents*

Disclosure was not ordered in *Intel's Patent* ([2002] RPC 957), it being stated that disclosure was not always necessary in amendment proceedings and that the obligation on the patentee to give full and frank "disclosure" as required in *Smith Kline & French v. Evans Medical* ([1989] FSR 561) was met in the first instance by the statement of reasons, and not by ordering "modern style disclosure".

Some limited disclosure under rule 106 was ordered in *University of Southampton's Applications* ([2002] RPC 906) concerning corresponding applications in other countries and of a draft application relevant to the issue of inventorship. Further disclosure was refused at this stage pending the filing of evidence, but further orders were made when the matter came back before the Comptroller at a later stage (BL O/456/02).

The provisions governing disclosure in proceedings before the Patents Court or Patents County Court formerly contained in CPR 49EPD 9 are now generally governed by CPR 63.8 (reprinted *infra* in § F 63.08) with the restrictions (formerly set out in CPR 49EPD 9) now being found in CPR 63PD 5 (reprinted *infra* at § F63PD.5).

72.52   *Appeals*

Under new CPR 63.17 (replacing CPR 49EPD 16), appeals from the Comptroller to the

Patents Court are now governed by the general rules for appeals set out in CPR 52, the main features of which are reprinted in the Main Work at §§ E52.1–E52PD.21. These features are discussed in §§ 97.12–97.18 in the Main Work and *infra*.

Costs   **72.53**

In *Ash & Lacy's Patent No. 2240559* (BL O/60/02), the Hearing Officer awarded costs against the claimant for having filed an inadequate statement of case, but in a later decision (BL O/144/02), when the patentee decided not to defend its patent, costs in an equal amount were awarded against it, so the costs orders cancelled out.

Following *Oystertec's application* (see § 72.15 *supra*) in which a revocation action was allowed to proceed in the name of a firm of patent agents, it was contended that the agents' firm should be treated as a litigant in person and therefore not be able to recover costs for work done by them. It was held (BL O/525/02) that this principle did not apply to proceedings before the Comptroller in which costs awarded "are not intended to compensate parties for their expenses but are merely a lump sum contribution to those expenses" and an appropriate award of costs was therefore made.

Putting validity in issue [Section 74]

SECTION 74—Proceedings in which validity may be put in issue   **74.01**

Subsection (8) was prospectively amended by Patents Act 2004 (c. 16, s. 13(2)) to read:

(8) It is hereby declared that for the purposes of this Act the validity of a patent is not be put in issue merely because—

    (a) the comptroller is considering its validity in order to decide whether to revoke it under section 73 above, **or**

    (b) its validity is being considered in connection with an opinion under section 74A below or a review of such an opinion.

COMMENTARY ON SECTION 74

Proceedings in which validity may be put in issue (subss. (1)–(3) and (8))   **74.03**

The prospective revision of subsection (8) (as noted in § 74.01 *supra*) will have effect to provide that proceedings under either section 74A (opinion as to validity or infringement) or section 74B (review of opinions under section 74A) are **not** ones which are deemed to have put the issue of validity in issue.

Opinions by Patent Office

SECTION 74A [ADDED]—Opinions as to validity or infringement   **74A.01**

(1) The proprietor of a patent or any other person may request the comptroller to issue an opinion—

    (a) as to whether a particular act constitutes, or (if done) would constitute, an infringement of the patent;

    (b) as to whether, or to what extent, the invention in question is not patentable because the condition in section l(l)(a) or (b) above is not satisfied.

(2) Subsection (1) above applies even if the patent has expired or has been surrendered.

(3) The comptroller shall issue an opinion if requested to do so under subsection (1) above, but shall not do so—

    (a) in such circumstances as may be prescribed, or

    (b) if for any reason he considers it inappropriate in all the circumstances to do so.

(4) An opinion under this section shall not be binding for any purposes.

(5) An opinion under this section shall be prepared by an examiner.

(6) In relation to a decision of the comptroller whether to issue an opinion under this section—

    (a) for the purposes of section 101 below, only the person making the request under subsection (1) above shall be regarded as a party to a proceeding before the comptroller; and

    (b) no appeal shall lie at the instance of any other person.

Note. New section 74A was prospectively added to the Act by the Patents Act 2004 (c. 16, s. 13(1)).

COMMENTARY ON SECTION 74A

74A.02 | *Scope of the section*

New section 74A, when brought into effect, will make available a new procedure for exploring issues of infringement and validity, which (while not leading to their final determination) is intended (according to the Explanatory Notes issued on the Bill which led to the Patents Act 2004, "the Explanatory Notes") to be of value in resolving actual or potential disputes. These Notes indicate that the new procedure will enable the Comptroller to issue, on request, non-binding opinions on questions of validity, although only on the issues of novelty or inventive step, as well as on questions of infringement. The Explanatory Notes also indicate the Government's belief that the ability to request such opinions from a neutral body should be helpful to parties who wish to settle disputes without launching full proceedings. It will also be possible to seek such opinions where there is no actual current dispute. The Explanatory Notes state that, *e.g.*, a person might want an opinion about whether a certain activity would infringe a patent, before investing resources in that activity; and a patent proprietor might want an opinion about whether "prior art" of which he has just become aware is relevant to his patented invention, before he decides whether to amend the scope of his patent.

The skeleton provisions set out in the new section remain to be fleshed out by detailed rules. According to the Explanatory Notes, it is envisaged that these rules will include the payment of a fee for providing an opinion under the section and that a simple, quick procedure will be prescribed, involving in most cases only the exchange of written submissions. It is, apparently, intended that a request for an opinion will be notified to the patent proprietor (where he has not himself made the request) and may also be notified to other persons. If the request is accepted, notice of that fact will be entered on the register of patents (as will notice of the opinion itself when it is delivered), for which rule-making power is being provided by an amendment of section 32(2), as noted in § 32.01 *supra*. After such entry has been made, any interested person will be able to submit observations on the issues raised in the request, but will not become a party to the proceedings and will have no right of appeal against a decision of the Comptroller to issue an opinion (see subs. (6)).

It is envisaged that the full text of the opinion, once it is delivered, will be open for inspection on the public file; and, if the findings contained in the opinion are superseded by subsequent litigation (or by a subsequent opinion), appropriate details will be entered on the register.

Subsections (1) and (2) define the scope of the new procedure. An opinion may be requested as to whether any act constitutes or would constitute an infringement of a patent, and as to whether (or to what extent) the patent is invalid. However, opinions on validity are limited to the question whether or not the invention is patentable, either because it is not new or because it does not involve an inventive step (within the meaning of section 1(1)(a) or (b)). An opinion may be requested in relation to any patent under the 1977 Act, except one which has been revoked. Accordingly, an opinion on infringement can be given even in relation to an act that has not taken place, and an opinion on infringement or validity can be given even in relation to a patent which has expired. Thus an opinion can be requested which will help someone decide whether it is safe to engage in a particular activity, or which concerns activity that might have taken place before a patent has expired. An opinion on validity may also be requested where the patent has been surrendered (for instance if a licensee wishes to argue that licence fees should be repaid).

Subsection (3) requires a request for an opinion to be accepted, except in prescribed circumstances or where the Comptroller considers that it would be inappropriate to do so; in those cases an opinion may not be issued. It is, apparently, envisaged that, *e.g.*, a request will not be able to be granted while the issue in question is being litigated in other proceedings, or where the request is considered to be frivolous or vexatious.

Subsection (4) ensures that an opinion under the section does not have binding legal effect for any purpose. According to the Explanatory Notes, it is intended that the procedure for delivering opinions will be as simple and quick as possible. This is intended to increase the likelihood of an opinion being helpful in assisting the early settlement of disputes; but an opinion based on such an abbreviated procedure will not be permitted to make a final binding determination of the issues concerned. However, it is considered that this bar on finality will not prevent the fact that an opinion had been given from being referred to in subsequent proceedings.

New subsection (5) requires an opinion to be prepared by an officer of the Patent Office holding the position of examiner. These are the officers who carry out the search and examination under sections 17 and 18.

Under subsection (6), when read with section 101, the requester of an opinion will have the right to be heard before a request under the section is refused; but no other person (including even the patentee) is to be regarded as a party to the proceedings and will have no right to be heard on the issues before the Examiner. The Explanatory Notes indicate that this is intended to prevent unnecessary delays in a procedure which is designed to be simple and rapid. However, new section 74B provides for a review of an opinion issued under section 74A, although only by the patentee or an exclusive licensee, as discussed in § 74B.02 *infra*.

Section 74(8) has been amended to make it clear that proceedings for an opinion under section 74A are not, as such, to be regarded as proceedings in which the validity of a patent is put in issue. Accordingly, questions of validity may be considered in the context of such proceedings, notwithstanding the exclusive list of proceedings in which the validity of a patent may be put in issue which is laid down by section 74(1) and (2).

Effect of the section   **74A.03**

Until the rules for operation of section 74A have been made, it is not possible to assess whether the new section will have its intended effect (as indicated in § 74A.02 *supra*), and whether it will be much used. Certainly, a patent proprietor or exclusive licensee would seem to have considerable apprehension over a one sided attack on his patent position brought about by a request for an opinion under the section because this is to be given without his ability to take part in a hearing and in a proceeding in which he may only make observations, presumably excluding the provision of evidence, and in which his powers of review may be limited and probably without a right of appeal (each as indicated in

§ 74B.02 *infra*). It therefore seems entirely possible that a patent proprietor will start proceedings before the court in order to have a hearing in which his defence on issues of invalidity and/or of non-infringement may be decided upon evidence. This could actually lead to an increase in litigation, rather than a decrease in it as hoped. While the proprietor or an exclusive licensee could seek (under section 74B) a review of the opinion given by the examiner under section 74A, it appears that the extent of such a review could be heavily circumscribed by rules made under that section as to make it unattractive, as discussed in § 74B.02 *infra*.

Nevertheless, probably where the section will most be used will be where a private inventor or small business entity is unwilling to accept a view from his patent agent that he has no case on infringement or that his patent is at least partly invalid for lack of novelty or clear obviousness and therefore wishes to have a second opinion, but without incurring considerable expense by seeking advice from counsel. Patent Agents could welcome the availability of such a proceeding, provided that the fee for seeking the opinion from the Patent Office is set at a reasonable level.

Although an opinion given under section 74A is to be "non binding", it would appear possible that this feature could be overridden by an agreement made between the parties. Care should therefore be taken in reaching **any** agreement as to the conduct of proceedings under section 74A to stress the continuing non binding nature of the result therefrom, if such be intended, in case some inference to the contrary would be possible, particularly where the agreement is an informal one reached in oral discussion.

74B.01   **SECTION 74B [ADDED]—Reviews of opinion under section 74A**

(1) Rules may make provision for a review before the comptroller, on an application by the proprietor or an exclusive licensee of the patent in question, of an opinion under section 74A above.

(2) The rules may, in particular—

(a) prescribe the circumstances in which, and the period within which, an application may be made;

(b) provide that, in prescribed circumstances, proceedings for a review may not be brought or continued where other proceedings have been brought;

(c) make provision under which, in prescribed circumstances, proceedings on a review are to be treated for prescribed purposes as if they were proceedings under section 61(1)(c) or (e), 71(1) or 72(l)(a) above;

(d) provide for there to be a right of appeal against a decision made on a review only in prescribed cases.

Note. New section 74B was prospectively added to the Act by the Patents Act 2004 (c. 16, s. 13).

COMMENTARY ON SECTION 74B

74B.02   *Scope of the section*

New section 74B provides for rules to be made to govern a review of an opinion in proceedings before the Comptroller governed by section 74A (as discussed in §§ 74A.02 and 74A.03) and the procedure to be adopted in such a review. The Explanatory Notes (as explained in § 74A.02) explain that it is envisaged that a review under section 74B will enable a full hearing to be obtained on the merits of the issues discussed in an opinion already given under section 74A. However, such a review will not be an appeal against that opinion and it may be requested only by the proprietor or an exclusive licensee of the patent. Although notice of a request for an opinion under section 74A, and the result thereof, are to be entered in the register, see § 74.02 *supra*, it is not entirely clear that information concerning proceedings for review, and the outcome thereof, are likewise to be entered.

Under subsection (2), certain matters, in particular, may be prescribed in those rules. Thus, under subsection (2)(a), such matters include the circumstances and time period in which an application for a review may be made; and paragraphs (b) and (c) of subsection (2) enable provision to be made concerning the relationship between such proceedings for review and other proceedings relating to the same issues so that rules may proscribe a review, or its continuance, where other proceedings have been brought.

The Explanatory Notes indicate that, in most cases, the existing procedures under the Act (those under ss. 61(1)(c), 71(1) or 72(1)(a)) should provide a sufficient means of reviewing the conclusions reached in an opinion. For example, where a person disagrees with an opinion that a patent is valid, he would be able to seek revocation of the patent under section 72; where a person disagreed with an opinion that a certain activity infringes a patent, it would be possible to seek a declaration of non-infringement under section 71; and a patent proprietor who disagrees with an opinion that certain activity does not infringe a patent would still be able to bring proceedings under section 61, if there is evidence of such activity; and an opinion that a patent is not valid could also be addressed in the proceedings for infringement.

But, it may be that, where there is no such existing or apprehended activity, a proprietor or exclusive licensee would (in the absence of section 74B) have available no existing mechanism for seeking a reconsideration of an opinion given under section 74A that the patent is invalid or that a particular act does not infringe the patent. Thus, where no proceedings under sections 61, 71 or 72 have been brought, subsection (2)(c) enables a review under the section to be treated. in appropriate cases, as proceedings brought under existing provisions of the Act. This will, for instance, enable provision to be made for treating proceedings for a review as revocation proceedings brought under section 72 for the purposes of giving relief under that section.

Section 74(8) has been amended to make it clear that proceedings for a review under section 74B of an opinion given under section 74A are not, as such, to be regarded as proceedings in which the validity of a patent is put in issue. Accordingly, questions of validity may be considered in the context of such review, notwithstanding the exclusive list of proceedings in which the validity of a patent may be put in issue which is laid down by section 74(1) and (2). However, that would not prevent the validity of the patent from being regarded as put in issue where (by virtue of rules made under section 74B(2)(c)) proceedings on a review come to be treated as proceedings under sections 61(1)(c) or (e), 71(1) or 72(1)(a).

While there is normally an automatic right of appeal from a decision of the Comptroller, section 97(4) removes that right in specific instances. Subsection (2)(d) provides for a right of appeal to exist from a decision of review under section 74B only in specified circumstances. The Explanatory Notes indicate that such an appeal may be inappropriate where the result of the review was merely to set aside the opinion).

Effect of the section   **74B.03**

As with section 74A, it remains to see what effect this new section will have. This will be heavily influenced by the nature and scope of the rules to be made for these review proceedings. *Prima facie*, a patentee could be expected to seek a review whenever an opinion is given under section 74A which is adverse to his interests. Nevertheless, if (as is apparently envisaged as indicated in § 74B.02 *supra*) reviews are to be discouraged in favour of a requirement for the opinion to be challenged (if that be possible) in proceedings to be commenced under one or more of sections 61, 71 and 72, that would increase the extent of litigation and increase the costs to the parties. It may, therefore, be that a patentee (unwilling to incur the costs of litigation) will not seek a review, but rather make it clear, in one way or another, that he disagrees with the opinion and stresses its non binding nature. In particular, although an opinion under section 74A has no binding effect, it is possible that a review under section 74B could result in an estoppel preventing re litigation of a finding of fact set out in the opinion or review.

75.01

SECTION 75—Amendment of patent in infringement or revocation proceedings

The Patents Act 2004 (c. 16, Sched. 2(19)) amended subsection (1), by replacing the word "is" (in line 2 of the reprint in the Main Work) by the words "may be", with effect from January 1, 2005 except in relation to proceedings brought before that date (S.I. 2004 No. 3205, aa. 2(f)(k) and 9(4)).

This Act (by s. 2(5)) also prospectively added new subsection 75(5), reading:

(5) In considering whether or not to allow an application proposed under this section, the court or the comptroller shall have regard to any relevant principles applicable under the European Patent Convention.

This prospective amendment will be brought into effect when the EPC revisions agreed in 2000 come into force.

Relevant Rule—Rule 78

75.02 Rule 78—Amendment of patent under section 75

With effect from April 1, 2003, Rule 40 was amended by the Patents (Electronic Communications) (Amendment) Rules 2003 (S.I. 2003 No. 513) to replace paragraphs (1) and (2) and add new paragraph (1A) together reading:

(1) Where in any proceedings before the comptroller a proposed amendment to the specification of a patent made under section 75 is to be delivered to the comptroller it shall, if it is reasonably possible, be delivered to the comptroller in electronic form or using electronic communications.

(1A) If the comptroller requires it, notice that a proposal has been made to amend the specification of a patent shall be advertised in the Journal and the advertisement shall state that any person may apply to the comptroller for a copy of the proposed amendment.

(2) Within two months of the date of the advertisement in the Journal, any person may give the comptroller notice of opposition to the proposed amendment on Patents Form 15/77.

Commentary on Section 75

75.03 *Scope of the section*

The term "amendment", as used throughout the Act, will (from the coming into force of new subsection 130(5A)) include any amendment made in the EPO (under new EPCa. 105A) by way of limitation of the claims of a granted European patent, see § 130.07 *infra*.

75.04 *Applicability of section 75*

The amendment of subsection (1) allows a proprietor to seek amendments under section

75 during the course of any proceedings in which it is possible (under s. 74(1)) and not merely when validity has actually been put in issue, thereby removing an uncertainty of the effect of the decision in *Norling v. Eez-Away* ([1997] RPC160) discussed in the Main Work.

Discretion   **75.06**

In *Ancare's Patent [New Zealand]* ([2001] RPC 335) it was held by the Court of Appeal of New Zealand that the possibility of amendment in revocation proceedings did not permit the validity of the patent to be supported in alternative versions. That was inconsistent with the requirement for the invention to be clearly defined and the need for competitors to know the scope of the monopoly.

In *Kirin-Amgen's Patent* ([2002] RPC 851) the court confirmed that "deleting" amendments to claims would normally be permitted, *i.e.* where there are claims which would be valid in the absence of the invalidity which has been established, but that delay should be taken into account and "any patentee who delays does so at his own risk"; conditions might be imposed on the amendment.

The insertion of new subsection (5) has the same intent and effect as that arising from new subsection 27(6), for which see § 27.05 *supra*.

Opposition (subs. (2))   **75.08**

CPR 49EPD 4 has been replaced by CPR 63.10 and CPR 63PD.12 (reprinted respectively at §§ F63.10 and 63PD.12 *infra*).

PRACTICE UNDER SECTION 75

Application to the court   **75.11**

Swintex v. Melba Products, cited in the Main Work, has been reported ([2000] FSR 39).

CPR 49EPD 4 has been replaced by CPR 63.10 and CPR 63PD.12 (reprinted respectively at §§ F63.10 and 63PD.12. CPR 63.10(3) now requires that the application notice (setting out the amendments sought) "must, if it is reasonably practical, be served on the Comptroller electronically". The same applies for applications made under section 75 to the Comptroller, see § 27.15 *supra*.

Allowance of amendment by the court   **75.12**

CPR 49EPD 4.8 has become CPR 63.10(8) (reprinted in § F63.10 *infra*). CPR 49EPD 4.9 has not been re-enacted, but an entry in the O.J. will appear following the required service on the Comptroller of the court order for amendment made under CPR 63.10(8).

Applications to the Comptroller   **75.13**

Under revised rule 78 (for which see § 75.02 *supra*), made under new section 124A (reprinted in § 124A.01 *infra*), an applicant seeking amendment is required to deliver the amendment (and where possible the reasons for making the amendment) to the Comptroller electronically. The procedure set out in § 27.15 *supra* applies *mutatis mutandis*. Likewise, the O.J. now carries only a notice that amendment is being sought, but any person may request a copy of the amendment and the reasons therefor which are then, if possible, transmitted to that person electronically.

In *Clear Focus Imaging v. Contra Vision* (BL C/54/01, *noted* IPD 25009) the court held that the issue of re-advertisement was a matter of discretion and did not affect an existing opponent who therefore had no interest in appealing this point. Unless the new amendment was one which would leave the claims significantly wider in scope than those originally proposed, it could not be said that anyone who had not opposed the original amendments could now wish to intervene.

76.01

SECTION 76—Amendments of applications and patents not to include added matter

The RRO (a. 13) amended subsections 76(1) and (3) and inserted new subsections (1A) and (4), as follows:

In subsection (1), the words "section 15(4)" were replaced by "section 15(9)". New subsection (1A) reads:

(1A) Where, in relation to an application for a patent

(a) a reference to an earlier relevant application has been filed as mentioned in section 15(1)(c)(ii) above; and

(b) the description filed under section 15(10)(b)(i) above discloses additional matter, that is, matter extending beyond that disclosed in the earlier relevant application,

the application shall not be allowed to proceed unless it is amended so as to exclude the additional matter

In subsection (2), the words "section 17(3)" were replaced by "section 15A(6)".

New subsection (4) reads:

(4) In subsection (lA) above "relevant application" has the meaning given by section 5(5) above.

Note. These amendments took effect from January 1, 2005, the Commencement Date of the RRO, but the previous version of the section continues to apply to patents and applications which were then "pending", a term defined in Note 3 to § 15.01 *supra*.

COMMENTARY ON SECTION 76

76.03 *Scope of the section*

Subsections (1) and (2) have been amended to replace the reference for divisional applications to section 15(9) (instead of to s. 15(4)) and the reference to the meeting of formal requirements to section 15A(6) (instead of to s. 17(3)), each because of the relocation of these provisions (as set out in §§ 15.01, 15A.01 and 17.01 *supra*).

Also, because it is now possible to initiate an application by filing a reference to a previous "relevant application" (as defined in s. 5(5)), instead of filing a description, new subsections (1A) and (4) provide that such an application is not to be allowed to proceed if it contains matter additional to that in the document used to initiate the application until that additional matter has been excluded from the description of the invention initially provided, all as discussed in § 15.08 *supra*.

Decisions involving alleged "additional matter"

76.07 *—The general principles*

In the quotation from *Bonzel v. Intervention (No.3)* ([1991] RPC 553) on page 730 the last two lines of sub-paragraph (3) should read:

"... subject-matter will be added *unless* such matter is clearly and unambiguously disclosed in the application either explicitly or implicitly."

—Amendments allowed without contravention of section 76   **76.08**

Monsanto v. Merck, cited in the Main Work, was published [2002] RPC 709, and was upheld on this point on appeal (cited as *Pharmacia v. Merck* ([2002] RPC 775)) the court holding that an amendment to restrict the claim to a substituent already described as optional would not add matter but be a disclaimer which the patentee is entitled to make. See § 72.26 *supra*.

In *Baker Hughes' Patents* (BL O/332/02) certain words which described (it was submitted, incorrectly) features mentioned in the patent as belonging to the prior art were allowed to be removed on the exercise of the Comptroller's discretion, on the basis that the amendments would not add new subject matter or extend the protection conferred by the claims. See also § 117.06. On appeal (BL C/49/02, *noted* IPD 26003) the court agreed, seeing no reason why the amendments should not be allowed, but observed that the matter could be revisited in revocation proceedings under s. 72(1)(d) as the present decision to allow the amendments would not create an estoppel.

—Introduction of subject-matter not specifically described   **76.10**

EPO Decision T 323/97, *UNILEVER/Disclaimer* ([2002] EPOR 427) held that the practice of permitting disclaimers having no support in the application as filed to make claimed subject matter novel by delimiting it against an accidental anticipation should not be maintained in the light of *EPO Opinion G* 2/98, *Requirement for claiming priority of the* "same invention" (OJEPO 2001, 413). However, this view, if maintained, would have had far reaching consequences and it appeared to be in conflict with other established case law of the Boards of Appeal. As a consequence, *EPO Decisions T* 507/99, *PPG/Disclaimers* (OJEPO 2003, 225; [2003] EPOR 291) and *T* 451/99, *GENETIC SYSTEMS/Synthetic antigen* ([2004] EPOR 127) each referred certain questions to the Enlarged Board of Appeal (respectively as *EPO Cases G* 1/03 and *G* 2/03) particularly in overcoming prior art under EPC Art. 54(3), where only novelty, and not inventive step, can be in issue. The resulting decisions were in identical terms so that only *EPO Opinion G* 1/03 (OJEPO 2004, 413; [2004] EPOR 331) need be consulted. These decisions largely discredited the decision in *T* 323/97 and set out the criteria for allowing a claim to have a disclaiming feature in the following headnote terms:

1. *An amendment to a claim by the introduction of a disclaimer may not be refused under Article 123(2) EPC for the sole reason that neither the disclaimer nor the subject-matter excluded by it from the scope of the claim have a basis in the application as filed.*

2. *The following criteria are to be applied for assessing the allowability of a disclaimer which is not disclosed in the application as filed:*

   2.1 *A disclaimer may be allowable in order to:*

   —restore novelty by delimiting a claim against state of the art under Article 54(3) and (4) EPC;

   —restore novelty by delimiting a claim against an accidental anticipation under Article 54(2) EPC; an anticipation is accidental if it is so unrelated to and remote from the claimed invention that the person skilled in the art would never have taken it into consideration when making the invention; and

   —disclaim subject-matter which, under Articles 52 to 57 EPC, is excluded from patentability for non-technical reasons.

   2.2 *A disclaimer should not remove more than is necessary either to restore novelty or to disclaim subject-matter excluded from patentability for non-technical reasons.*

2.3 *A disclaimer which is or becomes relevant for the assessment of inventive step or sufficiency of disclosure adds subject-matter contrary to Article 123(2) EPC.*

2.4 *A claim containing a disclaimer must meet the requirements of clarity and conciseness of Article 84 EPC.*

While these cases were pending, *EPO Decision T 525/99, LUBRIZOL/ Flourohydrocarbons* ([2004] EPOR 85; [2004] EPOR 85) stated that there is no addition of subject-matter where a disclaimer is inserted into a claim with wording taken solely and directly from a document which is prior art only under EPCa. 54(3). This now seems to be the general position under *Opinion G 1/03.*

An example of an allegation of added subject-matter being dismissed because the added matter consisted of technical matter which the skilled person would have known and taken for granted is *DSM's Patent* ([2001] RPC 675).

Addition of an explanation of the meaning of a trade mark as at the priority date contravenes EPCa. 123(2) (*EPO Decision T 480/98, CIUFFO GATTO/Trade mark* [2000] EPOR 494).

76.11 *—Addition of subject-matter by excision or alteration of text*

Monsanto v. Merck, cited in the Main Work, was published [2002] RPC 709, and was upheld on this point on appeal (cited as *Pharmacia v. Merck* ([2002] RPC 775)).

In *Fieldturf's Divisional Application* (BL O/192/02) the divisional was not accorded the filing date of its parent because the divisional claimed a two layer structure instead of the three layer structure of the parent application, omitting mention of a "base layer" which appeared from the parent to be essential.

76.13 *—Restriction to an intermediate generalisation*

Monsanto v. Merck, cited in the Main Work, was published [2002] RPC 709, and was upheld on this point on appeal (cited as *Pharmacia v. Merck* ([2002] RPC 775)), the court finding that the amendment in question amounted to making a new selection of compounds. See § 72.26.

In *EPO Decision T 812/97, SEARLE/Cyclooxygenase 2 inhibitors* ([2002] EPOR 443) (relating to the same European patent under opposition at the EPO), the Board of Appeal held that for an intermediate generalisation to be acceptable under the EPC, its limits "must themselves be directly and unambiguously derivable from the application as filed in the same was as any other amendment" and that the Boards "take a strict view here because to do otherwise would lead to applications being filed with broad speculative claims, the identification of the really significant features only being introduced by later amendments".

In *Tickner v. Honda* (BL C/68/01, *noted* IPD 25020) the proposed amendment was rejected as an intermediate generalisation adding matter by disclosing and claiming a new combination which the patentee had never contemplated. Likewise, in *EPO Decision T 422/00, MODINE/Heat exchanger* ([2004] EPOR 303), the EPO held that if the inclusion of an intermediate generalisation makes a technical contribution to the subject-matter to be claimed, the amendment is not one "clearly and unambiguously derivable from the original disclosure" as required by *EPO Decision G 1/93, ADVANCED SEMICONDUCTOR PRODUCTS/Limiting feature* (OJEPO 1994, 541; [1995] EPOR 97), on which see § 76.22 *infra.*

76.14 *—Acknowledgment of prior art*

The Court of Appeal judgment in *Cartonneries de Thulin v. CTP White Knight,* cited in the Main Work, has been reported ([2001] RPC 107). Here, the claims were construed differently in that it was held that the claim wording should not be impliedly limited by reference to the drawing and, on that different view, it was held that subject-matter had been added to the original disclosure, see § 125.15 *infra*.

See § 76.10 *supra* for comments on EPO practice regarding introducing disclaimers to deal with acknowledged prior art.

The possibility of claim broadening before grant   **76.16**

In *EPO Decision T* 311/91, *FUJITSU/Removal of organic resist* ([2000] EPOR 488), it was permitted to remove the word "used" from the claim phrase "for removing a used organic resist" as the description indicted that working on a "used resist" was only an advantageous, but not an essential, feature of the invention.

The concept of "additional matter" present in other provisions

—Relationship of "additional matter" to concept of novelty   **76.19**

In *EPO Decision T* 824/94, *INSTITUT PASTEUR/Lympdenopathy-associate virus* ([2000] EPOR 436), it was reiterated that the test for allowability of amendment under EPCa. 123(2) is the same as the test for novelty.

—Amendment extending the protection conferred (EPCa. 123(3) and subs.
(3)(b))   **76.22**

EPO Decision T 1149/97, *SOLATRON/Fluid transducer* (OJEPO 2000, 259) has now been published at [2001] EPOR 33.

In *Tickner v. Honda* (BL C/68/01, *noted* IPD 25020) an interesting argument was run that if claim 1 of the patent were invalid, the introduction of a claim narrower than the original claim 1 but broader than any of the sub-claims would result in the protection conferred by the patent being extended (the original claim 1, being invalid, conferring no protection). That argument was rejected, the court saying that "like patents themselves, the EPC and the Act must be construed purposively", but the proposed amendment was nevertheless found objectionable: see § 76.13, *supra*.

SECTION 76A—Biotechnological inventions   76A.01

Note. This added section was applied to the Isle of Man by S.I. 2003 No. 1249.

PART II   [SECTIONS 77–95]

PROVISIONS ABOUT INTERNATIONAL CONVENTIONS

SECTION 77—Effect of European Patent (UK)   77.01

The Patents Act 2004 (c. 16, Sched. 1(2)) prospectively amended subsection 77(5)(a) by inserting after the word "restored" the words "or is revoked by the Board of Appeal and is subsequently restored by the Enlarged Board of Appeal". This amendment will be brought into effect when the EPC revisions agreed in 2000 come into force.

RELEVANT RULES—RULE 80 AND SCHEDULE 4, PARAGRAPHS 1, 2, 5 AND 6

77.03   Schedule 4, paragraph 1—Translation of European patents (UK) filed under section 77(6)

In the reprinting of sub-paragraph 1(1) in the Main Work, "77(6)" should read " 77(6)(a) or 77(6)(b) ".

A new sub-paragraph 1(4A) was added (after sub-paragraph 1(4) to Schedule 4 to the Rules by S.I. 2003 No. 513 (effective from April 1, 2003), reading:

(4A) Where the translation filed under section 77(6) is delivered in electronic form or using electronic communcations, subparagraphs (3) and (4) shall not apply to the extent that they have been removed or varied by the comptroller in directions made under section 124A and the presentation of the translation shall comply with such directions.

77.05   Schedule 4, paragraph 5—Verification of translation

This paragraph was removed, with effect from January 12, 2005 (S.I. 2004 No. 2358, Sched. 2(13)), see § 123.43 *infra*.

COMMENTARY ON SECTION 77

77.10   *Effect of revocation or amendment of a European patent by the EPO (subss. (2), (4) and (4A))*

A final decision of an EPO Board of Appeal revoking a patent is conclusive and must be taken (at least within the EPO) as *res judicata* (*EPO Decision G* 1/97, *ETA/Request with review to revision* OJEPO 2000, 322; [2001] EPOR 1).

In the Scottish case of *ITP v. Coflexip Stena* (Court of Session (Inner House) November 19, 2004, 2004 SLT 1285, *noted*, *The Times*, November 29, 2004), there had been a finding of infringement at first instance, but then the patent in suit was revoked by a decision of an EPO Board of Appeal. The patentee made an application to the European Court of Human Rights for review of the decision in the light of alleged defects and sought a stay of the Scots proceedings pending that decision. The court held that it was clear that under s. 77(4A) of the Act the court had to accept the EPO decision as final notwithstanding any further challenge, and therefore the original decision on infringement must be overturned.

77.12   *Intervening rights on restoration of a European patent (UK) or application therefor (subs. (5))*

Subsection (5) has been amended to ensure that intervening rights are available to third parties when a European patent has been revoked and is later restored by the new procedure for a review of a decision of an EPO Board of Appeal under EPCa. 112A.

77.13   *Translation of European patents (UK) (subs. (6)–(9))*

The automatic extension of the period of time for filing of a translation under Schedule 4, paragraph 2 of the Rules which is available under revised rule 110(3) is now two months, with a further extension available with discretion under rule 110(4), see § 123.33 *infra*.

PRACTICE UNDER SECTION 77

77.17   *Filing and form of translations*

As indicated in § 77.33 *supra*, sub-paragraphs (3) and (4) of rule 1 of Schedule 4 to the

Rules will not apply, or apply only in modified form, to any permitted filing of a translation in electronic form or by way of an electronic communication under a direction given by the Comptroller, *q.v.* § 124A.02 *infra*.

Use of translation in legal proceedings   **77.18**

Former CPR 49EPD 8 has been subsumed into the general CPR, see particularly § E32.18 in the Main Work. References to the requirement to produce translations of foreign language documents are now to be found in CPR 63PD 11 and paragraph 9(b) of the *Patents Court Guide*, see respectively §§ F63PD.11 and G09 *infra*.

SECTION 78—Effect of filing an application for a European patent (UK)   **78.01**

The RRO (a. 14) amended subsection 78(3)(b) by replacing the words "specified in section 5(2) " by "allowed under section 5(2A)(a) ". This amendment took effect from January 1, 2005, the Commencement Date of the RRO, but the previous version of the section continues to apply to applications then "pending", a term defined in Note 3 to § 15.01 *supra*.

The Patents Act 2004 (c. 16, Sched. 1(3)) also prospectively amended subsections 78(5A), substituted a new form of subsection (6) and inserted new subsections (6A)-(6C) each as set out, or indicated, *infra*. These amendments will be brought into effect when the EPC revisions agreed in 2000 come into force.

In subsection (5A), there has been added to the end thereof the words:

"; and the occurrence of any event mentioned in subsection (5)(b) shall not prevent matter contained in an application for a European patent (UK) becoming part of the state of the art by virtue of section 2(3) above as regards other inventions where the event occurs before the publication of that application."

Subsection (6) and new subsections (6A)–(6C) will then read:

(6) Where, between [*those*] subsections **(1) to (3) above** ceasing to apply to **an application for a European patent (UK)** [*any such application*] and the re establishment of the rights of the applicant, a person—

    (a) begins in good faith to do an act which would [, *apart from section 55 above*] constitute an infringement **of the rights conferred by publication** of the application if those subsections then applied, or

    (b) makes in good faith effective and serious preparations to do such an act,

he shall have the **right to continue to do the act or, as the case may be, to do the act, notwithstanding subsections (1) to (3) applying again and notwithstanding the grant of the patent** [*rights conferred by section 28A(4) and (5) above, and subsections (6) and (7) of that section shall apply... accordingly*].

(6A) Subsections (5) and (6) of section 20B above have effect for the purposes of subsection (6) above as they have effect for the purposes of that section and as if the references to subsection (4) of that section were references to subsection (6) above.

(6B) Subject to subsection (6A) above, the right conferred by subsection (6) above does not extend to granting a licence to another person to do the act in question.

(6C) Subsections (6) to (6B) above apply in relation to the use of a patented invention for the services of the Crown as they apply in relation to

an infringement of the rights conferred by publication of the application (or, as the case may be, infringement of the patent).

"Patented invention" has the same meaning as in section 55 above.

RELEVANT RULE—RULE 80 AND SCHEDULE 4, PARAGRAPH 3

78.02   Schedule 4, paragraph 3—Translation of claims of applications for European patents (UK) filed under section 78(7)

Sub-paragraph (3) was amended by S.I. 2003 No. 513 (effective from April 1, 2003), by replacing the initial word "The" by "Subject to paragraph 1(4A) the", as to which see § 77.03 *supra*.

COMMENTARY ON SECTION 78

78.03   *Scope of the section*

When EPC(2000) is brought into effect, an application for a European patent will (under revised EPCa. 79) automatically be deemed to be an application for a European patent in each of the then Contracting States. The definition of "designate" in section 130(1) has been amended accordingly, see § 130.01 *infra*.

78.04   *Effect of application for European patent (UK) (subss. (1)–(4))*

The reference in subsection (3)(b) to "specified in section 5(2) " has been changed to "allowed under section 5(2A)(a) " in order to accommodate the possible allowed late filing of a priority declaration (by the EPO under a provision analogous to that now provided for an application under the Act, as described in § 5.03 *supra*.

78.05   *Effect of refusal, etc. and reinstatement (subss. (5), (5A) and (6))*

The amendment made to subsection (5A) will, when it is brought into force, ensure that an application for a European patent (UK) shall have prior art effect under section 2(3) upon publication, regardless of whether the UK remains designated at the time of its publication. This is a consequence of the fact that, under EPC(2000) every European patent application will, upon filing, be deemed to be an application for protection in all then contracting States (see revised EPCa. 79).

The amendments to subsection (6) and the new subsections (6A)–(6C) clarify and expand the previous provisions for intervening rights arising when a European patent application is terminated or refused, and subsequently reinstated, including where the reinstatement arises from a review of a decision of an EPO Board of Appeal under new EPCa. 112A, and conform to corresponding new provisions in respect of applications under the Act arising under new sections 20B and 117A.

Subsection (6C) applies these provisions also to a claim for compensation for Crown use of an invention covered by such a revived application.

PRACTICE UNDER SECTION 78

78.08   *Filing of translation of claims*

The amendment to paragraph 3(3) of Schedule 4 to the Rules (noted in § 78.02 *supra*) which applies new sub-paragraph 1(4A) to Schedule 4 to the Rules (for which see § 77.03

supra) means that the provisions of this paragraph 3 will not apply, or only apply in modified form, to any permitted filing of a translation in electronic form or by way of an electronic communication under a direction given by the Comptroller, *q.v.* § 124A.02 *infra*.

SECTION 80—Authentic text of European patents and patent applications | 80.01

The Patents Act 2004 (c. 16, Sched. 1(4)) prospectively substituted a new form of subsection 80(4) and inserted new subsections (5)–(7) each as set out below. These amendments will be brought into effect when the EPC revisions agreed in 2000 come into force.

Subsection (4) and new subsections (5)–(7) will then read:

(4) Where a correction of a translation is published under subsection (3) above and before it is so published a person—

    (a) begins in good faith to do an act which would not constitute an infringement of the patent [*or application*] as originally translated, **or of the rights conferred by publication of the application as originally translated**, but would [*(apart from section 55 above) constitute an infringement of it*] **do so** under the amended translation, or

    (b) makes in good faith effective and serious preparations to do such an act,

he shall have the **right to continue to do the act or, as the case may be, to do the act, notwithstanding the publication of the corrected translation and notwithstanding the grant of the patent** [*the rights conferred by section 28A(4) and (5) above, and subsections (6) and (7) of that section shall apply... accordingly*].

(5) Subsections (5) and (6) of section 28A above have effect for the purposes of subsection (4) above as they have effect for the purposes of that section and as if—

    (a) the references to subsection (4) of that section were references to subsection (4) above;

    (b) the reference to the registered proprietor of the patent included a reference to the applicant.

(6) Subject to subsection (5) above, the right conferred by subsection (4) above does not extend to granting a licence to another person to do the act in question.

(7) Subsections (4) to (6) above apply in relation to the use of a patented invention for the services of the Crown as they apply in relation to an infringement of the patent or of the rights conferred by the publication of the application.

"Patented invention" has the same meaning as in section 55 above.

RELEVANT RULES—RULE 80 AND SCHEDULE 4, PARAGRAPH 4

Schedule 4, paragraph 4—Corrected translations filed under section 80(3)   **80.02**

Sub-paragraph (2) was amended by S.I. 2003 No. 513 (effective from April 1, 2003), by replacing the initial word "The" by "Subject to paragraph 1(4A) the", as to which see § 77.03 *supra*.

COMMENTARY ON SECTION 80

80.07 *—Intervening rights (subs. (4))*

The replacement of previous subsection (4) and the addition of new subsections (5)–(7) are designed to make the provisions of section 80 consistent with the new subsections 78(6)–(6C), as explained in § 78.05 *supra*.

PRACTICE UNDER SECTION 80

80.10 *Filing of corrected translation (Rules, Sched. 4, para. 4)*

The amendment to paragraph 4(2) of Schedule 4 to the Rules (noted in § 80.02 *supra*), which applies new sub-paragraph 1(4A) to Schedule 4 to the Rules (for which see § 77.03 *supra*), means that the provisions of this paragraph 4 will not apply, or only apply in modified form, to any permitted filing of a translation in electronic form or by way of an electronic communication under a direction given by the Comptroller, *q.v.* § 124A.02 *infra*.

80.12 *Use of translation of European patent (UK) in proceedings before the court*

CPR 49EPD has been replaced by CPR 63 and the Practice Directions thereunder. These are reprinted in Appendix F *infra*. CPR 63PD11.2(3) requires that a copy of each document referred to in the 'Grounds of Invalidity' document, and where necessary a translation of the document, must be served with that document, see § 61.42 *supra*.

81.01   **SECTION 81—Conversion of European patent applications**

The RRO (a. 15) amended subsection (2)(c) by replacing the words "filing fee" by "application fee"; and amended subsection (3)(d) by inserting "15A," after the words "required by sections". These amendments took effect from January 1, 2005, but the previous version of the section continues to apply to applications then "pending", a term defined in Note 3(b) to § 15.01 *supra*, and sections 14(1A) and 15A have no effect thereon (RRO, a. 22).

Further amendments to section 81(1) and (2) were also prospectively made by the Patents Act 2004 (c. 16, Scheds. 1(5) and 3). These further prospective amendments (which include the removal of the now redundant subsections (1)(a) and (2)(a)) will be brought into effect when the EPC revisions agreed in 2000 come into force. When they come into effect, subsections 81(1) and (2) will read:

81.—(1) The comptroller may direct that on compliance with the relevant conditions mentioned in subsection (2) below an application for a European patent (UK) shall be treated as an application for a patent under this Act *[in the following cases: (a)... (b)... European Patent Office]* **where the application is deemed to be withdrawn under the provisions of the European Patent Convention relating to the time for forwarding applications to the European Patent Office.**

(2) The relevant conditions referred to above are *[that]* —

    [(a) . . .*relating to the application];*

    (b) *[in the case... subsection (4)(b) above]* **that** —

        (i) the applicant requests the comptroller within the relevant prescribed period (where the application was filed with the Patent Office) to give a direction under this section, or

   (ii) the central industrial property office of a country which is party to the convention, other than the United Kingdom, with which the application was filed transmits within the relevant prescribed period a request that the application should be converted into an application under this Act, together with a copy of the application; and

(c) **that** [*in either case*] the applicant within the prescribed period pays the **application** [*filing*] fee and if the application is in a language other than English, files a translation into English of the application and of any amendments previously made in accordance with the convention.

Section 81(3) remains unchanged.

RELEVANT RULES—RULES 81–83

Rule 81—Procedure for making request under section 81(2)(b)(i)   **81.02**

In the reprinting of rule 81(1) in the Main Work, the words "said notification and by" should have appeared before "prescribed fee" in line 4, and in the reprinting of rule 81(2) the third line should refer to the copy of the application and the request being sent "by the Comptroller".

By S.I. 2004 No. 2358 (Sched. 2(6)), paragraphs (3) and (4) of rule 81 were replaced (with effect from January 1, 2005) by:

(3) Where a request has been made under section 81(2)(b)(i), the period prescribed for the purposes of sections 13(2), 15(10)(d) and 81(2)(c) shall be the period of two months starting on the date the comptroller received the request mentioned in paragraph (1).

Rule 82—Procedure where section 81(2)(b)(ii) applies   **81.03**

By S.I. 2004 No. 2358 (Sched. 2(7)), paragraphs (3) and (4) of rule 82 were replaced (with effect from January 1, 2005) by:

(3) Where a request has been transmitted under section 81(2)(b)(ii), the period prescribed for the purposes of sections 13(2), 15(10)(d) and 81(2)(c) shall be the period of four months starting on the date of the notification under paragraph (2).

COMMENTARY ON SECTION 81

Scope of the Section   **81.06**

Subsection (1) is prospectively revised (for which see § 81.01) to remove the now redundant provision of original paragraph (a) thereof.

Procedure for conversion (subs.(2))   **81.07**

The amendments made or prospectively made to subsections (1) and (2) clarify the point that, where a European application is deemed to be withdrawn under the revised EPC(2000), because the application has not been forwarded to the EPO within the required time, it may be converted to a national UK application under the Act, provided that the conditions of revised subsection (2) are met. The term "filing fee" has been changed to "application fee" to accommodate the change discussed in § 14.08 *supra*.

Treatment of converted application (subs.3))   **81.08**

Reference to section 15A has been added to subsection (3)(d) to accommodate the relocation of the topic of "preliminary examination" into new section 15A, leaving section 17 dealing only with the topic of "search", see §§ 15A.03 and 17.07 *supra*.

PRACTICE UNDER SECTION 81

Procedure for conversion

81.09 | *—Initiation of conversion*

Where the request for conversion is one initiated by the applicant under section 81(2)(b)(i) the revision of rule 81 (for which see § 81.02 *supra*) results in the time within which there must be filed: PF 7/77; and PF 9A/77 (or the old PF 9/77 in the case of a "pending application, as defined in Note 3 to § 15.01 *supra*); and any required translation of the European application because this is not in the English language, each remaining at two months from the date when the Comptroller received the request for conversion under section 81(1).

Where the conversion involves the transmission to the Patent Office from another EPC country under section 81(2)(b)(ii), these periods are also unchanged and therefore remain at four months from the date of notification by the Comptroller to the applicant under rule 81(2).

The automatic extensions of the period of time for meeting the terms of revised rules 81(3) and 82(3) (reprinted respectively in §§ 81.02 and 81.03 *supra*) which are available under revised rule 110(3) is now two months, with a further extension available with discretion under rule 110(4) not exceeding two months (r. 110(8) and (10)), see § 123.33 *infra*.

81.10 | *—Requirements for priority documents and translations for converted application*

There is an error in the Main Work in that the commentary under this heading refers to the old version of rule 6(6). There is now no 21 month deadline for the filing of the translation as will be seen from the reprinting of the rule in § 5.02 *supra*. The translation is due before grant unless requested earlier by the Examiner. See § 5.19 *supra*.

81.11 | *Request for substantive examination on converted application*

An automatic extension of the period of time specified by rule 83(3) for requesting substantive examination of a European application converted under section 81 is available under revised rule 110(3) for a period not exceeding two months, with a further extension available with discretion under rule 110(4) not exceeding a further two months (r. 110(8) and (10)), see § 123.33 *infra*.

86.01 | **SECTION 86—Implementation of Community Patent Convention [Repealed]**

This section, which had never been brought into force, was repealed by the Patents Act 2004 (c. 16, Scheds. 1(6) and 3), with effect from January 1, 2005 (S.I. 2004 No. 3205. a. 2(g)(i))) as part of the removal from the Act of all references to the CPC which never came into force.

SECTION 87—Decisions on Community Patent Convention [Repealed] | 87.01

This section, which had never been brought into force, was repealed by the Patents Act 2004 (c. 16, Scheds. 1(6) and 3), with effect from January 1, 2005 (S.I. 2004 No. 3205, a. 2(g)(i)) as part of the removal from the Act of all references to the CPC which never came into force.

SECTION 89—Effect of international application for patent | 89.01

Subsection 89(4) was repealed by the Patents Act 2004 (c. 16, Scheds. 1(7) and 3) with effect from January 1, 2004 (S.I. 2004 No. 3205, a. 2(g)(i)).

Rule 120—Fees to be paid in sterling | 89.06

In the reprinting of the rule in the Main Work, the word "said" should be inserted before "Treaty".

COMMENTARY ON SECTION 89

The international phase

—International filing | 89.11

By amendment of the PCT Regulations, from January 1, 2000 all international applications are deemed to designate all PCT Contracting States. Also, when EPCa. 79 (as revised in EPC(2000)) is brought into effect, all European patent applications are, likewise, to be deemed to designate all EPC Contracting States. These changes are reflected in the revision of the definition of "designate" in section 130(1) (*q.v.* § 130.01 *infra*) and the insertion of a new subsection 130(4A) replacing section 89(4), as explained in § 89.29 *infra*.

United Kingdom Patent Office as an international authority

—Supply of certified copies | 89.20

Since November 1, 2004, the preparation of a certified copy of a priority document has been deemed to have been requested by indicating in Box VI on the PCT Request Form that priority from an application filed under the Act is claimed for the international application (O.J. November 17, 2004). Accordingly, when this indication has been given, the requisite certified copy will be prepared and transmitted to the International Bureau by the Patent Office without the need to file PF 23/77. This is possible, despite the wording of rule 119, because rule 4(2) permits the use of a form which is acceptable to the Comptroller and the aforesaid indication on the PCT Request Form is deemed to be such a form.

International applications designating the EPO (subs. (4)) | 89.29

The interpretation provision in new subsection 130(4A) (for which see § 130.01), when brought into force, makes subsection 89(4) redundant. Subsection 130(4A) defines an international application for a European patent (UK) as one not to be interpreted also as an international application for a patent (UK). Consequently, subsection 89(4) will then be repealed, but its general effect is unaltered by the replacement effect of subsection 130(4A). It is to be noted that, when EPC 2000 comes into effect, an international application (EP) will automatically designate all Contracting States, see revised EPCa. 79 and thus the term "application for a European patent (UK)" will then be meaningless. Because (since January 1, 2004) all international applications are deemed to designate all PCT Contracting States, the term "international application for a patent (UK)" has likewise become meaningless. These changes are dealt with by amendment of the term "designated" (for which see § 130.01 *infra*).

143

89.30 | *Patent Office review of refusal to accord international filing date (subs. (5))*

In *Penife International's International Application* (BL O/382/03) it was held that the international application could not be accorded a filing date because the application did not contain "a part which on the face of it appears to be a claim or claims" as required by PCTa. 11(1)(e)). This was upheld on judicial review ([2004] RPC 737) on the basis that a distinct claim, identified as such, had to be included in the application, and it was not sufficient that the description contained a "consistory clause" describing the invention.

SECTION 89A—International and national phases of application

RELEVANT RULE—RULE 85(1)–(7A)

89A.02 **Rule 85(1)–(7A)—International application for patents: Sections 89 and 89A**

Changes to rule 85 were made by S.I. 2001 No. 1412 and later by S.I. 2002 No. 529 consequent upon the amendment of PCTa. 22(1) to bring the period for entry into the national phase into conformity with that under PCTa. 39(1) when international preliminary examination is requested. Also, in accordance with practice under the EPC, this period is now set at 31 months, irrespective of whether international preliminary examination was requested. These changes took effect from April 1, 2002 in respect of all international applications where the national phase had not then begun and where the previous set period had not then expired.

Further changes to rule 85 were made by S.I. 2004 No. 2358 (Sched. 2(8)), taking effect from January 1, 2005, the RRO Commencement Date. These changes are shown in bold in the reprints of the relevant parts of rule 85 *infra* in which typographical corrections to rule 85(7A) as printed in the Main Work have also been made.

All these changes result in the following wording:

"(1) Subject to the provisions of this rule, in relation to an international application for a patent (UK) which is, under section 89, to be treated as an application for a patent under the Act, the prescribed period for the purposes of section 89A(3) and (5) is thirty one months calculated from the date which, by virtue of section 89B(1)(b), is to be treated as the declared priority date or, where there is no declared priority date, the date of filing of the international application for a patent (UK)."

Rule 85(2) now reads:

(2) Where, in accordance with paragraph 1 of Schedule 2, the information specified in subparagraphs (2)(a)(ii) and (iii) of that paragraph is added to an international application for a patent (UK) after the international filing date, rule 113(1) shall not apply in respect of that information; and where the translation of the information, the filing of which is required to satisfy the relevant conditions of section 89A(3), has not been filed at the Patent Office before the end of the period referred to in paragraph (1) above,—

(a) the comptroller shall give notice to the applicant at the address furnished by the applicant in accordance with rule 30 requiring the applicant to file the translation within three months commencing on the day on which the notice is sent; and

(b) the period referred to in paragraph (1) shall be treated in respect of the translation as not expiring until the end of the period specified in the notice given under subparagraph (a) above.

In rule 85(3), subparagraphs (b) to (e) have been replaced by a single subparagraph (b), and the further subparagraph (c) inserted by the 2002 revision was subsequently deleted. Thus, after subparagraph (a), there now follows only subparagraph (3)(b) reading:

(b) an applicant may comply with rule 5(2) at any time before the end of the period of thirty two months after the declared priority date or, if there is no declared priority date, the date of filing of the international application for a patent (UK).

In rule 85(4)(e), the word "relevant" has been twice deleted; and in paragraph (5A) the same amendments have been made as noted *supra* for rule 85(2).

Paragraph (7) has been replaced by:

"(7) In the case of an international application for a patent (UK) in respect of which the conditions specified in section 89A(3) are satisfied, the period prescribed for the purposes of sections 13(2), 15(10)(c) and (d), 17(1) and 18(1) shall be the period which expires thirty three months after the declared priority date or, if there is no declared priority date, the date of filing of the international application for a patent (UK).

(7A) In the case of an international application for a patent (UK) in respect of which the conditions specified in section 89A(3)(b) are satisfied, the period prescribed—

(a) for the purpose of section 13(2), shall be the period prescribed by rule 15(1) or two months from the date the said conditions are satisfied, whichever expires the later;

(b) for the purposes of section 15(10)(c) and (d) and 17(1) shall be the period prescribed by rule 25(2) or two months from the date on which the said conditions are satisfied whichever expires the later, and

(c) for the purposes of section 18(1), shall be the period prescribed by paragraph (7) above.

COMMENTARY ON SECTION 89A

Valid entry into the UK (subss. (2) and (3)(a))

—General   **89A.08**

There is now a uniform period of 31 months for entry into the national UK phase irrespective of whether international preliminary examination has been requested, see the amendments to rule 85 set out in § 89A.02 *supra*.

—Filing of translation of the international application   **89A.10**

Verification of a translation is now only required upon request by the Comptroller, see § 89A.19 *infra*.

—Time limit for entry into the UK phase   **89A.11**

There is now a uniform period of 31 months for entry into the national UK phase irrespective of whether international preliminary examination has been requested, see the amendments to rule 85 set out in § 89A.02 *supra*.

89A.15   *—Copy and translation of priority document*

Verification of a translation is now only required upon request by the Comptroller, see § 89A.19 *infra*.

89A.16   *Further formalities after entry into the UK phase*

There is now a uniform period of 31 months for entry into the national UK phase irrespective of whether international preliminary examination has been requested, see the amendments to rule 85 set out in § 89A.02 *supra*. Consequently, the period of 22 months referred to in the Main Work is no longer applicable. Moreover, the period of 32 months has been extended to 33 months (see r. 85(7), reprinted in § 89A.02 *supra*) and is now of uniform application to the further formalities discussed in the Main Work, *i.e.* to the times for the filing of PF 7/77, the payment of the application fee and the search fee and the filing of new PF 9A/77 (or old PF 9/77 in the case of an application which was pending on January 1, 2005, for which see Note 3 to § 15.01 *supra*) and PF 10/77. However, different periods are applicable, other than for filing PF 10/77, when early national processing is requested, see § 89A.23 *infra*.

Automatic extensions of the periods of time specified by rule 85(1), (5A), 7 and (7A) are now available under revised rule 110(3) for a period not exceeding two months, with a further extension available with discretion under rule 110(4) but not exceeding a further two months (r. 110(8) and (10)), see § 123.33 *infra*.

PRACTICE UNDER SECTION 89A

89A.17   *Valid entry into the UK phase*

There is now a uniform period of 31 months for entry into the national UK phase irrespective of whether international preliminary examination has been requested, see the amendments to rule 85 set out in § 89A.02 *supra*.

89A.18   *National fee*

There is now a uniform period of 31 months for entry into the national UK phase irrespective of whether international preliminary examination has been requested, see the amendments to rule 85 set out in § 89A.02 *supra*.

89A.19   *Translation of the international application*

There is now a uniform period of 31 months for entry into the national UK phase irrespective of whether international preliminary examination has been requested, see the amendments to rule 85 set out in § 89A.02 *supra*. It is no longer necessary to verify a filed translation. Instead new rule 2 (reprinted in § 123.11A) provides for the Comptroller to take action where he has reasonable doubts about the accuracy of any translation filed at the Patent Office, for which see § 123.43 *infra*.

89A.20   *Translation of amendments and explanatory statement*

The position is the same as that given in § 89A.19 *supra*.

89A.21   *Verification of translation of application*

The amendment to rule 85(3), noted in § 89A.02 *supra*, has removed the need to verify any translation filed at the Patent Office, but see § 89A.19 *supra*.

Early national processing (subs. (3)(b))   **89A.23**

Early national processing under section 89A(3)(b) is now governed by rule 89A(7A). This specifies that: (1) PF 1/77 must be filed within the period specified in rule 15(1) (for which see § 13.03 *supra*); and (2) the application and search fees and PF 9A/77 (or old PF 9/77) must be filed within the period specified in rule 25(2) (for which see § 15.04 *supra*). However, the period for filing PF 10/77 remains at the 33 months stated in subsection 89A(7) (reprinted in § 89A.02 *supra*).

Request for preliminary examination and search (PF 9/77)   **89A.24**

The period for filing PF 9A/77 (or old PF 9/77), as well as paying the application and search fees, is now thirty three months from the declared priority date or, if none, the date of filing of the international application for a patent (UK). However, a shorter period applies where early national processing is requested, see subs. (7A) and § 89A.23 *supra*.

Request for substantive examination (PF 10/77)   **89A.25**

The period for filing PF 10/77 to request substantive examination is now a uniform 33 months from the declared priority date or, if none, the date of filing of the international application for a patent (UK), even where early national processing is requested (subs. (7) and (7A), reprinted in § 89A.02 *supra*).

Statement of inventorship (PF 7/77)   **89A.28**

The period for filing PF 7/77 is now 33 months from the declared priority date or, if none, the date of filing of the international application for a patent (UK) (r. 85(7), reprinted in § 89A.02 *supra*). However, where early national processing is requested, this period is (when there is a declared priority date) the last to expire of the period of 12 months starting on the declared priority date or the period of two months starting on the date of filing of the application; and, if there is no such declared priority date, it is 12 months from the filing date (r. 85(7A), likewise reprinted).

Extensions of time   **89A.35**

The availability of extensions of time is now governed by the replaced rule 110 and new Schedule 4A to the Rules (for which see §§ 123.09 and 123.09A–123.09D *infra*). Each of the periods specified in rule 85 is extensible (at least with discretion under r. 110(1)), but extensions of the periods specified in rules 85(1), (5A), (7) and (7A) are only available for two months under rule 110(3) (Rules, Sched. 4A, Part 3), and not further under rule 110(4) because such extensions are (by Rules, Sched. 4A, Part 4) limited to two months and cannot be sought later than two months after the expiry of the period, or extended period, of time that has been prescribed under the rule (r. 110(8) and (10)).

SECTION 89B [ADDED]—Adaptation of provisions in relation to international applications   **89B.01**

The RRO (a. 16) amended subsection (1)(b) by replacing the words "specified in section 5(2) " by "allowed under section 5(2A)(a) above"; and amended subsection (5) by replacing the words "under section" by "under sections 15A, " These amendments took effect from January 1, 2005, but the previous version of the section continues to apply to international applications which at that date had already entered the national UK phase (as defined in s. 89A(3), see Note 3 to § 15.01 *supra*, and section 15A has no effect thereon (RRO, a. 22).

Also, subsection 89B(2) was amended by the Patents Act 2004 (c. 16, Sched. 1(8)) so that the words after " section 16 above when the" now read:

"national phase of the application begins or, if later, when published in accordance with the Treaty".

This amendment of section 89B(2) had effect from January 1, 2005, but only as regards applications which entered the UK national phase on or after that date (S.I. 2004 No. 3205, aa. 2(i), 9(5)).

89B.05 | *Declaration of priority (subs. (1)(b))*

The reference in subsection (1)(b) to "specified under section 5(2) " has been changed to "allowed under section 5(2A)(a) " in order to accommodate the possible allowed late filing of a priority declaration, as described in § 5.03 *supra*.

89B.08 | *Effect of international publication (subs. (2))*

The revision of subsection (2) (noted in § 89B.01 *supra*) makes it clear that provided that an international application has been published under the PCT then it is treated as published under section 16 even when the application enters the national UK phase early. However, if the application has not yet been published under the PCT then the application is not treated as published under section 16 until publication under the PCT has taken place.

89B.16 | *Examination in the UK phase (subs. (5))*

Reference to section 15A has been added to subsection (5) to accommodate the relocation of the topic of "preliminary examination" into new section 15A, leaving section 17 dealing only with the topic of "search", see §§ 15A.03 and 17.07 *supra*.

Convention countries [Section 90]

SECTION 90—Orders in Council as to convention countries

COMMENTARY ON SECTION 90

90.03 | *Countries designated as "convention countries"*

The Orders designating countries as "convention countries" for the purposes of section 5 have been consolidated into a new Order, the Patents (Convention Countries) Order (S.I. 2004 No. 3335), with previous such orders then being repealed. No distinction is here drawn between States which are "convention countries" by virtue of being members of the Paris Convention or because of their membership of the World Trade organisation. The countries newly added to those previously designated were: Andorra, Saudi Arabia, Serbia and Montenegro, and the Seychelles.

Miscellaneous [Sections 91–95]

91.01 | **SECTION 91—Evidence of conventions and instruments under conventions**

The Patents Act 2004 (c. 16, Sched. 2(20)) amended subsection 91(1)(b), with effect from January 1, 2005 (S.I. 2004 No. 3205, a. 2(f)(k)), by changing the words "or

Community patents kept under it" therein to "patents kept under the European Patent Convention".

COMMENTARY ON SECTION 91

Scope of the section **91.02**

The amendment to subsection (1), noted in § 91.01, *supra* is a consequence of the removal from the Act of references to the CPC which never came into force.

SECTION 92—Obtaining evidence for proceedings under the European Patent Convention

COMMENTARY ON SECTION 92 **92.03**

Operations under the Evidence (Proceedings in Other Jurisdictions) Act 1975 (c. 34) is now governed by CPR 34.21 (reprinted in § E34.21 *infra*).

PRACTICE UNDER SECTION 92 **92.04**

The reference to § E50R70 should now be changed to § E34.21 (reprinted *infra*).

SECTION 93—Enforcement of orders for costs **93.01**

Note. The amendment noted for sub-paragraph (d) is now a consequence of S.I. 2003 No. 1249.

SECTION 94—Communication of information to the European Patent Office, etc.

COMMENTARY ON SECTION 94

Disclosure by the Patents Court **94.05**

CPR 49EPD 17 has been replaced by CPR 63PD 14 (reprinted *infra* at § F63PD.14).

SECTION 95—Financial provisions **95.01**

The Patents Act 2004 (c. 16, Scheds. 2(21) and 3) amended section 95, with effect from January 1, 2005 (S.I. 2004 No. 3205, a. 2(f)(g)(k)), by: in subsection (1) omitting the words "the Community Patent Convention"; and, in subsection (2), for the words "either of these conventions" substituting the words "that convention".

COMMENTARY ON SECTION 95 **95.02**

The amendments to section 95, noted in § 95.01, *supra* are a consequence of the removal from the Act of references to the CPC which never came into force.

PART III [SECTIONS 96–132]—MISCELLANEOUS AND GENERAL

Legal proceedings [Sections 96–108]

96.01   **SECTION 96 [REPEALED]—The Patents Court**

Note. This section was also repealed for the Isle of Man by S.I. 2003 No. 1249.

COMMENTARY ON SECTION 96 [REPEALED]

96.06   *Scope of the section*

CPR 49EPD has been replaced by CPR 63 and the Practice Directions thereunder. These are reprinted in Appendix F *infra*. *The Patents Court Guide* has also been re-issued, for which see Appendix G *infra*, §§ G18 and G19 of which are relevant in the present context.

96.07   *Subject-matter jurisdiction of the Patents Court*

CPR 49EPD 1 has been replaced by CPR 63.1–63.3 (reprinted in §§ F63.1 – F63.33 *infra*).

96.08   *Nominated judges for the Patents Court*

In October 2003, Aldous LJ. retired and was replaced by the elevation of Jacob LJ. to the Court of Appeal. Laddie and Pumfrey JJ. are the principal Patents Judges. Neuberger LJ. has also now been appointed to the Court of Appeal. At the time of writing the other judges appointed to sit, as required, in the Patents Court are Patten, Lewison and Mann JJ. Contact details for all these judges are provided in § G03 *infra*.

Other former Patents Judges now sitting in the Court of Appeal are: Mummery and Chadwick LJJ.; and, in the House of Lords: Lords Nicholls, Hoffmann and Walker. Lord Hoffmann geve the leading judgment in the *Kirin-Amgen and SABAF* Cases, which were heard in the House of Lords in 2004.

Territorial jurisdiction of the Patents Court

96.09   *—The Brussels and Lugano Conventions*

The matter is now governed, for EU member states except Denmark, by Council Regulation 44/2001 of December 12, 2001 which came into force on March 1, 2002.

96.11   *—Extra-territorial jurisdiction*

CPR 49EPD 3.22 has been replaced by CPR 63.16(2) (reprinted in § F63.16 *infra*).

96.12   *Appointment of scientific advisers*

In *Kirin-Amgen v. Hoechst Marion Roussel* in the House of Lords ([2005] RPC 169), Professor Yudkin of Oxford University gave a series of seminars to the Law Lords *in camera* before the appeal was heard which was welcomed by Lords Hope and Hoffmann (and no doubt by the others too). Lord Hope suggested this might be adopted in future in cases "where the technology is complex and undisputed and the parties are willing to consent to it".

SECTION 97—Appeals from the Comptroller

97.01

Note. The amendment noted for subsection (2) is now, for the Isle of Man, a consequence of S.I. 2003 No. 1249.

RELEVANT RULES

97.02

CPR 49EPD 16 has been replaced by CPR 63.17 (reprinted *infra* at § 63.17) which subsumes the appeal procedure into that for all appeals as set out in CPR 52 and its Practice Directions, see § 97.12 *infra.*

COMMENTARY ON SECTION 97

Further appeals from the Patents Court after appeal from the Comptroller (subs.(3))

97.06

In *Baker Hughes' Patents* (BL C/49/02, *noted* IPD 26003) certain amendments were allowed under s.27 (see § 76.08). The court held that under the Access to Justice Act 1999 (c.22), which contains a prohibition against "second tier" appeals, the Patents Court has no discretion to grant leave for a further appeal despite the provisions of section 97, which were held to be overridden by the 1999 Act. However, in *McKenzie's Application* (BL C/4/04), a discrepancy was noted between section 97(3) which permits a further appeal of a decision of the Comptroller from the Patents Court to the Court of Appeal with leave given by the Patents Court, whereas CPR 52.13.1 requires permission from the Court of Appeal. It was held that in view of the explicit wording of section 97(3), there was jurisdiction to give leave for a second appeal, but that in the circumstances it would be refused.

Principles affecting exercise of appellate jurisdiction

—Weight given to the Comptroller's decision

97.09

In *Thibierge & Comar v. Rexam* ([2002] RPC 379) the court confirmed that "great weight" must be given to the Comptroller's decision even though the appeal is by way of re-hearing. The Civil Procedure Rules had not altered this position. The court quoted from the relevant paragraph of the former *Supreme Court Practice* and then, in *Clear Focus Imaging v. Contra Vision* (BL C/54/01), confirmed that it adopted the rule that "an appeal from the Office relating to an exercise of discretion requires that it should be shown that there was an error of principle. It has to be shown that the decision maker below exercised his discretion under a mistake of law, or disregard of principle, or under a misapprehension of the facts, or that he took into account irrelevant matters or failed to exercise his discretion, or the conclusion he reached in the exercise of his discretion was 'outside the generous ambit within which a reasonable disagreement is possible'". However, a notice in the O.J. for August 20, 2003 states that, under CPR 52.11, an appeal from a decision of the Comptroller is now a "review", rather than a "re-hearing". This brings the practice for patent appeals into line with that for other intellectual property appeals (*e.g.* trade mark appeals) and supersedes the previous case law.

PRACTICE UNDER SECTION 97

Appeals from the Comptroller to the Patents Court

—Lodging and serving of notice of appeal

97.12

Under new CPR 63.17 (reprinted at § F63.16 *infra* and replacing former CPR 49EPD 16), the procedure for bringing an appeal from the Comptroller to the Patents Court is now governed by the general procedures for appeals set out in CPR Part 52, the relevant rules of which are reproduced in §§ E52.1 – 52.13 of the Main Work. As the appeal is not from a county court or high court decision and it is a "statutory appeal" governed by CPR 52PD.17, no leave to appeal is required under CPR 52.3. The time for appeal is 28 days from the date of the Comptroller's decision, the Comptroller having no power to vary this period. Also (from CPR 52.6), the Comptroller no longer has power to extend this term as was possible under former CPR 49EPD 16.3, although an application may be made to the court to extend the term. Under CPR 52PD 5.1 (not reprinted herein), Court Form N171 (available on the court service website at www.hmcourts-service.gov.uk) should now be used for the Notice of Appeal rather than that set out in § F16A in the Main Work. Otherwise, the procedure set out in the Main Work appears essentially to be unchanged. A summary of the position as regards appeals is set out in Tribunal Practice Notice 1/2003 (revised) ([2003] RPC 817). *The Patents Court Guide* has been re-issued and is reprinted in Appendix G *infra*. Paragraph 7 thereof is particularly relevant to appeals from the Comptroller, which can (by agreement) be conducted as "appeals on paper only", see § G07 *infra*. In *Clear Focus Imaging v. Contra Vision* (BL C/54/01) the court noted that the opponent's appeal had been defective in naming "The Patent Office" as the respondent whereas it should have named the patentee as respondent with a copy being served on the Comptroller of Patents. A request for the appeal to be decided on the papers should have been made at the time of service of the appeal.

97.13   *—Respondent's notice and cross-appeal*

The procedural changes indicated in § 97.12 *supra* apply here *mutatis mutandis*. CPR 63.17 (replacing former CPR 49EPD 16) and paragraph 5 of the new *Patents Court Guide*, are particularly relevant, for which see §§ F63.17 and G05 *infra*.

97.14   *—Hearings and representation thereat*

Apart from the procedural changes indicated in § 97.12 *supra*, the position set out in the Main Work appears to be unchanged under CPR 63.17 which has replaced former CPR 49EPD 16. The *Patents Court Guide* has been re-issued and paragraph 3 thereof (reprinted at § G03 *infra*) is the provision now relevant to fixing the hearing and procedure thereat. Although former CPD 49EPD 16.16 has not been re-enacted as such, the rights of registered patent agents to conduct, and appear in, appeal proceedings from the Comptroller appears to be unchanged having regard to the provisions of section 102A (for which see § 102A.02 in the Main Work).

97.16   *—Admission of new evidence on appeal*

As procedure on appeals from the Comptroller to the Patents Court is now governed by CPR Part 52 (see CPR 63.17 reprinted *infra* at § F63.17), any admission of further evidence for the appeal will require the leave of the appellate body (here the Patents Court): the principles set out in the Main Work would appear to continue to apply.

The decision in *Coflexip v. Stolt Comex*, cited in the Main Work, has been reported ([2001] RPC 182); see § 125.15 *infra* for comment on further proceedings in this case.

In *Clear Focus Imaging v. Contra Vision* (BL C/54/01) a request to file new evidence was supported by a statement which was regarded as inadequate in stating that the opponent had only become aware of the existence of the person giving the statement a short time beforehand. This lack of awareness might have been due to a lack of diligence by the opponents. The hearing officer had exercised his discretion properly to exclude the new evidence.

97.18   *—Other relevant rules of court*

CPR 49EPD has been replaced by CPR 63 and the Practice Directions thereunder, for which see the entries under Appendix F *infra*.

Further appeals from the Patents Court to the Court of Appeal

—General   **97.19**

CPR 49EPD 3.2 has been replaced by CPR 63.16(2) (reprinted in § 63PD.16 *infra*).

In *Designers Guild v. Russell Williams* ([2001] FSR 113 at 122) the House of Lords said that an appeal court should only reverse a decision based on the facts and evidence if satisfied that an error of principle had been made, see also *Biogen v. Medeva* ([1997] RPC 1 (HL)). This approach is being adopted for appeals generally and has been followed by the Court of Appeal in several cases, see, *e.g. Instance v. Denny Bros.* ([2002] RPC 321), noted in more detail in §§ 3.02 and 3.04 *supra*, in an appeal against a finding of obviousness. As noted there, it is only the initial tribunal which has the benefit of assessing the witnesses first hand whereas the appeal tribunal must normally proceed only on the basis of transcripts of the evidence. The Court of Appeal emphasised and followed this principle also in *Pharmacia v. Merck* ([2002] RPC 775), and in *Merck's Patents [Alendronate product]* ([2004] FSR 330) took the matter further by saying that "in future when it is sought to challenge the trial judge's conclusions on anticipation or obviousness, the Grounds of Appeal should, in respect of each complaint, contain a succinct statement of the principle that the judge is said to have infringed, and ... unless the matter is self-evident, what is the authority for that principle".

In the light of these decisions, increased emphasis is now placed on CPR 52.11(3) (reprinted in the Main Work at § E52.1 1) and this is also reflected in the new requirement, set out in § E52PD.3 that the Notice of Appeal must differentiate appeals on matters of law from those on matters of fact.

In *AB Hässle's Patents* ([2003] FSR 413; [2003] IP&T 266) the Court of Appeal was presented with an unusual situation in which the patentee, instead of appealing the first instance judgment, sought a new trial on the ground that the trial judge's interventions during cross-examination of its expert showed apparent bias. The Court of Appeal decided that the amount of questioning by the judge was not unfair or oppressive and the judge's conduct of the trial was not, and would not be seen, to be such as to render the trial unfair. The application for a new trial therefore failed, and the decision below was upheld.

—Skeleton Arguments   **97.22**

The "supervising lord justice" for appeal from the Patents Court (or Comptroller) to the Court of Appeal is now Jacob LJ.

SECTION 98—Proceedings in Scotland

COMMENTARY ON SECTION 98

Jurisdiction of the Court in Scotland   **98.05**

For an article on Scottish procedure and jurisdiction see "The Scottish Courts—the tartan alternative for resolving IP disputes" by Gill Grassie [2004] *CIPA* 406. Note that this article states that in relation to an infringer based in Scotland, in order to obtain an injunction which is effective UK-wide, the infringer must be sued in the Scottish Court of Session. If the infringer is domiciled in Scotland but is sued in England, any injunction would not be enforceable in Scotland without further formal enforcement and recognition procedures. The article also makes the point that an attack on the validity of a registered IP right (such as a patent) can be mounted in the English or Scottish Court, irrespective of the domicile of either party (and any order for revocation would then be effective UK-wide as a matter of course).

SECTION 99A [ADDED]—Power of Patents Court to order report

COMMENTARY ON SECTION 99A

99A.05 *Opinion from the European Patent Office*

While CPR 49EPD 49 has been replaced by CPR 63 and the Practice Directions thereunder, these continue to contain no reference to the possible operation of EPCa. 25.

SECTION 101—Exercise of comptroller's discretionary powers

COMMENTARY ON SECTION 101

101.05 *Procedure for hearings*

Procedure for hearings is now dealt with in the Patent Hearings Manual, which now includes much of the material previously published in the Examining Manual concerning sections 101 and 107. The Patent Hearings Manual is available on the Patent Office web site www.patent.gov.uk/patents.

103.01

SECTION 103—Extension of privilege for communications with solicitors relating to patent proceedings

Notes.
1. By the Solicitors' Incorporated Practices Order 1991 (S.I. 1991 No. 2684, a. 4), the term "solicitor" as used in this section includes any body corporate recognised by the Council of the Law Society under section 9 of the Administration of Justice Act 1985 [c. 61].
2. The Patents Act 2004 (c. 16, Scheds. 2(22) and 3) amended subsection 103(2), with effect from January 1, 2005 (S.I. 2004 No. 3205, a. 2(f)(g)(k)), by omitting the words "the Community Patent Convention" therein.

103.02

COMMENTARY ON SECTION 103

As noted in § 103.01, the term "solicitor" as used in subsection (1) has been extended to include a solicitors' practice organised as a body corporate; and the amendment of subsection (2) is a consequence of the removal from the Act of references to the CPC which never came into force.

105.01

SECTION 105—Extension of privilege in Scotland for communications relating to patent proceedings

The Patents Act 2004 (c. 16, Scheds. 2(22) and 3) amended subsection 105(2), with effect from January 1, 2005 (S.I. 2004 No. 3205, a. 2(f)(g)(k)), by omitting the words "the Community Patent Convention"therein.

COMMENTARY ON SECTION 105

105.02 *Privilege under Scots law and scope of the section*

The amendment to subsection (2), noted in § 105.01 *supra*, is a consequence of the removal from the Act of references to the CPC which never came into force.

SECTION 106—Costs and expenses in proceedings before the court [under section 40] | 106.01

By the Patents Act 2004 (c. 16, s. 14), amendments were made to section 106. These amendments had effect from January 1, 2005 (S.I. 2004 No. 3205, a. 2(e)(g)), but (by subs. 14(4) of that Act) do not apply to proceedings commenced before that date. These amendments are: (1) the heading for the section was changed as indicated; (2) subsection (1) was amended by replacing the words "proceedings before the court... an appeal to the court" by "proceedings to which this section applies"; and (3) new subsection (1A) was added, reading:

(1A) This section applies to proceedings before the court (including proceedings on an appeal to the court) which are—
  (a) proceedings under section 40;
  (b) proceedings for infringement;
  (c) proceedings under section 70; or
  (d) proceedings on an application for a declaration or declarator under section 71.

COMMENTARY ON SECTION 106 | 106.02

The amendments to the section (for which see § 106.01 *supra*) provide the court with a discretion, when awarding costs, to take into account the financial position of the parties in proceedings, not only those under section 40, but also in: "proceedings for infringement" (which will usually be brought before the court under section 61(1)); and proceedings under section 70 (threats) and/or section 71 (a declaration, or declarator, of non-infringement). Proceedings for revocation, as such, are not included within the ambit of the amended section, but, where there is a counterclaim for revocation as part of infringement proceedings, it is thought that the costs of bringing, or defending, invalidity claims should fall therewithin.

These amendments provide a specific discretion to the court which is additional to that which at least the Patents Court already has (although the position may be different in Scotland or Northern Ireland) in relation to awards of costs under the CPR Part 44 (for which see §§ E44.2-E44PD13 in the Main Work. The revision is intended to redress somewhat the imbalance in the ability to bring, or defend, patent litigation when one party is an individual or an SME (small or medium sized enterprise), especially where the other party has large financial resources available to it. However, the section only provides a discretion which an individual or SME cannot expect to have exercised in his/its favour when he/it has behaved in an abusive or irresponsible manner, *e.g.* having commenced litigation on an unjustified basis. Also, under the section the court has to have regard, not only the financial position of the parties, but also "all the relevant circumstances".

It remains to be seen how the Patents Court will treat this amended section. One consequence could be that it will increase the litigation costs for an individual or SME as claims may require justification requiring preparation and presentation of evidence of his/its financial standing.

CPR 49EPD 14 (mentioned in the Main Work) has been replaced by CPR 63.12 and 63PD.13 (respectively reprinted below in §§ F63.12 and *F63PD.13*).

SECTION 107—Costs and expenses in proceedings before the comptroller | 107.01

The Patents Act 2004 (c. 16, s. 15) prospectively amended section 107 by substituting a new form of subsection (4) reading:

(4) The comptroller may make an order for security for costs or expenses against any party to proceedings before him under this Act if—

    (a) the prescribed conditions are met, and

    (b) he is satisfied that it is just to make the order, having regard to all the circumstances of the case;

and in default of the required security being given the comptroller may treat the reference, application or notice in question as abandoned.

Note. The amendment noted for subsection (6) is now a consequence of S.I. 2003 No. 1249.

COMMENTARY ON SECTION 107

107.02   *Scope of the section*

An award of costs was made in favour of a firm of patent agents acting in its own name in a revocation action in *Oystertec's Patent* BL O/525/02, see §§ 72.15 and 72.53 *supra*.

Procedure regarding awards of costs is now dealt with in the Patent Hearings Manual (see § 101.05 *supra*).

Extent of awards under section 107

107.04   *—Departures from the norm*

Stafford Engineering's Licence of Right (Copyright) Application, cited in the Main Work, has been reported ([2000] RPC 797).

107.05   *Security for costs (subs. (4))*

At present, subsection (4) does not provide a basis for security for costs to be given in proceedings under section 71 (*Ash & Lacy's Patent No. 2240558* [2002] RPC 939).

However, this will change when the revised form of the subsection (for which see § 107.01 *supra*) takes effect. There, will then be no restriction either to the requirement of the person ordered to give security to reside or carry on business in the United Kingdom, nor to the types of proceedings in which the Comptroller may order security to be given.

However, the subsection will be subject to the meeting of "prescribed conditions" and to the requirement that the giving of security is only to be ordered when the Comptroller "is satisfied that it is just to make the order, having regard to all the circumstances of the case". The subsection will then also permit security to be ordered to be given by an impecunious corporate body, *e.g.* one that has made a reference in entitlement proceedings.

The Explanatory Notes provided with the Bill which led to the Patents Act 2004 indicate that, as to the "prescribed conditions", it is intended to align the position of the Comptroller as far as possible with CPR 25.13 (reprinted in § E25.13 of the Main Work, as amended as noted below) so that, in particular, due account can be taken of the ability to enforce judgments in other jurisdictions under the Brussels and Lugano Conventions or under Regulation (EC) No. 44/2001.

Abdulhayogu's Application, mentioned in the Main Work, was in fact reported in [2000] RPC 18. In *McGarry and Lawson's Application* (BL O/262/03), it was held that the new Civil Procedure Rules had not altered the position since that case, thus s.107(4) of the Act was seen to provide a complete code as to the provision of security for costs in proceedings before the Comptroller.

109.01   **SECTION 109—Falsification of register, etc.**

Note. The amendment noted for sub-paragraph (b) is now a consequence of S.I. 2003 No. 1249. This section was applied to the Isle of Man by S.I. 2003 No.1249.

SECTION 117—Correction of errors in patents and applications

New subsections (3) and (4) were added to section 117 by the RRO (a. 17) with effect from January 1, 2005. These read:

(3) Where the comptroller is requested to correct an error or mistake in a withdrawal of an application for a patent, and—

(a) the application was published under section 16 above; and

(b) details of the withdrawal were published by the comptroller;
the comptroller shall publish notice of such request in the prescribed manner.

(4) Where the comptroller publishes a notice under subsection (3) above, the comptroller may only correct an error or mistake under subsection (1) above by order.

RELEVANT RULE—RULE 91

Rule 91—Correction of errors in patents and applications

Rule 91 was amended by S.I. 2004 No. 2358 (Sched. 2(10)), with effect from January 1, 2005, to add a new paragraph (3A) reading:

(3A) Where the comptroller is required to publish a notice under section 117(3), it shall be published in the Journal.

COMMENTARY ON SECTION 117

Scope of the section

New subsections (3) and (4) (reprinted in § 117.01 *supra*) provide for the Comptroller to allow, as a result of a request therefor, the correction of a withdrawal of an application which had been made in error or by a mistake. This correction is to be by way of resuscitation of the withdrawn application under new section 117A. If allowed thereunder, the resuscitation will have effect under the provisions of subsections 117(4)-(7), as summarised in § 117A.02 *infra*.

The new subsections (3) and (4) require that such a request for resuscitation of an application which has already been published under section 16 is to be published in the O.J. together with details of the withdrawal. Thereafter, any correction of an error or mistake in the earlier withdrawal is to be made by an order.

Nature of permissible corrections to specifications (r. 91(2))

In *Reeves Wireline's Application* (BL O/454/01) the Comptroller held that rule 91(2) imposes a stringent requirement for an allowable correction, namely (a) is it clear that there is an error? and (b) if so, is it clear that what is now offered is what was originally intended?

"Correction" as contrasted with "amendment"

In *Baker Hughes' Patents* (BL O/332/02) the amendments were allowed under section 27 but an alternative request to treat them as corrections under section 117 was refused. It was held that for a correction to be made under section 117 it has first to be clear that something is wrong, and that this was not so in the case where the amendment requested was to remove certain words which described features mentioned in the patent as belonging to the prior art. See also § 76.08 *supra*.

117A.01 | **SECTION 117A [ADDED]—Effect of reinstating a withdrawn application under section 117**

The RRO (a. 18) added new section 117A, and subsection (7) was later added (by Patents Act 2004, c. 16, Sched. 2(23)) which (by s. 17(2) and Sched. 2(23) of that Act) took effect on January 1, 2005 (the Commencement Date of the RRO).

117A.—(1) Where—

    (a) the comptroller is requested to correct an error or mistake in a withdrawal of an application for a patent; and

    (b) an application has been resuscitated in accordance with that request, the effect of that resuscitation is as follows.

(2) Anything done under or in relation to the application during the period between the application being withdrawn and its resuscitation shall be treated as valid.

(3) If the comptroller has published notice of the request as mentioned in section 117(3) above, anything done during that period which would have constituted an infringement of the rights conferred by publication of the application if the application had not been withdrawn shall be treated as an infringement of those rights if it was a continuation or repetition of an earlier act infringing those rights.

(4) If the comptroller has published notice of the request as mentioned in section 117(3) above and, after the withdrawal of the application and before publication of the notice, a person—

    (a) began in good faith to do an act which would have constituted an infringement of the rights conferred by publication of the application if the withdrawal had not taken place, or

    (b) made in good faith effective and serious preparations to do such an act, he has the right to continue to do the act or, as the case may be, to do the act, notwithstanding the resuscitation of the application and the grant of the patent; but this right does not extend to granting a licence to another person to do the act.

(5) If the act was done, or the preparations were made, in the course of a business, the person entitled to the right conferred by subsection (4) above may—

    (a) authorise the doing of that act by any partners of his for the time being in that business, and

    (b) assign that right, or transmit it on death (or in the case of a body corporate on its dissolution), to any person who acquires that part of the business in the course of which the act was done or the preparations were made.

(6) Where a product is disposed of to another in exercise of a right conferred by subsection (4) or (5) above, that other and any person claiming through him may deal with the product in the same way as if it had been disposed of by the applicant.

(7) The above provisions apply in relation to the use of a patented invention for the services of the Crown as they apply in relation to infringe-

ment of the rights conferred by publication of the application for a patent (or, as the case may be, infringement of the patent).

"Patented invention" has the same meaning as in section 55 above.

Note. This section applies even to applications which, on January 1, 2005 (the Commencement Date of the RRO), were "pending" as defined in Note 3 to § 15.01 *supra*.

COMMENTARY ON SECTION 117A

Scope of the section   117A.02

New section 117A specifies the provisions which apply when reinstatement of an application is allowed as a correction of a withdrawal of an application. These provisions generally follow those which apply under section 20B when a withdrawn application is reinstated under section 20A, as discussed in § 20B.02. However, the availability of "continuing rights" (under s. 117A(3) and (4)) starts on the date when the request for correction under section 117(3) was published rather than the date when the application was published under section 16. Otherwise, the commentary on section 20B (in § 20B.02) applies *mutatis mutandis* to the application of section 117A. As also noted in § 20B.02, these third party rights are generally similar to those which are imposed under section 28A when a lapsed patent is restored and under section 64 for prior secret users of an invention of a granted patent. The commentaries on these sections may, therefore, also be applicable to the situation of resuscitation of an application which has lapsed through error or mistake.

SECTION 117B [ADDED]—Extension of time limits specified by   117B.01
comptroller

The RRO (a. 18) introduced new section 117B, reading:

117B.—(1) Subsection (2) below applies in relation to a period if it is specified by the comptroller in connection with an application for a patent, or a patent.

(2) Subject to subsections (4) and (5) below, the comptroller shall extend a period to which this subsection applies if—

  (a) the applicant or the proprietor of the patent requests him to do so; and

  (b) the request complies with the relevant requirements of rules.

(3) An extension of a period under subsection (2) above expires—

  (a) at the end of the period prescribed for the purposes of this subsection, or

  (b) if sooner, at the end of the period prescribed for the purposes of section 20 above.

(4) If a period has already been extended under subsection (2) above—

  (a) that subsection does not apply in relation to it again;

  (b) the comptroller may further extend the period subject to such conditions as he thinks fit.

(5) Subsection (2) above does not apply to a period specified in relation to proceedings before the comptroller.

Note. This new section took effect on January 1, 2005 (even as to then "pending applications", as defined in Note 3 to § 15.01 above).

Relevant Rule—Rule 110A

117B.02 | **Rule 110A [Added]—Extension of time limits specified by comptroller**

110A.—(1) A request made under section 117B(2) shall be—

(a) in writing; and

(b) made before the end of the period prescribed by paragraph (2).

(2) The period prescribed for the purposes of section 117B(3) shall be the period of two months starting immediately after the expiry of the period to which section 117B(2) applies.

(3) A request made to the comptroller under section 117B(4)(b) to further extend a period shall be in writing.

Note. This new rule was added by S.I. 2004 No. 2358 with effect from January 1, 2005, the "RRO Commencement date".

Commentary on Section 117B

117B.03 | *Scope of the section*

New section 117B (reprinted in § 117B.01), which is to be read together with rule 110A (reprinted in § 117B.02), applies to time limits in relation to an application or a patent which have been set by the Comptroller, rather than by the Act or the Rules, (subs. 1)), but the section does not apply to periods set by the Comptroller during proceedings before him (subs. (5)).

The section provides for the extension of such a time limit upon a request therefor provided that the request complies with the relevant requirements of other rules (subs. (2)). The request must be in writing and made within the two months following the expiry of the time limit set by the Comptroller (r. 110A(1)). This period is inextensible (under Rules, Sched. 4A, Part 1 reprinted at § 123.09A), Any extension so granted cannot extend beyond the end of the period prescribed under section 20, *i.e.* the end of the "rule 34 period" (subs. (3) and r. 110A(2)), for which see § 18.10 in the Main Work. A further extension under section 117B is possible, but the Comptroller may make this subject to such conditions as he thinks fit (subs. (4)).

SECTION 118—Information about patent applications and patents, and inspection of documents

Commentary on Section 118

118.11 *Scope of the section*

CPR 5.4 (revised as noted *infra* in § E05.4) now specifies the documents of which copies may be obtained from court records by a party to proceedings, and by any other person, and the cases in which permission of the court is required to obtain a copy of a document. It also permits a party to proceedings, or other person identified in a claim form, to apply for an order restricting persons from obtaining a copy of the claim form.

118.12 *Availability of information on European Patents and applications and on international applications*

It is now possible to view details in relation to European patents and applications free of charge on the internet via http://register.epoline.org/espacenet/ep/en/srch-reg.htm. Information can be accessed via application or publication number, name of applicant, priority data, etc. and, for at least more recently filed applications, the full file of the application (and any opposition) can be inspected via this website.

The O.J. for December 31, 2003 contains a notice that, under new rule PCTr. 94.1(c), the UK Patent Office has made a request that, as from January 1, 2004, it be supplied with copies of Preliminary Examination Reports for international applications which have been published. These should then become available on the Patent Office file as and when the international application enters the UK national phase.

Access to register and to documents filed at the Patent Office (subs. (1))   **118.14**

In *Haberman v. Comptroller* ([2004] RPC 414) the claimant sought from the Patents Court an order for the Comptroller to receive evidence and determine the date of withdrawal of a UK application. A subsequent European application, claiming priority from a later filed UK application, had been found not entitled to its claimed priority date (and as a consequence had been revoked), on the ground that at the time of filing the UK priority application, the earlier UK application had not been withdrawn as required by Art. 87(4) EPC. There was uncertainty about the date of withdrawal because of possible errors in the agent's files, and the Patent Office had been unable to confirm the date of withdrawal because its own files relating to the withdrawn application had been destroyed in accordance with its normal practice. The deputy judge held that he had sympathy with the claimant, seeing no purpose in the requirement for withdrawal of the earlier application prior to filing of the later, but was unable to assist. Given that the question of entitlement to priority would be a matter for the EPO to determine, he said that her recourse was "to trust in the good sense of the Board of Appeal and those other tribunals before whom the question of the priority date may come".

Confidentiality   **118.19**

In further proceedings in *University of Southampton's Applications* (BL O/444/02 and O/456/02 —see also § 72.44 *supra*) confidentiality orders as to issues involving a third party were refused, on the principle that the subject matter in issue should be in the public domain, but the university was given time to decide whether it wished to withdraw its evidence as an alternative to making the information public.

PRACTICE UNDER SECTION 118

Information given on request

—Information concerning Supplementary Protection Certificates   **118.22**

The Patent Office website (www.patent.org.uk) now contains details of SPCs, which can be accessed via the SPC number or patent number.

SECTION 119—Service by post

COMMENTARY ON SECTION 119

Scope of the section   **119.03**

Since January 2, 2001, it has also been possible to file documents at the Patent Office by sending them to Hays Document Exchange addressed to "DX 722541 CLEPPA PARK 3".

Receipt at that address is deemed to be receipt at the Patent Office, see O.J. January 3, 2001. As filing in this way is not regarded as a use of the "post", rule 97 (and s. 119 itself) is inapplicable to this mode of filing, see § 119.04 *infra*.

119.04   *Delivery in the ordinary course of post (r. 97)*

The Postal Services Act 2000 (c. 26) has liberalised the meaning of the word "post". As a consequence, the Patent Office accept that rule 97 now applies to delivery of documents through "any commercial service which undertakes to deliver mail in exchange for a fee". Supporting evidence may be called for before a filing date is accorded under rule 97 so practitioners are advised to keep appropriate records of the date and means of despatch. Any doubts about whether a particular delivery service would qualify under rule 97 may be raised with the Patent Office, but this would presumably ultimately be for the courts to determine.

PRACTICE UNDER SECTION 119

119.06   *Filing by fax*

For a revised form of notice as regards filing by fax at the Patent Office, see the current web site www.patent.gov.uk, but the information given in the Main Work appears to be unaffected.

120.01   **SECTION 120—Hours of business and excluded dates**

The Patents Act 2004 (c. 16, Sched. 2(24)) amended subsection 120(1) and inserted new subsection (3), each with effect from September 22, 2004 (S.I. 2004 No. 2177) and then reading as follows:

(1) The Comptroller may give directions specifying [*Rules may specify*] the hour at which the Patent Office shall be taken to be closed on any day for purposes of the transaction by the public of business under this Act or any class of business, and **the directions** may specify days as excluded days for any such purposes.

(3) Directions under this section shall be published in the prescribed manner.

RELEVANT RULES—RULES 98 AND 99

120.02   **Rule 98—Hours of business**

This rule was repealed by S.I. 2004 No. 2177 with effect from September 22, 2004. However, the contents of the rule then merely became the directions issued by the Comptroller under the power of amended section 120, see § 120.04 *infra*.

120.03   **Rule 99—Excluded days**

This rule was repealed by S.I. 2004 No. 2177 with effect from September 22, 2004. However, the contents of the rule then merely became the directions issued by the Comptroller under the power of amended section 120, see § 120.04 *infra*.

COMMENTARY ON SECTION 120

120.04   *Scope of the section*

The amendments to section 120 removed from the ambit of the Rules details of the

Patent Office's hours of business and of "excluded dates", but required these to be replaced by directions issued by the Comptroller and published in the prescribed manner. These directions may be differential in character, *i.e.* specifying different hours for the receipt of new applications from those for other types of business.

These amendments were brought into effect from September 22, 2004 (S.I. 2004 No. 2177) with consequent repeal of rules 98 and 99. Under this S.I. the provisions of these two rules were then translated into Comptroller's directions deemed thereby to be worded in the same way.

New subsection (3) requires that these directions are to be "published in the prescribed manner", but S.I. 2004 No. 2177 only requires (under new rule 115(2)) such publication to be in the O.J., although it is expected that future directions will be published as a separate item on the Patent Office web site.

SECTION 121—Comptroller's annual report
121.01

The Patents Act 2004 (c. 16, Scheds. 2(25) and 3) amended subsection 121, with effect form January 1, 2005 (S.I. 2004 No. 3205, a. 2(f)(g)(k)), as follows:

The words "1st June" are replaced by "1st December"; the word "financial" is inserted before "year" on each occurrence; the words "the Community Patent Convention" are deleted; and the words "these conventions" are replaced by "that convention".

COMMENTARY ON SECTION 121
121.02

The changes made to section 121 (as noted in § 121.01 *supra*): (1) bring the date for the Comptroller's Annual Report into the section with consequential amendment of the Patent Office Trading Fund Order (see § 123.16 *infra*); and (2) are a consequence of the removal from the Act of references to the CPC which never came into force.

SECTION 123—Rules
123.01

The Patents Act 2004 (c. 16, Scheds. 2(26)(3) and (4)) inserted new subsection (2A) and deleted subsections (4) and (5). These provisions were given effect by S.I. 2004 No. 2177 from September 22, 2004. The new subsection (2A) reads:

(2A) The comptroller may set out in directions any forms the use of which is required by rules; and any such directions shall be published in the prescribed manner.

Also this 2004 Act (by Sched. 2(26)(2)) prospectively amended subsection (2) by replacing paragraph (i) to read:

(i) giving effect to an inventor's rights to be mentioned conferred by section 13, and providing for an inventor's waiver of any such right to be subject to acceptance by the comptroller.

This provision had yet to be given effect.

RELEVANT RULES—RULES 1–4, 100–102, 110, 111 AND 113–116

Rule 2—Interpretation
123.03

Two further definitions were added (by S.I. 2004 No. 2358 (Sched. 2(2)) to rule 2 in the appropriate places, with effect from January 1, 2005, as follows:

"the initiation date" shall be the date the new application was initiated by documents containing the information mentioned in any of paragraphs (a) to (c) of section 15(1) being filed at the Patent Office.

"Termination" has the meaning given in section 20B(7) and "terminated" shall be construed accordingly.

123.04 **Rule 3—Construction**

Rule 3(d) and Schedule 1 to the Rules were deleted (as from September 22, 2004) by S.I. 2004 No. 2177.

123.05 **Rule 4—Forms**

Paragraphs (1) and (2) of rule 4 were replaced (by S.I. 2004 No. 2177), with effect from September 22, 2004, by:

(1) The forms of which the use is required by these Rules are those set out in directions under section 123(2A) (but this is without prejudice to rule 121(1)).

(2) Such a requirement to use a form is satisfied by the use of —

    (a) a form which is a replica of the form set out in such directions; or

    (b) a form which is acceptable to the comptroller and contains the information required by the form as so set out.

(2A) Such directions shall be published in accordance with rule 115(2).

A new paragraph 4(3) (having effect from April 1, 2003) was added by S.I. 2003 No. 513 reading:

(3) A requirement under these Rules to use a form shall not apply if the comptroller, in directions made under section 124A, directs that the information required may be presented in some other manner.

123.05A **Rule 4A—Multiple copies**

Rule 4A (having effect from April 1, 2003) was inserted by S.I. 2003 No. 513 reading:

4A. Where a document is delivered to the comptroller in electronic form or using electronic communications, a requirement in these Rules for the document to be delivered to the comptroller with a copy or copies of that document or in duplicate or triplicate shall not apply if the requirement is removed or varied by the comptroller in directions made under section 124A.

123.08 **Rule 102—Remission of fees**

Consequent on the replacement of old section 15(4) by new section 15(9), the reference to "15(4)" in rule 102(1)(b) has been replaced by "15(9)" (S.I. 2004 No. 2358 (Sched. 2(3)).

123.09 **Rule 110 [Replaced]—Alteration of time limits**

Rule 110 was replaced, and Schedule 4A was added to the Rules (by S.I. 2004 No. 2358), as reprinted in §§ 123.09A-123.09D *infra*), both with effect from January 1, 2005, except for applications pending immediately before January 1, 2005 to which the unamended rule 110 continues to apply, see the RRO (aa. 20 22 and S.I. 2004 No. 2358, r. 20(3)). The replaced rule 110 reads:

110.—(1) The comptroller may, if he thinks fit, extend (or further extend) any period of time prescribed by these Rules except a period prescribed by the rules listed in Part I or 3 of Schedule 4A.

(2) The comptroller may, if he thinks fit, shorten any period of time prescribed by the rules listed in Part 2 of Schedule 4A.

(3) The comptroller shall extend, by a period of two months, any period of time prescribed by the rules listed in Part 3 of Schedule 4A where—

(a) a request is filed on Patents Form 52/77;

(b) no previous request has been made under this paragraph;

(c) that request is filed before the end of the period of two months starting on the date the relevant period of time expired.

(4) The comptroller may, if he thinks fit, extend (or further extend) any period of time prescribed by the rules listed in Part 3 of Schedule 4A where—

(a) a request is filed on Patents Form 52/77; and

(b) unless the comptroller otherwise directs, the person making the request has furnished evidence supporting the grounds of the request.

(5) Where the request under paragraph (4) has been granted the comptroller shall notify the person who made the request accordingly.

(6) Where a person is notified under paragraph (5) that his request has been granted he shall, before the end of the period of two months starting on the date of the notification, file Patents Form 53/77; otherwise the extension granted under paragraph (4) shall have no effect.

(7) A request under paragraph (3) or (4) for more than one time period to be altered may only be made on single form where, if the request were granted, all the altered time periods would expire on the same date.

(8) Any alteration made under paragraphs (1), (2) or (4) shall be made—

(a) after giving the parties such notice, and

(b) subject to such conditions,

as the comptroller may direct, except that a period of time prescribed by the rules listed in Part 4 of Schedule 4A may only be extended (or further extended) for a period of two months.

(9) Subject to paragraph (10), an extension may be granted under paragraph (1) or (4) notwithstanding the period of time prescribed by the relevant rule has expired.

(10) No extension may be granted in relation to the periods of time prescribed by the rules listed in Part 4 of Schedule 4A after the expiry of the period of two months starting immediately after the period of time as prescribed (or previously extended) has expired.

(11) Where—

(a) the period within which any party to a dispute may file evidence under these Rules is to begin after the expiry of any period in which any other party may file evidence under these Rules; and

(b) that other party notifies the comptroller that he does not wish to file any, or any further, evidence,

the comptroller may direct that the period within which the first party may file evidence shall begin on such date as may be specified in the direction and shall notify all parties to the dispute of that date.

SCHEDULE 4A TO THE PATENTS RULES 1995—
Alteration of time limits
(Added by S.I. 2004 No. 2358, with effect from January 1, 2005)

123.09A | **Rules, Schedule 4A, Part 1 [Added]**

Periods of time that cannot be altered

rule 6(2)(b) (declaration of priority for the purposes of section 5(2) made after the date fo filing)

rule 6A(1) period for making a request to the comptroller for permission to make a late declaration of priority)

rule 26 (extensions for new applications), so far as it relates to rules 6 and 6A

rule 36A(1) (application to reinstate a terminated application)

rule 39(1) and (2) (renewal of patents)

rule 40(2) (notice of opposition to application to amend the specification after grant)

rule 41(1) (application to restore a lapsed patent)

rule 43(2) (notice of opposition to the surrender of a patent)

rule 59(2) (application for compensation of employees for certain inventions)

rule 64(1) (application to cancel entry that patent licence is available as of right)

rule 65(1) (opposition to cancellation of entry that patent licence is available as of right)

rule 71(1) (opposition to a compulsory licence)

rule 78(2) (opposition to an amendment of patent under section 75)

rule 81(1) (request for a direction under section 81)

rule 82(1) (request from a foreign industrial property office for a direction under section 81)

rule 91(4) (opposition to the correction of an error in a patent or application)

rule 110A (extension of time limits specified by comptroller)

paragraph 5(2) and (4) of Schedule 2 (new deposits of biological material)

123.09B | **Rules, Schedule 4A, Part 2 [Added]**

Periods of time that may be shortened under rule 110(2)

rule 7(3) to (5) (entitlement to grant of a patent)

rule 8(3), (5), (6) and (7) (entitlement to right under the application)

rule 9(2) (request for a licence to work an invention after transfer)

rule 12(2) (service of counter statement in relation to a request under section 10 or 12(4))

rule 13(2) (objection to licence terms)

rule 14(3) (service of counter statement in relation to the mentioning of an inventor)

rule 40(4) (service of counter-statement in amendment proceedings)

rule 43(4) (service of counter-statement in surrender proceedings)

rule 54(3) to (5) (determination of right after grant) rule 56 (new applications) rule 57(1) (request for licence after transfer of a patent)

rule 58(2) (service of counter statement after reference under section 38(5))

rule 59(3) to (5) (application for compensation of employees)

rule 62(3) and (4) (proceedings involving licences of right)

rule 70(1) (request to be heard in respect of an application under section 48, 51 or 52)

rule 71(3) (service of counter-statement in opposition in proceedings relating to compulsory licences)

rule 72(3) to (7) (infringement proceedings before the comptroller)

rule 73(3) to (5) (validity in infringement proceedings before the comptroller)

rule 74(2) to (4) (procedure for a declaration of non-infringement)

rule 75(3) to (5) (procedure on application for revocation under section 72)

rule 77(1) (observations and opportunity to amend on revocation under section 73)

rule 88(1), (lA), (lB) and (3) (comptroller's discretionary powers)

Rules, Schedule 4A, Part 3 [Added]   123.09C

Periods of time that may be extended under rules 110(3) or 110(4)

rule 6B(1) and (2) (filing of information and priority documents)

rule 15(1) (filing of statement of inventorship and the right to be granted a patent) rule 23 (missing parts)

rule 25(1), (2) and (4)(a) (periods prescribed for the purposes of section 15(10) and 17(1))

rule 26 (extensions for new applications), except so far as it relates to rule 6 and 6A

rule 33(2), (3) and (5) (request for substantive examination)

rule 34 (period for putting an application in order)

rule 41(4) (payment of unpaid renewal fee after restoration)

rule 81(3) (filing of a request and fee to convert an application for European patent (UK))

rule 82(3) (filing a request and fee to convert an application from another convention country)

rule 83(3) (request for substantive examination when section 81(2) applies)

rule 85(1), (5A), (7) and (7A) (international applications for patents)

paragraph 1(3) of Schedule 2 (filing of information in relation to the deposit of biological matter)

paragraph 2 of Schedule 4 (filing of a translation of European patent (UK) specifications)

Rules, Schedule 4A, Part 4 [Added]   123.09D

Periods of time to which rule 110(8) and (10) relate

rule 15(1) (filing of statement of inventorship)

rule 16(1B) and (6) (filing of name and address and translations)

rule 24 (new applications under section 15(9))

rule 25 (periods prescribed for the purposes of section 15(10) and 17(1))

rule 26 (extensions for new applications), so far as it relates to rule 15(1) rule 33 (request for substantive examination under section 18)

rule 34 (period for putting application in order)

rule 81(3) (request under section 81(2)(b)(i))

rule 82(3) (request under section 81(2)(b)(ii))

rule 83(1) (request for substantive examination when section 81(2) applies)

rule 85(1), (2)(a), (5A), (7), (7A)(a) to (c) (international applications for patents)

123.10A **Rule 112A [Added]—Copies kept at the Patent Office**

Rule 112A was added by S.I. 2004 No. 2358, effective from January 1, 2005, and reading:

112A.—(1) This rule applies when an applicant is required to file a copy of an application that has been filed at the Patent Office because that application or a copy of that application is already kept at the Patent Office.

(2) Where this rule applies the comptroller shall make a copy (or further copy) of that application.

123.11 **Rule 113—Translations**

Rule 113 was amended by S.I. 2004 No. 2358, with effect from January 1, 2005, as follows:

(i) Rule 113(1) was amended to read:

(1) Subject to the provisions of rules 6 to 6C, 16, 22A, 40, 81, 82 and 85 and paragraph (3) of Schedule 4, where any document or part of a document which is in a language other than English is filed at the Patent Office or sent to the comptroller in pursuance of the Act or these Rules, it shall be accompanied by a translation into English of the document or that part.

(ii) In each of rules 113(3)–(5) the words "verified to the satisfaction of the comptroller as corresponding to the original text thereof" were deleted.

(iii) Rule 113(6) was deleted.

123.11A **Rule 113A [Added]—Establishing the accuracy of translations**

Rule 113A was added by S.I. 2004 No. 2358, effective from January 1, 2005, and reading:

113. If the comptroller has reasonable doubts about the accuracy of any translation that has been filed at the Patent Office by any person in accordance with the Act or these Rules—

(a) he shall notify that person of the reasons for his doubts; and

(b) he may require that person to furnish evidence to establish that the translation is accurate,

and where that person fails to furnish evidence the comptroller may, if he thinks fit, take no further action in relation to that document.

123.15 **Rule 115—The Journal**

By S.I. 2004 No. 2177 (effective from September 22, 2004), the existing rule was renumbered as paragraph (1) and new paragraph (2) was inserted, reading:

(2) The comptroller shall publish in the Journal any directions he gives under section 120(1) or 123 (2A).

PATENT OFFICE TRADING FUND ORDER 1991 | **123.16**

(S.I. 1991 No. 1796)

Article 6 of this Order was revoked by the Patents Act 2004 (c. 16, s. 16(3)), with effect from January 1, 2005 (S.I. 2004 No. 3205, a. 2(h)). This is consequent on the changes made at the same time to section 121, as noted in § 121.01 *supra*.

Commentary on Section 123

Definitions to Patents Rules (rr. 2 and 3) | **123.18**

Under new subsection 123(2A) (for which see § 123.01 *supra*), as made effective on September 22, 2004 by S.I. 2004 No. 2177, it is no longer required for the forms to be used in business with the Patent Office to be prescribed formally by the Patents Rules, but instead they are now prescribed under Directions issued by the Comptroller and published in the O.J. Consequently, this S.I. repealed rule 3(d) and Schedule 1 to the Rules (as reprinted in §§ 140.01–140.54 in the Main Work and below). Although the initial directions given by the Comptroller were deemed (by S.I. 2004 No. 2177) to be identical with the forms in force on this repeal date, a Direction issued December 2, 2004 revoked that provision and replaced it with a list of the now operative forms, the contents of which are made available on the web site "www.patent.gov.uk/patent/forms/ ", from which the Forms may be freely downloaded. In view of this availability, and the possibility of future changes, the Forms are no longer being reprinted in this Work, see § 140.00 *infra*.

Form and content of documents (subs. (2)(a)) | **123.19**

Where electronic filing of a form may be permitted (as discussed in the separate commentaries for such forms), rules 4(4) and 4A (for which see §§ 123.05 and 123.05A *supra*) modify the requirements for forms and in particular disapply the need to provide multiple copies of such forms. The supply of a single copy of a required form is generally necessary where a fee needs to be paid therewith.

It is to be noted that rule 4(2) is broad enough to cover the use of any indication which satisfies the Comptroller of the intention of the applicant, see *e.g.* § 89.20 *supra* where an indication on the PCT Request Form that priority is being claimed is sufficient to obviate the need to file PF 23/77 requesting a certified copy of the priority application to be made and transmitted to the International Bureau.

Relief under rule 100 is discretionary and may be conditional | **123.23**

Eveready Battery's Patent, cited in the Main Work, has been reported ([2000] RPC 852).

Fees and remission of fees (subss. (2)(c) and (4))

—Fees | **123.25**

The repeal of subsection (4) (for which see § 123.01) and the consequent amendment of the "Trading Fund Status" of the Patent Office (for which see § 123.50 in the Main Work), means that the specific consent of the Treasury is no longer required for rules setting the level of fees charged by the Patent Office. However, these fees still need to be made by rules signed by the Secretary of State and to be subject to annulment by a resolution of either House of Parliament.

For the current level of fees, see § 142.02 in the Main Work and below.

123.30 | *Advisers (subss. (2)(g) and (5))*

The repeal of subsection (5) (for which see § 123.01), and the consequent amendment of the "Trading Fund Status" of the Patent Office (for which see § 123.50 in the Main Work), means that the remuneration to be paid to an adviser no longer needs the consent of the Treasury, although it remains to be determined by the Secretary of State.

Time limits (subs. (2)(h) and rr. 110 and 111)

123.31 | *—Scope of rules 110 and 111*

In addition to the provisions for time extension set out in the Main Work, new section 117B formalises the position that, besides the position as to time periods specified in the Act and Rules, extensions can be granted by the Comptroller of time limits set by him (other than in proceedings before him), see §§ 117B.01–117B.03 *supra* where the conditions applicable to such extensions are explained.

Also, new section 20A permits the reinstatement of an application that has been terminated by failure to meet the time periods required by the rules, and new section 117A permits the resuscitation of an application which had been withdrawn by error or mistake, in each case subject to the possible imposition of third party rights, as set out and described respectively in §§ 20A.01–20B.02 and 117A.01–117A.02 *supra*.

Rule 110 therefore deals with the alteration of those time periods which are specified in the Rules, which (if not complied with) will lead to a deemed withdrawal of the application. As stated in the Main Work, in principle, any such period can be extended, unless this is precluded or limited by other provisions set out in rule 110 (r. 110(1)). Those rules which are inextensible are now listed in Part 1 of Schedule 4A to the Rules (reprinted at § 123.09A *supra* and discussed in § 123.32 *infra*).

However (under r. 110(2)), the Comptroller has power to shorten certain time periods, viz. the periods specified in the rules listed in this Part 2 of this Schedule 4A (reprinted in § 123.09B *supra* and discussed in § 123.36 *infra*).

Moreover (under r. 110(3)), automatic extensions by two months of the periods specified in those rules which are listed in Part 3 of this Schedule 4A (reprinted in § 123.09C *supra* and discussed in § 123.33 *infra*) are possible upon request to the Comptroller and payment of the prescribed fee, but provided that the request is one being made under rule 123(3) for the first time and is made within a period of two months of the date when the relevant period expired.

Further extensions under the rules specified under rule 123(3), *i.e.* those listed in Part 3 of Schedule 4A) are possible (under r. 123(4), as discussed in § 123.34 *infra*), if a request therefor is made and supported by evidence following which the Comptroller exercises his discretion and, if he allows the request, a further fee is then paid.

However, in respect of some of the rules which are listed in this Part 3, Part 4 of Schedule 4A (reprinted in § 123.09D *supra*) limits the possible extension period to only two months (r. 110(8)) and then only if the extension is granted within the two months following the expiry of the period, or extended period, of time prescribed by the relevant rule (r. 123(10)), as discussed in § 123.34 *infra*.

Where a period of time is one not specified in the lists of any part of Schedule 4A, a discretionary extension should be available under rule 123(1), as discussed in § 123.36 in the Main Work and below, but any such extension under rule 16(1B) and (6) (filing of name and address and translations); or rule 24 (divisional applications) may not exceed two months (Rules, Sched. 4A, Part 4).

An extension can be granted under either of rules 123(1) or (4) notwithstanding that the period prescribed by the rules has already expired (s. 123(3A) and r. 123(9)).

Under rule 110(8), the Comptroller may, if he thinks fit, alter any period of time under any of rules 110(1)–(4) upon such notice and upon such terms as he may direct. However, presumably, this is intended to be a general rule making power, rather than one to be exercised in specific cases and simply obviates the need for a formal S.I. amending any of these time limits. Thus, it is thought that the power of rule 110(8) should not be used to nullify the normal application of rules 110(1)–(4) without appropriate notice given well in advance of the intention to alter specified time periods set out in the Rules, subject to appropriate transitional provisions.

Rule 110(11) relates to time periods applicable in proceedings before the Comptroller and is discussed in § 72.34 *supra*.

—The inextensible time periods under rule 110 (Rules Sched. 4A, Part 1)   123.32

The rules which specify time limits that cannot be extended are now those of replaced rule 110(1) as listed in Part 1 of Schedule 4A to the Rules (reprinted at § 123.09A *supra*). The only changes made to this list in these revisions of the rules concerns the renumbering of the rules relating to the making of priority declarations, former rule 6 having been replaced by reference to replaced rule 6 and new rule 6A.

—Automatic limited extension of certain time periods (r. 110(3))   123.33

The rules which specify time limits under which automatic extensions of time can be obtained under replaced rule 110(3) are now those listed in Part 3 of Schedule 4A to the Rules (reprinted at § 123.09C *supra*), but the extensions available under replaced rule 110(3) are now a uniform two months, rather than one month as previously. Otherwise, there are no substantive changes to this list of rules applicable to the operation of rule 110(3); the changes made are merely a consequence of the renumbering or relocation of some these numbered rules, leading to the new references to rules 6B, 23, 25(2) and (4), 81(3) and 82(3).

An extension request under rule 110(3) must be made on PF 52/77 (which has been revised from the form shown at page 1141 of the Main Work, see § 140.52) and before the end of the period of two months following the date when the time period expired (r. 110(3)(a) and (c)), although the Comptroller has power to alter this two month period under rule 110(8) upon such notice and terms as he may direct.. Only one extension under rule 110(3) is possible in respect of each period to be extended (r. 110(3)(b)) so that any further extension of the same period must be sought under rule 110(4), for which see § 123.34.

However, under rule 110(8) and (10), in certain cases only a single extension (or further extension) of two months can be granted and then only if the request therefor is made within the two month period immediately following the expiry of the period, or extended period, under the relevant rule. This is the position for those rules listed in Part 4 of Schedule 4A to the Rules (reprinted in § 123.09D). These are the periods set by:

rule 15(1) (filing of PF 7/77);

rule 16(1B) and (6) (filing of name and address and translations);

rule 24 (new applications under section 15(9);

rule 25 (filing of claims, abstract, priority documents and the search request);

rule 26 (so far as r. 15(1) applies to divisional and replacement applications);

rule 33 (request for substantive examination under section 18);

rule 34 (period for putting application in order);

rule 82(3) (request under section 81(2)(b)(i));

rule 83(1) (request for substantive examination when section 81(2) applies); and

rule 85(1), (2)(a), (5A), (7) and (7A)(a)–(c) (international applications for patents).

Where multiple parallel extensions are requested on the same application, they may be made on a single PF 52/77 provided that all the periods sought to be extended would then expire on the same date (r. 110(7)).

The statement in the Main Work that if PF 52/77 is not filed during the one-month extension period that the application is deemed to be withdrawn should refer to the *normal* period (not the "normal extended period")— *cf.* § 18.10.

123.34 —*Request for discretionary extension of the time periods covered by rule 110(3), 110(4)–(6)*

The provisions for allowing a further discretionary extension of a period to which an automatic limited extension can be obtained under rule 110(3) (as discussed in § 123.33 *supra*) are now set out in replaced rules 110(4)–(6), as reprinted in § 123.09 *supra*.

The allowance of an extension under rule 110(4) requires the filing of a further PF 52/77 (in its now revised form from that shown on page 1141 of the Main Work, see § 140.00) togther with evidence supporting the request. Such an extension may be granted notwithstanding that the prescribed period of time had already expired at the date of the extension request (r. 110(9)), but this is not possible for the rules listed in Part 4 of Schedule 4A (for which see § 123.33 *supra*). For extensions under these listed rules. an extension request must be made within the two month period immediately following the expiry date of the period (or extended period) prescribed by the relevant rule (see r. 110(10), as discussed in § 123.33 *supra*).

Once the request for a discretionary further extension has been granted, this if to be notified to the applicant (r. 110(5)) and then, within two months of the date of the notification, PF 53/77 must be filed: otherwise the granted extension has no effect (r. 110(6)).

As with extensions requested under r 110(3), multiple requests for extensions under different rules can be made on the same form, but only if all the altered time periods would expire on the same date (r. 110(7)).

In *Meunier's International Application* (BL O/13/01), an application to grant an extension of time under these rules to allow late entry of an international application into the UK phase was refused. The applicant was seen to have changed his mind in having instructed his agent to pursue protection only via the EPO, and it was unfortunate that the European designation for the United Kingdom had later been dropped as a result of a mistake by his agent.

A similar case is *Pilat's International Application* ([2003] RPC 253) in which the applicant had intended to pursue protection in the UK via the "Euro- PCT " route but due to an error the PCT request form did not include a European regional designation. By the time this was realised it was too late to correct the request form and so the applicant sought an extension of the period for entering the UK national phase under rule 110(4). This was refused as it was held that the applicant had no continuing underlying intention to pursue the national phase route for protection in the UK so that to allow the extension would have given him the opportunity effectively to change his mind.

In *MacMullen's Application* (BL O/307/03) evidence of the applicant's efforts to raise money to pay the fee for form 9/77 was accepted as evidence of a continuing underlying intention to file the request and pay the fee and discretion was exercised in favour of the applicant.

—Discretionary extension without fee and restriction of time limits (r. 110(1) **123.36**
and (2))

Under rule 110(1), any time period which is prescribed by a rule is extensible with the
exercise of discretion by the Comptroller provided that the rule is **not** one of those listed
under the Rules, Schedule 4A, Parts 1 and 3 (reprinted in §§ 123.09A and D *supra*). Such
an extension can be granted notwithstanding that the prescribed period under the relevant
rule has already expired (s. 123(3A) and r. 110(9)). However, any such extension of the
periods specified in rule 16(1B) and (6), or in rule 24, may not exceed two months, see
§ 123.31 *supra*.

In addition to the power provided by rule 110(9) to alter a time period arising under any
part of rule 110(1)–(4) (as stated in § 123.31 *supra*), rule 110(2) provides specific power
to the Comptroller to shorten the time period prescribed in certain rules, should he see fit.
The rules under which this power can be used are those listed in Part 2 of Schedule 4A to
the Rules (printed at § 123.09B). These rules are the same as those listed at the end of
§ 123.36 in the Main Work, save that the reference to rule 8(7) (for which see § 8.03 in the
Main Work) has been omitted; and references to rule 74(2)–(4) have been added (for
which see § 71.02 in the Main Work). These changes perhaps arise from inadvertent
omissions when former rule 110(2A) was added in 1999.

In *Abbott Laboratories' SPC Application* ([2004] RPC 391) the period for applying for
an SPC in the UK was extended under r.110(1); see Appendix B12 *infra*.

Naming of inventor (subs. (2)(i)) **123.41**

The prospective amendment to paragraph (2)(i) (noted at § 123.01 *supra*) permits rules
to be made setting out the way in which an inventor may be identified in respect of a patent
or application therefor and also the terms upon which an inventor may (subject to
acceptance by the Comptroller) waive his rights to be mentioned as such (as provided for
in s. 13(1)), on which see § 13.04 *supra*.

Translations (subs. (2)(j) and r. 113) **123.42**

The subject-matter of former rule 6(6) has been omitted from the rules revised as a
consequence of the RRO. No translation of a priority application is now required to be
filed unless and until a direction may be made by the Comptroller requiring this to be filed,
and then only if the validity of the priority claim is regarded as relevant to whether of not
the claimed invention is novel and involves an inventive step, see Rule 6C (reprinted in
§ 5.02C and discussed in § 5.08 *supra*). When an initial filing is made involving reference
to an earlier application in lieu of a formal description, a certified copy of that earlier
application is required to be filed (unless a copy thereof is already on file in the Patent
Office), together with a translation of this if not in the English language, all as also
discussed in § 5.08 *supra*, However, no verification of such a translation is required, but
see § 123.42 *infra*.

—Verification of translations **123.43**

New rule 113A (reprinted at § 123.11A *supra*) takes the place of the previous rule
requirements that translations filed at the Patent Office should be "verified to the satisfaction of the comptroller" and rule 113 (and Rules, Sched, 4(5)) have been amended
accordingly to remove the references therein to verification (see §§ 123.11 and 77.05
respectively). Instead, new rule 113A provides that, where the comptroller has "reasonable
doubts about the accuracy of any [such] translation", he may notify the person who has
filed the translation of the reasons for his doubts and he may also require that person to
furnish evidence that the translation is accurate. If this is not done, then the Comptroller is
empowered, if he thinks fit, to take no further action in relation to that document.

123.47   *The Journal (subs. (6))*

Since August 2, 2000 the O.J. has been placed on the Patent Office web site www.patent.gov.uk.

123.48   *Patent law reports (subs. (7))*

Practice Direction (Form of Judgments, Paragraph Marking and Neutral Citation) of January 11, 2001 ([2001] 1 WLR 194; [2001] 1 All ER 193) and Practice Direction (Neutral Citations) of January 14, 2002 ([2002] 1 WLR 346) provide for numbering of all High Court judgments with a unique number. Patents Court decisions will be numbered for example " [2002] EWHC 123 (Pat)" and general Chancery decisions as " [2002] EWHC 123 (Ch)". Since decisions are now being issued with numbered paragraphs, a full citation of a particular paragraph would include the paragraph number thus: *Smith v. Jones* [2002] EWHC 123 at [59]. Although the Practice Directions indicate that it is intended that this form of citation be used as much as possible, the main series of patent law reports, RPC and FSR, still adopt their own citation references which are used in the Main Work and in this Supplement. Unreported judgments continue to be referred to by their British Library (BL) reference numbers or references to other sources (*e.g.* IPD or *The Times*) where available. Neutral citations are now given in this Work for unpublished decisions not available in the British Library collection.

123.49   *Address of the Patent Office*

Correspondence with individuals at the Patent Office may be made by email, but such emails should be restricted to correspondence only and, in particular, should not attach other documents. The standard email address for all Patent Office staff now ends with "… @patent.gov.uk" and not "… @ukpats.org.uk". The same applies to the "enquiries" email address. A notice in the O.J. of July 11, 2001 gives general information on communicating with patents staff by email, and supersedes the one referred to in this paragraph in the Main Work.

124A.01

SECTION 124A [ADDED]

Use of electronic communications

124A.—(1) The comptroller may make directions as to the form and manner in which documents to be delivered to the comptroller—

   (a) in electronic form; or

   (b) using electronic communications, are to be delivered to him.

(2) A direction under subsection (1) may provide that in order for a document to be delivered in compliance with the direction it shall be accompanied by one or more additional documents specified in the direction.

(3) If a document to which a direction under subsection (1) applies is delivered to the comptroller in a form or manner which does not comply with the direction the comptroller may treat the document as not having been delivered.

(4) Subsection (5) applies in relation to a case where—

   (a) a document is delivered using electronic communications, and

   (b) there is a requirement for a fee to accompany the document.

(5) The comptroller may make directions specifying—

   (a) how the fee shall be paid;

(b) when the fee shall be deemed to have been paid.

(6) The comptroller may make directions specifying that a person who delivers a document to the comptroller in electronic form or using electronic communications cannot treat the document as having been delivered unless its delivery has been acknowledged.

(7) The comptroller may make directions specifying how a time of delivery is to be accorded to a document delivered to him in electronic form or using electronic communications.

(8) A direction under this section may be given—

(a) generally;

(b) in relation to a description of cases specified in the direction;

(c) in relation to a particular person or persons.

(9) In a case falling within subsection (8)(a) or (b), the direction must be published in such manner as the comptroller considers appropriate for the purpose of bringing it to the attention of the persons affected by it.

(10) In a case falling within subsection (8)(c), the direction must be notified to that person or those persons in such manner as may be agreed between that person or those persons and the comptroller.

(11) A direction under this section may be varied or revoked by a subsequent direction under this section.

(12) A direction under this section may include incidental, supplementary, saving and transitional provisions.

(13) Where the comptroller delivers a document using electronic communications then, unless the contrary intention has been specified by the comptroller, the delivery is deemed to be effected by the comptroller properly addressing and transmitting the electronic communication.

(14) Where the comptroller makes a direction under this section which applies in addition to or in place of rules, to the extent that the direction applies—

(a) "prescribed" in this Act includes prescribed by the direction;

(b) references in this Act to compliance with rules or requirements of rules include compliance with the direction or requirements of the direction.

(15) In this section—

(a) references to a document include anything that is or may be embodied in paper form;

(b) references to delivery to the comptroller include delivery at, in, with or to the Patent Office;

(c) references to delivery by the comptroller include delivery by the Patent Office;

and cognate expressions must be construed accordingly.

Note. Section 124A was added by the Patents Act 1977 (Electronic Communications) Order 2003 (S.I. 2003 No. 512) with effect from April 1, 2003. This section was applied to the Isle of Man by S.I. 2003 No. 1249.

DIRECTIONS UNDER SECTION 124A OF THE PATENTS ACT 1977 | **124A.02**

Directions for the filing of patent applications by electronic means were first issued by the Comptroller on December 19, 2003 on a trial basis and amended in September 2004. However, these were entirely replaced in January 2005 by the following version:

Filing Patent Applications by Electronic Means

Introduction

1. The comptroller has made the following Directions under section 124A of the Patents Act 1977 ("the Act") to direct the form and manner in which patent application and certain other documents may be delivered to him in electronic form or using electronic communications.

2. These Directions come into force on 23 January 2005.

3. The Directions made on 19th December 2003 and on 27th September 2004 are hereby revoked.

Interpretation

4. In these Directions:
"appropriate hardware" means either:
   (a) a smart card reader and the smart card supplied by the Office; or
   (b) a smart card reader and smart card supplied by any other person and which are acceptable to the Office;
"appropriate software" means version 2.20 of the UK epoline® software;
"digital media" means a compact read-only optical disk that can contain electronic data and conforms to ISO 9660: 1988;
"electronic application" means:
   (a) an application for a patent under the Act; or
   (b) in relation to an international application for a patent (UK), a request to enter the national phase;
   processed using the appropriate software and appropriate hardware;
"EPO" means the European Patent Office;
"the Office" means the Patent Office or, where appropriate, the comptroller;
"online", in relation to a document being delivered, refers to a document that has been transmitted from one device to another by means of an electronic communications network (within the meaning of section 32 of the Communications Act 2003);
"original format", in relation to a document, means a document in the file format in which it was originally created before it was converted into a PDF file;
"priority application" has the meaning given by rule 6(6) of the Rules;
"submission session" means the time during which the user communicates with the Office using the appropriate software and appropriate hardware for the purposes of delivering an electronic application;
"the Rules" means the Patents Rules 1995;
"user" means a person using the appropriate software and appropriate hardware to deliver an electronic application;
"WIPO" means the World Intellectual Property Organisation;
"wrapped" means one or more files contained in a single ZIP file.

5. In these Directions, "Patents Form" shall be construed as a reference to a document containing the information required by the relevant Patents Form as set out in directions under section 123(2A) of the Act.

6. In these Directions, "delivered" and related expressions, means delivered to the Office and for the purposes of the Act and the Rules a document shall be treated as filed at the time it was delivered.

Filing of patent applications

7. An electronic application may be delivered either online or on digital media, except that no electronic application may be delivered by a person who has not registered with the Office.

8. An electronic application delivered online shall be submitted using the appropriate software.

9. An electronic application may only be sent from a computer that uses a version of Microsoft Windows® supported by the Office.

Preparation of documents

10. An electronic application, including any documents listed in paragraphs 18 or 19, shall be wrapped, signed and encrypted using the appropriate software and appropriate hardware.

11. The user may deliver documents related to the electronic application in their original format. These documents shall be wrapped and shall be delivered at the same time as the electronic application.

12. The documents mentioned in paragraph 11 shall not be part of the application. They shall only be used in the subsequent processing of the electronic application for verification of its contents at the time it was delivered.

13. Any requirement of the Rules—
   (a) to deliver more than one copy of a document; or
   (b) to use a particular form;
shall not apply where the document is delivered to the comptroller in accordance with these Directions.

Sequence listings

14. Where sequence listings form part of an electronic application the listings shall comply with WIPO standard ST.25 ASCII.

Illegible or incomplete documents and infected files

15. Where part or all of a document delivered under these Directions is illegible or incomplete, the whole document shall be treated as not complying with these Directions.

16. Where a document delivered under these Directions is reported as having a virus (or other malicious software) by the Office's virus checking software, the document shall be treated as not complying with these Directions.

17. Where a document is treated as not having been delivered under paragraph 15 or 16, provided the user can be identified, he shall be notified of this fact by the Office.

Other documents

18. In relation to an application for a patent under the Act, the following documents may be delivered at the same time as the electronic application:

    Patents Form 3/77

    Patents Form 7/77

    Patents Form 8A/77

    Patents Form 9A/77

    Patents Form 10/77

    Patents Form 23/77

    a copy of a priority application where that application was filed with the United States Patent and Trademark Office translations of priority applications covering letter.

19. In relation to a request for an application for an international patent (UK) to enter the national phase, the following documents may be delivered at the same time as the electronic application:

    Patents Form 7/77

    Patents Form 9A/77

    Patents Form 10/77

    Patents Form 23/77

    translation of the international application

    translation of information relating to the deposit of a micro-organism

    translation of amendment under the Patent Cooperation Treaty

    translations of priority applications

    copy of the application under the Patent Cooperation Treaty

    copy of amendment under the Patent Cooperation Treaty covering letter.

Signatures

20. Where a document requiring a signature is delivered online or on digital media, it shall only be treated as signed where the signature takes the form of a facsimile signature, a text string signature or an enhanced electronic signature.

21. In paragraph 20:

    "facsimile signature" means a TIFF or JPEG image of the signatory's signature;

    "text string signature" means a string of characters, preceded and followed by a forward slash (/), selected by the signatory to provide evidence of his identity and of his intent to sign the document in question;

    "enhanced electronic signature" means a signature created using an electronic PKI-based certificate issued by the Office, the EPO or recognised by either.

Online filing

22. A user may only deliver an electronic application online if he has:

(a) an account with the Office;

(b) registered with the Office;

(c) registered for PKI certification; and

(d) successfully completed a service trial.

23. An electronic application shall be sent online to the electronic address (URL address) provided to the user for that purpose by the Office.

24. An electronic application can be sent online at any time, except between 01.00 and 06.30 hours UK time.

Filing using digital media

25. An application for a patent delivered on digital media must be accompanied by a paper document identifying:

(a) that the digital media contains an application for a patent;

(b) the person applying for a patent or contain information sufficient to enable that person to be contacted by the Office;

(c) a list of the Patents Forms and documents making up the application (or which can be delivered at the same time as the application (as listed in paragraph 18 or 19)) which are stored on the digital media.

Acknowledgment and time of delivery

26. Where an electronic application has been delivered online, in accordance with these Directions, the electronic acknowledgement ("the receipt") will be issued to the user electronically during the submission session.

27. Where no receipt is electronically issued in accordance with paragraph 26, the electronic application will be treated as not having been delivered.

28. The receipt will specify:

(a) the date and time of delivery at the office;

(b) the application number allocated to the electronic application; and

(c) a list of the Patents Forms and documents delivered at the same time as the electronic application.

29. The receipt for an electronic application delivered on digital media will include the information referred to in paragraph 28, but will be sent to the user by post.

Payment of fees

30. Where a Patents Form or other document is required by the Patent (Fees) Rules 1998 to be accompanied by a fee, that Patents Form or document shall be treated as not complying with these Directions until the fee has been paid.

31. Fees may be paid by one of the following methods:

(a) from a deposit account held with the Office;

(b) by a credit-card or debit-card registered with the Office for that purpose;

(c) by bank transfer to Bank of England account number 25011006 (sort code 10–00–00, swift code BKENGB2L); or

(d) by cheque made payable to "The Patent Office".

RON MARCHANT
Comptroller—General of Patents,
Designs and Trade Marks
19 January 2005

Notes to the Directions

The Directions (as made available on the web site "www.patent.gov.uk/patent/notices/ index.htm " contain some guidance and explanatory notes, the more important of which are:

Applications under the Patent Cooperation Treaty and the European Patent Convention

(d) These Directions do not include provision for an international application for a patent to be filed electronically under the Patent Cooperation Treaty ("PCT") or for a European patent application to be filed under the European Patent Convention.

(e) The conditions and requirements for the electronic filing of European patent applications were advertised by the EPO in OJEPO 11/2002 pp. 543–548.

(f) The conditions and requirements for the initial electronic filing of international applications under the PCT are given in Part 7 and Annex F of the PCT Administrative Instructions available on the WIPO web site [http://www.wipo.int/pct/en/texts/index.htm].

Registration

(g) The online filing service is only available to those who have registered with the Office and have the required system specification to run the appropriate software.

(h) Details of the registration procedure for the secure electronic filing system may be obtained from the Office's IT Helpdesk: Telephone: +44 (0)1633 813500; Fax: +44 (0)1633 814907; Email: eolf.support@patent.gov.uk; Mail: IT Helpdesk, Room 3B07, The Patent Office, Concept House, Cardiff Road, Newport, NP10 8QQ, South Wales.

(i) Details of versions of Microsoft Windows® supported by the Office will be issued to the user during the registration procedure, or on request.

(j) The electronic address mentioned in paragraph 23 is provided to the user by the Office as part of the registration process.

Paperless filing

(k) No paper confirmation is required for documents delivered online or on digital media. A paper document is required, for the purposes of identification, to accompany an electronic application delivered on digital media (see paragraph 25 of the Direction).

Sequence Listing

(l) Details of the ST.25 ASCII standard, mentioned in paragraph 14 of the Direction, can be obtained from the WIPO website [http://www.wipo.int/scit/en/ standards/standards.htm].

Payment of fees

(m) The appropriate software requires the user to specify both a method of payment and a payment reference.

(n) Where a fee has been not be paid, or paid only in part, then the applicant will be notified by the Office of this fact.

Enquiries

(o) Helpdesk support for online filing will be available between 08.00 and 17.00 hours Monday to Friday excluding bank holidays.

(p) Any queries about this Direction should be addressed to: Andrew Hughes, The Patent Office, Concept House, Cardiff Road, Newport, South Wales, NP10 8QQ, United Kingdom Tel: +44 (0)1633 814728; Email: andrew.hughes@patent.gov.uk.

COMMENTARY ON SECTION 124A

124A.03

Section 124A was introduced into the Act in order to facilitate the use of electronic communications with the Patent Office by providing enabling powers for new Rules or for amended Rules having this objective.

The first changes made for this purpose were made by the Patents (Electronic Communications) (Amendment) Rules 2003 (S.I. 2003 No. 513) and mainly involved the insertion into the Rules of provisions enabling the Comptroller to issue directions for the filing of applications and other documents in electronic form or by electronic communication. The only amendments so made which were immediately effective were to rules 40 and 78 (for which see §§ 27.15 and 75.13 *supra*) providing that amendments to a granted patent which are sought from the Comptroller under either of sections 27 and 75 should, whenever possible, be supplied to the Comptroller in electronic form.

Subsequently, Directions for the Filing of Patent Applications by Electronic Means were published and later amended (as indicated in § 124A.02 *supra*). It is important to note that such e-filing requires prior authorisation from the Patent Office. As these Directions may be changed at short notice, the current state of the requirements therefor should be ascertained from the Patent Office website "www. patent.gov.uk/patent/notices/ index.htm ", or enquiries made to an address as set out in paragraph (h) of the Notes to the Directions.

SECTION 125—Extent of invention

COMMENTARY ON SECTION 125

Meaning of "invention" in section 125

125.05

In *DSM's Patent* ([2001] RPC 675), claims to a gene sequence were not seen as a mere discovery in relation to a known enzyme, see also §§ 125A.14 and 125A.19 *infra*, but the claims were otherwise held invalid for lack of inventive step (see § 3.19 *supra*) and for insufficiency (see § 14.17 *supra*).

The "Gillette Defence"

125.07

The Court of Appeal decisions in *Cartonneries de Thulin v. CTP White Knight* and *American Home Products v. Novartis*, each cited in the Main Work as respectively BL C/19/00 and C/31/00, have been respectively reported ([2001] RPC 107 and 159).

The effect of subsection (3)

125.08

In *Hewlett Packard v. Waters* (BL C/42/01; [2002] IP&T 5, *noted* IPD 24071) the court said that it was "not in general possible finally to come to a conclusion as to the proper construction of the claim until the nature of the alleged infringement has been considered". This was stated to be because of "the need [arising from the *Catnic* and *Improver* cases] to identify variants from the literal which are represented by the alleged infringement." However, on appeal, a different construction was given to the claims and infringement was then found (BL C/18/02; [2003] IP&T 143, *noted* IPD 25044). [*Editor's note*: it is not clear that the same approach would be taken following *Kirin-Amgen v. Hoechst Marion Roussel* ([2005] RPC 169—see § 125.16 *infra*)].

In *Merck v. Generics [Alendronate process]* ([2004] RPC 607), the judge examined the meaning of the Protocol to EPCa. 69 in some detail. He explained this in terms of a balance between width of protection and validity, and said that "it is up to the patentee to choose the level of risk he wishes to run". The monopoly sought by the patentee must be discernible from the patent, and it "cannot be right that [the reader] needs to carry out experiments to determine the width of the monopoly". "The Protocol is directed at allowing protection for the discernible intention of the patentee, to be derived from the words used to express that intention". The Protocol "says expressly that the context may be looked at even when no question of ambiguity of the claim arises. What it does not say … is that by looking at the claims in the context of the specification the exclusive rights can be extended beyond that which the patentee wanted to cover". The concept of fair protection for the patentee was seen in the context of the disadvantages that the patentee might suffer if his claim were construed more broadly than he intended: "There is no cannon of construction which would justify the courts in granting a patentee more protection than that which, objectively assessed, he indicated he wanted. Indeed to do so would not be "fair" to the patentee. It could expose him to a greater risk of invalidity than he was prepared to shoulder". See also § 125.16 *infra*.

The meaning of terms used in the description (subs. (1))

125.10   *—The general position under the common law*

For a synopsis of the canons of construction to be applied to the interpretation of patent claims, see *Dyson v. Hoover* ([2001] RPC 473). For comment on this decision, see A. Inglis and S. Cotrill (*Patent World* 128, December 2000/January 2001, 15).

In *Kirin-Amgen v. Roche Diagnostics* ([2002] RPC 1) the court felt that the rules for construction of patents did not differ substantially from those for other legal documents. The fact that a patent was a unilateral document did not seem to the court to be a relevant distinction since the approach to the construction of notices (*i.e.* other unilateral documents) was the same as for the construction of contracts.

125.11   *—Claim construction is a question of law*

In *Sara Lee v. Johnson Wax* (BL C/60/01, *noted* IPD 25008) the Court of Appeal deplored that the parties had "inflicted upon the judge" evidence of professors as to the meaning of the terms "liquid-permeable closure" and "porous mass". As these were not technical terms, their construction was entirely a matter for the court, and could not be delegated to scientific witnesses.

125.12   *—The patent must be read as a whole*

SmithKline Beecham's [Paroxetine Anhydrate] Patent (BL C/28/02, *noted* IPD 25083) involved the court in a lengthy consideration of the meaning of the phrase "substantially free of bound organic solvent", reference back to the specification being made for guidance, and the court making some criticism of the drafting. The decision was upheld on appeal ([2003 RPC 855; [2004] IP&T 846—see § 2.09 *supra*).

The first instance decision in *Sara Lee v. Johnson Wax*, cited in the Main Work, was reported at [2001] FSR 261.

125.13   *—The meaning to be given to technical terms*

Kimberley-Clark v. Procter & Gamble (No. 2) (BL C/25/00, *noted* IPD 23087) has been reported in [2001] FSR 339.

In the EPO the term "substantially free" has been held to be construed according to the circumstances of the case (*EPO Decision T 79/99, GASCO/Solid lipid microspheres*, [2000] EPOR 419) which here required the phrase to mean "free in so far as is practically and realistically feasible". Also, the term "naizatidine" included not only the pure chemical but also the "real product" sold under that generic name (*EPO Decision T 55/99, ELI LILLY/Naizatidine* [2000] EPOR 430).

The court in *Kirin-Amgen v. Roche Diagnostics* ([2002] RPC 1) considered that "[q]uestions as to the meaning of words in documents can rarely, if ever, be determined by reference to dictionaries". Dictionary definitions are "shorn of any relevant context" and "represent the view of a particular person who is required to summarise a definition in a few words". Expressions "may have slightly different meanings to different scientists in the field".

In the Court of Appeal decision in *Dyson v. Hoover* ([2002] RPC 465) the court did not find the evidence of professors as to the meaning of words and phrases in the claims helpful as "they did not seek to attribute to these the meaning required by the Protocol". See also *Sara Lee v. Johnson Wax* (BL C/60/01, *noted* IPD 25008), referred to at § 125.11 *supra*, in which the Court of Appeal said that scientific witnesses are not experts in the construction of patent specifications and their expertise "which requires precise use of words, is not useful when applying the Protocol".

The broader meaning given to a term in a claim by the Court of Appeal in *Coflexip v. Stolt Comex* (BL C/32/00 and [2001] RPC 182) led to the patent subsequently being held invalid over different prior art (*Rockwater v. Coflexip* (BL C/15/03, *noted* IPD 26039)) —see the case comment on this case by N. Coulson and D. Brown at *Patent World* No. 153 (June 2003)). However, on appeal, the decision on invalidity was reversed, and the patent again found valid and infringed (*Technip's Patent* ([2004] RPC 919)) —see § 125.15 *infra*, and the case comment by Katharine Stephens in [2004] *CIPA* 224).

—Claim construction must be sensible   **125.14**

In *EPO Decision T 79/96, APV ANHYDRO/Granulation by spray drying* ([2001] EPOR 309), the EPO said that when assessing the novelty of claimed subject matter, an expression in a claim should be given its broadest technically sensible meaning.

Claim construction must be "purposive"   **125.15**

The Court of Appeal decision in *Cartonneries de Thulin v. CTP White Knight*, cited in the Main Work, has been reported ([2001] RPC 107). The decision in *Buchanan v. Alba Diagnostics [Scotland]*, also cited in the Main Work, was upheld on appeal ([2001] RPC 851), but it was opined that, in the circumstances of the case, the onus of proof of non-infringement should have been held to have lain with the defender. The decision was also upheld on appeal to the House of Lords ([2004] RPC 681), see § 31.05 *supra*.

It is not appropriate to narrow down the proper meaning of claims by importing limitations not to be found in those claims, but only in the description, as such does not provide the required "reasonable certainty for third parties" (*Cadcam Technology v. Proel* BL CC/61/00).

As a matter of principle, according to the court in *Kirin-Amgen v. Roche Diagnostics* ([2002] RPC 1), questions of claim construction and infringement of the claim are separate, and there are "obvious dangers" in determining construction having regard to the infringement. But "some issues of construction only arose because of the nature of the alleged infringement". In the same case the court said that expressing something in non-quantitative terms could lead to uncertainties, difficulties and difference of opinion, but these "fuzzy edges" were inevitable in science and technology and it would be unrealistic to construe a patent in an unnatural way "simply because it would otherwise result in the odd occasion" in which there could be such uncertainties, etc.

In the Court of Appeal decision in *Dyson v. Hoover* ([2002] RPC 465) the test of the Protocol was applied to the meaning of the term "frustro-conical" which it was held should not be given a precise mathematical definition, but construed purposively to encompass a shape, generally frustro-conical, which achieved the effect desired by the patent. Contrast, however, *EPO Decision T 728/98, ALBANY/Pure Terfenidine* ([2002] EPOR 1) in which the EPO held that claims comprising unclear technical features entailed doubts as to the subject matter covered by the claim, particularly where the unclear feature was essential for delimiting the claimed subject-matter from the prior art. For example, purity as such is an unreliable characteristic in the pharmaceutical field and is a "rather hazy concept having a variable meaning shifting with time and progress in analytical chemistry". So a term such as "substantially pure" was unclear and did not allow determination of the scope of the claim without ambiguity.

The Court of Appeal in *Pharmacia v. Merck* ([2002] RPC 775) elaborated on the approach to the construction of patent claims under the Protocol in some detail, comparing it with the approaches to construction of contracts, statutes and wills, and finding both similarities and differences. In that the court had to determine the intentions of the patentee, there was most similarity with the interpretation of wills. However, this was only one step in the process because the court was required by the Protocol to balance the interests of the patentee with that of third parties. Under the Protocol, it might be necessary to fill in a gap or to depart from the precise terms of the patent in suit but only if the court was satisfied that this could be done as a matter of interpretation. The weight to be given to the concepts of reasonableness and fairness under the Protocol has yet to be articulated by the courts but may be guided by policy considerations such as that identified by Lord Hoffmann in *Biogen v. Medeva*: "... care is needed not to stifle further research and healthy competition by allowing the first person who has found a way of achieving an obviously desirable goal to monopolise every other way of doing so ...". However the court acknowledged that "it would be unfair to the patentee to construe a patent beyond its intended ambit.... To do so may make his patent invalid." See also the article *Purposive Construction of Unambiguous Terms in a Claim* by L. Kempton and A. Cooke ([2002] *CIPA* 24).

The court applied these principles in *Tickner v. Honda* (BL C/68/01 *noted* IPD 25020) in finding non-infringement where the claimant's alleged construction would have given "more than fair protection to the patentee, covering something he never envisaged either specifically or generally". It also would not give third parties reasonable certainty "catching them even though what they do owes nothing to the inventor's conception in its widest form".

In *Technip's Patent* ([2004] RPC 919), in overturning the decision of the Patents Court in *Rockwater v. Coflexip* (BL C/15/03, *noted* IPD 26039) in which the Patents Court had held invalid, over new prior art, the patent previously held valid in *Coflexip v. Stolt Comex* (BL C/32/00 and [2001] RPC 182), the Court of Appeal commented on the concept of "doctrine of equivalents" in the context of the Protocol and the principle of purposive construction. In holding that no general "doctrine of equivalents" is created by the Protocol, the court said "... purposive construction can lead to a conclusion that a technically trivial or minor difference between an element of a claim and the corresponding element of the alleged infringement nonetheless falls within the meaning of the element when read purposively. This is not because there is a doctrine of equivalents: it is because that is the fair way to read the claim in context". [*Editor's note*: this comment would seem to confine the ambit of purposive construction, and thus, presumably, the application of the "Protocol" or "*Improver*" questions, to "technically trivial or minor" variants between the claim and the alleged infringement; *cf.* the House of Lords' review of the *Improver* questions in *Kirin-Amgen v. Hoechst Marion Roussel*, § 125.16 *infra*.]

125.16   *The Catnic/Improver questions*

In *Kirin-Amgen v. Hoechst Marion Roussel* in the House of Lords ([2005] RPC 169), Lord Hoffmann took the opportunity to review the whole field of claim construction and "equivalents" and to place the *Improver/Protocol* questions (Lord Hoffmann uses the latter term for the three questions as formulated in *Improver*) in their proper context. In the course of a thorough review of historical and recent cases on construction, including case law from Germany, the Netherlands and the United States, he summarises the approach of the Protocol and Art. 69 as being "so far as is possible in an imperfect world, not to disappoint the reasonable expectations" of the patentee or third parties. To that end, a construction which would give fair protection to the patentee would be one "which would give him the full extent of the monopoly which the person skilled in the art would think he was intending to claim". Likewise, reasonable certainty for third parties would be achieved by a principle "which would not give the patentee more than the full extent of the monopoly which the person skilled in the art would think that he was intending to claim". Having set forth these basic principles, Lord Hoffmann refers to the questions formulated (by him) in *Improver* as being "only guidelines, more useful in some cases than in others". They ought not to be treated as "legal rules"; "the determination of the extent of protection conferred by a European patent is an examination in which there is only one compulsory question, namely that set by Art. 69 and its Protocol: what would a person skilled in the art have understood the patentee to have used the language of the claim to mean? Everything else ... is only guidance to a judge in trying to answer that question". Lord Walker of Gestingthorpe, in concurring with the opinion of Lord Hoffmann, went further in noting that neither *Catnic* nor *Improver* were concerned with high technology inventions and saying that "in a rapidly developing, high-technology field the *Improver* questions may have no useful function, and may be a distraction from the one compulsory question set by Art. 69 and its Protocol". Clearly, the remaining commentary in this supplement and in the Main Work needs to be read with this in mind and the whole judgment in *Amgen* should be carefully studied for a comprehensive and authoratative exposition of the law in this area by the judge who "invented" the *Improver* questions in the first place.

The decision on infringement in *Rocky Mountain Traders v. Hewlett Packard*, cited in the Main Work, was upheld on appeal ([2002] FSR 1), the Court considering, in particular, that the third *Improver* question had been answered correctly in the negative to find infringement, had the claim been valid (on which see § 3.13 *supra*).

The *Catnic/Improver* questions are now being termed the "Protocol Questions", see *Amersham v. Amicon* (BL C/49/00, *noted* IPD 24011). However one of the judges in the Court of Appeal in *Pharmacia v. Merck* ([2002] RPC 775) uses the term " *Improver* questions" when referring to the questions as formulated in that case, and says that they "are no more than guidelines: the final conclusion on interpretation must be found by asking the Protocol questions"—by which is presumably meant the two limbs of fairness for the patentee and reasonable certainty for third parties as mandated under the Protocol itself.

In *Sara Lee v. Johnson Wax* (BL C/60/01, *noted* IPD 25008), the Court of Appeal said that the second "Protocol" question was designed to ensure a reasonable degree of certainty for third parties. "To be fair to the patentee a party cannot necessarily avoid infringement by taking the invention in a disguised but equivalent form. However to be fair to the public the equivalence must be clear or obvious to the skilled addressee ... He should not have to build the device and test it ... if the variant is not obviously immaterial, it would normally be wrong for the public to be prevented from making that variant. It is the patentee who chooses the words of the claim".

The Court of Appeal in *Pharmacia v. Merck* (*supra*) developed this theme further by viewing the *Improver* questions as analogous to the process of filling in gaps in statutes. They are used as a tool of analysis and the disciplined approach offered promotes consistency and transparency. But "the touchstone for a variant to be within a patent is not so that it is necessary so that the monopoly granted by the patent is effective ... the variant must be immaterial, obvious and consistent with the language of the patent". The court then applied the *Improver* questions to conclude that the claim in this case ought to be construed to cover the variant (the *keto* tautomer), thus overturning the first instance decision (cited as *Monsanto v. Merck* ([2002] RPC 709)) on this point. Another way in which this is put in the same case is that the Protocol (*i.e. Improver*) questions are normally a useful tool to arrive at the middle ground required by the Protocol. But sometimes the questions cannot be used without modification. The court then appears to have used a direct application of the Protocol's desideratum of fairness to the patentee to reach the same result (that the variant was included), and to conclude that so to do would not prevent there being a reasonable degree of certainty for third parties.

In *Kirin-Amgen v. Roche Diagnostics* ([2002] RPC 1), infringement by one defendant was found on a literal reading of the claim. The other defendant used different technology but was also found to infringe based on an application of the "Protocol" questions, the defendant having made use of the "technical contribution" of the patent. On appeal (*Kirin-Amgen v. Transkaryotic Therapies* [2003] RPC 31) this decision was overturned as incompatible with EPC Art. 69 and the Protocol. See the case comment by H. Sheraton and A. Sharples [2002] EIPR 596. In the House of Lords ([2005] RPC 169), the finding of non-infringement was upheld following Lord Hoffmann's review of the law referred to *supra*.

In the appeal in *City Technology v. Alphasense* (BL C/13/02; [2002] IP&T 767, *noted* IPD 25038), referred to in § 125.20 *infra*, the defendant conceded that the variant present in its device had no material effect on the way the invention worked and that this had been obvious, thus answering the first two *Improver* questions in the patentee's favour. It argued however that the patentee had indicated, by the words used in the specification, that it intended strict compliance with the words of the claim, *i.e.* that the third question should be answered in the defendant's favour. That submission was rejected, the court holding that the specification followed a "familiar pattern" for mechanical inventions, and there was nothing to indicate that fair protection for the patentee should be limited to a literal interpretation. The court said that it did not believe that third parties would be surprised by that conclusion (thus, presumably, implying that the test of certainty for third parties was also fulfilled).

In *Merck v. Generics [Alendronate process]* ([2004] RPC 607), referred to in § 125.08, the patent concerned the use of sulphonic acids in a manufacturing process. The claim specified methanesulphonic acid (MSA), but the patentee sought to show by experiments that it was possible to substitute other sulphonic acids without having any material effect on the process, and that this would have been obvious to the skilled reader at the relevant date, in an attempt to see that the first two *Improver* questions would be answered in its favour. The judge referred to the *Improver* questions as "normally useful tools", but said that there was nothing to suggest that they were intended as "a rigid checklist with three boxes, each of which needs to be ticked appropriately for there to be infringement. ... They are not a substitute for the Protocol". Given that the patentee had clearly limited the acid in the claim to MSA, he was deemed to have made a decision not to seek protection for other sulphonic acids, whether or not he was aware of their existence or whether or not they might work. The third "*Improver*" question was therefore answered in favour of this construction.

The judge went on to consider the first two *Improver* questions in accordance with the more usual "structured" approach, in case the matter went to appeal. He concluded that it was not obvious that the other acids would work in the same way, thus answering the first question in the negative. In answering the second question also in the negative, he said that the test for obviousness in *Improver* question (2) could not be the same test as used to invalidate a patent over published prior art, and that when seeking to broaden the patent monopoly to cover variants, "a higher degree of confidence of success must be involved. The reader must have little or no doubt that the variant will, not may, work in the same way to produce the same results". He found that the evidence fell short of that requirement.

[*Editor's Note*: Laddie J.'s reservations about the *Improver* questions turned out to be well founded in view of Lord Hoffmann's review of the whole of this field in *Kirin-Amgen*. The *Merck* Case indicates an increased emphasis on the third Improver question, and it is that third question which comes closest to Lord Hoffmann's formulation of looking at what the person skilled in the art would think the patentee was intending to claim. Literal construction is of course banned by the Protocol, but this does not mean that departure from the plain words of the claim should be permitted on a routine basis. If a precise expression is used, the meaning of which would be clear to the person skilled in the art (such as the name of a specific chemical compound), the patentee will be deemed to have chosen it with due regard for that meaning. Where less precise expressions are used, there may be more scope for arguing about the patentee's intentions. This presumably still applies to words like "vertically", as in *Catnic*. The *Merck* Case has been criticised by P.G. Mole in [2004] *CIPA* 50 as a case which should never have been brought, and he is also critical of the drafting of the claims. Patent attorneys should first and foremost be skilled draftsmen, and despite repeated references in the cases to the intentions of the patentee, it is inevitably a patent attorney who chooses the language of the claims. The *Improver* questions are not a substitute for the Protocol, as the judge says, but nor should the Protocol be seen as a substitute for good drafting. The judge's barbed comment in *Merck* that "the courts are not a branch of the social services whose job it is to help the infirm or the unwise and the Protocol does not require them to be so" should be noted.]

A review of cases on the protocol by H. Dunlop was published in [2003] EIPR 342 under the title "Court of Appeal gets to grips with the Protocol", and provides a detailed analysis of many decisions given by the English courts during the period 1993–2003, but not the most recent *Merck* Case mentioned above or the House of Lords' decision in *Kirin-Amgen*, which were of course published after that article went to press.

Decisions on claim construction under subsection (3)   **125.18**

The Court of Appeal decision in *Wheatley v. Drillsafe*, cited in the Main Work as BL C/30/00, has been published ([2001] RPC 133); and the Court of Appeal decision in *American Home Products v. Novartis*, cited in the Main Work as BL C/31/00, has been published ([2001] RPC 159).

See the case comment by G. Thomson and L. Kempton [2002] EIPR 591 on the recent Court of Appeal decisions on the "protocol questions".

—Decisions finding non-infringement   **125.19**

The Court of Appeal decision in *Wheatley v. Drillsafe*, cited in the Main Work as BL C/30/00, has been published ([2001] RPC 133). The first instance decision in *Rohm & Haas v. Collag*, there noted, has been published ([2001] FSR 426) and was upheld on appeal ([2002] FSR 445), but with some additional remarks relevant to the issue of "file wrapper estoppel—see § 125.26 *infra*. In *Amersham v. Amicon* (BL C/49/00, *noted* IPD 24011), it was argued that the stated object of the invention could be ignored as not being correct, but the court held that there could be no infringement in such a situation. In the Court of Appeal (BL C/32/01, *noted* IPD 24078) the judgment was upheld on this point and it was commented that the Protocol did not introduce "a doctrine of infringement by equivalent effect by use of a different mechanism. That may be for the future." and "third parties should be able to discern, from the terms of the patent, which equivalent mechanisms, if any, are included within the claim".

Infringement (in the context of an application under s. 71) had been found in *Impro's Patent* ([1998] FSR 299) (see § 71.05 *supra*). In *Arjo and Impro v. Liko* (BL C/52/01, *noted* [2001] *CIPA* 575, 628 and IPD 25006) the court disagreed with the construction placed on the patent in the previous case (by a different judge), holding that the Protocol Questions could not be used to "allow one to ignore limitations in the claim which a skilled reader would understand to have been deliberately included to achieve a particular, stated and wanted, technical effect". Certain features previously determined as inessential were held to be essential features, being "features which the inventor put forward as central to his alleged technical contribution to the art", even though it appeared that these features were not in fact essential to the working of the invention.

In *Sara Lee v. Johnson Wax* (BL C/60/01, *noted* IPD 25008), infringement was not found where the defendant's device used a feature which could not be held to be a "liquidpermeable closure" as required by the words of the claim. Accordingly the words of the claim were not apt to cover the alleged infringement, which operated in a different way. There may have been "equivalence of result, but not of construction"; see also § 125.16 *supra*.

In finding non-infringement "on the basis of "variants" in *Wesley Jesson v. Coopervision* ([2003] RPC 355), having already found non-infringement on a literal construction, the judge of the Patents County Court took account of amendments made during prosecution of the patent application before the EPO in drawing conclusions as to the significance of an integer of the claim. He referred in this context to the words of Hoffmann L.J. in *Société Technique de Pulverisation STEP v. Emson* ([1993] RPC 513) quoted in the Main Work in § 125.16 *supra*, in particular that "the patentee may have had some reason of his own" for introducing the amendment. The patentee had introduced a more restricted term "dots" instead of "pattern" in response to prior art cited by the EPO and it was acknowledged by the defendants' counsel that if the claim had remained in its original form, he might have been in difficulty as to this aspect of his non-infringement case. This seems to be an example of "file wrapper estoppel" emerging in an English case—see § 125.26 *infra*.

125.20 *—Decisions finding infringement*

Stoves v. Baumatic (BL C/27/00) has been noted (IPD 23086). A similar decision is *City Technology v. Alphasense* (BL C/42/00; [2001] IP&T 326, *noted* IPD 23102) where the word "wick" was interpreted functionally and as not limited to a unitary element. The decision was upheld on appeal (BL C/13/02; [2002] IP&T 767, *noted* IPD 25038); see § 125.16 *supra*.

Infringement was found by the Court of Appeal in *Pharmacia v. Merck* ([2002] RPC 775) overturning the first instance decision (cited as *Monsanto v. Merck* ([2002] RPC 709)) on this point, see § 125.16 *supra*.

125.21 *—Limitation of literal wording*

The Court of Appeal decision in *Cartonneries de Thulin v. CTP White Knight*, cited in the Main Work, has been reported at [2001] RPC 107.

The patent in issue in *Coflexip v. Stolt Comex* (BL C/32/00 and [2001] RPC 182 (CA)) was subsequently invalidated over different prior art because of the claim construction applied on appeal (*Rockwater v. Coflexip* (BL C/15/03, *noted* IPD 26039))—see the case comment on this case by N. Coulson and D. Brown at *Patent World* No. 153 (June 2003)). However, on appeal, the decision on invalidity was reversed, and the patent again found valid and infringed (*Technip's Patent* ([2004] RPC 919))—see § 125.15 *supra*, and the case comment by Katharine Stephens in [2004] *CIPA* 224).

125.23 *—Reference numerals in claims*

In *Russel Finex v. Telsonic* ([2004] EWHC 589 (Pat), BL C/26/04; IPD 27050), the judge commented that reference numerals in the claim "may, depending on the circumstances, help to illustrate that the inventor intended a wide or narrow scope for his claim", but "cannot be used to import into the claim restrictions which are not foreshadowed by the language of the claim itself".

125.24 *Claims containing a statement of purpose*

The Court of Appeal decision in *Bristol-Myers Squibb v. Baker Norton*, cited in the Main Work, has now been reported at [2001] RPC 1.

File wrapper estoppel **125.26**

In the Appeal in *Rohm & Haas v. Collag* ([2002] FSR 445) a key issue in the case was the meaning of the word "surfactant". A question was raised whether statements made in a letter to the EPO in the course of prosecution of the patent should be taken into account in construing the claims. The Court of Appeal (in a statement which would appear to be *obiter*) said that had it been necessary to take account of the letter in order to resolve the issue of construction, the judge would have been entitled to do so. Some commentators (see L. Cohen [2001] *CIPA* 571 and A. Rich [2001] *CIPA* 583) have seen this as a step towards the acceptance of a general doctrine of file wrapper estoppel in the United Kingdom along the lines of the United States model, but it is submitted that the decision (apart from being *obiter* on this point) may go no further than *Furr v. Truline* ([1985] FSR 553) noted in the Main Work in which the patentee was not allowed to resile from an "admission against interest" held to have been made in the Patent Office file.

In *Wesley Jesson v. Coopervision* ([2003] RPC 355) the judge of the Patents County Court took account of amendments made during prosecution of the patent application before the EPO in reaching a finding of non-infringement under the Protocol—see 125.19 *supra*. However, in *Machinery Developments v. St Merryn Meat* (PAT 03 061, BL C/50/04), he explained that decision as relating to a "key word" in the claims, and in which he had reached his conclusion on infringement without reference to the prosecution file such that this was "a makeweight point". In stating that he did not find the notion of prosecution history estoppel helpful in deciding the issues in the case before him, the judge echoed the cautionary comments of Jacob J. in *Celltech*, *infra*, as to the undesirability of introducing such a doctrine into English law, particularly in the context of cases to be decided in accordance with the procedures of the Patents County Court, which "was set up to cater for the needs of litigants ... of modest means".

In *Celltech Chiroscience v. Medimmune* (BL C/36/01, *noted* IPD 24074), a judge of the English High Court had to construe the claims of a US patent in order to determine whether payment of royalties was due under a licence (which was under English law, but required royalties to be paid in respect of products falling within the US patent). In this initial decision the determination of this question was stayed pending the decision of the US Supreme Court in *Festo Corp v. Shoketsu Kinzoku* (*infra*). In subsequent proceedings (*Celltech (Adair's) US Patent* [2003] FSR 433), when the scope of the US doctrine of file wrapper estoppel had been clarified by the *Festo* decision, the English court found that the patent was not infringed, the application of the doctrine of equivalents having been precluded by arguments made during prosecution, "argument estoppel". On appeal ([2004] FSR 35), the Court of Appeal upheld (by a majority) the judge's finding on "argument estoppel" but also allowed the defendant's cross-appeal that the assertion of infringement was precluded by "amendment estoppel" as well. The case is also of interest in view of remarks made by the judge at first instance about the undesirability of introducing a doctrine of file wrapper estoppel into European law. These views were reinforced by a different judge in the Patents Court in *Russel Finex v. Telsonic* ([2004] EWHC 589 (Pat), BL C/26/04; IPD 27050), in saying that "Patents and their claims are meant to be statements made by the patentee to the relevant public. Their meaning and effect should be discernible from the face of the document". In this case, the judge declined to rule on the issue because the meaning of the claim appeared clear to him without resorting to the prosecution history.

The same conclusion (as to non-infringement) was reached when the case again came before the Patents Court (*Celltech R & D v. Medimmune* [2004] EWHC 1124 (Pat), BL C/55/04) for a finding on the same facts but in relation to the corresponding European patent and under the German law relating to infringement. The German law was seen as broadly in line with the *Improver* approach, and in particular the statement by the German Supreme Court in *Custodial* II (GRUR 2002, 527) that "the German law of infringement does not allow one to correct mistakes made by the patentee. If the patentee has imposed a clear limit on his monopoly which addressees recognise as being unnecessary or based on mistaken science, it is still effective" was seen as involving essentially the same test as the third *Improver* question.

The final word on the role (or lack of it) in English law of any doctrine of prosecution history or "file wrapper" estoppel may have been uttered by Lord Hoffmann in *Kirin-Amgen v. Hoechst Marion Roussel* ([2005] RPC 169), in which he says that *Catnic* and Art. 69 "firmly shut the door on any doctrine which extends protection outside the claims". Lord Hoffmann referred to the *Festo* litigation (*infra*) as suggesting that American litigants "pay dearly for results which are no more just or predictable than could be achieved by simply reading the claims".

Festo Corp v. Shoketsu Kinzoku, reported at [2003] FSR 154, is a very important US case on the scope of the doctrine of equivalents and file wrapper estoppel in US law. The Court of Appeals for the Federal Circuit had held that estoppel arose from any amendment that narrowed a claim to comply with the Patent Act and when estoppel applied it stood as a complete bar against any claim of equivalence for the element that was amended. This caused concern that the doctrine of equivalents was effectively abolished for any element of a claim which had undergone amendment during prosecution. The US Supreme Court held that estoppel required an examination of the subject matter surrendered by the amendment. To establish a rule barring all equivalence was inconsistent with the purpose of applying the estoppel, namely to hold the inventor to the representations made during prosecution and the inferences that might reasonably be drawn from the amendment. By amending, the inventor was deemed to concede that the patent did not extend as far as the original claim. It did not follow, however, that the amended claim became so perfect in its description that no-one could devise an equivalent. Language remained an "imperfect fit" for invention. The narrowing amendment might demonstrate what the claim was not, but it might still fail to capture precisely what the claim was. When the court was unable to determine the purpose underlying a narrowing amendment, the patentee should bear the burden of showing that the amendment did not surrender the particular equivalent in question.

[*Editor's Note*: in the light of the remarks of Jacob J. and Laddie JJ. in *Celltech* and *Russel Finex* and the judgment of Judge Fysh in *Wesley Jesson* it would seem to remain an open question whether any doctrine of "file wrapper" or "prosecution history" estoppel forms part of English patent law. Given the further judgment of Judge Fysh in *Machinery Developments*, it would seem that the judicial view as to the evils of such a doctrine is hardening, see also the *Kirin-Agmen* House of Lords judgment, *supra*. Perhaps the courts will restrict it to clear cases of "admissions against interest", as already suggested above.]

125A.01

SECTION 125A [ADDED]—Disclosure of invention by specifications: availability of samples of biological material

Note. The amendments noted for the title and subsections (1) and (2)(a) were each applied to the Isle of Man by S.I. 2003 No. 1249.

RELEVANT RULES—RULE 17 AND SCHEDULE 2

125A.02 **Rule 17—Biological material**

Note. Rule 17 was amended by S.I. 2001 No. 1412 (with formal effect from July 6, 2001) to replace "require for their performance the use of micro-organisms" by "involve the use of or concern biological material". As explained in § 125A.09 in the Main Work, this amendment may have had effect from at least July 28, 2000 when section 125A was likewise amended.

PATENTS RULES 1995—SCHEDULE 2: BIOLOGICAL MATERIAL

Note. Schedule 2 was extensively amended by The Patents (Amendment) Rules 2001 (S.I. 2001 No. 1412), with effect from July 6, 2001. The new form of Schedule 2 is set out in §§ 125A.03 – 125A.07 *infra*. However, the former form (as set out in these sections of the Main Work) continues to have effect in relation to applications with dates of filing from January 7, 1991 up to July 6, 2001, as to which see § 125A.09 of the Main Work.

Paragraph 1—Application

1.—(1) The specification of an application for a patent, or of a patent, for an invention which involves the use of or concerns biological material—

(a) which is not available to the public at the date of filing the application; and

(b) which cannot be described in the specification in such a manner as to enable the invention to be performed by a person skilled in the art,

shall, in relation to the biological material itself, be treated for the purposes of the Act as disclosing the invention in such a manner only if one of the conditions set out in subparagraph (2) below is satisfied and the application as filed contains such relevant information as is available to the applicant on the characteristics of the biological material.

(2) The conditions referred to in subparagraph (1) above are—

(a) a condition that,—

(i) not later than the date of filing of the application, the biological material has been deposited in a depositary institution which is able to furnish a sample of the biological material; and

(ii) the name of the depositary institution and the accession number of the deposit are given in the specification of the application; and

(iii) where the biological material has been deposited by a person other than the applicant, the name and address of the depositor are stated in the application and a document is filed satisfying the comptroller that the depositor has authorised the applicant to refer to the deposited material in the application and has given his unreserved and irrevocable consent to the deposited material being made available to the public in accordance with this Schedule; and

(b) a condition, in the case of a European patent (UK), an application for a European patent (UK) or an international application for a patent (UK) which is treated, by virtue of section 77, 81 or 89 as a patent under the Act, or, as the case may be, an application for a patent under the Act, that the corresponding provisions of the Implementing Regulations to the European Patent Convention or, as the case may require, the Patent Co-operation Treaty have been complied with,

and, where paragraph 5 below applies, a further condition that a new deposit has been made in accordance with that paragraph and the applicant or proprietor has made the request referred to in subparagraph (2)(b) of that paragraph within the period referred to in subparagraph (2) or, if applicable (4), of that paragraph.

(3) Where the information specified in subparagraph (2)(a)(ii) or (iii) above is not contained in an application for a patent as filed, it shall be added to the application—

(a) before the end of the period of 16 months after the declared priority date or, where there is no declared priority date, the date of filing of the application;

(b) where a request is made by the applicant to the comptroller to publish the application before the end of the period prescribed for the purposes of section 16(1), on or before the date of the request; or

(c) where the comptroller sends notification to the applicant that, in accordance with subsection (4) of section 118, he has received a request by any person for information and inspection of documents under subsection (1) of that section, before the end of one month after his sending to the applicant notification of his receipt of the request,

whichever is the earliest.

(4) The giving of the information specified in subparagraph (2)(a)(ii) above shall constitute the unreserved and irrevocable consent of the applicant to the depositary institution with which biological material (including a deposit which is to be treated as having always been available by virtue of paragraph 5(2) below) is from time to time deposited making the biological material available on receipt of the comptroller's certificate authorising the release to the person who is named therein as a person to whom the biological material may be made available and who makes a valid request therefor to the institution.

Notes.

1. This form of paragraph 1 has effect from July 6, 2001.
2. Former subparagraph (6), which continues to have effect, now appears as paragraph 6 of the Schedule (see § 125A.06A *infra*).

125A.04   Paragraph 2—General availability of biological material

2.—(1) Save where paragraph 3 below has effect, a request may be made to the comptroller to issue a certificate authorising a depositary institution to make available a sample of biological material—

    (a) before publication of the application for a patent, to a person who has made a request under section 118(1) in the circumstances mentioned in paragraph 1(3)(c) above; and

    (b) at any later time, to any person (notwithstanding revocation or cancellation of the patent).

(2) A request under subparagraph (1) above shall be made on Patents Form 8/77 (which shall be filed in duplicate together, in the case of biological material which is deposited under the Budapest Treaty with an international depositary authority, with the form provided for by the Regulations under that Treaty).

(3) On receipt of a valid request under subparagraph (1) above, the comptroller shall send copies of the form or forms lodged with him under subparagraph (2) above and of his certificate authorising the release of the sample—

    (a) to the applicant for, or proprietor of, the patent;

    (b) to the depositary institution; and

    (c) to the person making the request.

(4) A request under subparagraph (1) above shall comprise, on the part of the person to whom the request relates, undertakings for the benefit of the applicant for, or proprietor of, the patent—

    (a) not to make the biological material, or any material derived from it, available to any other person; and

    (b) not to use the biological material, or any material derived from it, otherwise than for experimental purposes relating to the subject matter of the invention,

and both undertakings shall have effect—

        (i) during any period before the application for a patent has been withdrawn, has been taken to be withdrawn, has been treated as having been withdrawn, has been refused or is treated as having been refused (including any further period allowed under rule 100 or rule 110(1) or (4) but excluding, where an application is reinstated under either of those rules, the period before it is reinstated);

(ii) if a patent is granted on the application, during any period for which the patent is in force and during the period of six months referred to in section 25(4).

(5) For the purpose of enabling any act specified in section 55 to be done in relation to the biological material for the services of the Crown, the undertakings specified in subparagraph (4) above—

(a) shall not be required from any government department or person authorised in writing by a government department for the purposes of this paragraph; and

(b) shall not have effect in relation to any such person who has already given them.

(6) An undertaking given pursuant to subparagraph (4) above may be varied by way of derogation by agreement between the applicant or proprietor and the person by whom it is given.

(7) Where, in respect of a patent to which an undertaking given pursuant to subparagraph 4 above has effect,

(a) an entry is made in the register under section 46 to the effect that licences are to be available as of right; or

(b) a compulsory licence is granted under section 48,

that undertaking shall not have effect to the extent necessary for effect to be given to any such licence.

(8) In subparagraph (4) above, references to material derived from deposited biological material are references to material so derived which exhibits those characteristics of the deposited biological material essential for the performance of the invention.

Notes.

1. This form of paragraph 2 has effect from July 6, 2001.

2. The form provided for by the Regulations under the Budapest Treaty, referred to in sub-paragraph 1, remains as Form BP/12, reprinted at § 141.03.

Paragraph 3—Restriction of availability of biological material to experts   **125A.05**

3.—(1) Subject to subparagraph (3) below, where before the preparations for publication under section 16 of an application for a patent have been completed, the applicant gives notice to the comptroller on Patents Form 8A/77 of his intention that a sample of the biological material should be made available only to an independent expert, the provisions of this paragraph shall have effect.

(2) The comptroller—

(a) shall publish, with the application, notice that the provisions of this paragraph have effect; and

(b) notwithstanding paragraph 2 above, shall not:

(i) until the grant of the patent or, where applicable,

(ii) for 20 years from the date on which the patent application was filed if the application has been withdrawn, has been taken to be withdrawn, has been treated as having been withdrawn, has been refused or is treated as having been refused, issue any certificate authorising release of a sample otherwise than under paragraph 4 below.

(3) Where an applicant for an international application for a patent (UK) gives notice in writing to the International Bureau under rule 13bis.3 of the Regulations under the Patent Co-operation Treaty before the technical preparations for international publication of the application are complete of his intention that a sample of the biological material should be made available only to an expert, he shall be treated by the comptroller for the purposes of this paragraph as having complied with the conditions in subparagraph (1) above and subparagraph (2)(a) above shall not apply.

Notes.

  1. This form of paragraph 3 has effect from July 6, 2001.
  2. In this amendment of paragraph (3), former sub-paragraphs (3)–(9) were transferred to a new paragraph 4, for which see § 125A.05A *infra.*

125A.05A   **Paragraph 4—Request for a sample to be made available to an expert**

4.—(1) Where the availability of samples is restricted to independent experts by paragraph 3 above, any person wishing to have a sample of the biological material made available ("the requester")—

> (a) shall apply to the comptroller on Patents Form 8/77 (which shall be filed in duplicate together, in the case of biological material which is deposited under the Budapest Treaty with an international depositary authority, with the form provided for by the Regulations under that Treaty) nominating the person ("the expert") to whom he wishes the sample to be made available; and
>
> (b) shall at the same time file undertakings by the expert as set out in subparagraph (4) of paragraph 2 above and the provisions of that paragraph relating to undertakings shall also apply to the undertakings given by the expert.

(2) The comptroller shall send a copy of Patents Form 8/77 filed under subparagraph (1) above to the applicant for the patent and shall specify the period within which the applicant may object, in accordance with subparagraph (3) below, to a sample of the biological material being made available to the expert.

(3) Unless, within the period specified by the comptroller under subparagraph (2) above (or within such longer period as the comptroller may, on application made to him within that period, allow), the applicant for the patent sends notice in writing to the comptroller that he objects to a sample of the biological material being made available to the expert and gives his reasons for his objection, the comptroller shall send a copy of any form lodged with him under subparagraph (1)(a) above and of his certificate authorising the release of the sample—

> (a) to the applicant for the patent,
>
> (b) to the depositary institution concerned,
>
> (c) to the requester, and
>
> (d) to the expert.

(4) Where, in accordance with subparagraph (3) above, the applicant for the patent sends notice to the comptroller of his objection to the issue of a certificate in favour of the expert, the comptroller—

> (a) shall decide, having regard to the knowledge, experience, independence and technical qualifications of the expert and to any other factors he

considers relevant, whether to issue his certificate in favour of the expert; and

(b) if he decides to authorise the release of the sample to the expert, shall send to the persons referred to in subparagraph (3) above a copy of any form lodged with him under subparagraph (1)(a) above and of his certificate authorising the release of the sample to the expert.

(5) Before making a decision in accordance with subparagraph (4) above, the comptroller shall afford the applicant and the requester the opportunity of being heard.

(6) If the comptroller decides under subparagraph (4) above not to issue his certificate in favour of the expert, the requester may, by notice in writing to the comptroller and the applicant, nominate another person as the expert for the purposes of this paragraph; and the comptroller shall give such directions as he shall think fit with regard to the subsequent procedure.

(7) Nothing in this paragraph or paragraph 3 above shall affect the rights under section 55 of any government department or any person authorised in writing by a government department.

Notes.
1. This new paragraph has effect from July 6, 2001.
2. Paragraph 4 consists of renumbered former sub-paragraphs 3(3)–(9).
3. The form provided for by the Regulations under the Budapest Treaty, referred to in subparagraph 1, is Form BP/12, reprinted at § 141.03 in the Main Work.

Paragraph 5—New deposits   **125A.06**

5.—(1) This paragraph applies where—

(a) biological material ceases to be available from the institution with which it was deposited because—
  (i) the biological material is no longer viable, or
  (ii) for any other reason the institution is unable to supply samples, or

(b) the depositary institution ceases to be recognised for the purposes of this Schedule —
  (i) ceases to be a depositary institution for the purposes of this Schedule, either entirely or for the kind of biological material to which the deposited sample belongs, or
  (ii) discontinues, temporarily or permanently, the performance of its functions as regards deposited biological material,

and no sample of the biological material has been transferred to another depositary institution, from which it continues to be available.

(2) An interruption in availability of the biological material shall be deemed not to have occurred if within a period of three months from the date on which the depositor was notified of the interruption by the depositary institution—

(a) the depositor (or applicant or proprietor if different) makes a new deposit of a sample of that biological material; and

(b) the applicant or proprietor makes a request for amendment of the specification under section 19 or section 27, as the case may be, so as to indicate the accession number of the new deposit and, where applicable, the name of the depository institution with which the deposit was made.

(3) In the case provided for in subparagraph (1)(a)(i) above, the new deposit

shall be made with the depositary institution with which the original deposit was made; in the cases provided for in subparagraphs (1)(a)(ii) and (1)(b), it may be made with another depositary institution.

(4) Where in a case to which subparagraph (1)(b) applies, no notification of the interruption of availability of the biological material from the depositary institution is received by the depositor within six months from the date of such event, the three-month period referred to in subparagraph (2) shall begin on the date on which this event is announced in the Journal.

(5) Any new deposit shall be accompanied by a statement signed by the person making the deposit certifying that the sample of biological material newly deposited is of the same biological material as was the sample originally deposited.

Notes.
1. This paragraph has effect from July 6, 2001.
2. It replaced former paragraph 4 (for which see § 125A.06 in the Main Work).

125A.06A   **Paragraph 6—Transitional Provisions**

6. In relation to an application for a patent filed before 7th January 1991, rule 17 of the Patents Rules 1982 [S.I. 1982 No. 717] shall continue to have effect notwithstanding its revocation by rule 123(3) of the Patents Rules 1990 [S.I. 1990 No. 2384].

Notes.
1. Paragraph 6 has effect from July 6, 2001, but in fact it duplicates former paragraph 1(6) (reprinted in § 125A.03 *supra*).
2. Rule 17 [1982] is reprinted at § 125A.08 in the Main Work.

125A.07   **Paragraph 7—Interpretation of Schedule**

7.—(1) In this Schedule —
"the Budapest Treaty" means the Treaty on the International Recognition of the Deposit of Micro-organisms for the purposes of Patent Procedure done at Budapest in 1977; and
"international depositary authority" means a depositary institution which has acquired the status of international depositary authority as provided in Article 7 of the Budapest Treaty.

(2) For the purposes of this Schedule a "depositary institution" is an institution which, at all relevant times,
(a) carries out the functions of receiving, accepting and storing biological material and the furnishing of samples thereof; and
(b) conducts its affairs in so far as they relate to the carrying out of those functions in an objective and impartial manner.

Notes.

Paragraph 7 has effect from July 6, 2001,

COMMENTARY ON SECTION 125A

125A.09   *Scope of the section*

The revisions of rule 17 and of Schedule 2 to the Rules implemented Articles 13 and 14 of the Biotechnology Directive (reprinted in §§ C13 and C14 of the Main Work), although only with formal effect from July 6, 2001 and only in respect of applications (and patents granted thereon) with dates of filing on or after this date. At the same time this Schedule was brought into conformity with the analogous provisions of the EPC and PCT, although it is possible that some minor discrepancies with those provisions may remain.

The challenge to the legality of the Biotechnology Directive by the Dutch Government referred to in the Main Work (*Kingdom of the Netherlands v. European Parliament* (Case C–377/98 ECJ) [2002] FSR 574; OJEPO 2002, 231; [2002] IP&T 121) failed on all counts, the ECJ holding that there was no legal uncertainty in the Directive and no breach of international obligations. It has since been reported (European Commission, July 10, 2003) that the Commission has decided to refer Germany, Austria, Belgium, France, Italy, Luxembourg, the Netherlands and Sweden to the European Court of Justice for failure to implement the Directive, although it is understood that Germany has now taken steps to amend its law to comply.

Reference might be made to Kamstra, *et al., Patents on Biotechnological Inventions: The* European Directive *—Special Report* (Sweet & Maxwell, 2001).

—Types of claim   **125A.10**

A 3rd edition of the book by H.-R. Jaenichem referred to in the Main Work has been published. A paper entitled "recent developments in the patenting of biotechnology inventions, including the scope of protection for patents on genes" by U. Kinkeldy was published in OJEPO (Special Edition No. 2) 140.

Particular forms of claim applicable to biotechnology

—Recombinant DNA   **125A.14**

In *DSM's Patent* ([2001] RPC 675), claims to a gene sequence were not seen as a mere discovery in relation to a known enzyme, see also § 125A.19 *infra*, but the claims were otherwise held invalid for lack of inventive step (see § 3.19 *supra*) and for insufficiency (see § 14.17 *supra*).

For a discussion on patenting genes and aspects of gene therapy, see N. Jenkins (*Patent World*, 128, December 2000/January 2001, 21).

—Plants and Animals   **125A.15**

The decision of the Opposition Division in *HARVARD/Onco-mouse* referred to in the Main Work has been published (OJEPO 2003, 473). The oppositions were rejected subject to the claims being limited to the creation of transgenic rodents. The decision has been appealed. See the article by A. Sharples and D. Curley [2002/2003] 1 BSLR 26 for further comment on this case.

Prior art issues applicable to biotechnology

—Claims to a desideratum or to matters "obvious to try"   **125A.19**

In *DSM's Patent* ([2001] RPC 675), claims to a gene sequence of a known enzyme were not seen as either a mere *desideratum* or as something obvious as such a try, see also § 125A.19, but the claims were otherwise held invalid for lack of inventive step (see § 3.19 *supra*) and for insufficiency (see § 14.17 *supra*).

EPO Decision T 145/95 *BTG/Newcastle disease virus*, referred to in the Main Work, has been reported at [2003] EPOR 390.

Insufficiency issues in relation to biotechnology

125A.23 | —*Sufficient description of method of performing the invention*

The decision of the Opposition Division in *HARVARD/Onco-mouse* referred to in the Main Work (given in 2001) has been published (OJEPO 2003, 473). The oppositions were rejected subject to the claims being limited to the creation of transgenic rodents. The decision has been appealed. See the article by A. Sharples and D. Curley [2002/2003] 1 BSLR 26 for further comment on this case.

125A.24 | —*The need for a deposit to establish sufficiency*

In *EPO Decision T* 816/90 *ALKO/CBH II* ([2003] EPOR 414), certain sub-claims were held invalid for insufficiency because the required deposits had not been made, even though the main claim (on which the sub-claims were dependent) was allowed as relating to a process which was inventive in itself.

125A.25 *Breadth of claim issues in relation to biotechnology*

Monsanto v. Merck, cited in the Main Work, was published [2002] RPC 709. Also see the appeal in this case cited as *Pharmacia v. Merck* ([2002] RPC 775).

In *DSM's Patent* ([2001] RPC 675), two claims were seen as of undue breadth and were held invalid for insufficiency (see § 14.17 *supra*). If the claim, which referred to hybridized material, was of broad scope (as was held), it was admitted to be unworkable and to extend to material unrelated to the inventive concept; and, if a narrower functional imitation were to be impliedly read into the claim wording (as the patentee contended), then the patent provided no teaching as to the appropriate conditions which should be used to achieve the production of only related DNA material. However, if the claims had been valid, they would not have been seen as limited to the precise sequences discovered and it was recognised that a patent draftsman has a problem in identifying the "relation" between the natural product in issue "so as to be clear and sufficient on the one hand, while, on the other hand, putting forward a formula which has commerical efficacy".

125A.27 *Deposit of biological material (Rules, Sched. 2, para. 1)*

The revision of paragraph 1 to Schedule 2 of the Rules (noted in § 125A.03 *supra*), effective with regard to applications (and patents granted thereon) having dates of filing on or after July 6, 2001 introduced (in sub-para. (1)) the new requirement that "the application as filed contains such relevant information as is available to the applicant on the characteristics of the biological material deposited". Read literally, this requirement is a very onerous one and could leave any patent to which it applies vulnerable to possible revocation for non-compliance if it comes to light that the proprietor had, at the date of filing, information on the characteristics of the biological material additional to that present in the specification at its filing date. It will be all too easy to overlook the apparent requirement to update the information on these characteristics contained in a priority document by additional information which came to the applicant's attention between the priority and filing dates. However, the missing information must be "relevant", and presumably this applies to the characteristics of the biological material which are necessary for practice of the invention or for the biological material to be identified, for example in an alleged infringement situation. For some discussion on the meaning of "relevance" in this context, see *EPO Guideline* C-III, 6.3 (1999 revision), the *EPH* (§ 18.6.2) and the wording of the Budapest Treaty and its Implementing Regulations (reprinted in Chapter 88 of the *EPH*). This EPO Guideline suggests that "relevant information" includes "the classification of the biological material, significant differences from known biological material, morphological and biochemical characteristics and the proposed taxonomic description, all in accordance with standard textbooks". It would not seem to be possible to add further information on such characteristics to the specification after filing, because to do so would apparently result in the addition of subject-matter contrary to section 76, thereby making a patent granted on the application revocable under section 72(1)(d).

For applications filed under the Act, the further conditions are set out in paragraph 1(2)(a) to Schedule 2 of the Rules. They are that: (i) not later than the filing date, a sample of the biological material has been deposited with a depositary institution able to furnish a sample thereof; (ii) the name of that institution and the accession number of the deposit are given in the specification; and (iii) where the deposit was made by a person other than the applicant (a practice which is generally undesirable), the name and address of the depositor is stated in the application and a document is filed evidencing that the depositor has given his unreserved and irrevocable consent to the deposited material being made available to the public as if the deposit had been made by the applicant.

The amendments made to paragraph 1(2) by the Patents (Amendment) Rules 2001 were intended to bring the requirements for depositing biological material into line with EPCr. 28(1)(d): (a) by the introduction of point (iii) (for the reason discussed in § 125A.33); (b) by removing the former requirement (in point (ii)) that the date of deposit should also appear in the specification; and (c) by deletion of the requirement (in Rules, Sched. 2, former para. 1(5)) that the specification should mention any international agreement (*viz.* the Budapest Treaty) under which the deposit has been made.

While the conditions of point (i) (in addition to the general condition contained at the end of para. (1) and discussed *supra*) must be satisfied at the date of filing, the requirements of points (ii) and (iii) may be met at a somewhat later date, *viz.*: (a) up to 16 months after the earliest declared priority date (or, if none, the filing date); or (b) earlier than the date when early publication is requested; or (c) where early access to the specification has been requested under section 118(4), then within one month of the Comptroller notifying the applicant of that request (Rules, Sched. 2, para. 1(3)). The periods specified in paragraph 1(3) are now automatically extensible by two months under rule 110(3), with further extension possible with discretion under rule 110(4), see § 123.33 *supra*. In the case of a divisional or replacement application under sections 8(3), 12(6), 15(4) or 37(4), the requirements of paragraph 1(2) must be met at least by the actual date of filing thereof, if not already met in the parent application (r. 26(1)(b)), but again a discretionary extension may be available, see § 15.22.

It is not clear what happens when the application/patent is assigned. Such may cause the depositor and the applicant to be different persons, even if this not so originally, and anyway will cause the required consent under point (iii) no longer relevant. It is prudent that, with or following any assignment of the application/patent, the new proprietor should furnish to the Patent Office a document providing his unreserved and irrevocable consent to the deposited material being made available to the public in accordance with point (iii) *supra*, on which see also § 125A.34.

Rule 17 of the Patents Rules 1981 (as reprinted in the Main Work at § 125A.08) continues to have effect in respect of applications filed before January 7, 1991. For applications filed on or after this date and before July 6, 2001, the provisions of Schedule 2 to the 1995 Rules (as printed in the Main Work at §§ 125A.03–125A.07) continue to apply.

Obtaining a sample of deposited biological material by a non-expert (Rules,   **125A.28**
Sched. 2, para. 2)

As set out in revised Schedule 2, paragraph 2 to the Rules (reprinted in § 125A.04 *supra*), where a request is made for release of a sample of deposited material, that request must include undertakings continuing during the life of the application patent: (a) not to make the sample supplied, or any material derived from it, available to any other person; and (b) not to use the sample, or any material derived from it, for other than experimental purposes related to the subject-matter of the invention (Rules, Sched. 2, para. 2(4)). These undertakings may be varied by way of derogation by an agreement between the applicant or proprietor and the person giving the undertaking (see Rules, Sched. 2, para. 2(6)).

125A.29 *—Obtaining a sample when access has been restricted to an expert (Rules, Sched. 2, paras 3 and 4)*

Since July 6, 2001, it has been possible (under revised Rules, Sched. 2, para. 3(2)(b)(ii), reprinted in § 125A.05A *supra*) not only to apply the "expert solution" (*i.e.* that provision of a sample of deposited material shall be limited to an expert) for the period between publication and grant or failure of the application, in the latter case, but also that such provision shall apply during the period of 20 years from the date of filing he application where the application was withdrawn, taken to be withdrawn, refused or taken to be refused before grant, *i.e.* when the application fails and does not proceed to grant. Thus, under this second aspect of the "expert solution", an applicant may eventually have the choice between: (1) allowing the application to proceed to grant, whereafter the deposited sample will become available to anyone; or (2) withdrawing the application, or otherwise allowing this to fail, and thereby retain limitation of access to the deposited material to an expert for the remainder of the 20 year period running from the filing date of the application.

To implement this "expert solution" for these effects, it is necessary to file PF 8A/77 before the "technical preparations for publication have been completed" (Rules, Sched. 2, para. 3(1)). For the meaning of this quoted phrase, see § 16.06 *supra*. Once the preparations for publication of the application under section 16 have been completed, it will be impossible to request the "expert solution" to be applied.

Where the "expert solution" is requested under paragraph 3, a notice thereof is published with the application (Rules, Sched. 2, para. 3(2)(a)). In the case of a European application, any application of the "expert solution" is published in the EPB. Possibly, this information will also appear in the EPIDOS data base of European applications/patents. Note also that the second (20 year) aspect of the restriction to an expert following failure of an application was made available for European applications from an earlier date in 1999.

When the "expert solution" has been applied, the Comptroller may not issue a certificate directed to the depositary institution for release of deposited material except in conformity with the provisions of paragraph 4 of Schedule 2 to the Rules (reprinted at § 125A.05A *supra*). The procedure for this is generally the same as when the "expert solution" does not apply (for which see § 125A.39 in the Main Work) and has not altered from that under the former form of Schedule 2 to the Rules. However, as the numbering of the various provisions has changed in the new form of Schedule 2, these provisions are summarised below.

Thus, the application for a sample of the deposited material to be made available is made on PF 8/77 (reprinted at § 140.08 *infra*) and this must nominate the "expert" to whom release is requested and, at the same time, undertakings by that expert are to be supplied (Rules, Sched. 2, para. 4(1)(b)). These undertakings are to be to the same effect as those specified for release to a non-expert, for which see paragraph 2(3) of Schedule 2 to the Rules, as discussed in § 125A.28 *supra*, but there is no provision for variation of these undertakings as there is where the "expert solution" does not apply (for which see Rules, Sched. 2, para. 2(5)).

Following the filing of PF 8/77, together with the required undertakings from the nominated expert, the Comptroller supplies a copy to the applicant for the patent, or the proprietor as the case may be, specifying the period within which the applicant/proprietor may object to the deposited biological material being made available to the nominated expert (Rules, Sched. 2, para. 4(2)), but this does not affect the rights of Crown user under section 55 (Rules, Sched. 2, para. 4(7)).

The applicant then has the period so specified within which he can send to the Comptroller a written objection to a sample of the deposited biological material being sent to the nominated expert and giving his reasons for that objection. In the absence of such objection, the Comptroller must then send a copy of PF 8/77, together with a certificate authorising release of the sample to: (a) the applicant; (b) the depositary institution concerned; (c) the requester; and (d) the expert (Sched. 2, para. 4(3)). If, however, the applicant lodges a written objection (within the period specified under para. 4(2)), which period may be extended, under para. 4(3), upon request made within that period), the Comptroller is required to adjudicate upon the suitability of the expert, having regard to his knowledge, experience, independence and technical qualifications (para. 4(4)). The applicant and the requester have the opportunity to be heard before the Comptroller makes his decision on the objection (para. 4(5)). If the objection is rejected, the notification procedure of paragraph 4(3) is then followed; and, if the objection is sustained, the requester may nominate another expert, whereupon the Comptroller will give such directions as he thinks fit as to the subsequent procedure (para. 4(6)), see also § 125A.39 in the Main Work.

Renewal of deposited biological material (Rules, Sched. 2, para. 5)　　　　**125A.30**

Under the new form of Schedule 2 to the Rules, the requirements for a renewal of deposited biological material (previously to be found in Rules, Sched. 2, para. 4) are now to be found in paragraph 5 thereof (reprinted at § 125A.06 *supra*). These provisions were operative from July 6, 2001 but would seem to apply to deposits made under the former regime where, after this date, a sample of deposited material ceases to be available from the institution with which it was deposited because it is either no longer viable, or "for any other reason the depositary institution is unable to supply samples"; and, in either situation, no transfer of the deposited material to another depositary institution, where it continues to be available, has occurred (Rules, Sched. 2, para. 5(1)).

This paragraph 5 implements Article 14 of the Biotechnology Directive (reprinted at § C14) which requires that a new deposit of the material (a "redeposit") has to be permitted on the same terms as those laid down in the Budapest Treaty. These include that any such redeposit must be accompanied by a certificate signed by the depositor certifying that the newly deposited material "is the same as that originally deposited" (see Rules, Sched. 2, para. 5(5)), a phrase which presumably means that the material at least has essentially the same biological activity. The term "depositary institution" is defined in paragraph 5(2) of Schedule 2 to the Rules (reprinted in § 125A.07 *supra*).

In accordance with the Budapest Treaty, sub-paragraph (2) sets out the circumstances in which an interruption of availability is deemed not to have occurred. If the conditions of this sub-paragraph are not met, then the interruption in availability is not condoned and, accordingly, the patentability of the application, or validity of the patent, as the case may be may then be impugned for insufficiency under either of sections 14(3) or 72(1)(c).

If the original depositary institution should notify the depositor that it has already transferred the deposited material to another depositary institution, all the applicant/ proprietor need do is to satisfy himself that the new institution can carry out its required storage of the sample in a satisfactory manner, except that it is also necessary for an application to be made to amend the application/patent so as to include therein informa- tion as to the new deposit number and name of the new depositary institution, as to which see *infra*.

If the depositor should be notified the original institution cannot now satisfy a valid request to make a sample of the deposited material available, "for any reason", then a fresh deposit must be made and, where the notification is that the originally deposited sample "is no longer viable", the redeposit must be made with the same institution, but otherwise a new institution may be chosen (Rules, Sched. 2, para. 5(3)). Note the require- ment to supply a certificate that the redeposited material "is the same as that of the original deposited material", see *supra*.

When the applicant or proprietor is notified by the relevant depositary institution that its ability to supply samples of the deposited material has been interrupted, the redeposit must take place (again with a certificate of identity), and an application must be made to amend the application or patent to provide details of the redeposit, within three months of the date of that notification (Rules, Sched. 2, para. 5(2)). This three months period is inextensible (see Rules, Schedule 4A, Part 1, reprinted at § 123.09A *supra*). However, where the original depositary institution (a term which presumably includes a depositary institution which has already been validly substituted therefor, with the application/patent amended to record that fact) ceases to be recognised for the purposes of Schedule 2 to the Rules, or has discontinued its performance, whether temporarily or permanently, of its functions as regards deposited biological material, and notice thereof from the depositary institution is not received within six months of that event occurring, the above-mentioned three month period begins only on the date when that event is announced in the O.J. (Rules, Sched. 2, para. 5(4)). This period is also inextensible under Rules, Schedule 4A, Part I, see § 123.09A *supra*.

To avoid a loss of rights arising from a failure to note such an entry in the O.J., it would be prudent to file a *caveat* requesting that notification of any such entry in the O.J. should be provided thereunder, for which see §§ 118.20 – 118.22 *supra*. The filing of such a *caveat* will be particularly important where the applicant/proprietor is not (or is no longer) the person recognised by the depositary institution as the depositor because an official notification from that institution may then never reach the applicant/proprietor. The notification may also not reach the applicant/proprietor if that person has changed his address. However, even the filing of a *caveat* may not be sufficient when this occurs, unless the address for reply thereto is amended upon that change of address.

Paragraph 5(2)(b) to Schedule 2 of the Rules requires that, where a new deposit is made following notification of an interruption in the availability of a deposited sample, a request for amendment of the application or patent (specified to be made under s. 19 or s. 27, but presumably not precluding application under s. 75 when court proceedings are pending) must also be made so as to include therein the accession number of the new deposit and the name of the new depositary institution (Rules, Sched. 2, para. 5(2)(c)). Again, this period is inextensible (Rules, Schedule 4A, Part 1).

125A.31 *Comparison with EPC and PCT provisions*

Since 1999, EPCr. 28 and PCTr. 13 *bis* have provided (as Sched. 2 to the Rules now also does) that, if the applicant has so requested, during the period following publication of the patent application up to grant of a patent, or for 20 years from the filing date if the application is refused or withdrawn, and a request therefor was filed before the technical preparations for publication of the application had been completed, the sample may only be made available to a nominated expert. This option (sometimes called the "expert solution") is virtually equivalent to maintaining inaccessibility of the deposit during whichever of those periods should apply, because the expert is independent and must not make the culture available to the requester or any other third party. Whereas, under the Act, a time limit exists for putting the application in order for grant (s. 20, r. 34, see § 18.10), no such time limit is provided under the EPC. Therefore, an applicant wishing to keep his deposit inaccessible for as long as possible might continue to find the EPC or the Euro- PCT route more advantageous than the national or the PCT (UK) route.

While, under the United Kingdom rules, an applicant has an almost unlimited choice of depositary institutions, under the EPC the depositary institution has to be one named in the prescribed list, see § 125A.27 *supra*. The Biotechnology Directive requires that this institution shall be a "recognised" one, but this does not necessarily mean that there should be a recognised list, and the current form of Schedule 2 to the Rules continues to permit the recognition of any depositary institution chosen by the applicant. However, problems can arise if a non-recognised institution is chosen for the initial deposit and the application under the Act is then abandoned but used as a priority document for a European or Euro-PCT application.

Procedure for deposit of biological material

—Factors influencing choice of depositary institution   **125A.36**

The name of the depositary institution listed under item (1) in the Main Work does not include the word "Ltd.".

SECTION 126—Stamp duty   126.01

Note. Section 126 was repealed by the Finance Act 2000 (c. 17, s. 156 and Sched. 40, Pt III) consequent upon the abolition (by s. 129 of that Act) of stamp duty on instruments for the sale, transfer or other disposition of intellectual property, see § 30.10 in the Main Work.

SECTION 130—Interpretation   130.01

Subsection 130(1) has been amended, or prospectively amended, as follows:

(1) A new definition was inserted (by the RRO, a. 19), reading:

> **"application fee" means the fee prescribed for the purposes of section 14(1A) above;**

> with the definition of "filing fee" then being deleted. These two amendments relate to the amended form of section 14 and are discussed in § 14.08. They took effect from January 1, 2005 (the RRO Commencement Date), but the definition "filing fee" (rather than "application fee") continues to apply to applications then "pending", a term defined in Note 3 to § 15.01 *supra*.

(2) The terms "application for a European patent (UK)" and "international application for a patent (UK)" were each amended (Patents Act 2004, c. 16, Sched. 1(9)), with effect from January 1 2005 (S.I. 2004 No. 3205, a. 2(i)) to read:

> "application for a European patent (UK) and (**subject to subsection (4A) below**) 'international application for a patent (UK)' each mean an application of the relevant description which, on its date of filing, designates the United Kingdom."

(3) In the definition of "Community Patent Convention", the words "and 'Community patent' means a patent granted under that convention" were prospectively deleted; and, in the definition of "relevant convention court", the words "the Community Court" were deleted (Patents Act 2004, c. 16, Scheds. 2(27) and 3), with effect from January 1, 2005 (S.I. 2004 No. 3205, a. 2(f)(g)(k)), as a consequence of the removal from the Act of references to the CPC which never came into force.

(4) The definition of "designate" was prospectively amended (Patents Act 2004, c. 16, Sched. 1(9)(2)(b)) by adding at the end of the definition the words:

> **"and includes a reference to a country being treated as designated in pursuance of the convention or treaty."**

> This definition was given effect on January 1, 2005, but only in respect of applications under the Patent Cooperation Treaty (S.I. 2004 No. 32025. a. 2(i)(j)). The amended definition at present does not apply to the EPC. It will be brought into effect when the revised form of the EPC comes into force.

(5) After the definition of "designate", a new definition was inserted by the Patents Act (Electronic Communications) Order, S.I. 2003 No. 512), with effect from April 1, 2003, reading:

> **"electronic communication" has the same meaning as in the Electronic Communications Act 2000 (c. 7).**

> This amendment is discussed in §§ 124A.01 and 124A.02 above.

(6) New subsection (4A) was inserted by the Patents Act 2004 (c. 16, Sched. 1(9)(3)), reading, with effect from January 1, 2005 (S.I. 2004 No. 3205), reading:

(4A) An international application for a patent is not, by reason of being treated by virtue of the European Patent Convention as an application for a European patent (UK), to be treated also as an international application for a patent (UK).

(7) New subsection (5A) was prospectively inserted by the Patents Act 2004 (c. 16, Sched. 1(9)(4)), reading:

(5A) References in this Act to the amendment of a patent or its specification (whether under this Act or by the European Patent Office) include, in particular, limitation of the claims (as interpreted by the description and any drawings referred to in the description or claims).

This amendment will be brought into effect when the revised form of the EPC comes into force.

Note. The definitions of "court" (as respects the Isle of Man), "biotechnological invention", "electronic communication" and "enactment" were each applied to the Isle of Man by S.I. 2003 No. 1249.

COMMENTARY ON SECTION 130

130.03 | *Specific definitions*

In the list of specific definitions set out in the Main Work:
(1) the term "Community Patent Convention" has been deleted as a consequence of the removal from the Act of references to the CPC which never came into force.
(2) a new term "Electronic communication" should be inserted with cross-references for the Main Commentary to § 124A.02 and to its mention in section 124A;
(3) the term "filing fee" should be replaced by the term "application fee" with the same cross references supplemented by a reference to section 15; and
(4) the term "relevant convention court" has been amended (for which see § 130.01) as a consequence of the removal from the Act of references to the CPC which never came into force.

130.07 | *Miscellaneous further definitions (subss. (2)–(5A))*

New subsection (4A) makes it clear that an international application which is treated as an application for a European patent (UK) is not also to be treated as an international application for a patent (UK).

New subsection (5A), when given effect, puts a gloss on the term "amendment" (of a patent, but not of an application) whenever this (and cognate terms) appears in the Act so as to include an amendment which limits the scope of the claims whether under either of s ections 27 or 75 or by way of limitation proceedings before the EPO of a European patent as a whole under new EPCa. 105A.

131.01 | **SECTION 131—Northern Ireland**

The Patents Act 2004 (c. 16, Sched. 2(28)) added new paragraph (f) to section 131, with effect from January 1, 2005 (S.I. 2004 No. 3202, a. 2(f)(k)) reading:

(f) any reference to a claimant includes a reference to a plaintiff.

COMMENTARY ON SECTION 131   **131.03**

Jurisdiction of the court in Northern Ireland

CPR 49EPD 49 has been replaced by CPR 63 and its Practice Directions and the *Patents Court Guide* re-issued, for which see Appendices F and G *infra*. However, these do not apply, as such, to proceedings in the courts of Northern Ireland. New paragraph (f) was added to the section because the term "plaintiff" continues to be used in Northern Ireland, whereas the term "plaintiff" has been changed to "claimant" in the other sections 60, 63 and 70 where the term "plaintiff" formerly appeared.

SECTION 131A [ADDED]—Scotland   **131A.01**

New section 131A was added by The Scotland Act 1998 (Consequential Modifications) (No. 2) Order 1999 (S.I. 1999 No. 1820, art. 4, Sched. 2, Pt I, para. 58) in the following terms—

131A. In the application of this Act to Scotland—

   (a) **"enactment" includes an enactment comprised in, or in an instrument made under, an Act of the Scottish Parliament;**

   (b) **any reference to a government department includes a reference to any part of the Scottish Administration; and**

   (c) **any reference to the Crown includes a reference to the Crown in right of the Scottish Administration.**

SECTION 132—Short title, extent, commencement consequential amendments and repeals

Application of the 1977 Act to the Isle of Man   **132.02**

Further modifications of the Act in relation to its application to the Isle of Man have been made by The Patents Act 1977 (Isle of Man) Order 2003 (S.I. 2003 No. 1249) effective from June 10, 2003 in order to have the Act (as already amended) made applicable with necessary modifications also to the Isle of Man as indicated in the commentaries herein on sections 1, 5, 22, 23, 41, 44, 45, 48, 48A, 48B, 50, 51, 52, 54, 58, 60, 76A, 94, 96, 97, 107, 124A, 125A, 130, Schedules A1 and A2. This new Order also replaced (and revoked) S.I. 1978 No. 621 and S.I. 1990 No. 2285, with paragraph 4 of this 1990 Order being repeated (without change) in paragraph 3 of the new 2003 Order.

The amendments made to the 1977 Act by the RRO and the Patents Act 2004 (c. 16), as set out and discussed above in relation to the sections thereby amended, each apply also in the application of the 1977 Act to the Isle of Man (Patents Act 2004, c. 16, s. 18(2) and RRO, a. 1(3)).

SCHEDULE 5 [SECTION 132]—Consequential amendments   **135.01**

The references in the Main Work to former paragraph 7 of Schedule 5, and its subsequent replacement by Schedule 7, para. 15 [1988], are now redundant as this provision of the 1988 Act was repealed by the Enterprise Act 2002 (c. 40, Sched. 26), as mentioned in § 44.04 *supra*.

SCHEDULE A1 [SECTION 60]—Derogation from patent protection in   **137.01**
respect of biotechnological inventions

Note. This added Schedule was applied to the Isle of Man by S.I. 2003 No. 1249.

138.01   SCHEDULE A2 [SECTION 76A]—Biotechnological inventions

Note. This added Schedule was applied to the Isle of Man by S.I. 2003 No. 1249.

138.02   COMMENTARY ON SCHEDULE A2

The Patent Office has announced (O.J. May 7, 2003) that patents will not be granted for processes of obtaining stem cells for human embryos, nor for human totipotent cells, these being considered unpatentable under paragraphs 3(d) and 3(a) respectively of Schedule A2. However, the notice indicates that these restrictions on patentability will not extend to inventions involving pluripotent stem cells.

The Patents Rules 1995

Entries for the following new rules should be added, in the appropriate places, as follows:

Rule		*Reprinted at §*
6A	Request to the comptroller for permission to make a late declaration under section 5(2B)	5.02A
6B	Filing of priority documents to support a declaration under section 5(2)	5.02B
6C	Translation of priority documents	5.02C
22A	References under section 15(1)(c)(ii)	15.01A
28A	Search under section 17	17.02
36A	Reinstatement of applications under section 20A	20A.02
110A	Extension of time limits specified by comptroller	117B.02
112A	Copies kept at the Patent Office	123.10A
113A	Establishing the accuracy of translations	123.11A
Sched.4A	Alteration of time limits	123.09A–123.09D

Notes on Patents Rules 1995   139.02

The Patents Rules 1995 were further amended by:

(1) The Patents (Amendment) Rules 2001 (S.I. 2001 No. 1412), with effect from July 6, 2001; and

(2) The Patents (Amendment) Rules 2002 (S.I. 2002 No. 529), with effect from April 1, 2002.

(3) The Patents Act 2004 (Commencement No. 1 and Consequential and Transitional Provisions) Order 2004 (S.I. 2004 No. 2177), effective from September 22, 2004;

(4) The Patents (Amendment) Rules 2004 (S.I. 2004 No. 2358) made in association with the Regulatory Reform (Patents) Order (S.I. 2004 No. 2357), each effective from January 1, 2005; and

(5) The Patents Act 2004 (Commencement No. 2 and Consequential and Transitional Provisions) Order 2004 (S.I. 2004 No. 3205), effective from January 1, 2005.

FORMS   140.00

The Forms for use in business before the Patent Office were those set out in Schedule 1 to the Patents Rules 1995 (as subsequently amended and reprinted in the Main Work). However, under the authority of new subsection 123(2A) (for which see § 123.05 *supra*), the forms are no longer prescribed by formal rules, but are based upon directions issued by the Comptroller (for which see § 123.18 *supra*). As these forms may change in the future by simple direction from the Comptroller, and because they are now readily available by downloading them (in their current forms) from the Patent Office website http://www.patent.gov.uk/patent/forms/, the Forms are no longer being reproduced herein. The above web site should therefore be consulted instead. Consequently, the contents of pages 1105-1151 of the Main Work should now be ignored. As at January 1, 2005, the current forms include changes to PF 1/77, 23/77, 52/77, 53/77, 54/77 and NP1, each as printed in the Main Work, and also include the new forms PF 3/77, 9A/77 and 14/77.

FEES

142.02

PATENTS FEES RULES 1998

The level of fees set out in the Main Work remains effective (as of January 1, 2005). However, changes and additional entries to the Patents (Fees) Rules 1998 (S.I. 1998 No. 1778, as amended by S.I. 1999 No. 1093) have been introduced by The Patents (Amendment) Rules 2004 (S.I. 2004 No. 2358, Sched. 3). These changes are:

(1) the omission of the entry for PF 1/77;

(2) the insertion of entries for new PF 3/77 being:

   (i) On making a declaration for the purposes of section 5(2), after the date of filing, in relation to an earlier relevant application filed during the period allowed by section 5(2A)(a) (rule 6(2))   £40

   (ii) On request for permission to make a late declaration of priority under section 5(2B) (rule 6A)   £150

(3) amending the entry for PF 9/77 to read:

   (i) On request for a further search under section 17(6) or payment for a supplementary search under section 17(8)   £100

(4) inserting entries for new PF 9A/77 being:

   (i) On request for a search under section 17(1):

      (a) in respect of an international application for a patent (UK) which is treated as an application for a patent under the Act and which has already been the subject of a search by the International Searching Authority in accordance with the Patent Co-operation Treaty.   £80

      (b) in respect of any other application   £100

   (ii) request for a further search under section 17(6) or payment for a supplementary search under section 17(8).   £100

(5) inserting an entry for new PF 14/77 being:

   (i) On making a request for reinstatement of a terminated application £100

(6) adding or amending the following entries to the final miscellaneous section:

   (i) inserting:

      The application fee:

      (a) in respect of an international application for a patent (UK) which is treated as an application for a patent under the Act —

      (b) in respect of any other application (including an application treated as an application under the Act following a direction under section 81)   £30

(ii) Amending the entry "On entry of an international application for a patent (UK) into the national phase (section 89A(3))" from a fee of £10 to a fee of £30.

Copyright, Designs and Patents Act 1988 (c. 48)

PART V [Sections 274–286]

PATENT AGENTS AND TRADE MARK AGENTS

Patent Agents [Sections 274–281]

SECTION 274 [1988]—Persons permitted a carry on business as a patent agent

Relevant Rule—Rule 90

Rule 90—Agents

In the reprinting of rule 90(2)(b) in the Main Work, the word "substituted" should read "previously appointed".

Commentary on Section 274 [1988]

Representation by an agent

—Liability of agents for negligence

Arbiter Group v. Gill Jennings & Every, cited in the Main Work, was reported ([2001] RPC 67).

In *Kalsep v. X-Flow* (BL C/13/01) terms in a patent licence agreement (which failed to provide for termination of the licence or any warranty as to patent validity and where the relevant application had not proceeded to grant) as being "grossly improvident" and the court opined that English advisers if instructed and aware of the facts would have been negligent in not advising the licensee not to terminate the agreement.

SECTION 275 [1988]—The Register of Patent Agents

Commentary on Section 275 [1988]

Examinations for entry into the Register of Patent Agents

Certain partial exemptions are possible for those who have gained similar qualifications in other jurisdictions, see *e.g.* as to exemption from the general law paper as set out in the O.J. of March 24 2004. Enquiry about the availablity of these exemptions should be made to the Chartered Institute of Patent Agents.

The Chartered Institute and "Chartered Patent Agents" **275.06**

The background to the disciplinary procedures and the Special Rules of Professional Conduct of the Chartered Institute has been explained ([2000] *CIPA* 383). Its former Professional Conduct Committee has been replaced by a Disciplinary Panel containing also lay persons and representatives of the Law Society, see [2000] *CIPA* 481.

SECTION 280—Privilege for communications with patent agents

COMMENTARY ON SECTION 280 [1988]

The nature of privilege

—General and the grounds of privilege **280.05**

The provisions of former CPR 49EPD 9 are now to be found in CPR 63PD 5, see also CPR 63.8 (reprinted respectively *infra* in §§ F63PD.5 and F63.8)

PART VI [SECTIONS 287–295]

PATENTS

Patents county courts [Sections 287–292]

SECTION 287 [1988]—Patents county courts: special jurisdiction

COMMENTARY ON SECTION 287 [1988]

The history of the development of the Patents County Court jurisdiction **287.04**

His Honour Judge Michael Fysh Q.C. was appointed the judge of the Patents County Court, on 18 October 2001 following the earlier retirement of His Honour Judge Peter Ford. Cases in the intervening period were handled by deputy judges as required. Speeches of welcome for the new judge are reported at [2002] FSR 79.

SECTION 289 [1988]—Transfer of proceedings between the High Court and Patents County Court

COMMENTARY ON SECTION 289 [1988]

Criteria for transfer between the High Court and Patents County Court **289.03**

In *Kimberley-Clark v. Procter & Gamble* (Pat 040109, 30.7.04; BL O/91/04, IPD 27088) The defendant sought a transfer to the Patents Court. The subject-matter of the litigation was seen to be well within the capability of the Patents County Court in terms of its technical content, but sales of the patented products were alleged to be over $50m in the UK and actions had been commenced in other European countries. Accordingly this was seen to be a case more suited to the Patents Court and transfer was ordered.

289.04 *Factors which influence applications for transfer in practice*

Transfer from the PCC to the High Court was refused in *Wesley Jessen Corp. v. Coopervision* (BL C/31/01) the court holding that the onus for transfer lay with he who sought it. There is no case for transfer just because the parties are big or that expert and experimental evidence is in prospect.

SECTION 291 [1988]—Proceedings in patents county court

COMMENTARY ON SECTION 291 [1988]

291.04 *Procedure in the Patents County Court*

New CPR Part 63 and the Practice Directions thereunder (reprinted *infra* at §§ F63.1–F63PD.16) have replaced CPR 49EPD and (apart for appeals from the Comptroller) apply equally to claims made in the Patents County Court as they apply to claims made in the Patents Court. The *Patents Court Guide* has also been re-issued, as reprinted in §§ G00–G22A.19 *infra*. Thus, the procedures set out under Practice under Sections 61 (for infringement proceedings) and 72 (for invalidity proceedings) apply *mutatis mutandis* to claims made in the Patents County Court, for which see §§ 61.41–61.62 and 72.31–72.53 in the Main Work and *infra*, as these apply to proceedings before the Patents Court.

291.06 *—Interim and trial procedures in the Patents County Court*

In *Cadcam Technology v. Proel* (BL CC/61/00) the court decided to deal with certain matters at a preliminary hearing to reduce the length of the trial.

SECTION 292 [1988]—Rights and duties of registered patent agents in relation to proceedings in patents county court

COMMENTARY ON SECTION 292 [1988]

292.04 *"Authorised litigators" and "authorised advocates"*

Lawyers (of any category) are no longer exempt from jury service (Criminal Justice Act 2003, c. 44, Sched. 33).

APPENDIX A—HISTORICAL BACKGROUND TO PATENTS ACT 1977
AND THE PATENT OFFICE

The three modes for obtaining United Kingdom patents under the Act

—The "European and Euro-PCT routes"   **A04**

Turkey became a Member State of the EPC on November 1, 2000. Bulgaria, the Czech Republic, Estonia and the Slovak Republic also became Member States on July 1, 2002, Slovenia on December 1, 2002, Hungary on January 1, 2003, Romania on March 1, 2003 and Poland on March 1, 2004.

APPENDIX B—SUPPLEMENTARY PROTECTION CERTIFICATES

COMMENTARY ON SUPPLEMENTARY PROTECTION CERTIFICATES

Definition of "product" for which a supplementary protection certificate can be granted   **B09**

In *BASF v. BIE* (ECJ Case C-258/99 [2002] RPC 274), the ECJ dismissed an appeal by BASF against refusal of the Netherlands Patent Office (upheld on national appeal) to grant an SPC for a plant protection product with less impurities than a corresponding product for which a marketing authorisation had been granted in 1987. BASF argued that a product within the meaning of Regulation No 1610/96 includes the active substance and the impurities. There is therefore a different product where the proportion of active substance to impurities is substantially altered. It was argued therefore that the earlier marketing authorisation should not prevent an SPC based on the later process patent. The ECJ held that the SPC Regulation covers chemical elements and their compounds, as they occur naturally or by manufacture, including any impurity inevitably resulting from the manufacturing process, and that two products, which differ only in the proportion of the active chemical compound to the impurity they contain, must be regarded as the same product within the meaning of the Regulation. The fact that a marketing authorisation must be obtained for the new product is not relevant for the purposes of establishing whether or not the products are the same for this purpose. The conditions laid down in Article 3(1)(a) and (d) of the Regulation are therefore not satisfied where a product differs from a previously authorised product only in the proportion impurity it contains. It would seem therefore that the reference in the SPC Regulations to protection provided by a process patent applies only to the case where the process results in a new active entity which for some reason has not been patented *per se*.

In *Takeda Chemical Industries' SPC Applications (No. 3)* ([2004] RPC 37), requests for SPCs covering combinations of lansoprazole and an antibiotic were refused because the basic patent related to lansoprazole itself and not the combination, which was not protected by a basic patent and therefore did not comply with article 3(a).

Definition of "basic patent" upon which a supplementary protection certificate can be granted   **B10**

In *Takeda's SPC Applications (No.2)* ([2004] RPC 20) it was held that under Article 3(c) of the SPC Regulation, which states that an SPC can only be granted where "the product has not already been the subject of a certificate", applications for SPCs based on different marketing authorisations for combinations containing the patented active ingredient were refused as the relevant "product" was the same in each case, namely the active ingredient which was the subject of the patent.

In *Chiron and Novo-Nordisk's SPC Application* (BL O/343/04) two other companies had already obtained SPCs relating to a particular product under different patents, and the present applicants sought a further SPC under their own patent which had been granted subsequently. Article 3(c) was here given a "teleological" interpretation as limited to the situation where multiple SPCs would be granted to the same applicant, but not where different applicants were involved. The present application was therefore allowable, and could be distinguished from *Takeda, supra*.

Note: it appears that relationships between companies will be disregarded in determining whether SPCs should be granted to multiple applicants. Thus it may be possible to obtain multiple SPCs by filing in the name of different companies in the same group.

B11   *Effect of a supplementary protection certificate*

CPR 49EPD 1 has been replaced by CPR 63.1–63.3 (reprinted in §§ F63.1–F63.3 *infra*).

For a possible exemption from infringement of an SPC by the carrying out of work of an experimental nature to enable further marketing once the SPC has expired, note the references to the need for an amendment to the Act to conform with EU Directives 2004/27/EC and 2004/28/EC (OJEC L136/34 and 58) in § 60.14.

B12   *Period within which application for a supplementary protection certificate in the United Kingdom must be filed*

In *Abbott Laboratories' SPC Application* ([2004] RPC 391) the period for applying for an SPC in the UK was extended by six days, the application having been late filed because of genuine misunderstandings (occasioned by a transfer of rights) and prompt action having been taken once the position had been revealed. It was therefore decided that the relevant period (which was held to run from the actual date of grant of the marketing authorisation, and not from the (later) date of publication of the authorisation in the London Gazette) could be extended at the Comptroller's discretion under rule 110(1).

B14   *Duration of a supplementary protection certificate*

The Comptroller's decision in *Novartis' Supplementary Protection Certificates* (BL O/44/03) supports the view (expressed in the Main Work) that because marketing authorisations granted in Switzerland extend to Liechtenstein (which is a member of the EEA), Switzerland is a country to be taken into account in determining the country for which the "first marketing authorisation" was issued. On appeal against this decision, questions relating to the status of Swiss marketing authorisations in the EEA were referred to the ECJ (Pumfrey, J., May 5, 2003) and assigned reference Case C–207/03, but the ECJ concurred in the above view.

PRACTICE CONCERNING SUPPLEMENTARY PROTECTION CERTIFICATES

B17   *Procedure for obtaining a supplementary protection certificate*

See the paper by J. Bellia (Patent Office Examiner) on "SPC Contentious Issues", *Pharma Patent Bulletin*, December 2002, Vol.5(6), page 5.

B20   *Inspection of documents filed at the Patent Office in connection with supplementary protection certificates and applications therefor*

Information about SPCs is now available on the Patent Office website "www.patent.gov.uk".

APPENDIX D—THE COMMUNITY TREATY

COMMENTARY ON THE COMMUNITY TREATY

D11   *The meaning of "The Community Treaty"*

On May 1, 2004 ten new member states joined the European Union. These are Cyprus, Czech

Republic, Estonia, Hungary, Latvia, Lithuania, Malta, Poland, Slovakia and Slovenia. The Union now consists of 25 member states. The "Association Agreements" for these countries referred to in the Main Work have therefore been replaced by the Accession Agreements with the relevant countries. At present, the accession of Bulgaria and Romania is being considered for 2007, and of Turkey possibly at a later date.

For the new position on the Brussels and Lugano Conventions, see § 96.09.

Interpretation of the Treaty by the European Court of Justice　　　　　　　　　　**D12**

In the Court of Appeal Decision in *British Horseracing Board v. William Hill* (noted IPD 24059) referral was made to the ECJ largely because a Swedish court had reached an opposite conclusion to that of the judge at first instance [2001] RPC 31. Accordingly the Court of Appeal felt that the issue could not be "*acte claire* ".

The principle of free trade between EEA Member States (CTaa. 28–30)

—"Exhaustion of rights" in international trade　　　　　　　　　　　　　　**D16**

The ECJ in *Zino Davidoff v. A&G Imports* ([2002] RPC 403) upheld the rule in *Silhouette* that there is no principle of international exhaustion of rights in relation to trade marks in Community law and Member States are not at liberty to impose their own rules of international exhaustion. The facts must unequivocally demonstrate that the proprietor has renounced his right to oppose placing of the goods on the market within the EEA before his consent to su ch marketing can be implied.

In the Swiss case of *Kodak v. Jumbo Market* ([2001] ENPR 321) the Swiss court drew distinctions between patents and other intellectual property rights in concluding that there should be no rule of international exhaustion for patent rights in Switzerland, even though international exhaustion applied to trade mark rights in Swiss law.

The Technology Transfer Regulation　　　　　　　　　　　　　　　　　**D20**

The Technology Transfer Regulation No. 240/96 ("the TTR") was repealed and replaced by the Technology Transfer Block Exemption Regulation (E.C.) No. 772/2004 made April 7, 2004 ("the TTBER") ([2004] OJEC L123/11 and L127/158). The TTBER became effective on May 1, 2004 and is to run until April 30, 2014 (Arts 9 and 11).

Apart from the transitional provision in Article 10 for existing agreements (for which see § D33, *infra*), the new Regulation renders obsolete the contents of §§ D20-D33 in the Main Work, for which the following §§ D20 – D33 should be read instead. While the TTBER (like the TTR) is peripheral to this Work, the following replacement paragraphs provide a re-print of the main recitals and each of the Articles of the TTBER (see §§ D22 – D28, infra), followed (in §§ D29 – D33, *infra*) by brief commentaries on these provisions. As before, for a full appreciation of the TTBER, specialist books should be consulted.

The TTBER continues to provide block exemption, under CTa. 81(3), to various provisions in technology transfer agreements having effect within the EEA, particularly licences for the exploitation of patents, software copyrights, know-how or similar IP rights (other than trade mark rights and other forms of copyright). However, it does not deal with licensing agreements for the purpose of sub-contracting research and development, nor with licensing agreements for the pooling of technologies with the purpose of licensing the created package of IP rights to third parties (Recital (7)). However, the Regulation does apply to provisions contained in technology transfer agreements that do not constitute the primary object of such agreements, but are directly related to the application of the licensed technology (Recital (9)).

Recital (12) is of particular importance as it indicates that an exclusive licensing agreement between non-competing undertakings will often not fall within the general prohibition of CTa 81(1). For these, and other, significant Recitals, see § D21, *infra*. For definitions of the terms used in the TTBER, see Article 1 (reprinted in § D22, *infra*, and discussed briefly in § D29, *infra*).

Articles 2 and 3 (each reprinted in § D23, *infra*) provide a general exemption for agreements which permit the production of contract products, on the condition that a specified market threshold is not exceeded, this being calculated as set out in Article 8 (reprinted in § D27, infra), but with the exemption being disapplied in circumstances set out in Article 5 (reprinted in § D25, *infra*). These Articles are discussed in § D30, *infra*.

Article 4 (reprinted in § D24, *infra*, and discussed in § D31, *infra*) sets out a relatively short list of licence terms which are considered to be ineligible for exemption, the so-called "hardcore restrictions", and consequently cause the entire agreement to be excluded from the block exemption otherwise provided by Article 2, see Recital (13). Articles 6 and 7 (reprinted in § D26, *infra*) provide respectively for withdrawal of an exemption in individual cases, or non-application of the Regulation in certain circumstances. These provisions are discussed in § D32, *infra*.

The remaining Articles 9–11 are reprinted in § D28, *infra*. Article 10 provides an important transitional provision (as discussed in § D33, *infra*) while Article 9 repeals the TTR and Article 11 brought the Regulation into force on May 1, 2004.

An important feature of the TTBER is that the onus of compliance is now even more firmly set upon the parties with no formal provision for seeking individual exemption or for opposition to an exemption provided as under the former TTR regime. Thus, the brunt of challenge to a term in a licence agreement alleged to be in breach of CTa. 81 can be expected to lie with a party to an agreement or to an entity affected thereby, made by way of complaint under national laws of competition to a court or competition authority in an EEA Member State, or made by complaint to the European Commission.

It is to be noted that, unlike the TTR, the TTBER does not contain a list of "white clauses", *i.e.* clauses which are considered not to be restrictive of competition and therefore not capable of falling within CTa. 81(1). Recital (8) (not reprinted in § D21, *infra*) explains that this omission provides the Regulation with greater flexibility. However, it can also be seen as providing the Commission with greater power to hold certain agreement provisions, previously seen to be non-objectionable, as anti-competitive. Also, Articles 6 and 7 (discussed in § D26, *infra*) potentially provide the Commission with relatively unfettered power to withdraw or disapply the exemption provided by Article 2 in circumstances where it reaches the view that there exists a situation to which CTa. 81(3) ought not to apply, these Articles 6 and 7 setting out only illustrative instances when these powers may be exercised. Thus, the terms of the TTBER are far less precise than those of the TTR and, particularly in view of the terms of Recital (12) there must be considerable uncertainty whether particular provisions in a technology transfer agreement can be regarded as entitled to exemption under CTa. 81(3).

Article 10 provides a two year period during which agreements can continue to enjoy exemptions available under the TTR but not under the TTBER, see § D33, *infra*.

Moreover, as with the TTR, Recital (20) of the new TTBER provides that this Regulation has no effect in relation to an infraction of CTa. 82 (abuse of a dominant position), for which see § D37 in the Main Work.

D21 | —*Recitals*

Several of the Recitals to the TTBER are explanatory of the basic law under CTa. 81 and the rationale and basis for the following substantive Articles. Those recitals which are seen to have more significance are now reprinted below.

(5) Technology transfer agreements concern the licensing of technology. Such agreements will usually improve economic efficiency and be pro-competitive as they can reduce duplication of research and development, strengthen the incentive for the initial research and development, spur incremental innovation, facilitate diffusion and generate product market competition.

(6) The likelihood that such efficiency-enhancing and pro-competitive effects will outweigh any anti-competitive effects due to restrictions contained in technology transfer agreements depends on the degree of market power of the undertakings concerned and, therefore, on the extent to which those undertakings face competition from undertakings owning substitute technologies or undertakings producing substitute products.

(7) This Regulation should only deal with agreements where the licensor permits the licensee to exploit the licensed technology, possibly after further research and development by the licensee, for the production of goods or services. It should not deal with licensing agreements for the purpose of subcontracting research and development. It should also not deal with licensing agreements to set up technology pools, that is to say, agreements for the pooling of technologies with the purpose of licensing the created package of intellectual property rights to third parties.

(9) The benefit of the block exemption established by this Regulation should be limited to those agreements which can be assumed with sufficient certainty to satisfy the conditions of Article 81(3). In order to attain the benefits and objectives of technology transfer, the benefit of this Regulation should also apply to provisions contained in technology transfer agreements that do not constitute the primary object of such agreements, but are directly related to the application of the licensed technology.

(10) For technology transfer agreements between competitors it can be presumed that, where the combined share of the relevant markets accounted for by the parties does not exceed 20% and the agreements do not contain certain severely anti-competitive restraints, they generally lead to an improvement in production or distribution and allow consumers a fair share of the resulting benefits.

(11) For technology transfer agreements between non-competitors it can be presumed that, where the individual share of the relevant markets accounted for by each of the parties does not exceed 30% and the agreements do not contain certain severely anti-competitive restraints, they generally lead to an improvement in production or distribution and allow consumers a fair share of the resulting benefits.

(12) There can be no presumption that above these market-share thresholds technology transfer agreements do fall within the scope of Article 81(1). For instance, an exclusive licensing agreement between non-competing undertakings does often not fall within the scope of Article 81(1). There can also be no presumption that, above these market-share thresholds, technology transfer agreements falling within the scope of Article 81(1) will not satisfy the conditions for exemption. However, it can also not be presumed that they will usually give rise to objective advantages of such a character and size as to compensate for the disadvantages which they create for competition.

(13) This Regulation should not exempt technology transfer agreements containing restrictions which are not indispensable to the improvement of production or distribution. In particular, technology transfer agreements containing certain severely anti-competitive restraints such as the fixing of prices charged to third parties should be excluded from the benefit of the block exemption established by this Regulation irrespective of the market shares of the undertakings concerned. In the case of such hardcore restrictions the whole agreement should be excluded from the benefit of the block exemption.

(14) In order to protect incentives to innovate and the appropriate application of intellectual property rights, certain restrictions should be excluded from the block exemption. In particular. exclusive grant back obligations for severable improvements should be excluded. Where such a restriction is included in a licence agreement only the restriction in question should be excluded from the benefit of the block exemption.

(19) This Regulation should cover only technology transfer agreements between a licensor and a licensee. It should cover such agreements even if conditions are stipulated for more than one level of trade, by, for instance, requiring the licensee to set up a particular distribution system and specifying the obligations the licensee must or may impose on resellers of the products produced under the licence. However, such conditions and obligations should comply with the competition rules applicable to supply and distribution agreements. Supply and distribution agreements concluded between a licensee and its buyers should not be exempted by this Regulation.

(20) This Regulation is without prejudice to the application of Article 82 of the Treaty.

—*Article 1: Definitions*   **D22**

1. For the purposes of this Regulation, the following definitions shall apply:

(a) 'agreement' means an agreement, a decision of an association of undertakings or a concerted practice;

(b) 'technology transfer agreement' means a patent licensing agreement, a know-how licensing agreement, a software copyright licensing agreement or a mixed patent, know-how or software copyright licensing agreement, including any such agreement containing provisions which relate to the sale and purchase of products or which relate to the licensing of other intellectual property rights or the assignment of intellectual property rights, provided that those provisions do not constitute the primary objective of the agreement and are directly related to the production of the contract products; assignments of patents, know-how, software copyright or a combination thereof where part of the risk associated with the exploitation of the technology remains with the assignor, in particular where the sum payable in consideration of the assignment is dependent on the turnover obtained by the assignee in respect of products produced with the assigned technology, the quantity of such products produced or the number of operations carried out employing the technology, shall also be deemed to be technology transfer agreements;

(c) 'reciprocal agreement' means a technology transfer agreement where two undertakings grant each other, in the same or separate contracts, a patent licence, a know-how licence, a software copyright licence or a mixed patent, know-how or software copyright licence and where these licences concern competing technologies or can be used for the production of competing products;

(d) 'non-reciprocal agreement' means a technology transfer agreement where one undertaking grants another undertaking a patent licence, a know-how licence, a software copyright licence or a mixed patent, know-how or software copyright licence, or where two undertakings grant each other such a licence but where these licences do not concern competing technologies and cannot be used for the production of competing products;

(e) 'product' means a good or a service, including both intermediary goods and services and final goods and services;

(f) 'contract products' means products produced with the licensed technology;

(g) 'intellectual property rights' includes industrial property rights, know-how, copyright and neighbouring rights;

(h) 'patents' means patents, patent applications, utility models, applications for registration of utility models, designs, topographies of semiconductor products, supplementary protection certificates for medicinal products or other products for which such supplementary protection certificates may be obtained and plant breeder's certificates;

(i) 'know-how' means a package of non-patented practical information, resulting from experience and testing, which is:

   (i) secret, that is to say, not generally known or easily accessible,

   (ii) substantial, that is to say, significant and useful for the production of the contract products, and

   (iii) identified, that is to say, described in a sufficiently comprehensive manner so as to make it possible to verify that it fulfils the criteria of secrecy and substantiality;

(j) 'competing undertakings' means undertakings which compete on the relevant technology market and/or the relevant product market, that is to say:

   (i) competing undertakings on the relevant technology market, being undertakings which license out competing technologies without infringing each others' intellectual property rights (actual competitors on the technology market); the relevant technology market includes technologies which are regarded by the licensees as interchangeable with or substitutable for the licensed technology, by reason of the technologies characteristics, their royalties and their intended use,

   (ii) competing undertakings on the relevant product market, being undertakings which. in the absence of the technology transfer agreement, are both active on the relevant product and geographic market(s) on which the contract products are sold without infringing each others' intellectual property rights (actual competitors on the product market) or would, on realistic grounds, undertake the necessary additional investments or other necessary switching costs so that they could timely enter, without infringing each others' intellectual property rights. the(se) relevant product and geographic market(s) in response to a small and permanent increase in relative prices (potential competitors on the product market); the relevant product market comprises products which are regarded by the buyers as interchangeable with or substitutable for the contract products, by reason of the products' characteristics, their prices and their intended use:

(k) 'selective distribution system' means a distribution system where the licensor undertakes to license the production of the contract products only to licensees selected on the basis of specified criteria and where these licensees undertake not to sell the contract products to unauthorised distributors;

(l) 'exclusive territory' means a territory in which only one undertaking is allowed to produce the contract products with the licensed technology, without prejudice to the possibility of allowing within that territory another licensee to produce the contract products only for a particular customer where this second licence was granted in order to create an alternative source of supply for that customer;

(m) 'exclusive customer group' means a group of customers to which only one undertaking is allowed actively to sell the contract products produced with the licensed technology;

(n) 'severable improvement' means an improvement that can be exploited without infringing the licensed technology.

2. The terms 'undertaking', 'licensor' and 'licensee' shall include their respective connected undertakings.

'Connected undertakings' means:

(a) undertakings in which a party to the agreement, directly or indirectly:

    (i) has the power to exercise more than half the voting rights, or

    (ii) has the power to appoint more than half the members of the supervisory board, board of management or bodies legally representing the undertaking, or

    (iii) has the right to manage the undertaking's affairs:

(b) undertakings which directly or indirectly have, over a party to the agreement, the rights or powers listed in (a);

(c) undertakings in which an undertaking referred to in (b) has, directly or indirectly, the rights or powers listed in (a);

(d) undertakings in which a party to the agreement together with one or more of the undertakings referred to in (a), (b) or (c), or in which two or more of the latter undertakings, jointly have the rights or powers listed in (a);

(e) undertakings in which the rights or the powers listed in (a) are jointly held by:

    (i) parties to the agreement or their respective connected undertakings referred to in (a) to (d), or

    (ii) one or more of the parties to the agreement or one or more of their connected undertakings referred to in (a) to (d) and one or more third parties.

—Articles 2 and 3: Exemption and Market-share thresholds

—Article 2: Exemption

D23

Pursuant to Article 81(3) of the Treaty and subject to the provisions of this Regulation, it is hereby declared that Article 81(1) of the Treaty shall not apply to technology transfer agreements entered into between two undertakings permitting the production of contract products.

This exemption applies to the extent that such agreements contain restrictions of competition falling within the scope of Article 81(1). The exemption shall apply for as long as the intellectual property right in the licensed technology has not expired, lapsed or been declared invalid or, in the case of know-how, for as long as the know-how remains secret, except in the event where the know-how becomes publicly known as a result of action by the licensee, in which case the exemption shall apply for the duration of the agreement.

—Article 3: Market-share thresholds

1. Where the undertakings patty to the agreement are competing undertakings, the exemption provided for in Article 2 shall apply on condition that the combined market share of the parties does not exceed 20% on the affected relevant technology and product market.

2. Where the undertakings party to the agreement are not competing undertakings, the exemption provided for in Article 2 shall apply on condition that the market share of each of the parties does not exceed 30% on the affected relevant technology and product market.

3. For the purposes of paragraphs 1 and 2, the market share of a party on the relevant technology market(s) is defined in terms of the presence of the licensed technology on the relevant product market(s). A licensor's market share on the relevant technology market shall be the combined market share on the relevant product market of the contract products produced by the licensor and its licensees.

—Article 4: Hardcore restrictions

D24

1. Where the undertakings party to the agreement are competing undertakings, the exemption provided for in Article 2 shall not apply to agreements which, directly or indirectly, in isolation or in combination with other factors under the control of the parties, have as their object:

(a) the restriction of a party's ability to determine its prices when selling products to third parties:

(b) the limitation of output, except limitations on the output of contract products imposed on the licensee in a non-reciprocal agreement or imposed on only one of the licensees in a reciprocal agreement;

(c) the allocation of markets or customers except:

    (i) the obligation on the licensee(s) to produce with the licensed technology only within one or more technical fields of use or one or more product markets,

    (ii) the obligation on the licensor and/or the licensee, in a non-reciprocal agreement, not to produce with the licensed technology within one or more technical fields of use or one or more product markets or one or more exclusive territories reserved for the other party,

    (iii) the obligation on the licensor not to license the technology to all other licensee in a particular territory,

    (iv) the restriction, in a non-reciprocal agreement, of active and/or passive sales by the licensee and/or the licensor into the exclusive territory or to the exclusive customer group reserved for the other party,

    (v) the restriction, in a non-reciprocal agreement, of active sales by the licensee into the exclusive territory or to the exclusive customer group allocated by the licensor to another licensee provided the latter was not a competing undertaking of the licensor at the time of the conclusion of its own licence,

    (vi) the obligation on the licensee to produce the contract products only for its own use provided that the licensee is not restricted in selling the contract products actively and passively as spare parts for its own products,

    (vii) the obligation on the licensee, in a non-reciprocal agreement, to produce the contract products only for a particular customer, where the licence was granted in order to create an alternative source of supply for that customer:

(d) the restriction of the licensee's ability to exploit its own technology or the restriction of the ability of any of the parties to the agreement to carry out research and development, unless such latter restriction is indispensable to prevent the disclosure of the licensed know-how to third parties.

2. Where the undertakings party to the agreement are not competing undertakings, the exemption provided for in Article 2 shall not apply to agreements which, directly or indirectly, in isolation or in combination with other factors under the control of the parties, have as their object:

(a) the restriction of a party's ability to determine its prices when selling products to third parties, without prejudice to the possibility of imposing a maximum sale price or recommending a sale price, provided that it does not amount to a fixed or minimum sale price as a result of pressure from, or incentives offered by, any of the parties;

(b) the restriction of the territory into which, or of the customers to whom, the licensee may passively sell the contract products, except:

    (i) the restriction of passive sales into an exclusive territory or to an exclusive customer group reserved for the licensor,

    (ii) the restriction of passive sales into an exclusive territory or to an exclusive customer group allocated by the licensor to another licensee during the first two years that this other licensee is selling the contract products in that territory or to that customer group,

    (iii) the obligation to produce the contract products only for its own use provided that the licensee is not restricted in selling the contract products actively and passively as spare parts for its own products,

    (iv) the obligation to produce the contract products only for a particular customer, where the licence was granted in order to create an alternative source of supply for that customer,

    (v) the restriction of sales to end-users by a licensee operating at the wholesale level of trade,

    (vi) the restriction of sales to unauthorised distributors by the members of a selective distribution system;

(c) the restriction of active or passive sales to end-users by a licensee which is a member of a selective distribution system and which operates at the retail level, without prejudice to the possibility of prohibiting a member of the system from operating out of an unauthorised place of establishment.

3. Where the undertakings party to the agreement are not competing undertakings at the time of the conclusion of the agreement but become competing undertakings afterwards, paragraph 2 and not paragraph 1 shall apply for the full life of the agreement unless the agreement is subsequently amended in any material respect.

—Article 5: Excluded restrictions   **D25**

1. The exemption provided for in Article 2 shall not apply to any of the following obligations contained in technology transfer agreements:
   (a) any direct or indirect obligation on the licensee to grant an exclusive licence to the licensor or to a third party designated by the licensor in respect of its own severable improvements to or its own new applications of the licensed technology;
   (b) any direct or indirect obligation on the licensee to assign, in whole or in part, to the licensor or to a third party designated by the licensor, rights to its own severable improvements to or its own new applications of the licensed technology;
   (c) any direct or indirect obligation on the licensee not to challenge the validity of intellectual property rights which the licensor holds in the common market, without prejudice to the possibility of providing for termination of the technology transfer agreement in the event that the licensee challenges the validity of one or more of the licensed intellectual property rights.

2. Where the undertakings party to the agreement are not competing undertakings, the exemption provided for in Article 2 shall not apply to any direct or indirect obligation limiting the licensee's ability to exploit its own technology or limiting the ability of any of the parties to the agreement to carry out research and development, unless such latter restriction is indispensable to prevent the disclosure of the licensed know-how to third parties.

—Articles 6 and 7: Withdrawal in individual cases and Non-application of the Regulation

—Article 6: Withdrawal in individual cases   **D26**

1. The Commission may withdraw the benefit of this Regulation, pursuant to Article 29(1) of Regulation (EC) No 1/2003, where it finds in any particular case that a technology transfer agreement to which the exemption provided for in Article 2 applies nevertheless has effects which are incompatible with Article 81(3) of the Treaty, and in particular where:
   (a) access of third parties' technologies to the market is restricted, for instance by the cumulative effect of parallel networks of similar restrictive agreements prohibiting licensees from using third parties' technologies;
   (b) access of potential licensees to the market is restricted, for instance by the cumulative effect of parallel networks of similar restrictive agreements prohibiting licensors from licensing to other licensees;
   (c) without any objectively valid reason, the parties do not exploit the licensed technology.

2. Where, in any particular case, a technology transfer agreement to which the exemption provided for in Article 1 applies has effects which are incompatible with Article 81(3) of the Treaty in the territory of a Member State, or in a part thereof, which has all the characteristics of a distinct geographic market., the competition authority of that Member State may withdraw the benefit of this Regulation. pursuant to Article 29(2) of Regulation (EC) No 1/2003. in respect of that territory, under the same circumstances as those set out in paragraph 1 of this Article.

—Article 7: Non-application of this Regulation

1. Pursuant to Article 1a of Regulation No 19/65/EEC, the Commission may by regulation declare that, where parallel networks of similar technology transfer agreements cover more than 50% of a relevant market, this Regulation is not to apply to technology transfer agreements containing specific restraints relating to that market.

2. A regulation pursuant to paragraph 1 shall not become applicable earlier than six months following its adoption.

—Article 8: Application of the market-share thresholds   **D27**

1. For the purposes of applying the market-share thresholds provided for in Article 3 the rules set out in this paragraph shall apply.

The market share shall be calculated on the basis of market sales value data. If market sales value data are not available, estimates based on other reliable market information, including market sales volumes, may be used to establish the market share of the undertaking concerned.

The market share shall be calculated on the basis of data relating to the preceding calendar year.

The market share held by the undertakings referred to in point (e) of the second subparagraph of Article 1(2) shall be apportioned equally to each undertaking having the rights or the powers listed in point (a) of the second subparagraph of Article 1(2).

2. If the market share referred to in Article 3(1) or (2) is initially not more than 20% respectively 30% but subsequently rises above those levels, the exemption provided for in Article 2 shall continue to apply for a period of two consecutive calendar years following the year in which the 20% threshold or 30% threshold was first exceeded.

—Articles 9–11: Repeal; Transitional period and Period of validity

D28   *—Article 9: Repeal*

Regulation (EC) No. 240/96 is repealed.
References to the repealed Regulation shall be construed as references to this Regulation.

—Article 10: Transitional period

The prohibition laid down in Article 81(1) of the Treaty shall not apply during the period from 1 May 2004 to 31 March 2006 in respect of agreements already in force on 30 April 2004 which do not satisfy the conditions for exemption provided for in this Regulation but which, on 30 April 2004, satisfied the conditions for exemption provided for in Regulation (EC) No 240/96.

—Article 11: Period of validity

This Regulation shall enter into force on 1 May 2004.
It shall expire on 30 April, 2014.

This Regulation shall be binding in its entirety and directly applicable in all Member States.

Commentary on the Technology Transfer Block Exemption Regulation ("the TTBER")

D29   *—Definitions within the TTBER (Art. 1)*

The definitions (reprinted in § D22, *supra*) are all-important in determining the scope of the TTBER and should be consulted whenever particular agreement wording is under consideration for compliance with the Regulation. Particularly important are the following:

The term "agreement" is given a broad meaning to include decisions and concerted practices (Art. 1(1)(a)).

The term "technology transfer agreement" applies also to agreements for the sale and purchase of products which relate to the licensing of other IP rights, although only if such licensing or assignment is a primary object of the agreement, and is not (in the case of an assignment) directly related to the production of contract products. The term also applies to an assignment of IP rights where part of the risk associated with the exploitation of the technology remains with the assignor, in particular where a royalty is payable based on a specified turnover or volume of the assignee's activities (Art. 1(1)(b)).

The term "intellectual property rights" includes "industrial property rights, know-how, software copyright and neighbouring rights" (Art. 1(1)(g)); the term "patents" includes also utility models, designs, semiconductor topographies, supplementary protection certificates, plant breeder's rights and applications for any of these rights (Art. 1(1)(h)); and "know-how" means a package of non-patented practical information which must be "secret", "substantial" and "identified", each as further defined in Article 1(1)(i).

The term "undertaking" includes entities which have the power to influence its actions in the ways set out in Article 1(2).

D30   *—Block exemptions and conditions applying thereto (Arts. 2, 3, 5 and 8)*

First (by Art. 2, reprinted in § D23, *supra*), it is declared that CTa. 81(1) does not apply to agreements for the production of "contract products" (the term "product" including services, see Art. 1.1(e)), although only to the extent that such agreements contain restrictions within the scope of CTa. 81(1) and provided that the IP right in the licensed technology has not expired or been invalidated; and, in the case of know-how, that this remains secret unless having become publicly known as a result of action by the licensee where the exemption continues to apply for the duration of the agreement. The limitation of the block exemption to agreements for the "production of contract products" means that agreements whereby one party agrees not to assert its IP rights against the other, or for settlement of an inter partes dispute, each without involving the production of "contract products" falls outside the terms of the block exemption provided by Article 2 and are thus subject to individual scrutiny.

However (by Art. 5, reprinted in § D25, *supra*), these general exemptions do not apply to any obligation placed upon a licensee to grant an exclusive licence, or to assign, to the licensor or a third party, rights in its own severable improvements or its own new application of the licensed technology; or to an obligation not to challenge the validity of such rights, although it is possible to provide for termination of the agreement in the event of any such challenge being made. Nevertheless, any restriction which falls within the terms of Article 5 is not prohibited as such, but merely does not enjoy the block exemption provided by Article 2 and is therefore subject to individual assessment. Note also that "non-compete" clauses are no longer black-listed and are therefore permitted when the applicable "market-share threshold" is satisfied, as discussed below.

With these provisos, the TTBER provides for a general block exemptions, although only on condition that a specified "market-share" is not exceeded. These "market-share thresholds" are set out in Article 3 (also reprinted in § D23, *supra*). They depend upon whether the parties to the agreement are "competing undertakings" for which see the definition thereof in Article 1(1)(j) (reprinted in § D22, *supra*), or are not such. For agreements between "competing undertakings", the exemptions apply only if the combined market share of the parties does not exceed 20% of the relevant technology and product market; whereas, if the parties are "competing undertakings", the threshold is 30% of that market. This "market share" is to be determined according to the presence of the licensed technology on the relevant product market(s); and (by Art. 3(3)) a licensor's market share of that market is "the combined market share on the relevant product market of the contract products produced by the licensor and [all?] its licensees", presumably within the EEA. However, there is no presumption that, above these percentage limits, the agreement is necessarily caught by CTa. 81(1) or not entitled to exemption under CTa. 81(3), merely that individual assessment is then required.

The determination of that market-share is governed by the rules set out in Article 8 (reprinted in § D27, *supra*). These require calculations on the basis of market sales value data for the preceding calendar year (or, if unavailable, on estimates thereof). However, exactly what is meant by "market sales value data" is rather unclear, but presumably will include the sales value of products (or services) which are competitive in the market, or substitutable therefor (see Art. 1.1(j)(i)), even though not identical with the "contract product" [or service].

In the case of "connected undertakings", where the rights are jointly held, the data is to be apportioned equally between the entities where one of them has control over the other, see Article 8(1) referring to the definition of such "connected undertakings" set out in Article 1(2)(a) and (3).

Where this market share is initially below the stated threshold but subsequently rises above it, the exemption of Article 2 continues to apply for two consecutive calendars years following that in which the threshold was exceeded (Art. 3(2)).

—Hardcore restrictions on the block exemptions (Art. 4) **D31**

Article 4 sets out licence terms which, if present, cause the entire agreement to be outside the terms of the block exemption provided by Article 2, see Recital (13). These forbidden provisions ("hardcore restrictions") vary according to whether the parties are "competing", or "non-competing" undertakings.

If the agreement parties are competing undertakings, even when they have a combined market-share not greater than 30% of the relevant market, Article 4(1) provides that the block exemption (provided by Art. 2) does not apply:

(1) where there is a restriction on a party's ability to determine its prices when selling to third parties; or

(2) where there is a limitation on output (*e.g.* preventing a licensee using its own technology), each as regards the output of contract products imposed on the licensee in a "non-reciprocal agreement" or imposed on only one of the licensees in a "reciprocal agreement" *(e.g.* a cross-licensing agreement), these terms being defined in Article 1(1)(c) and (d); or

(3) where the parties agree to a particular allocation of markets or customers, other than as defined in Art. 4(1)(c).

When the agreement parties are not "competing undertakings", even when they have a combined market-share of not greater than 20% of the relevant market, Article 4(2) provides that the block exemption otherwise provided by Article 2 is lost when the agreement has an object:

(1) the restriction of a party's ability to determine its prices to third parties, other than the possibility of imposing a maximum sale price which does not amount to a fixed or minimum sales price arising from pressure applied by a party or an incentive offered thereby (Art. 3(2)(a));

(2) a restriction of the territory into which sales may be made, other than passive sales made into an exclusive territory reserved to the licensor; or (for two years) to an exclusive territory allocated to another; or an obligation to produce contract products for its own use, provided that the licensee is not restricted from supplying spare parts; or an obligation to provide products for a particular customer in order to create an alternative supply source therefor; or a restriction on sales to end users by a wholesaler licensee; or a restriction on sales to unauthorised distributers (Art. 3(2)(b)); or

(3) a restriction on a licensee, who is a member of a selective distribution system operating at the retail level, from active or passive sales, except where such member is prohibited from operating out of an unauthorised place of establishment (Art. 4(2)(c)).

These restrictions to not appear to prohibit, as such, "field of use" or "captive use" restraints. Also, in the case of a "non-reciprocal agreement", territorial and customer restrictions appear possible.

Where the undertakings are not "competing undertakings" when the agreement is concluded, but become such at a later date, Article 4(2) (rather than Art. 4(1)) applies for the full life of the agreement (Art. 4(3)).

D32 — *Individual withdrawal of exemptions and non-applicability of the Regulation (Arts. 6 and 7)*

Articles 6 and 7 (reprinted in § D26, *supra*) provide the Commission with power to withdraw the benefit of the TTBER where it finds in any particular case that a technology transfer agreement, despite being eligible for exemption under Article 2, is incompatible with CTa. 81(3). This power is open-ended, but three examples are set out in Article 6(1) illustrative of when the power may be used: *viz.*

(1) where access of third parties' technologies, or

(2) of potential licensees, each to the market is restricted by parallel networks of other agreements, or

(3) where the parties do not exploit the licensed technology without an "objectively valid reason".

Article 6(2) enables national competition authorities power to withdraw the benefit of the TTBER in respect of the territory of a Member State or of part of it.

Given (as noted in § D20, *supra*) that there is now no "white list" of acceptable non-competitive provisions (as previously set out in the TTR), it can be seen that the TTBER potentially gives the Commission unlimited power to adjust its position on the effect of CTa. 81(1) and (3) as and when it may deem this appropriate.

Article 7 also permits the Commission, by way of a new Regulation, to disapply the TTBER in circumstances where "parallel networks of similar technology transfer agreements cover more than 50% of a relevant market".

D33 — *Transitional provision (Art. 10)*

Article 10 (reprinted in § D28, *supra*) contains an important transitional provision in respect of provisions in existing agreements (*i.e.* agreements in force on April 30, 2004) which enjoyed exemption under the TTR and CTa. 81(3), but which are not entitled under the TTBER to such exemption. Such agreements can continue to enjoy their previous exemption for a period of two years ending April 30, 2006.

APPENDIX E—CIVIL PROCEDURE RULES (Extracts)

INTRODUCTION

E00.2 **Scope of this Appendix**

The extracts from the CPR, and their Practice Directions, are subject to frequent variation and, therefore if important, the current state of any particular rule or Practice Direction should be checked. This can conveniently be done on the web site of the Department of Constitutional Affairs http://www.dca.gov.uk/civil/procrules_fin/menus/rules.htm.

Noted below are the significant changes that have been made, up to April 1, 2003, to those extracts from the CPR and its Practice Directions which were reprinted in the Main Work.

Parts of the Civil Procedure Rules (as relevant to this Work)   E00.3

Part 63, with the Practice Directions thereunder (each reproduced in Appendix F *infra* in so far as these relate to patent claims), was introduced on April 1, 2003 replacing (for these claims) the former Practice Directions E under CPR Part 49 (reproduced in Appendix F of the Main Work), these then ceasing to have effect.

PART 2—APPLICATION AND INTERPRETATION OF THE RULES

Interpretation   E02.3

In rule 2.2, the word "relevant" has been corrected to "rule or".

PART 5—COURT DOCUMENTS

Supply of documents from court records   E05.4

CPR 5.4 has been amended to read:

5.4—(1) A court or court office may keep a publicly accessible register of claims which have been issued out of that court or court office.

(2) Any person who pays the prescribed fee may, during office hours, search any available register of claims. (The practice direction contains details of available registers.)

(3) A party to proceedings may, unless the court orders otherwise, obtain from the records of the court a copy of—

(a) a statement of case;

(b) a judgment or order given or made in public (whether made at a hearing or without a hearing);

(c) an application notice, other than in relation to—

(i) an application by a solicitor for an order declaring that he has ceased to be the solicitor acting for a party; or

(ii) an application for an order that the identity of a party or witness should not be disclosed;

(d) any written evidence filed in relation to an application, other than a type of application mentioned in sub-paragraph (c)(i) or (ii);

(e) a notice of payment into court;

(f) an appellant's notice or respondent's notice.

(4) A party to proceedings may, if the court gives permission, obtain from the records of the court a copy of any other document filed by a party or communication between the court and a party or another person.

(5) Any other person may—

(a) unless the court orders otherwise, obtain from the records of the court a copy of—

(i) a claim form, subject to paragraph (6) and to any order of the court under paragraph (7);

(ii) a judgment or order given or made in public (whether made at a hearing or without a hearing), subject to paragraph (6); and

(b) if the court gives permission, obtain from the records of the court a copy of any other document filed by a party, or communication between the court and a party or another person.

(6) A person may obtain a copy of a claim form or a judgment or order under paragraph (5)(a) only if—

(a) where there is one defendant, the defendant has filed an acknowledgment of service or a defence;

   (b) where there is more than one defendant, either—

     (i) all the defendants have filed an acknowledgment of service or a defence;

     (ii) at least one defendant has filed an acknowledgment of service or a defence, and the court gives permission;

   (c) the claim has been listed for a hearing; or

   (d) judgment has been entered in the claim.

(7) The court may, on the application of a party or of any person identified in the claim form—

   (a) restrict the persons or classes of persons who may obtain a copy of the claim form;

   (b) order that persons or classes of persons may only obtain a copy of the claim form if it is edited in accordance with the directions of the court; or

   (c) make such other order as it thinks fit.

(8) A person wishing to obtain a copy of a document under paragraph (3), (4) or (5) must pay any prescribed fee and—

   (a) if the court's permission is required, file an application notice in accordance with Part 23; or

   (b) if permission is not required, file a written request for the document.

(9) An application for permission to obtain a copy of a document, or for an order under paragraph (7), may be made without notice, but the court may direct notice to be given to any person who would be affected by its decision.

(10) Paragraphs (3) to (9) of this rule do not apply in relation to any proceedings in respect of which a rule or practice direction makes different provision.

PART 6—SERVICE OF DOCUMENTS

I. GENERAL RULES ABOUT SERVICE

E06.5   **Address for service**

At the end of rule 6.5 the following words have been added:

" (Rule 42.1 provides that if the business address of his solicitor is given that solicitor will be treated as acting for that party)."

PART 16 PRACTICE DIRECTION—STATEMENTS OF CASE

The defence

E16PD.11   **General**

This Practice Direction has become No. 10.

E16PD.12   **Statement of truth**

This Practice Direction has become No. 11.

E16PD.14   **Other matters**

This Practice Direction has become No. 13.

PART 20 PRACTICE DIRECTION—COUNTERCLAIMS AND OTHER PART 20 CLAIMS

E20PD.3   **General**

A minor change has been made to this paragraph.

PART 22—STATEMENTS OF TRUTH

Documents to be verified by a statement of truth   **E22.1**

Sub-paragraphs (d)–(f) have been added to rule 22.1(1).

PART 22 PRACTICE DIRECTION—STATEMENTS OF TRUTH

Penalty   **E22PD.5**

A minor change has been made to this paragraph.

PART 25—INTERIM REMEDIES AND SECURITY FOR COSTS

II. SECURITY FOR COSTS

Conditions to be satisfied   **E25.13**

In rule 25.13(2), sub-paragraphs (a) and (b) have been replaced by:

    (a) "the claimant is—
        (i) resident out of the jurisdiction; but
        (ii) not resident in a Brussels Contracting State, a Lugano Contracting State or a Regulation State, as defined in section 1(3) of the Civil Jurisdiction and Judgments Act 1982 [c. 27, as amended by the Civil Jurisdiction and Judgments Act 1991 (c. 12) and by S.I. 1989/1346; S.I. 1990/2591; S.I. 1993/603; S.I. 2000/1824 and S.I. 2001/3929]; "

PART 29—THE MULTI-TRACK

Pre-Trial Check list (listing questionnaire)   **E29.6**

Rule 29.6 (including its title) has been replaced by:

    "(1) The court will send the parties a pre-trial check list (listing questionnaire) for completion and return by the date specified in directions given under rule 29.2(3) unless it considers that the claim can proceed to trial without the need for a pre-trial check list.
    (2) Each party must file the completed pre-trial check list by the date specified by the court.
    (3) If—
    (a) a party fails to file the completed pre-trial check list by the date specified;
    (b) a party has failed to give all the information requested by the pre-trial check list; or
    (c) the court considers that a hearing is necessary to enable it to decide what directions to give in order to complete preparation of the case for trial,
the court may give such directions as it thinks appropriate."

Pre-trial review   **E29.7**

In rule 29.7 the words "listing questionnaire" have been replaced by "pre-trial check list".

E29.8 Setting a trial timetable and fixing or confirming the trial date or week

In rule 29.8(a) the words "listing questionnaire" have been replaced by "pre-trial check list".

PART 31—Disclosure and Inspection of Documents

E31.14 Documents referred to in statements of case, etc.

Rule 31.14 has been amended to read:

"**31.14**—(1) A party may inspect a document mentioned in—
    (a) a statement of case;
    (b) a witness statement;
    (c) a witness summary; or
    (d) an affidavit.
    (2) Subject to rule 35.10(4), a party may apply for an order for inspection of any document mentioned in an expert's report which has not already been disclosed in the proceedings.
(Rule 35.10(4) makes provision in relation to instructions referred to in an expert's report)"

PART 31 Practice Direction—Disclosure and Inspection

E31PD.4 Disclosure statement

There has been added to the end of 31PD 4.3 the words:

"or the basis upon which he makes the statement on behalf of the party".

E31PD.5 Specific disclosure

Practice Direction CPR PD 5.5(1) has been amended to read:

"**5.5(1)**– An order for specific disclosure may in an appropriate case direct a party to—
    (1) carry out a search for any documents which it is reasonable to suppose may contain information which may—
        (a) enable the party applying for disclosure either to advance his own case or to damage that of the party giving disclosure; or
        (b) lead to a train of enquiry which has either of those consequences; and
    (2) disclose any documents found as a result of that search."

E31PD.7 Inspection of documents mentioned in expert's report (rule 3.14(e))

Paragraph E31PD.7 has been replaced by:

"**7.1** If a party wishes to inspect documents referred to in the expert report of another party, before issuing an application he should request inspection of the documents informally, and inspection should be provided by agreement unless the request is unreasonable.

7.2 Where an expert report refers to a large number or volume of documents and it would be burdensome to copy or collate them, the court will only order inspection of such documents if it is satisfied that it is necessary for the just disposal of the proceedings and the party cannot reasonably obtain the documents from another source."

False disclosure statement   E31PD.8

A new paragraph 8 has been added, reading:

"**8.** Attention is drawn to rule 31.23 which sets out the consequences of making a false disclosure statement without an honest belief in its truth, and to the procedures set out in paragraph 28.1–28.3 of the practice direction supplementing Part 32. "

PART 32—Evidence

Availability of witness statements for inspection   E32.13

In paragraph (1), the words "unless the court otherwise directs during the course of the trial" have been substituted for "during the course of the trial unless the court otherwise directs".

PART 34—Witnesses, Depositions and Evidence for Foreign Courts

Order under 1975 Act, as applied by Patents Act 1977   E34.21

34.21 —Where an order is made for the examination of witnesses under section 1 of the 1975 Act [the Evidence (Proceedings in Other Jurisdictions) Act 1975, c. 34] as applied by section 92 of the Patents Act 1977 [c. 37] the court may permit an officer of the European Patent Office to—
    (a) attend the examination and examine the witnesses; or
    (b) request the court or the examiner before whom the examination takes place to put specified questions to them.

PART 35—Experts and Assesors

Discussions between experts   E35.12

A minor change has been made to rule 12(1).

Expert's right to ask court for directions   E35.14

Minor changes have been made to rules 14(2) and (3).

Assessors   E35.15

A minor change has been made to rule 15(7).

Part 35 Practice Direction—Experts and Assessors

Experts evidence—general requirements   E35PD.0

A new paragraph 1 has been inserted reading:

"**1.1** It is the duty of an expert to help the court on matters within his own expertise: rule 35.3(1). This duty is paramount and overrides any obligation to the person from whom the expert has received instructions or by whom he is paid: rule 35.3(2).

1.2 Expert evidence should be the independent product of the expert uninfluenced by the pressures of litigation.

1.3 An expert should assist the court by providing objective, unbiased opinion on matters within his expertise, and should not assume the role of an advocate.

1.4 An expert should consider all material facts, including those which might detract from his opinion.

1.5 An expert should make it clear:
(a) when a question or issue falls outside his expertise; and
(b) when he is not able to reach a definite opinion, for example because he has insufficient information.

1.6 If, after producing a report, an expert changes his view on any material matter, such change of view should be communicated to all the parties without delay, and when appropriate to the court."

E35PD.1   Form and content of expert's reports

Former paragraph 1 has been renumbered as paragraph 2 and sub-paragraphs 2.1 and 2.2 have been revised to read:

"**2.1** An expert's report should be addressed to the court and not to the party from whom the expert has received his instructions.

2.2 An expert's report must:
(1) give details of the expert's qualifications;
(2) give details of any literature or other material which the expert has relied on in making the report;
(3) contain a statement setting out the substance of all facts and instructions given to the expert which are material to the opinions expressed in the report or upon which those opinions are based;
(4) make clear which of the facts stated in the report are within the expert's own knowledge;
(5) say who carried out any examination, measurement, test or experiment which the expert has used for the report, give the qualifications of that person, and say whether or not the test or experiment has been carried out under the expert's supervision;
(6) where there is a range of opinion on the matters dealt with in the report—
(a) summarise the range of opinion, and
(b) give reasons for his own opinion;
(7) contain a summary of the conclusions reached;
(8) if the expert is not able to give his opinion without qualification, state the qualification; and
(9) contain a statement that the expert understands his duty to the court, and has complied and will continue to comply with that duty."

E35PD2–5   *Note.* Paragraphs 2–5 of 35PD (as reprinted in the Main Work) have been respectively renumbered as paragraphs 3–6, with the reference to paragraph 1.2(8) in former paragraph 3 (now paragraph 4) being changed to " paragraph 2.2(3) ".

PART 44—GENERAL RULES ABOUT COSTS

E44.13   Special situations

Rule 44.13(1) has been amended to read:

"(1) Where the court makes an order which does not mention costs—
(a) the general rule is that no party is entitled to costs in relation to that order; but

(b) this does not affect any entitlement of a party to recover costs out of a fund held by him as trustee or personal representative, or pursuant to any lease, mortgage or other security."

Court's powers in relation to misconduct   E44.14

A minor change has been made to rule 14(1)(a).

PART 48—Costs—Special Cases

II. Costs relating to Solicitors and other Legal Representatives

Basis of detailed assessment of solicitor and client costs   E48.8

Paragraph (1) of CPR 48.8 has been replaced by:

"(1) This rule applies to every assessment of a solicitor's bill to his client except a bill which is to be paid out of the Community Legal Service Fund under the Legal Aid Act 1988 [c. 34] or the Access to Justice Act 1999 [c. 22]. ";

and, after paragraph (2), there has been inserted:

"(3) Where the court is considering a percentage increase, whether on the application of the legal representative under rule 44.16 or on the application of the client, the court will have regard to all the relevant factors as they reasonably appeared to the solicitor or counsel when the conditional fee agreement was entered into or varied."

(4) In paragraph (3), "conditional fee agreement" means an agreement enforceable under section 58 of the Courts and Legal Services Act 1990 [c. 41] at the date on which that agreement was entered into or varied. "

Part 49 Practice Direction E—Patents etc.   E49EPD.0

The Practice Directions of CPR 49EPD were replaced (from April 1, 2003) by a new CPR Part 63 and Practice Directions thereunder. These are reprinted Statute *infra* as a new Appendix F replacing that Appendix as printed in the Main Work.

PART 50—Application of the Schedules   E50.0

The entries in the Main Work under Part 50 have ceased to be applicable, having been replaced by CPR Part 34, Section II. In particular, former RSC O. 70, r. 2 has been re-enacted as CPR 34.21, reprinted in § 34.21 *supra*.

PART 52—Appeals

I. General Rules about Appeals

Non-disclosure of Part 36 offers and payments   E52.12

Paragraph (1) of CPR 52.12 has been replaced by:

(1) The fact that a Part 36 offer or Part 36 payment has been made must not be disclosed to any judge of the appeal court who is to hear or determine—

(a) an application for permission to appeal; or

(b) an appeal,

until all questions (other than costs) have been determined.

PART 52 PRACTICE DIRECTION—APPEALS

E52PD.9   Re-hearings

Paragraph 9.1 has been amended to read:

"9.1 The hearing of an appeal will be a re-hearing (as opposed to a review of the decision of the lower court) if the appeal is from the decision of a minister, person or other body and the minister, person or other body—

(1) did not hold a hearing to come to that decision; or

(2) held a hearing to come to that decision, but the procedure adopted did not provide for the consideration of evidence."

E63.0   PART 63—PATENTS AND OTHER INTELLECTUAL PROPERTY CLAIMS

CPR Part 63, and its Practice Directions have replaced former CPR 49EPD and, in so far as these apply to proceedings in the Patents Court or the Patents County Court, they are reprinted Statute *infra* in a replacement Appendix F.

PRACTICE DIRECTION—PROTOCOLS

EPrPD.4   Pre-action behaviour in other cases

4. The following paragraphs have been added to paragraph 4:

"4A.1 Where a person enters into a funding arrangement within the meaning of rule 43.2(1)(k) [not reprinted in the Main Work] he should inform other potential parties to the claim that he has done so.

4A.2 Paragraph 4A.1 applies to all proceedings whether proceedings to which a pre-action protocol applies or otherwise.

(Rule 44.3B(1)(c) provides that a party may not recover any additional liability for any period in the proceedings during which he failed to provide information about a funding arrangement in accordance with a rule, practice direction or court order.)"

The Second Cumulative Supplement made reference to proposals for pre-action protocols specific to intellectual property matters. It is understood that these proposals have been shelved but the courts will expect the General pre-action protocol to be adhered to as far as possible.

APPENDIX F—CIVIL PROCEDURE RULES FOR THE PATENTS COURT   F00

Note. Appendix F, as printed in the Main Work, is no longer operative. It was replaced, with effect from April 1, 2003, by the provisions reprinted below.

PART 63—PATENTS AND OTHER INTELLECTUAL PROPERTY CLAIMS   F63.0

(Effective from April 1, 2003)

Note. CPR 63 and its Practice Directions deal generally with litigation on intellectual property claims, but reproduced below are only those provisions which apply to patent litigation.

Scope of this Part and interpretation   F63.1

63.1—(1) This Part applies to all intellectual property claims including—
(a) registered intellectual property rights such as—
(i) patents;
   ...

(2) In this Part—
(a) "the 1977 Act" means the Patents Act 1977 [c.37];
(b) "the 1988 Act" means the Copyright, Designs and Patents Act 1988 [c. 48];
(c) ...
(d) "the Comptroller" means the Comptroller General of Patents, Designs and Trade Marks;
(e) "patent" means a patent under the 1977 Act and includes any application for a patent or supplementary protection certificate granted under—
   (i) the Patents (Supplementary Protection Certificates) Rules 1997 [S.I. 1997 No. 64];
   (ii) the Patents (Supplementary Protection Certificate for Medicinal Products) Regulations 1992 [S.I. 1992 No. 3091]; and
   (iii) the Patents (Supplementary Protection Certificate for Plant Protection Products) Regulations 1996 [S.I. 1996 No. 3120];
(f) "Patents Court" means the Patents Court of the High Court constituted as part of the Chancery Division by section 6(1) of the Supreme Court Act 1981 [c. 54];
(g) "Patents County Court" means a county court designated as a Patents County Court under section 287(1) of the 1988 Act;
(h) "the register" means whichever of the following registers is appropriate—
   (i) patents maintained by the Comptroller under section 32 of the 1977 Act; ...
(i) ...

Application of the Civil Procedure Rules   F63.2

63.2 These Rules and their practice directions apply to intellectual property claims unless this Part or a practice direction provides otherwise.

I. PATENTS AND REGISTERED DESIGNS

Scope of Section I   F63.3

63.3—(1) This Section of this Part applies to claims in—

(a) the Patents Court; and

(b) a Patents County Court.

(2) Claims in the court include any claim relating to matters arising out of—

(a) the 1977 Act;

...

F63.4 Specialist list

63.4 Claims in the Patents Court and a Patents County Court form specialist lists for the purpose of rule 30.5.

F63.5 Starting the claim

63.5 Claims to which this Section of this Part applies must be started—

(a) by issuing a Part 7 claim form; or

(b) in existing proceedings under Part 20.

F63.6 Defence and reply

63.6 Part 15 applies with the modification—

(a) to rule 15.4 that in a claim for infringement under rule 63.9, the defence must be filed within 42 days of service of the claim form; and

(b) to rule 15.8 that the claimant must—

(i) file any reply to a defence; and

(ii) serve it on all other parties,

within 21 days of service of the defence.

F63.7 Case management

63.7—(1) Claims under this Section of this Part are allocated to the multi-track.

(2) Part 26 and any other rule that requires a party to file an allocation questionnaire do not apply.

(3) The following provisions only of Part 29 apply—

(a) rule 29.3(2) (legal representatives to attend case management conferences);

(b) rule 29.4 (the court's approval of agreed proposals for the management of proceedings); and

(c) rule 29.5 (variation of case management timetable) with the exception of paragraph (1)(b) and (c).

(4) As soon as practicable the court will hold a case management conference which must be fixed in accordance with the practice direction.

F63.8 Disclosure and inspection

63.8 Part 31 is modified to the extent set out in the practice direction.

F63.9 Claim for infringement and challenge to validity

63.9—(1) In a claim for infringement or an application in which the validity of a patent or registered design is challenged, the statement of case must contain particulars as set out in the practice direction.

(2) In a claim for infringement, the period for service of the defence or Part 20 claim is 42 days after service of the claim form.

Application to amend a patent specification in existing proceedings F63.10

63.10—(1) An application under section 75 of the 1977 Act for permission to amend the specification of a patent by the proprietor of the patent must be made by application notice.

(2) The application notice must—

    (a) give particulars of—

        (i) the proposed amendment sought; and

        (ii) the grounds upon which the amendment is sought;

    (b) state whether the applicant will contend that the claims prior to amendment are valid; and

    (c) be served by the applicant on all parties and the Comptroller within 7 days of its issue.

(3) The application notice must, if it is reasonably possible, be served on the Comptroller electronically.

(4) Unless the court otherwise orders, the Comptroller will forthwith advertise the application to amend in the journal.

(5) The advertisement will state that any person may apply to the Comptroller for a copy of the application notice.

(6) Within 14 days of the first appearance of the advertisement any person who wishes to oppose the application must file and serve on all parties and the Comptroller a notice opposing the application which must include the grounds relied on.

(7) Within 28 days of the first appearance of the advertisement the applicant must apply to the court for directions.

(8) Unless the court otherwise orders, the applicant must within 7 days serve on the Comptroller any order of the court on the application.

(9) In this rule, "the journal" means the journal published pursuant to rules made under section 123(6) of the 1977 Act.

Court's determination of question or application F63.11

63.11 Where the Comptroller—

    (a) declines to deal with a question under section 8(7), 12(2), 37(8) or 61(5) of the 1977 Act;

    (b) declines to deal with an application under section 40(5) of the 1977 Act; or

    (c) certifies under section 72(7)(b) of the 1977 Act that the court should determine the question whether a patent should be revoked,

any person seeking the court's determination of that question or application must issue a claim form within 14 days of the Comptroller's decision.

Application by employee for compensation F63.12

63.12—(1) An application by an employee for compensation under section 40(1) or (2) of the 1977 Act must be made—

    (a) in a claim form; and

    (b) within the period prescribed by paragraphs (2) and (3).

(2) The prescribed period begins on the date of the grant of the patent and ends one year after the patent has ceased to have effect.

(3) Where a patent has ceased to have effect as a result of failure to pay the renewal fees within the period prescribed under rule 39 of the Patents Rules 1995 [S.I. 1995 No. 2093], and an application for restoration is made to the Comptroller under section 28 of the 1977 Act, the period prescribed under paragraph (2) —

    (b) if restoration is ordered, continues as if the patent had remained continuously in effect; or

    (c) if restoration is refused, is treated as expiring one year after the patent ceased to have effect, or six months after the refusal, whichever is the later.

III. Service

F63.16 **Service**

63.16—(1) Subject to paragraph (2), Part 6 applies to service of a claim form and any document under this Part.

(2) A claim form relating to a registered right may be served—

(a) on a party who has registered the right at the address for service given for that right in the United Kingdom Patent Office register, provided the address is within the jurisdiction; or

(b) in accordance with rule 6.19(1) or (1A) on a party who has registered the right at the address for service given for that right in the appropriate register at—

(i) the United Kingdom Patent Office; or

(ii) the Office for Harmonisation in the Internal Market.

IV. Appeals

F63.17 **Appeals from the Comptroller**

63.17—(1) Part 52 applies to appeals from the Comptroller.

(2) Patent appeals are to be made to the Patents Court, ...

(3) Where Part 52 requires a document to be served, it must also be served on the Comptroller or registrar, as appropriate.

PART 63 PRACTICE DIRECTION—PATENTS AND OTHER INTELLECTUAL PROPERTY

This Practice Direction supplements CPR Part 63

F63PD.1 **Contents of this practice direction**

1.1 This practice direction is divided into three sections—

Section 1—Provisions about patents and registered designs

...

F63PD.2 *I. Provisions about Patents and Registered Designs*

2.1 This Section of this practice direction applies to claims in the Patents Court and a Patents County Court.

2.2 The following claims must be dealt with in the court—

(1) any matter arising out of the 1977 Act, including—

(a) infringement actions;

(b) revocation actions;

(c) threats under section 70 of the 1977 Act; and

(d) disputes as to ownership;

...

F63PD.3 **Starting the claim (rule 63.5)**

3.1 A claim form to which this Section of this Part applies must be marked in the top right hand corner "Patents Court" below the title of the court in which it is issued.

Case management (rule 63.7)   F63PD.4

4.1 The following parts only of the practice direction supplementing Part 29 apply —

(1) paragraph 5 (case management conferences)—

(a) excluding paragraph 5.9; and

(b) modified so far as is made necessary by other specific provisions of this practice direction; and

(2) paragraph 7 (failure to comply with case management directions).

4.2 Case management shall be dealt with by—

(1) a judge of the court; or

(2) a Master or district judge where a judge of the court so directs.

4.3 The claimant must apply for a case management conference within 14 days of the date when all defendants who intend to file and serve a defence have done so.

4.4 Where the claim has been transferred, the claimant must apply for a case management conference within 14 days of the date of the order transferring the claim, unless the court—

(1) held; or

(2) gave directions for

a case management conference, when it made the order transferring the claim.

4.5 Any party may, at a time earlier than that provided in paragraphs 4.3 and 4.4, apply in writing to the court to fix a case management conference.

4.6 If the claimant does not make an application in accordance with paragraphs 4.3 and 4.4, any other party may apply for a case management conference.

4.7 The court may fix a case management conference at any time on its own initiative.

4.8 Not less than 4 days before a case management conference, each party must file and serve an application notice for any order which that party intends to seek at the case management conference.

4.9 Unless the court orders otherwise, the claimant, or the party who makes an application under paragraph 4.6, in consultation with the other parties, must prepare a case management bundle containing—

(1) the claim form;

(2) all statements of case (excluding schedules), except that, if a summary of a statement of case has been filed, the bundle should contain the summary, and not the full statement of case;

(3) a pre-trial timetable, if one has been agreed or ordered;

(4) the principal orders of the court; and

(5) any agreement in writing made by the parties as to disclosure,

and provide copies of the case management bundle for the court and the other parties at least 4 days before the first case management conference or any earlier hearing at which the court may give case management directions.

4.10 At the case management conference the court may direct that—

(1) a scientific adviser under section 70(3) of the Supreme Court Act 1981 be appointed; and

(2) a document setting out basic undisputed technology should be prepared.

(Rule 35.15 applies to scientific advisers)

4.11 Where a trial date has not been fixed by the court, a party may apply for a trial date by filing a certificate which must—

(1) state the estimated length of the trial, agreed if possible by all parties;

(2) detail the time required for the judge to consider the documents;

(3) identify the area of technology; and

(4) assess the complexity of the technical issues involved by indicating the complexity on a scale of 1 to 5 (with 1 being the least and 5 the most complex).

4.12 The claimant, in consultation with the other parties, must revise and update the documents referred to in paragraph 4.9 appropriately as the case proceeds. This must include making all necessary revisions and additions at least 7 days before any subsequent hearing at which the court may give case management directions.

F63PD.5   Disclosure and inspection (rule 63.8)

5.1 Standard disclosure does not require the disclosure of documents where the documents relate to—

(1) the infringement of a patent by a product or process if, before or at the same time as serving a list of documents, the defendant has served on the claimant and any other party—

(a) full particulars of the product or process alleged to infringe; and

(b) drawings or other illustrations, if necessary;

(2) any ground on which the validity of a patent is put in issue, except documents which came into existence within the period—

(a) beginning two years before the earliest claimed priority date; and

(b) ending two years after that date; and

(3) the issue of commercial success.

5.2 Where the issue of commercial success arises, the patentee must, within such time limit as the court may direct, serve a schedule containing—

(1) where the commercial success relates to an article or product—

(a) an identification of the article or product (for example by product code number) which the patentee asserts has been made in accordance with the claims of the patent;

(b) a summary by convenient periods of sales of any such article or product;

(c) a summary for the equivalent periods of sales, if any, of any equivalent prior article or product marketed before the article or product in sub-paragraph (a); and

(d) a summary by convenient periods of any expenditure on advertising and promotion which supported the marketing of the articles or products in sub-paragraphs (a) and (c); or

(2) where the commercial success relates to the use of a process—

(a) an identification of the process which the patentee asserts has been used in accordance with the claims of the patent;

(b) a summary by convenient periods of the revenue received from the use of such process;

(c) a summary for the equivalent periods of the revenues, if any, received from the use of any equivalent prior art process; and

(d) a summary by convenient periods of any expenditure which supported the use of the process in sub-paragraphs (a) and (c).

F63PD.6   Short applications

6.1 Where any application is listed for a short hearing, the parties must file all necessary documents, skeleton arguments and drafts of any orders sought, by no later than 3.00pm on the preceding working day.

6.2 A short hearing is any hearing which is listed for no more than 1 hour.

F63PD.7   Timetable for trial

7.1 Not less than one week before the beginning of the trial, each party must inform the court in writing of the estimated length of its—

(1) oral submissions;

(2) examination in chief, if any, of its own witnesses; and

(3) cross-examination of witnesses of any other party.

7.2 At least four days before the date fixed for the trial, the claimant must file—

(3) the trial bundle; and

(4) a Reading Guide for the judge.

7.3 The Reading Guide filed under paragraph 7.2 must—

(1) be short and, if possible, agreed;

(2) set out the issues, the parts of the documents that need to be read on each issue and the most convenient order that they should be read;

(3) identify the relevant passages in text books and cases, if appropriate; and

(4) not contain argument.

Jurisdiction of Masters

F63PD.8

8.1 A Master may deal with—

(1) orders by way of settlement, except settlement of procedural disputes;

(2) orders on applications for extension of time;

(3) applications for leave to serve out of the jurisdiction;

(4) applications for security for costs;

(5) other matters as directed by a judge of the court; and

(6) enforcement of money judgments.

Experiments

F63PD.9

9.1 Where a party seeks to establish any fact by experimental proof conducted for the purpose of litigation he must, at least 21 days before service of the application notice for directions under paragraph 9.3, or within such other time as the court may direct, serve on all parties a notice—

(1) stating the facts which he seeks to establish; and

(2) giving full particulars of the experiments proposed to establish them.

9.2 A party served with notice under paragraph 9.1 —

(2) must within 21 days after such service, serve on the other party a notice stating whether or not he admits each fact; and

(3) may request the opportunity to inspect a repetition of all or a number of the experiments identified in the notice served under paragraph 9.1.

9.3 Where any fact which a party seeks to establish by experimental proof is not admitted, he must apply to the court for permission and directions by application notice.

Use of models or apparatus

F63PD.10

10.1 Where a party intends to rely on any model or apparatus, he must apply to the court for directions at the first case management conference.

Claim for infringement and challenge of validity (rule 63.9)

F63PD.11

11.1 In a claim for infringement of a patent—

(1) the statement of case must—

(a) show which of the claims in the specification of the patent are alleged to be infringed; and

(b) give at least one example of each type of infringement alleged; and

(2) a copy of each document referred to in the statement of case, and where necessary a translation of the document, must be served with the statement of case.

11.2 Where the validity of a patent or … is challenged—

(1) the statement of case must contain particulars of—

(a) the relief sought; and

(b) the issues except those relating to validity of the patent …;

(2) the statement of case must have a separate document annexed to it headed 'Grounds of Invalidity" specifying the grounds on which validity of the patent is challenged;

(3) a copy of each document referred to in the Grounds of Invalidity, and where necessary a translation of the document, must be served with the Grounds of Invalidity; and

(4) the Comptroller must be sent a copy of the Grounds of Invalidity and where any such Grounds of Invalidity are amended, a copy of the amended document, at the same time as the Grounds of Invalidity are served or amended.

11.3 Where, in an application in which validity of a patent or ... is challenged, the Grounds of Invalidity include an allegation—

(1) that the invention is not a patentable invention because it is not new or does not involve an inventive step, the particulars must specify such details of the matter in the state of art relied on, as set out in paragraph 11.4;

(2) that the specification of the patent does not disclose the invention clearly enough and completely enough for it to be performed by a person skilled in the art, the particulars must state, if appropriate, which examples of the invention cannot be made to work and in which respects they do not work or do not work as described in the specification; or

(3) ...

11.4 The details required under paragraph 11.3(1) and ... are—

(1) in the case of matter or ... made available to the public by written description the date on which and the means by which it was so made available, unless this is clear from the face of the matter; and

(2) in the case of matter or ... made available to the public by use—

(a) the date or dates of such use;

(b) the name of all persons making such use;

(c) any written material which identifies such use;

(d) the existence and location of any apparatus employed in such use; and

(e) all facts and matters relied on to establish that such matter was made available to the public.

11.5 In any proceedings in which validity of a patent is challenged—

(1) on the ground that the invention did not involve an inventive step, a party who wishes to rely on the commercial success of the patent must state the grounds on which he so relies in his statement of case; and

(2) the court may order inspection of machinery or apparatus where a party alleges such machinery or apparatus was used before the priority date of the claim.

F63PD.12   Application to amend a patent specification in existing proceedings (rule 63.10)

12.1 Not later than two days before the first hearing date the applicant, the Comptroller if he wishes to be heard, the parties to the proceedings and any other opponent, must file and serve a document stating the directions sought.

12.2 Where the application notice is served on the Comptroller electronically under rule 63.10(3), it must comply with any requirements for the sending of electronic communications to the Comptroller.

F63PD.13   Application by employee for compensation (rule 63.12)

13.1 Where an employee applies for compensation under section 40(1) or (2) of the 1977 Act, the court must at the case management conference give directions as to—

(1) the manner in which the evidence, including any accounts of expenditure and receipts relating to the claim, is to be given at the hearing of the claim and if written evidence is to be given, specify the period within which witness statements or affidavits must be filed; and

(2) the provision to the claimant by the defendant or a person deputed by him, of reasonable facilities for inspecting and taking extracts from the accounts by which the defendant proposes to verify the accounts in sub-paragraph (1) or from which those accounts have been derived.

F63PD.14   Communication of information to the European Patent Office

14.1 The court may authorise the communication of any such information in the court files as the court thinks fit to—

(1) the European Patent Office; or

(2) the competent authority of any country which is a party to the European Patent convention.

14.2 Before authorising the disclosure of information under paragraph 14.1, the court shall permit any party who may be affected by the disclosure to make representations, in writing or otherwise, on the question of whether the information should be disclosed.

Order affecting entry in the register of patents …   F63PD.15

15.1 Where any order of the court affects the validity of an entry in the register, the court and the party in whose favour the order is made, must serve a copy of such order on the Comptroller within 14 days.
15.2 Where the order is in favour of more than one party, a copy of the order must be served by such party as the court directs.

Claim for rectification of the register of patents …   F63PD.16

16.1 Where a claim is made for the rectification of the register of patents or …, the claimant must at the same time as serving the other parties, serve a copy of—

(1) the claim form; and

(2) accompanying documents

on the Comptroller or …, as appropriate.
16.2 Where documents under paragraph 16.1 are served on the Comptroller or …, he shall be entitled to take part in the proceedings.

APPENDIX G—PATENTS COURT GUIDE

Purpose of the Patents Court Guide   G00

The following announcement was issued by Jacob J., on March 3, 2003:

"New Rules for Intellectual Property come into force on 1st April 2003. Part 49 will cease to apply to IP. Instead there is a new Part 63 (Patents and other Intellectual Property Claims) and associated Practice Direction. There are no transitional provisions. A problem arising from that is the fact that the time for appealing from a decision of the Comptroller is reduced from 6 weeks to 2 weeks (the latter following from the fact that Part 52 will apply to all appeals). [*Spent announcement omitted*]. What follows is the Patents Court Guide for all patent proceedings (existing and to be commenced) for on and after 1st April 2003 in both the Patents Court and the Patents County Court. Particular attention is drawn to the provision for a streamlined procedure and to the duty of legal advisors to inform their clients of the provision. It is new to this Guide and agreed by a sub-committee of the Intellectual Property Court Users' Committee."

The new Patents Court Guide (as amended August 5, 2003) is reprinted below to replace the now inoperative form set out in Appendix G of the Main Work.

1. Introduction   G01

The general guidance applicable to matters in the Chancery Division, as set out in the Chancery Guide, also applies to patent actions unless specifically mentioned below. "PD 63'" refers to the Practice Direction—Patents and Other Intellectual Property Claims which supplements CPR Part 63. This Guide applies as appropriate to both the Patents Court and the Patents County Court.

2. General   G02

Actions proceeding in the Patents Court are allocated to the multi-track (CPR 63.7(1)). Attention is drawn to CPR 63(7) and its associated PD (case management).

3. The Patents Judges   G03

The Patents Judges and their clerks are as set out below.

Laddie J (Clerk: Peter Smith—telephone 020 7947 6518, fax 020 7947 6439
e-mail: peter.smith@courtservice.gsi.gov.uk)
Pumfrey J. (Clerk: Bob Glen—telephone 020 7947 7482, fax 020 7947 6593
e-mail: robert.glen@courtservice.gsi.gov.uk)
Patten J. (Clerk: Richard Trout—telephone 020 7947 7617, fax 020 7947 6650
e-mail: richard.trout@courtservice.gsi.gov.uk)
Lewison J. (Clerk: Denise Dolan—telephone 020 7947 6039, fax 020 7947 6894
e-mail: denise.dolan@courtservice.gsi.gov.uk)
Mann J. (Clerk: Amanda Dennis—telephone 020 7947 7964, fax 020 7947 6739
e-mail: amanda.dennis@courtservice.gsi.gov.uk)

G04   4. Patents County Court

The Patents County Court

Claims forms for the Patents County Court and general enquiries relating to procedure, fees and forms may be addressed to:

The Specialist Section
Central London Civil Justice Section
26 Park Crescent
London
W1N 4HT
Tel: 020 7917 7821
Fax: 020 7917 7935

Enquiries relating to listing and existing patents cases may be addressed to:

Clerk His Honour Judge Fysh QC
Field House
15-25 Breams Buildings
London
EC4A 1DZ
Tel: 020 7073 4251
Fax: 020 7073 4253

G05   5. Arrangements for Listing

The Chancery Listing Officer is responsible for the listing of all patents work.

The Chancery Listing Officer and his staff are located in Room WG04 in the Royal Courts of Justice. The office is open to the public from 10.00am to 4.30pm each day. The telephone numbers are 0207 947 6778/6690 and the fax number is 0207 947 7345.

Appointments to fix trials and interlocutory applications are dealt with on Mondays and Thursdays between 11.00am and 12.00 noon. The applicant should first obtain an appointment from the Chancery Listing Officer and notify all interested parties of the date and time fixed.

Short applications (before the normal court day starts at 10.30am) can be issued and the hearing date arranged at any time by attendance at the Chancery Listing Office.

These are listed for hearing before the normal court day starts at 10.30, for instance at 9.30 or 10 a.m. Attention is drawn to PD63.6. Accurate time estimates are essential and a guillotine may be imposed on oral submissions if estimates show signs of being exceeded.

G06   6. September Sittings

The Patents Court will endeavour, if the parties so desire and the case is urgent, to sit in September.

G07   7. Appeals from the Comptroller General of Patents, Trade Marks and Designs

Patents

By virtue of statute these lie only to the High Court and not the Patents County Court. They are now governed by CPR Part 52 (see CPR 63.17). Permission to appeal is not required. Note that the

Comptroller must be served with a Notice of Appeal (CPR 63.17(3)). The appellant has the conduct of the appeal and he or his representative should within 2 weeks of lodging the appeal, contact the Chancery Listing Officer with a view to arranging a hearing date. The appellant shall ensure that the appeal is set down as soon as is reasonably practicable after service of the notice of appeal. Parties are reminded that the provisions about the service of skeleton arguments apply to appeals from the Comptroller.

Trade Marks

These are assigned to the Chancery Division as a whole, not the Patents Court (CPR 63.17(2)). Permission to appeal is not required.

Appeals on Paper only

The Court will hear appeals on the papers only if that is what the parties desire. If the appellant is willing for the appeal to be heard on paper only, he should contact the respondent and the Patent Office at the earliest opportunity to discover whether such a way of proceeding is agreed. If it is, the Chancery Listing Office should be informed as soon as possible. The parties (and the Chancery Listing Officer if he/she so desires) should liaise amongst themselves for early preparation of written submissions and bundles and provide the court with all necessary materials.

Appeals concerning Registered Designs

These go to the Registered Designs Appeal Tribunal. This consists of one of the patent judges sitting as a tribunal. The CPR and PD do not apply to such appeals. Where such an appeal is desired, contact should be made direct to the Chancery Listing Officer.

8. Applications without Notice   **G08**

A party wishing to apply without notice to the respondent(s) should contact the Chancery Listing Office. In cases of emergency in vacation or out of normal court hours the application should be made to the duty Chancery Judge. In the Patents County Court, contact should be made with the Court Office.

9. Documents   **G09**

(a) Bundling is of considerable importance and should be approached intelligently. The general guidance given in Appendix 2 of the Chancery Guide should be followed. Solicitors or patent agents who fail to do so may be required to explain why and may be penalised personally in costs.

(b) Copies of documents referred to in a statement of case (e.g. an advertisement referred to in a claim of infringement form or documents cited in Grounds of Invalidity) should be served with the statement of case. Where any such document requires translation, a translation should be served at the same time.

(c) If it is known which Judge will be taking the case, papers for the case should be lodged directly with that Judge's clerk. Faxed documents of significance (and particularly skeleton arguments) should be followed up by clean direct prints. By agreement documents may also be sent by e-mail to the clerk of the Judge concerned.

(d) It is the responsibility of both parties to ensure that all relevant documents are lodged with the clerk of the Judge who will be taking the case by noon two days before the date fixed for hearing unless some longer or shorter period has been ordered by the judge or is prescribed by this Guide.

(e) The Judges request that all important documents also be supplied to them on disk in a format convenient for the Judge's use (normally Microsoft Word 7 for Windows). These will include skeleton arguments, the witness statements and expert reports.

10. Streamlined Procedure   **G10**

(a) Nature of a streamlined procedure.

A streamlined procedure is one in which, save and to the extent that it is otherwise ordered:
   i. all factual and expert evidence is in writing;

ii. there is no requirement to give disclosure of documents;

iii. there are no experiments,

iv. cross-examination is only permitted on any topic or topics where it is necessary and is confined to those topics;

v. the total duration of the trial fixed is and will normally be not more than one day;

vi. the date for trial will be fixed when the Order for a streamlined trial is made and will normally be about six months thereafter.

A streamlined procedure also includes minor variants of the above (e.g. disclosure confined to a limited issue).

(b) Criteria for a streamlined procedure

The court will order a streamlined procedure by agreement or, in the absence of agreement, where application of the overriding objective indicates that it is appropriate. Particular emphasis will be placed on proportionality, the financial position of each of the parties, degree of complexity and the importance of the case.

(c) When to apply for streamlined procedure

Any party may apply at any time after commencement of the action for a streamlined procedure. Any such application should be made at the earliest time reasonably possible, which will generally be at the case management conference required by PD63 within 14 days after service of the defence.

(d) How to apply for a streamline procedure

A party wishing for a streamlined procedure should, in the first instance, invite the other party(ies) to agree, setting out the proposed procedural steps in a draft Order. If there is agreement, the court will normally make the Order on a written application signed on behalf of each party. The parties should liase with each other and the Chancery Listing Officer or the Patents County court concerning a date for trial so that this can be fixed.

If there is no agreement, the party wishing for a streamlined procedure must make an application for it, setting forth the proposed procedural directions in his application notice and requesting that the application be determined on paper. He should support the application by a witness statement addressing the criteria in CPR Rule 1.1(2). The opposing party must, unless he obtains an extension of time (by consent or from the court) make and serve on the opposite party a witness statement in response within 10 days of service upon him of the application notice.

The court will determine the matter provisionally on paper alone and make a provisional judgment and order accordingly. Unless either side seeks an oral hearing the provisional order will come into effect 7 days after its service on the parties.

If a party is desirous of an oral hearing, it must, within 7 days of service upon it of the provisional order, seek an oral hearing in the immediate future by contacting the Chancery Listing Officer. Such an oral hearing will fixed as soon as is practicable, either by way of a telephone hearing or a short application.

(e) Duty to inform clients

The parties' legal advisers must draw their clients' attention to the availability of a streamlined procedure in the Patents Court and the Patents County Court.

G11 11. Timetable for trial, Reading Guide, Time Estimates, common general knowledge

Attention is drawn to PD 63.7. Further the parties should endeavour to produce a composite document setting forth the matters alleged to form part of the common general knowledge and, where they disagree, what that disagreement is.

G12 12. Narrowing of Issues

As early as possible the patentee should identify which of the claims of its patent are contended to have independent validity and which of those claims are said to be infringed and should communicate a list of those claims to the other party.

This position should be kept under constant review. If there is any alteration in the number of claims said to have independent validity the patentee must forthwith notify the other parties.

13. Admissions G13

With a view to early elimination of non-issues, practitioners are reminded of the necessity of making admissions in accordance with CPR Rule 32.18 at an early stage. It should be done as early as possible, for instance, in a defence or reply. Thus in a defence a party may admit the acts complained of or that his article/process has certain of the features of a claim. In a reply a patentee may be able to admit prior publication of cited documents.

Parties should also consider making a request to identify points not in dispute. Technically a request seeking admissions in respect of particular integers of a claim may involve a mixed question of fact and law and so not be within the rules about admissions. By asking whether or not the defendant disputes that his article/process has certain features of the claim the real dispute can be narrowed. Thus the ambit of disclosure and of witness and expert statements will be narrowed.

14. Skeleton Arguments, Pre-Trial and after the Evidence G14

In addition to the Reading Guide parties should lodge skeleton arguments in time for the Judge to read them before trial. That should normally be at least two days before commencement of the trial, but in substantial cases a longer period (to be discussed with the clerk to the Judge concerned) may be needed. It is desirable that each party should summarise what it contends to be the common general knowledge of the man skilled in the art.

Following the evidence in a substantial trial a short adjournment may be granted to enable the parties to summarise their arguments in writing before oral argument.

In trials where a transcript of evidence is being made and supplied to the Judge, the transcript should be accompanied by a version on disk.

15. Jurisdiction of Masters G15

Masters have only a limited jurisdiction in patent matters (see PD 63.8). Generally it is more convenient for consent orders (on paper or in court) to be made by a Judge even where a Master has jurisdiction to do so.

Where a Master makes a consent order disposing of an action which has been fixed, it is the duty of all the parties' representatives to inform the Chancery Listing Office that the case has settled.

16. Agreed Orders G16

The court is normally willing to make consent orders without the need for the attendance of any parties. A draft of the agreed order and the written consent of all the parties' respective solicitors or counsel should be supplied to the Chancery Listing Officer. Where a draft has been substantially amended by hand, it is helpful for a disk of the unamended version to be supplied in accordance with paragraph 9.6 of the Chancery Guide. Unless the Judge considers a hearing is needed he will make the order in the agreed terms by initialling it. It will be drawn up accordingly and sent to the parties.

17. Telephone Applications G17

For short (20 minutes or less) matters, the Patents Judges are willing, unless a matter of general public importance is involved, to hear applications by telephone conference in accordance with the Practice Direction under CPR Part 23.

It is possible for the application to be recorded, and if recording by the Patents Court rather than by British Telecom (or other service provider) is requested arrangements should be made with the Chancery Listing Officer. The recording will not be transcribed. The tape will be kept by the clerk to the judge hearing the application for a period of six months. Arrangements for transcription, if needed, must be made by the parties.

This procedure should be used where it will save costs.

18. Patents Judges able and willing to sit out of London G18

If the parties so desire, for the purpose of saving time or costs, the Patents Court will sit out of

London. Before any approach is made to the Chancery Listing Officer, the parties should discuss between themselves the desirability of such course. If there is a dispute as to venue the court will resolve the matter on an application. Where there is no dispute, the Chancery Listing Officer should be contacted as soon as possible so that arrangements can be put in place well before the date of the proposed hearing. The Patents County Court may also be able to sit out of London.

G19 19. Intellectual Property Court Users' Committee

This considers the problems and concerns of intellectual property litigation generally. Membership of the committee includes the principal Patents Judges, the Patents County Court Judge, a representative of each of the Patent Bar Association, the Intellectual Property Lawyers Association, the Chartered Institute of Patent Agents, the Institute of Trade Mark Agents and the Trade Marks Designs and Patents Federation. It will also include one or more other Chancery Judges. Anyone having views concerning the improvement of intellectual property litigation is invited to make his or her views known to the committee, preferably through the relevant professional representative on the committee. The Patents County Court also has a Users' Committee.

G20 20. Orders following judgment

Where a judgment is made available in draft before being given in open court the parties should, in advance of that occasion, exchange drafts of the desired consequential order. It is highly undesirable that one party should spring a proposal on the other for the first time when judgment is given. Where the parties are agreed as to the consequential order and have supplied a copy of the same signed by all parties or their representatives, attendance at the handing down of the judgment is not necessary.

G21 21. Applications for interim remedies: trial dates

When an application for an interim remedy is made the claimant should, where practicable, make prior investigations as to the estimated length of trial and possible trial dates.

G22 22. Specimen minute of order for directions

The general form minute of order for directions annexed to this practice direction has the approval of the Patents Judges. It is intended only as a guide and may need adaptation for particular circumstances.

ANNEX—STANDARD FORM OF ORDER FOR DIRECTIONS

G22A (* indicates a provision which may be necessary when a rule has not been compiled with, for example, standard disclosure in accordance with the Practice Direction supplementing CPR Part 63.)
[RECITALS AS NECESSARY]

Transfer

G22A.1 1. [This Action and Counterclaim be transferred to the Patents County Court.] (If this order is made, no other Order will generally be necessary, though it will generally be desirable for procedural orders to be made at this time to save the costs of a further conference in the County Court.)

Proof of Documents

G22A.2 2. Legible copies of the specification of the Patent in suit [and any patent specifications or other documents cited in the Particulars of Objections] may be used at the trial without further proof thereof or of their contents.

Amendments to Pleadings

G22A.3 3. The Claimants have leave to amend their Claim Form shown in red on the copy [annexed to the Application Notice/as signed by the solicitors for the parties/annexed hereto] and [to re-serve the

246

same on or before [date]/and that re-service be dispensed with] and that the Defendants have leave to serve a consequentially amended Defence within [number] days [thereafter/hereafter] and that the Claimants have leave to serve a consequentially amended Reply (if so advised) within [number] days thereafter.

4. (a) The Defendants have leave to amend their Defence [and Part 20 Claim and Grounds of Invalidity] as shown in red on the copy [annexed to the Application notice/as signed by the solicitors for the parties/annexed hereto] and [to reserve the same within [number] days/on or before[date]] [and that re-service be dispensed with] and that the Claimants have leave to serve a consequentially amended Reply (if so advised) within [number] days thereafter. **G22A.4**

(b) The Claimants do on or before [date] elect whether they will discontinue this Claim and withdraw their Defence to Part 20 Claim and consent to an Order for the revocation of Patent No… ("the patent in suit") AND IF the Claimants shall so elect and give notice thereof in the time aforesaid IT IS ORDERED THAT the patent in suit be revoked [and that it be referred to the Costs Judge to assess the costs of the Defendants and this Action and Grounds of Invalidity up to and including [date] being the date of service of the [amended] Grounds of Invalidity and Part 20 Claim to the date of this Order [except so far as the same have been increased by the failure of the Defendants originally to deliver the Defence and Grounds of Invalidity in its amended form], and to assess the costs of the Claimants in this Action and Part 20 Claim from [date] [insofar as they have been increased by the failure of the Defendants aforesaid] AND IT IS ORDERED that the said Costs Judge is to set off the costs of the Defendants and of the Claimants when so assessed as aforesaid and to certify to which of them the balance after such set-off is due.]/[Order for payment of sums determined by the Court on a summary assessment].

Further Information and Clarification

5. (a) The [Claimants/Defendants] do on or before [date] serve on the [Defendants/Claimants] the Further Information or Clarification of the [specify Statement of case] as requested by the [Claimants/ Defendants] by their Request served on the [Defendants/Claimants] on [date] [and/or] **G22A.5**

(b) The [Claimants/Defendants] do on or before [date] serve on the [Defendants/Claimants] a response to their Request for Further Information or Clarification of the [identify statement of case] served on the [Defendants/Claimants] on [date].

Admissions*

6. The [Claimants/Defendants] do on or before [date] state in writing whether or not they admit the facts specified in the [Defendants'/Claimants'] Notice to Admit facts dated [date]. **G22A.6**

Security

7. The Claimants do provide security for the Defendants' costs in the sum of £[state sum] by [specify manner in which security to be given] and that in the meantime all further proceedings be stayed. **G22A.7**

Lists of Documents*

8. (a) The Claimants and the Defendants respectively do on or before [state date] make and serve on the other of them a list in accordance with form N265 of the documents in their control which they are required to disclose in accordance with the obligation of standard disclosure in accordance with CPR Part 31 as modified by paragraph 5 of the Practice Direction—Patents etc. supplementing CPR Part 63. **G22A.8**

(b) In respect of those issues identified in Schedule [number] hereto disclosure shall be limited to those [documents/categories of documents] listed in Schedule [number].

Inspection*

9. If any party wishes to inspect or have copies of such documents as are in another party's control it shall give notice in writing that it wishes to do so and such inspection shall be allowed at all reasonable times upon reasonable notice and any copies shall be provided within [number] working days of the request upon the undertaking of the party requesting the copies to pay the reasonable copying charges. **G22A.9**

*Experiments**

G22A.10   10. (a) Where a party desires to establish any fact by experimental proof, including an experiment conducted for the purposes of litigation or otherwise not being an experiment conducted in the normal course of research, that party shall on or before [date] serve on all the other parties a notice stating the facts which it desires to establish and giving full particulars of the experiments proposed to establish them.

(b) A party upon whom a notice is served under the preceding sub-paragraph shall within [number] days, serve on the party serving the notice a notice stating in respect of each fact whether or not that party admits it.

(c) Where any fact which a party wishes to establish by experimental proof is not admitted that party shall apply to the Court for further directions in respect of such experiments.

[Or where paragraph 9 of the Practice Direction—Patents etc. supplementing CPR Part 63 has been complied with.]

G22A.11   11 (a) The Claimants/Defendants are to afford to the other parties an opportunity, if so requested, of inspecting a repetition of the experiments identified in paragraphs [specify them] of the Notice[s] of Experiments served on [date]. Any such inspection must be requested within [number] days of the date of this Order and shall take place within [number] days of the date of the request.

(b) If any party shall wish to establish any fact in reply to experimental proof that party shall on or before [date] serve on all the other parties a notice stating the facts which it desires to establish and giving full particulars of the experiments proposed to establish them.

(c) A party upon whom a notice is served under the preceding sub-paragraph shall within [number] days serve on the party serving the notice a notice stating in respect of each fact whether or not that party admits it.

(d) Where any fact which a party wishes to establish by experimental proof in reply is not admitted the party may apply to the Court for further directions in respect of such experiments.

Notice of Models, etc.

G22A.12   12 (a) If any party wishes to rely at the trial of this action upon any model, apparatus, drawing, photograph, cinematograph or video film whether or not the same is contained in a witness statement, affidavit or expert's report that party shall on or before [date] give notice thereof to all the other parties; shall afford the other parties an opportunity within [number] days of the service of such notice of inspecting the same and shall, if so requested, furnish the other party with copies of any such drawing or photograph and a sufficient drawing photograph or other illustration of any model or apparatus.

(b) If any party wishes to rely upon any such materials in reply to any matter of which notice was given under sub-paragraph (a) of this paragraph, that party shall within [number] days after the last inspection to be made in pursuance of the said sub-paragraph (a) give to the other parties a like notice, and if so requested within [number] days of delivery of such notice shall afford like opportunities of inspection which shall take place within [number] days of such request; and shall in like manner furnish copies of any drawing or photograph and illustration of any such model or apparatus.

(c) No further or other model apparatus drawing photograph cinematograph or video film shall be relied upon in evidence by either party save with consent or by leave of the Court.

Written evidence

G22A.13   13. (a) Each party may call up to [number] expert witnesses in this Action and Part 20 Claim provided that the said party:

(i) supplies the name of such expert to the other parties and to the Court on or before [date]; and

(ii) no later than [date/[number days] before the date set for the hearing of this Action and Part 20 Claim] serve upon the other parties a report of each such expert comprising the evidence which that expert intends to give at trial.

(b) Each party shall on or before [date] serve on the other parties [signed] written statements of the oral evidence which the party intends to lead on any issues of fact to be decided at the trial, such statements to stand as the evidence in chief of the witness unless the Court otherwise directs;

(c) The parties shall [here insert the particular directions sought, e.g. within 21 days after service of the other party's expert reports and written statements state in writing the facts and matters in those reports and statements which are admitted].

Admissibility of Evidence

14. A party who objects to any statements of any witness being read by the Judge prior to the hearing of the trial, shall serve upon each other party a notice in writing to that effect setting out the grounds of the objection.

G22A.14

Non-Compliance

15. Where either party fails to comply with the directions relating to experiments and written evidence it shall not be entitled to adduce evidence to which such directions relate without the leave of the Court.

G22A.15

Trial Bundles

16. Each party shall no later than [number] days before the date fixed for the trial of this Action and Counterclaim serve upon the parties a list of all the documents to be included in the trial bundles. The Claimants shall no later than [number] days before the date fixed for trial serve upon the Defendants … sets of the bundles for use at trial.

G22A.16

Trial

17. The trial of these proceedings shall be before an Assigned Judge alone in [London], estimated length [number] days and a pre-reading estimate for the Judge of [number] days.

G22A.17

Liberty to Apply

18. The parties are to be at liberty on two days' notice to apply for further directions and generally.

G22A.18

Costs

19. The costs of this Application are to be costs in the Action and Part 20 Claim.

G22A.19

APPENDIX I—REGULATIONS FOR EXAMINATIONS FOR REGISTRATION OF PATENT AGENTS

Schedule II

I10

The comptroller has decided that those who pass the patent papers in the QMW or Manchester University course, although failing those examinations as a whole, shall be exempted from Papers P2 and P5. Likewise, partial passes in the design and copyright and law papers in those examinations shall provide exemption from the D&C and Law Foundation papers respectively: see O.J. August 20, 2003. Exemption from the "Law" paper is also available for those who have gained a law qualification in certain other countries the laws of which are based on the principles of common law (see O.J. March 24, 2004). For further information on exemptions from the examination requirements, see the web site www.cipa.org.uk.

APPENDIX J—RULES OF PROFESSIONAL CONDUCT OF THE CHARTERED INSTITUTE OF PATENT AGENTS

General

Guidelines to rules 1 and 2

J01.02G

Guideline A.4(ii) was amended in April 2003 to read:

"(ii) Members have a duty to charge only fees which are reasonable, that is to say generally in line with professional fees elsewhere. Factors which may be taken into account are the time spent, the costs of running a practice, the urgency of the situation and any special circumstances. All this should be specified to the client before any work is done.

New clients and those who wish should be advised of the hourly rates for different classes of work, and of the anticipated costs of pieces of work, both individually and as a whole job. All clients should be advised as to costs at frequent intervals, and particularly when an estimate looks likely to be exceeded.

There is an increasing demand for fixed-price quotations for particular pieces of work. The work for which a quotation is given should be precisely defined, and a member should seek to keep the time-period covered by the quotation as short as possible in the interest of predictability, but the additional risk involved will anyway make a quotation higher than a cost-plus estimate. A quotation may be accompanied by a request for payment before work is started, and this will have the advantage that it will be less likely for the client subsequently to argue that the charge was unreasonable."

SUPPLEMENTARY INDEX

This Index is supplementary to that at the end of the Main Work and refers to the section (§) numbers therein. Thus, both Indexes should be consulted and then the indicated sections studied in both the Main Work and this Supplement. In this Supplementary Index, an asterisk indicates that citation is additional to corresponding citation in the Main Work.

Admissibility,
    evidence, of, G22A.14

* **Admissions,**
    infringement proceedings, and, 61.58
    Patent Court procedure, and, G13
    standard form of order for directions, G22A.6

* **Adviser,**
    appointment, 96.12

* **Agents,**
    registration qualifications, I10
    rights and obligations in Patents County Court, 291.06

* **Amendment,**
    pleadings, of, G22A.3–G22A.4

* **Animals and animal variety,**
    biotechnology, 1.19, 1.20

* **Appeal,**
    Comptroller, from,
        appellate jurisdiction, principles affecting, 97.08–97.11
        composition of Patents Court, and, 97.05
        further appeals to Court of Appeal, 97.06, 97.19–97.23
        legal aid, and, 97.24
        Patents Court, to, 97.12–97.18, F63.17, G07
        right of appeal, 97.04
        Scottish proceedings, 97.07
    re-Hearings, E52PD.9
    revocation proceedings, 72.52

* **Application,**
    correction of errors, 117.01–117.14

Assessors,
    expert evidence, E35PD.0–E35PD.5

* **Biotechnology,**
    public policy, 1.19
    scope of protection, 125A.10

Case management,
    multi-track procedure, and, E29.2–E29.4
    Patent Court procedure, and, F63.7, F63PD.4
Chancery Division,
    listing office, G05, G07
    practice guide, G01
* **Chemical compounds,**
    inventive step, and, 3.36–3.37
* **Claims,**
    categories, 14.23
    purpose and requirements, 14.22
Commercial success,
    inventive step, and, 3.44
Common design,
    joint tortfeasance, and, 60.25
* **Common general knowledge,**
    prior art, 3.06
* **Comptroller,**
    appeals from,
        appellate jurisdiction, principles affecting, 97.08–97.11
        composition of Patents Court, and, 97.05
        further appeals to Court of Appeal, 97.06, 97.19–97.23
        legal aid, and, 97.24
        Patents Court, to, 97.12–97.18, F63.17, G07
        right of appeal, 97.04
        Scottish proceedings, 97.07
Compulsory licences,
    failure to supply, 48A.07
    plant breeders' rights, and, 48A.04
    WTO proprietors, and, 48A.01–48A.11
Computer implemented inventions,
    protection of, 1.14, 1.15
* **Correction,**
    divisional applications, 15.32
    translation, filing of, 80.10
* **Costs,**
    misconduct, and, E44.14
    Patent Court procedure, and, G16
    revocation proceedings, 72.53
    solicitor and client costs,
        basis of assessment, E48.8
    standard form of order for directions, G22A.19
    trustees, funds held by, E44.13
Counter-claims,
    civil procedure rules, and, E20.1–E20PD.6
Court of Session,
    report, power to order, 99B.01–99B.02
Declaration,
    infringement, of, 61.13
    revocation, of, 61.13
* **Disclaimer,**
    amendments, 76.10
Disclosure,
    amendment of specification after grant, 27.06
    documents, of,
        civil procedure rules, and, E31.2–E31PD.7

Disclosure—*cont.*
    Patents Court, by, 94.05, F63.8, F63PD.5
Discretion,
    amendment of specification after grant, 27.05
*   **Divisional application,**
    corrections, 15.32
Doctrine of equivalents, 125.15–125.16
Documents,
*   disclosure and inspection of, E31.2–E31PD.7
    form and content of,
        electronic filing, 123.19
    inspection of, 118.11
    list of, G22A.8
    Patents Court, and, G09
    proof of, G22A.2
    size and presentation of, 14.05
    specification. *See* **Specification**
    supply of court records, E05.4
Electronic communications,
    use of, 124A.01–124A.02
Electronic filing,
    documents, form and content of, 123.19, 124A.02
Employee inventions,
*   compensation for,
        Patent Court procedure, and, F63.12, F63PD.13
Equivalents, 125.15–125.16
*   **European Application (UK),**
    corrected translation, filing of, 80.10
*   **European Patent Office,**
    communication of,
*   information to, F63PD.14
*   **Evidence,**
    admissibility of, G22A.14
    expert evidence,
        practice direction, E35PD.0–E35PD.5
    witness statements,
        availability for inspection, E32.13
    written, G22A.13
Exempt acts,
    infringement, and, 60.12–60.19
*   **Exclusive licence,**
    defined, 67.03
*   **Exclusive licensee,**
    right to sue, 67.04
*   **Experiments,**
    Patent Court procedure, and, F63PD.9
    standard form of order for directions, G22A.10–G22A.11
Expert evidence,
    practice direction, E35PD.0–E35PD.5
*   **Extent of protection,**
    patentee's choice, 125.08
Foreign proceedings,
    examination of witnesses, E34.21
*   **Forms,**
    multiple copies, 125.05
    rules concerning, 123.17

Grace periods,
    consultation by Patent Office, 2.29
Grounds of Invalidity document, 61.42
High Court,
    transfers to and from, 289.03
* **Improvements,**
    security under Scots law, 31.05
Infringement,
    damages, 61.24–61.28
    declaration of, 61.13
    exempt acts, 60.12–60.19
    interim injunctions, 61.09–61.21
    laches, acquiescence and estoppel, 60.21
    proceedings for,
        admissions, 61.58
        before Patents Court, 61.41, F63.9, F63PD.11
        disclosure, 61.49–61.56
        evidence, 61.60
        experiments, 61.59
        groundless threats, remedy for, 70.01–70.09
        inspection of property, 61.57
        non-registration, effect of, 68.01–68.04
        preliminary points, 61.45
        stay of proceedings, 61.46
        striking out of pleadings, 61.43–61.44
        trial procedure, 61.62
    'proprietor', 61.04
    prototype, making of, 60.12
    'without prejudice' settlements, 61.60
* **Inspection,**
    documents, of,
        civil procedure rules, and, E31.2–E31PD.7
        court records, E.05.4
        in court proceedings, 118.11
        standard form of order for directions, G22A.9
Intangibles,
    taxation of, 30.12
* **Intellectual Property Court Users' Committee,**
    constitution of, G19
Interim injunctions,
    infringement, and, 61.09–61.21
Interim remedies,
    civil procedure rules, and, E25.1
    Patent Court procedure, and, G21
* **International application,**
    review of filing date, 89.30
    time, extensions of, 89A.35
International application (UK),
*   preliminary examination of, 89A.02
    prescribed periods, 89A.02
    translation
        verification of, 89A.21
*   UK phase
        time limits for, 89A.16–89A.21, 89A.23–89A.25, 89A.28

Invention,
    computer implemented
        protection of, 1.14, 1.15
*   **Inventor,**
    identification, 13.04
*   **Inventive step,**
    chemical compounds, and, 3.36–3.37
    commercial success, 3.44
    discovery of problem, 3.30–3.32
    solution, assessment of, 3.33–3.35
Jurisdiction,
    Comptroller, appeals from, 97.08–97.11
    Masters, F63PD.8, G15
    Patents Court, 96.06–96.11
*   **Language of filing,**
    patent applications, and, 14.12
Liberty to apply,
    standard form of order for directions, G22A.18
Listing questionnaire,
    multi-track procedure, E29.6
Masters,
    jurisdiction of, F63PD.8, G15
Media neutral citations,
    patent reports, and, 123.48
Misconduct,
    costs, and, E44.14
Models, use of,
    notice of, G22A.12
    Patent Court procedure, and, F63PD.10
Multi-track procedure,
    case management, E29.2–E29.4
    listing questionnaire, E29.6
    pre-trial review, E29.7
    trial timetable, setting a, E29.8
Multiple copies,
    forms, and, 125.05
Negligence,
    agents liability for, 274.09
Non-compliance,
    standard form of order for directions, G22A.15
*   **Novelty,**
    EPC requirements, 14.27
    ex post facto analysis, 3.15
Obvious to try test, 3.11
Office of Fair Trading,
    draft guidelines
        application of Competition Act 1998, 44.04
Orders,
    Patent Court procedure, and, G20, G22–G22A.19
Part 36 offers and payments, E52.12
*   **Patent,**
    amendment, procedure for, 27.15–27.20
    lapsed patents, restoration of, 28.01–28.15
    Patents Court,
        practice direction, E49.0, E63.0, F63.0–F63PD.6

Patent applications,
    Welsh language, and, 14.12
Patent Office,
    email correspondence with, 123.49
*   filing by
        Document Exchange at, 119.03
        fax at, 119.06
    grace periods, consultation on, 2.29
*   website, 123.47
Patent reports,
    media neutral citations, and, 123.48
* **Patentable invention,**
    methods of doing business, 1.14
* **Patents County Court,**
    address for communications, G04
    patent agents, 291.06
    proceedings in, 291.01–291.09
    transfer to, from, 289.03
* **Patents Court,**
    admissions, G13
    agreed costs, G16
    appeals, composition for, 97.05
    case management, F63.7, F63PD.4
    Comptroller, appeals from, 97.12–97.18, F63.17, G07
    correction of errors, 117.01–117.14
    defences, F63.6
    determination by court, F63.11
    disclosure and inspection, 94.05, F63.8, F63PD.5
    documents, and, G09
    employee compensation, F63.12, F63PD.13
    EPO, communication of information to, F63PD.14
    experiments, F63PD.9
    infringement, 61.41, F63.9, F63PD.11
    interim remedies, trial date for, G21
    jurisdiction, 96.06–96.11
    Masters' jurisdiction, F63PD.8, G15
    Models, use of, F63PD.10
    narrowing of issues, G12
    orders following judgment, G20
    orders for directions, G22–G22A.19
    register of patents, and, F63PD.15–F63PD.16
    report, power to order, 99A.01–99A.05
    September sittings, G06
    service, F63.16
    short applications, F63PD.6, G05
    sitting outside London, G18
    skeleton arguments, G14
    specialist list, F63.4
    specification, amendment to, F63.10, F63PD.12
    starting claims, F63.5, F63PD.3
    streamlined procedure, G10
    telephone applications, G17
    timetable for trial, F63PD.7, G11
    validity, challenges to, F63.9, F63PD.11
    without notice applications, G08

Payments into court, E52.12

Plant breeders' rights,
    compulsory licences, and, 48.04

* **Plant variety,**
    infringements, 62.02

Pleadings,
    amendment of, G22A.3–G22A.4

Preliminary examination,
*   formal requirements, 17.04

Pre-trial review,
    multi-track procedure, E29.7

* **Prior art,**
    common general knowledge, 3.06
    date of publication, 2.06

* **Priority document,**
    certification, 32.37

* **Proprietor,**
    defined, 61.04

Public policy, 1.19

* **Publication,**
    avoidance by withdrawal, 16.06

Rectification,
*   register of,
        claims for, F63PD.16

* **Register of Patent Agents**, 275.04

Register of patents,
    orders affecting entries in, F63PD.15
    rectification, claims for, F63PD.16

Re-hearings,
    appeals, and, E52PD.9

Relevant application,
    priority claim form, 5.15

* **Restoration,**
    employee error, 28.07

* **Revocation,**
    appeals, and, 72.52
    costs, and, 72.53
    declaration of, 61.13

* **Scots law,**
    effect of revocation, 77.10
    jurisdiction, 98.05

* **Search,**
    new examination procedures, 18.07

* **Security for costs,**
    civil procedure rules, and, E25.12–E25.15

September sittings,
    Patent Court proceudre, and, G06

* **Service,**
    documents, E06.2–E06PD.6
    Patent Court procedure, and, F63.16

Short applications,
    Patent Court procedure, and, F63PD.6, G05

Sittings outside London,
    Patent Court procedure, and, G18

* **Skeleton arguments,**
    Patent Court procedure, and, G14

Software. *see* **Computer programs**

Solution, assessment of,
   inventive step, and, 3.33–3.35

Specialist list,
   Patent Court procedure, and, F63.4

* **Specification,**
   amendment after grant, 27.01–27.20

* **Statement of case,**
   civil procedure rules, and, E16.2–E16PD.14

Statement of truth,
   civil procedure rules, and, E22.1–E22PD.5

* **Stay of proceedings,**
   infringement proceedings, and, 61.46

Streamlined procedure,
   Patent Court procedure, and, G10

Striking out,
   infringement proceedings, and, 61.43–61.44

* **Substantive examination,**
   'examination opinions', 18.07

Synergistic effects, 3.11

Taxation,
   intangibles, and, 30.12

* **Technical character,**
   required of patentable invention, 1.12, 1.14

Telephone applications,
   Patent Court procedure, and, G17

Trade Marks,
   use of in claim, 14.28, 76.10

* **Transfer,**
   between High Court and Patents County Court, 289.03
   standard form of order for directions, G22A.1

Trial bundles,
   standard form of order for directions, G22A

Trial timetable,
   multi-track procedure, E29.8
   Patent Court procedure, and, F63PD.7, G11

* **Validity,**
   challenges to,
      Patent Court procedure, and, F63.9, F63PD.11

* **Welsh language,**
   patent applications, and, 14.12

Withdrawal,
   avoidance of publication, 16.06
   prior conflicting application, 2.26

Without notice applications,
   Patent Court procedure, and, G08

* **Witness statements,**
   availability for inspection, E32.13

Witnesses,
   examination of in foreign proceedings, E34.21

Written evidence,
   standard form of order for directions, G22A.13

* **WTO proprietors,**
   compulsory licences, 48A.01–48A.11